Johann Joseph Ignaz von Döllinger

Studies in European History

Being Academical Addresses

Johann Joseph Ignaz von Döllinger

Studies in European History
Being Academical Addresses

ISBN/EAN: 9783742895523

Manufactured in Europe, USA, Canada, Australia, Japa

Cover: Foto ©Thomas Meinert / pixelio.de

Manufactured and distributed by brebook publishing software
(www.brebook.com)

Johann Joseph Ignaz von Döllinger

Studies in European History

J. Doellinger

IN

EUROPEAN HISTORY

BEING

ACADEMICAL ADDRESSES

DELIVERED BY

JOHN IGNATIUS VON DÖLLINGER, D.D.

LATE PROFESSOR OF ECCLESIASTICAL HISTORY
IN THE UNIVERSITY OF MUNICH

TRANSLATED AT THE REQUEST OF THE AUTHOR

BY

MARGARET WARRE

WITH PORTRAIT

LONDON
JOHN MURRAY, ALBEMARLE STREET
1890

TRANSLATOR'S PREFACE

The translation of the following Addresses was undertaken at the request of the late Professor Dr. von Döllinger, who himself selected those which he wished to be published in England and in English.

It was not without much hesitation that the responsibility entailed by such a task was accepted. It is not without apprehension lest the original may have lost much in the translation that the work is now offered to the public.

The venerable author of the Addresses saw only a part of the translation. His long and eminent career was brought to a close before it could be completed; and thus the work has suffered the irreparable loss of his criticism and correction.

The grateful acknowledgments of the Translator are due in the first place to the Rev. Alfred Plummer, D.D., of Durham University, who most kindly read through and revised the MS. of the translation; to Mr. F. W. Cornish, of Eton College; to Mr. John Murray, jun., and his sister

Miss MURRAY, who have looked through and corrected the proof sheets; and to the Rev. Dr. WARRE, Head Master of Eton, who (in the absence of the Translator abroad) has revised the whole, and has seen the work through the press. Lastly, it is to the great kindness of the Right Hon. W. E. GLADSTONE, M.P. that the work is indebted for the frontispiece, which is copied from a picture in his possession—an excellent likeness of the venerable and learned author.

CONTENTS

ACADEMICAL ADDRESSES

I

THE SIGNIFICANCE OF DYNASTIES IN THE HISTORY OF THE WORLD[1]

The beginnings of national and political life lie beyond our recollection, yet it is certain that the oldest known form under which they appeared was monarchical, not republican. Now whether this form was of the nature of a patriarchate, the paternal rule in the family, of a theocratic priesthood, a military leadership, or a civil judgeship; or whether, now and then, royalty appeared at the very outset as a pure uncompromising despotism, the preference for monarchy asserts itself as a law in human nature, as the primitive manifestation of political instincts.

The transition from the single ruler to the king, that is to say, to hereditary monarchy, is likewise the result of a law universally implanted in human nature. Purely elective monarchies, which ignore the hereditary principle, are beacons of warning in history; they have invariably contained the germs of corruption and dissolution, and their formation has frequently betokened a period of political and moral decay in a nation. They have always been

[1] Lecture delivered March 20, 1880, at the public meeting of the Royal Bavarian Academy of Science. Printed now for the first time, it may serve as an introduction to the lecture which follows, which was delivered some months later at the meeting of the Academy upon the occasion of the commemoration of the 700th year of the reign of the house of Wittelsbach in Bavaria.

conducive to bribery in one form or another, for electors have been prone to turn the privilege of a vote into a matter of personal profit. Elective bodies have besides always been apt to fall a prey to party divisions, and to elect, not the worthiest candidate, but the man most likely to prove useful to his party. It is of the highest importance to a political organism that the unity, the unbroken continuity, of supreme authority, should, by embodiment in a ruling family, be preserved in the eyes of all against the unstable wills of passing generations. The king born to the throne, and he alone, is the representative of the nation in past and present, the living tradition of political organisation. The hereditary monarch not only bears the responsibility of the past; he is accountable also for the future. He is conscious that his sins of omission and commission must, for good or for evil, bear fruit for those who come after him. It has been remarked that the subjects of elective states and spiritual principalities exhibit, as a rule, no attachment to their princes. The news of the death of a pope was always received with indifference in the States of the Church, and it was not otherwise in the German ecclesiastical states. Personal loyalty has been exclusively reserved for the rulers who belonged to an hereditary dynasty.

The great monarchies whose historical traditions reach back for as many as twenty or thirty centuries before Christ, have embalmed the remembrance of a long series of dynasties.

Twenty-six dynasties are reckoned to have reigned in Egypt before the year 525 B.C., when by the Persian conquest the fall of the Pharaohs was achieved. Mere names for the most part; yet to some of these, such as Sethos and Ramses II., splendour still attaches, whilst mighty architectural remains and inscriptions survive to testify to the grandeur and exploits of others amongst these monarchs.

Little insight can be gained into the history of the

two Asiatic empires, the Assyrian and the Babylonian; yet in both alike polygamy and the life of the harem are already perceptible in full development, producing consequences which, in subsequent periods as well, have never failed to attend them.

During a period of 230 years, eighteen kings of the house of the Achæmenidæ successively ruled the Persian Monarchy, and the dynasty ranks pre-eminent as the most brilliant of the pre-Christian era. The religion of Zoroaster imparted a spirit of conquest to the monarchs of this race, by whom the national energy was quickened through continual foreign wars. A policy of conquest was the principle which upheld the dynasty. Two monarchs, however, Cyrus and Darius I., were likewise religious reformers. The fact that so long a period should have elapsed in the hereditary states of Persia, unmarked either by rebellion or a change of dynasty, may very properly be attributed to the protection afforded to the monarch by the religious aspect in which he was regarded. The internal history of the family was, however, in sharp contrast with the outward splendour of its career; revealing a tissue of bloody crimes and unnatural atrocities—marriages with sisters and daughters, and such frequent murder of relatives, that, according to the expression of Justinus, parricide and fratricide had become the established custom of the race. Only two Persian Monarchs died a natural death. Meanwhile the law of Persia had decreed that the king might justifiably act in all ways as he pleased. This is the first signal instance in history in which it may be seen to what a depth of moral corruption a dynasty, and through it a people, can be brought by the atmosphere of the harem and the intrigues of eunuchs.

The Persian Monarchy is more aptly termed an empire than a monarchy. It extended over the greater part of the known world, and in one, at least, of its monarchs the ambition was aroused of founding a universal monarchy.

The features which characterise the development of most Oriental states and dynasties are already apparent in the Persian Monarchy. The ruler becomes transformed from the warrior chief and tribal king into the court-king, screened by an obsequious nobility from the sight and approach of his people. An elaborate ceremonial, rigidly enforced, serves at once to isolate him and at the same time to give him the semblance of real authority.

The Greeks began their historical career with restricted monarchy, which, however, soon passed into republics in each town. On the other hand, two Semitic races, the Jews and the Arabs, followed an opposite course in their national development. Each, under very different circumstances, passed from democratic conditions, in which the distinction of tribe and family presented the only organisation, into a state of monarchy. The Jews, when a considerable time had elapsed since their migration into Palestine, were moved, in imitation of the surrounding nations, whose hostility they dreaded, to unite themselves under the centralising bond of a supreme head. David, their second king, was the first to found a dynasty, the vitality of which was sustained henceforward by the glory of its founder and the hope of the promises made to him. The monarchs of this royal house moved freely amongst the people, and were at all times accessible to those who applied to them for assistance. But amongst them also polygamy bore poisonous fruits, nor were intrigue and violence wanting, after the fashion of Oriental courts.

The spirit of disruption re-awoke no later than under David's grandson; the ten tribes rebelled, and formed a separate kingdom which lasted until the captivity, a kingdom nevertheless, according to the prophet Hosea, not of God's grace, but of His wrath. Twenty kings reigned in succession, springing from nine different houses, a change of dynasty being usually accompanied by bloodshed. Both kingdoms perished through their own fault, yet it is worthy of notice that Judah with her single royal house survived the hostile sister kingdom and her nine dynasties by about a century and a half.

The Roman Empire during the whole period of its existence, which was little short of five hundred years, established no regular succession to the throne, nor any genuine dynasty. This may in part be attributed to the disordered state of family ties, many emperors not having, nor indeed desiring to have, sons, as well as to the political hypocrisy with which the imperial government was introduced and established by Augustus and his immediate successors; the legal foundation of an hereditary succession being incompatible with the retention of republican forms. Hence the custom arose for an emperor to designate his successor by adoption, by investing him with the title of Cæsar, or by associating him during his own lifetime in the regency. Once only did the senate arrive at making a free choice; the elevation of an emperor, as well as his deposition and death, rested, as a rule, chiefly in the hands of the Prætorian Guards and of the legions. The introduction and triumph of Christianity brought about no essential change in this respect. The numerous family of Constantine, which seemed to bespeak a lasting dynasty, wrought out its own destruction in the space of fifty years.

The Græco-Byzantine Empire affords instances of the son succeeding the father, or the nephew the uncle, more frequently when the father had during his lifetime associated the son with himself as co-emperor or Cæsar, or when the son happened to have been *porphyrogennetos*, born in the purple, *i.e.* after his father's accession to imperial honours. But breaks in the succession were not wanting, whenever the army or the fleet interfered to set up the emperor of its choice. The house of Heraclius managed to retain the imperial power for a considerable period, and so also did the Isaurian house of Iconoclast emperors, both founded by successful generals. In instances where the father on his deathbed appointed a regent to govern during the minority of his son, it usually fell out that the young prince was murdered, blinded, or forced to adopt the monastic tonsure.

During the one thousand years that this empire endured, the house of the Comneni must be cited as the most vigorous. At a time of great pressure during the twelfth century, three highly-gifted emperors of that race rescued the tottering empire from destruction. The fresh splendour with which these rulers surrounded the Byzantine throne was, however, speedily obscured by the Latin conquest, a catastrophe from which the Eastern Empire was never again able to rise to strength and prosperity.

Wide as is the difference that severs the Asiatic from the European mind, and Islam from Christendom, it does not exceed the distinction which sunders the dynasty of the Moslem world from the character of the ruling families of Christendom. The successors of the Prophet, brandishing the Koran in one hand and the sword in the other, priest-kings and warriors, outwardly pledged to respect the precepts of the Koran, but virtually possessed of unlimited power, received the title of Kaliph, and were chosen by election in accordance with the Arab custom of setting up or deposing tribal chiefs. A legally established hereditary succession there was not. Amongst as many as fourteen sovereigns chosen from the Ommiades, four only were succeeded by their sons, and amongst the first twenty-four kaliphs not more than six. The election became more and more a mere form, and as a rule it was the reigning kaliph who nominated his successor, and caused him to be forthwith formally recognised. Not long after the death of Mohammed the question of the succession to the kaliphate led to the great schism of the Sunnis and Shiites, which is still kept up with undiminished bitterness.

Amongst empires which owe their greatness and vitality to the energetic spirit of a ruling dynasty, that of the Osmanli stands pre-eminent. Under a succession of sultans, all alike men of intellect and activity, the Osman

Empire grew and flourished, until it surpassed in might and extent the empire of Charles the Great. The culminating pinnacle of power and magnificence was attained under Suleiman II., the contemporary of Charles V., when, after the taking of Constantinople, he assumed the kaliphate, and the Shereef of Mecca transmitted to him the keys of the Kaaba in acknowledgment of the spiritual and temporal supremacy of the monarch. The Sultans, without exception, belonged to the race of Osman; but their mothers were, in most cases, slaves. Islam, indeed, owed much to the support of renegade Christian slaves, who became most serviceable instruments in the hands of their masters. The inmates of the Sultan's harem, including crowds of concubines and odalisques, supplied him with numerous descendants. In default of any fixed law of succession, the father could nominate any one of his sons to follow him upon the throne. Mohammed the Conqueror, moved by fear of the constant intrigues of mothers and sons—the saying of Tacitus, 'solita fratrum odia,' holds good in the harem—and by the dangers of civil war and palace revolutions, issued a dynastic decree compelling future monarchs, 'for the peace of the world,' immediately upon accession, to put their brothers to death. A similar object was attained in Persia by causing them to be blinded. This decree proved ineffectual to prevent the downfall of the Osman dynasty. Sultans began to adopt the fatal policy of retaining their sons as prisoners in the harem, instead of sending them as hitherto to be governors in the provinces. Hence it came to pass that the throne of an empire of which the fabric had been founded and sustained entirely by the personal qualities of its rulers was filled by a succession of weaklings.

The sultans ceased henceforth to attend the divan in person, and left the direction of affairs in the hands of their viziers. The deposition, imprisonment, and murder of these phantom sovereigns soon became a matter of frequent occurrence. Systematically educated in incapacity, they fell under the guidance of an hereditary oligarchy, the Effendis of Stamboul, who knew how to render themselves indispensable by ministering to their vices. No dynasty can in the end withstand the baneful effects of polygamy and of education in the hareem. The fate of the empire was predestined by the Koran and the religious traditions of the Sunnis. Where polygamy, slavery, murder, religious oppression and persecution are unassailable principles, sanctified by the example of the Prophet himself, no reform and no recovery is possible for a body politic thus sick unto death.

The Mongols, before whose world-wide conquests and desolating power Asia and Europe alike trembled in the thirteenth century, failed nevertheless in the attempt to weld together the various tribes by the establishment of a lasting dynasty. Genghis Khan, after the fashion of the Slav 'Seniorat,' removed the tribal chieftain, a relative of his own, who ruled under the title of Chakan or 'Prince of princes,' to substitute his own third son Ogotai; and the right of the latter was recognised in a great popular assembly in 1228.

One of the most extraordinary transformations recorded in history was accomplished amongst this people. The Buddhist religion converted these rude nomad tribes into a harmless, peaceable people, not, however, without their being considerably reduced in numbers. A third of the male population still lives under monastic vows, and spends its days in prostration before the Dalai-lama of Thibet. For in Thibet, where the religion of Buddha found free space for development, being neither fettered by political restraints nor contaminated by earlier forms of faith, the supreme power is vested in the hands of the Lamas, the largest priestly hierarchy upon earth, whose chief, worshipped as the incarnation of the Godhead, unites in his person both the spiritual and the temporal power. His office has now become dependent upon the imperial court of Pekin. So long as marriage was permitted to the high priest, and he held his dignity by inheritance, the dynasty was one of divine incarnations. The successor was always the same Priest-God, who in dying was immediately born again. But with the introduction of celibacy it became needful to provide for the succession in some other way, and out of three boys selected for the purpose, one is now chosen by lot.

The royal dynasty of Japan is peculiarly constituted, and cannot be compared with the dynastic institutions of other states. Its history commences with that of the nation in B.C. 660. The Japanese, like the Egyptians, claim to have been originally governed by a divine race of kings, from whom their later sovereigns were likewise descended. From the above-mentioned date, 122 mikados or emperors have followed in unbroken succession upon the throne. Their jurisdiction was both spiritual and temporal. The grafting of Buddhism upon the Sintu or ancient religion of the country in the sixth century after Christ, brought no alteration in the position and twofold supremacy of the mikado.

During hundreds of years Christian states have repeatedly failed in establishing an uninterrupted succession of monarchs to the throne, but this difficulty was obviated in Japan by the appointment of four imperial families from among whom, upon the failure of the direct line, a mikado might be given to the state. This has not, however, prevented boys and women and even young girls from occasionally occupying the throne. The mikado became in process of time more and more pushed into the background by the relatives who surrounded him, offshoots of the numerous royal wives and concubines, until, in A.D. 1292, Shogun, general in chief of the imperial forces, succeeded in making his own office hereditary and in concentrating in it for himself and his descendants the whole of the governing power. From that moment the mikado, overwhelmed with ceremonial homage, and fettered by an elaborate and wearisome court etiquette, retained scarcely the shadow of power. The constitutional reform of 1868 has put an end to this state of things, when even Japan recognised the necessity of abolishing the law which prohibited foreigners from admission into the country.

Amongst nations of Teutonic race in the earliest stage hereditary sovereignty and self-government through elected magistrates are both observable. Most of the tribes which at the period of the great migration settled upon Roman territory brought their kings with them,—most, I say, for the Alemanni, for instance, had none. The kings were created by election, the choice being usually confined to one particular family, or they forthwith became founders of such a family. As, however, by contact and mingling of the Roman population with their German conquerors, new relations were formed, the princes found it necessary to adapt their rule to the needs of a people accustomed to other laws and customs. Their administration consequently grew more and more into conformity with Roman practice, and monarchy, as we find it amongst the Visigoths, Ostrogoths, and Merovingians, assumed a more absolute form. The close relations which sprang up between the royal dynasties and the church operated in the same direction. The pernicious practice of partitioning the kingdom amongst the sons of the sovereign was the frequent occasion of fratricidal and civil strife both amongst the Merovingians in Gaul and the Lombards in Italy. These evils were avoided in Spain by the Visigoths, who maintained the principle of the integrity of the kingdom. Nevertheless neither amongst the Visigoths nor the Lombards did any family succeed in securing hereditary possession of the throne; and regicide was not unfrequent either amongst these two or amongst the Merovingians. Seven violent changes in the succession were made by the Visigoths during the period of their monarchy, which comprises a list of thirty-five kings. The facility with which the Moslem invaders from Africa annihilated the Visigothic Kingdom in a single battle was plainly the result of internal decadence. Spain owed her ruin to the want of an hereditary line of kings, just as from the same cause the Lombard Kingdom in Italy ingloriously succumbed not long afterwards to the shock of the Franco-Gallic invasion.

Two dynasties, possessing otherwise few features in common, resemble one another in this, that in both cases an unparalleled rise and continued growth was followed suddenly by an irretrievable downfall. The Carlovingian family, beginning with the elder Pepin, rose during the lifetime of three great men, Charles Martel, Pepin II., and Charles the Great, to the dignity of the imperial title, and to the sovereignty over the whole of civilised or half-barbarian Europe. But even under Louis the Pious, the son of Charles the Great, decay had set in; it is sufficiently marked by the difference between the father and son. During the 173 years that the Carlovingian race still continued on the throne, it produced not a single other prince of high capacity. Charles the Simple died despised and forgotten; his grandsons Lothar and Louis the Child were poisoned. The mighty inheritance of Charles the Great was reduced to the single town of Noyon and the surrounding territory. And so the Franks turned their backs upon the Carlovingian house from which their affections had become estranged, and, passing over the claim of the rightful heir Duke Charles of Lorraine, let the royal power fall into the hands of a new dynasty, the Capetian, which thus began its course of 800 years. The Germans meanwhile, repudiating the claims of the elder house, had elected Duke Conrad of Franconia as their king. The Carlovingians had merited their fate. Continually engaged in fratricidal wars and in quelling the rebellions of their sons, they overlooked the growing power of their vassals, who assiduously fomented these family quarrels which led to the final downfall of the house.

When Germany by the expulsion of the Carlovingians became an independent kingdom, with which the imperial title was soon afterwards combined, the Teutonic custom of election by the nobles, and of preserving at the same time the hereditary line of succession, continued in force. The formal election of the sovereign was in fact no more than the confirmation of his title by the nation, or by the nobles who represented the nation. The kings further sought to secure their position by causing the election and coronation of the son during the father's lifetime. But whilst in France elective rights were entirely swallowed up by those of hereditary succession (the unity and strength of the kingdom and the development of monarchical power being thus guaranteed), affairs took a contrary course in Germany and led to a different result. The momentous turning-point was reached when, in 1077, at the Convent of Forchheim, the rebellious princes, in connivance with Rome, decreed that the election of a king should be henceforth governed by arbitrary choice regardless of hereditary claims.

After the fall of the house of Hohenstaufen the Ecclesiastical Electors, at the instigation of the papacy, found means during a whole century to prevent the transmission of the crown from father to son, or the accession even of a relative of the deceased monarch; a policy effectually calculated to weaken and ruin both kingdom and empire. For henceforward every imperial election became an object of traffic, and electors bartered their votes for sums of money and political privileges. At length, when monarchy had declined to a shadow, and nothing remained of the royal German or of the imperial power but empty forms, the succession was once more suffered to become hereditary, first in the Luxemburg, and then in the Habsburg family.

The development of the German principalities took a different course. The offices of duke and count having become hereditary, the princely houses to whom they appertained were not backward in strengthening and widening their own power by appropriating the spoils of the empire and the crown. The Golden Bull provided that the electoral principalities should not be subdivided. But the other princes set themselves in general to secure two objects: to provide a landed inheritance for each son, and to preserve as far as possible the independence of their possessions. Every trace of derived official power had before long disappeared from amongst the hereditary landed nobility; who, assuming more and more of independent governing power, ventured upon yet more unscrupulous partitions. It was during that period of the eclipse of the empire, after 1254, that, in defiance of imperial law, the most arbitrary subdivisions were rapidly accomplished. The first instance took place in 1255. In 1190 there had been twenty-two reigning princes in Germany; a century later the number had been doubled. Thus the ancient ties of race were rent asunder, and Germany was aimlessly dismembered, just as chance or family convenience suggested. A host of dukedoms, counties, bishoprics, and abbeys, and presently also of free towns and knightly manors (*Rittersitze*), sprang into independent existence. Besides this, not a single province of Germany was defined by natural geographical and political demarcations, nor was the population animated by any public spirit or desire for the welfare of nation or empire. The nation languished under the multitude of reigning dynasties. The number of sovereigns finally amounted to 1,800, viz. 314 imperial and 1,374 knightly territories.

The deficiency of princely houses amongst the Slav nations forms a striking contrast with the abundant dynasties of the German states. In every Slav country the native dynasties have either died out or been deposed, and their place has been taken by foreign lines. Even in Russia, during the last hundred years, the sceptre has remained in the hands of a German family, the house of Holstein-Gottorp. Curiously enough, however, in North-western Germany the primitive Slav dynasty still survives, in Mecklenburg. An ancestor of the reigning house, the Obotritenfürst Pribislaw, having received baptism and sworn fealty as a vassal to Germany, was reinstated in his dominions. The country nevertheless was Germanised, and the Wend language soon died out.

In Bohemia the dynasty of Premysl, having occupied the throne during several centuries, suddenly rose to unexpected splendour under Ottocar II., to whom was even made the offer of the German crown. However, upon the death of his son Wenzel, murdered by his vassals in 1306, the old race became extinct. The Luxemburg dynasty replaced it upon the throne for the space of a century, and in 1526 the Bohemians elected Ferdinand of Habsburg, the husband of Anna the last king's daughter, to reign over them. Having attested thereby their right of election, they again asserted it in 1618 by proclaiming the Elector Palatine in opposition to the house of Habsburg. This led to the annihilation of religious and political freedom in Bohemia, and was the immediate cause of the Thirty Years' War, whereby the country was utterly laid waste.

The Bulgarians, a race of purely Slavonic origin, whose liberation and elevation into a new state governed by a German prince we have ourselves lately witnessed, had in 1018 erected a kingdom, which, despite the hostile pressure from either side, of Byzantium and Hungary, maintained its existence until 1392, when it succumbed before the advance of the Ottoman power.

A similar fate overtook the most warlike and powerful amongst the Slavonic races, the Servians. The dynasty of the Nemanias, which governed Servia for 212 years, created a powerful kingdom, which, under the great emperor Stephen Duschan, who adopted the title of Czar, comprised from 1347 to 1355 the whole Græco-Illyrian peninsula with the exception of the Peloponnesus and Roumelia. The constitutional code of which Stephen was the author conceded to his people privileges unexampled in those days. But the dynasty came to an end with his son Urosch V., and, after a century of internal trouble and unsuccessful warfare, Servia, in common with the remaining Slav states, was swallowed up in the darkness and misery of Turkish oppression.

Fully to account, however, for the rapidity with which the Slavonic principalities of the Balkan, despite the defensive advantages of their situation, fell a prey to Turkish oppression, it must be borne in mind that the most effectual help to the Turks, and the most deadly foe to the Slavs, was found in Western Christendom. The doom of the Slavonic peoples was written in the fact that they belonged to the Greek Church, and that Latins and Turks consequently joined hands in their destruction. Any one who reflects upon this will not fail to perceive wherein the deeper root of Panslavism lies at the present day, and the magnitude of the danger which it involves for Austria.

The tenth and eleventh centuries witnessed the rise of a great Slavonic kingdom under Norman rule. Nevertheless, being subject to the partitions customary amongst Slavonic peoples, and likewise to the Slavonic institution of the Seniorat, the Kingdom of Russia quickly fell to pieces. In 1054 Jaroslav, repeating the policy of the first Christian monarch Wladimir, divided the kingdom amongst his five sons, to one of whom he gave the title of 'Grossfürst' or chief of all the royal princes, without, however, investing him with any actual power over the rest. The endeavour of each subordinate prince to wrest this dignity for himself, was the cause of constant civil wars. Russia became an extensive but powerless confederation, continually on the decline, until infinite subdivisions and the dissensions of her princes led to her easy subjection by the Monguls.

Whilst attempting to portray the leading features of dynasties, and to note the conditions under which they exist, I may as well observe that of all the great royal houses, that which best understood and put in practice a true dynastic policy was that of the Capets in France. The Salic Law, originally enacted merely to exclude daughters from inheriting private property, came after a time to be applied to the crown, and it was held that its provisions excluded females from the succession to the throne. It must be admitted that the sex has taken ample vengeance for the slight put upon it, for in no European country has female rule, open or secret, been so long maintained or so powerfully felt as in France. During the first centuries of consolidation of the French Kingdom and dynasty, the effect of the Salic Law was doubly beneficial. Not only did it protect the kingdom from dismemberment and from the introduction of foreign dynasties; it enabled the kings through the law of settlements to establish their brothers or sons as counts or dukes over newly acquired provinces, and by such means to ensure an heir to the throne through some collateral branch of the dynasty in the event of failure in the direct line. The German Emperor Otto the Great had sagaciously endeavoured to strengthen his house by bestowing vacant dukedoms upon his sons and sons-in-law. But in this case such a policy only resulted in the rebellion of sons and relatives against the head of the family. Amongst the French princes the welfare and unity of the kingdom was of higher interest. The attempt, at a later time, of Philip II., in defiance of Salic Law, to impose a king upon France whose claim to the succession was derived through the female line, was frustrated. Germans assuredly have not forgotten the fearful devastation by fire and sword of the Palatinate in 1689, the pretext for which was the claim to the inheritance of German territory raised, contrary to all right, by a French prince who had married the daughter of the Elector Palatine.

In the Pyrenean peninsula, where female succession was valid, history took a different course. By the marriage, in 1234, of the heiress Blanca to Thibaut Count of Champagne, the Kingdom of Navarre passed for the first time into the hands of a French dynasty, and was afterwards united to France by the marriage of Philippe le Bel with Joanna. It again became independent under a French dynasty founded by Philip Count of Evreux, who married Joanna II.; and subsequently, after a brief connection with Aragon, was once more subjected to the rule of French princes in the persons of the Counts of Foix and the Lords of Albret, until it was forcibly annexed by Ferdinand King of Aragon to his dominions.

Spain received a Burgundian dynasty in the twelfth century, through the marriage of Queen Urraca of Castille with Raymond of Burgundy; a German dynasty in the sixteenth century by the accession of the son of the Emperor Maximilian to the throne; and a Bourbon dynasty in the eighteenth century. Despite the exclusive tendencies of Spain, the French princes in the peninsula kept up the intercourse between the more highly civilised sister-country and the land of their adoption. They opened the door to intellectual influences, and it was thus made easier to the French Cluniac monks to inspire fresh tendencies into the Spanish Church, and to lay the foundation of those principles which actuated the behaviour of Spain in ecclesiastical matters from the time of Ferdinand and Isabella, and which continued to guide the policy of Philip II. and his successors.

Reverting to the dynastic policy of the Capets, we find that in the year 1270 the royal house of France was only indirectly in possession of the greater part of modern France, that is to say, through the eight dynasties which were offshoots from it. The provinces apportioned by settlement to these families gradually reverted to the crown. Some collateral branches died out. The parent stem itself was four times on the point of extinction, and each time was revived through the indirect lines. Upon the death of Henry III. not only did the main line of the Capets disappear with the Valois branch, but by that time more than sixteen of the princely lines derived from it had come to an end. Meanwhile, within the space of 700 years the monarchs of the house of Capet had completed the task of extending the Kingdom of France up to its natural territorial limits. Once indeed a serious deviation from the policy of consolidation took place, when King John erected into principalities, for three of his sons, provinces which had previously been united to the crown. This retrograde step was punished by the rise of the Burgundian and Armagnac factions, which led to a civil war, threatening the very existence of the French Kingdom.

Matrimonial alliances play an important part in dynastic policy.

The fortune of the Habsburg family in marriage is proverbial. Yet to Europe at large these marriages were a source of trouble, since twice—in the sixteenth and again in the eighteenth century—the alliances formed with distant countries possessing no natural ties of interest, and the quarrels consequent upon disputed claims of inheritance, plunged Europe into protracted wars, in which Italy, Belgium, Spain, and Germany were visited with all the horrors of desolation.

France fared better with the marriages of her kings. Her matrimonial policy had undoubtedly led the nation into the Hundred Years' War with England, and into fruitless conflicts with Italy; yet it was nevertheless through marriage that Philippe Auguste acquired Artois; Philippe le Bel, Champagne and Brie; Louis XII., Brittany; and Louis XV., Lorraine. Queens thus brought with them as dowries acquisitions which must otherwise have been striven for upon the field of battle. Spain also was indebted for her union and political greatness to the marriage of Ferdinand of Aragon with Isabella of Castille.

Placed in a most difficult situation, the Dukes of Savoy found it greatly to their advantage to ally themselves by a double marriage with the most powerful monarchical houses of Europe. The house of Nassau-Dillenburg-Orange long flourished under a singularly favourable star, almost every marriage bringing with it an increase of territory and population.

But marriages have not infrequently produced momentous and mischievous consequences to royal races. The union of near relatives, frequent inter-marriage between two families, or, as in the case of the Habsburgs, between two branches of the same family, are causes which have been mainly accountable for the decay and extinction of dynasties. To the proverb of the middle ages—*aut non vives, aut non dives, aut non proles*—that is to say, to the early death, or poverty, or sterility which are consequent upon such marriages, another evil result may be added—mental weakness and disorder. That to the people, to whom their princes should at any rate be patterns, should be set an example of marriage between nephew and aunt or uncle and niece, is a dark stain in the history of Christian nations. The German Habsburgs did not numerically fail in offspring. The Emperor Maximilian had sixteen children by his cousin Maria, only daughter of Charles V., amongst whom were the Emperors Rudolph and Matthias; Maximilian the Grand Master of the Teutonic order and elective King of Poland; and Albert the Regent of Belgium. None of these left his inheritance to his son. The marriage of Charles of Styria with Maria of Bavaria was as fruitful as that of his father Ferdinand I. who had fifteen children; Ferdinand II. had seven; Ferdinand III., eleven; Leopold I. by three wives had sixteen sons and daughters, yet his son the Emperor Charles VI. was the last of the race; for in him the house of Habsburg came to an end, forty years after the extinction of the Spanish branch.

Effectual means have been devised to reduce princes into a state of acquiescence with idleness and incapacity; viz. the perpetual ceremonial and wearisome *etiquette* which like a net surrounds and trammels their daily life. The result attained has been similar to that produced by education in an Eastern hareem amongst women, eunuchs, and slaves. In Spain especially, but also in Vienna, the monotony of royal life under the unvarying restraint of court etiquette with its rigid mechanism, had an irresistible influence upon the minds of the princes fatal to all thought. Saint-Simon, who had known Philip V., the first Bourbon to ascend the Spanish throne, as a young and lively prince at the court of France, was astonished, upon a visit to Madrid, at the change which had come over the young monarch, whom he found just as mechanical, silent, melancholy, and hypochondriacal as his predecessors of the house of Habsburg.

The house of Habsburg had mentally and physically deteriorated in Spain with each succeeding generation. The portraits of the kings from Charles I. (V.) to Charles II. convey the impression of the progressive degradation of the race. Philip II. held the reins of government in his own hands; his son and his grandson, Philip III. and Philip IV., resigned them into the hands of their ministers, and their successor Charles II., a pitiable weakling, stunted in mind and body, was unable to continue the line. To his father Philip IV., besides several legitimate children, thirty-two bastards had been born. We find the same in the Stuart king, Charles II. of England, who had twelve illegitimate, but no legitimate children; Louis XIV., again, saw his sons, four daughters, grandson, and great-grandson precede him to the grave; one great-grandson alone, Louis XV., upon whom the destinies of France hung, survived him. His physician is said to have pointed out to him the cause: the children born of merely conventional marriages to worn-out voluptuaries are wanting in vital power, impoverished in blood, and as a rule short-lived. Many a princely race can show a similar result from a similar cause.

Old dynasties, like nations, have their source of vitality in the past, springing out of the remembrance of one or more famous ancestors, who for their great deeds—as national benefactors, or as wise and noble princes, or, acting in accordance with the popular sentiment, as conquerors who have added to the dominions of their country—survive in the grateful remembrance of the people. The image of the pious and just, tender yet strong Louis IX., shining through the troubled ages like a beneficent sunbeam, fostered the warmth of national loyalty towards the dynasty to which he belonged; and his name rather than any other is still invoked in any attempt to stir up sympathy with the old monarchy in the hearts of Frenchmen—an attempt useless enough now, since loyalty towards a dynasty is a sentiment that has been torn up by the very roots from the minds of the masses in France. The name of Bourbon has become associated in the popular mind with indistinct but deeply execrated memories of the *ancien régime* as the personification of arbitrary oppression and extortion. The fame of the earlier Louis has been obscured by the misdeeds of the XIVth and XVth representatives of the name. Such an entire revolution in the sentiments of a great people is one of the most striking phenomena of history. During a long period the French were not only loyal subjects, but enthusiastic worshippers of their king. In 1272 the Venetian ambassador remarked: 'Frenchmen neither can nor will exist out of their own country, for they know no other god but their king; the populace falls down to worship him upon bended knee whenever he passes.'

Just as the memory of the saintly Louis retained its glow in France, so did that of Alfred the Great in England, and to an even greater degree that of Edward the Confessor. Towards the latter, indeed, long after his death, and when romance had thrown an additional halo around him, the people were wont to look back with yearning affection, heightened by contrast with the hatred which they bore to the yoke of their Norman and Angevin masters. Such posthumous popularity has not attended any later sovereign, although Elizabeth, both during her life and after death, was a popular favourite. The people of England, with strong loyalist sentiments, are yet apt to call their monarchs to a strict account.

Amongst the gloomy pictures of the past, I reckon those dynasties which slowly or swiftly have compassed their own destruction. In a history of dynasties a section should be reserved for examples of this kind of suicide. The catastrophe may be brought about in three ways. First, by the murder of relatives so that the race perishes for want of an offshoot; an instance of this was the annihilation of the great Isaurian race of emperors by the Empress Irene, the murderess of her own son. Oriental history, both ancient and Mohammedan, is rife with similar occurrences.

Secondly, ruling houses have courted ruin by their vices, by unbridled lust and manifold crimes. Upon the death of Henry II. in 1559, the hopes of the house of Valois rested upon the four sons of that monarch, of whom three, Francis II., Charles IX., and Henry III., ascended the throne in turn. None of these left a legitimate son. Two of them shed streams of French blood in cowardly assassinations, and upon the death of Henry, a vicious king, who himself fell a victim to the hand of an assassin, the family became extinct.

There is a third way by which a ruling house achieves self-destruction. The Bourbons, especially Louis XIV. and XV., have trodden it. It was they who prepared the way for the general catastrophe of the Revolution and the downfall of their own dynasty—made them, in fact inevitable. Constant usurpations in favour of unlimited despotism; the undermining and dissolution of all protective rights and institutions for the people; encroachment by the cabinet upon the administration of justice, coupled with banishment of refractory judges; arbitrary imprisonment through innumerable *lettres-de-cachet*; sale of state and court offices, and consequent inability of government to control its functionaries; estrangement between classes through the hateful privileges of some, and the irreconcilable interests of others; above all, oppression and extortion practised against the mass of the people, *i.e.* the peasantry, to an extent almost inconceivable in our day: this was the inheritance which these three predecessors left to the well-meaning but ill-starred Louis XVI. It is doubtful whether the most highly-gifted monarch, supported by the most able statesmen, could have carried out a reformation amid disorders so profound, or have arrested the impending disaster. The weak, short-sighted Louis XVI. was by no means fitted for the giant task; it swept him into the abyss.

Ernst Moritz Arndt, a man whose name will remain ever dear to Germans, expressed in 1844 great anxiety at the fact that Germany was called upon to provide dynasties and princes for all Europe. 'Germany,' he said, 'has become a nursery for princes. Out of this eagle's nest have flown sovereigns to fill the English, Russian, and Scandinavian thrones, and empresses and queens are sought for in it. A melancholy prospect is hence opened of disputed claims and contested rights, which may possibly in the future divide and sap the strength of the fatherland.' Arndt dwelt much upon the importance of a general German law, a Pragmatic Sanction, being passed, which should make it impossible for a German state to accept any foreign prince, or any German prince occupying a foreign throne, as its leader. Had he lived to witness the events of 1871, he would have learnt to regard the future with greater confidence. The German federal union, the empire, is, and, let us hope, will remain, firmly and strongly cemented. The Salic Law remains in force, and a disruption of the provinces of Germany could only take place as the result of disastrous wars. German princes will yet again and again be summoned to fill foreign thrones. There is always a greater demand in the world for princes and dynasties than for republics and demagogues. We have given a Coburg prince to Portugal and a Hohenzollern prince to Roumania, and let us hope for the establishment of their power, and increased prosperity to their adopted countries.

Les dynasties s'en vont! was an exclamation made fifty years ago, and one which is often repeated at the present day in France and throughout Latin Europe. We have seen the fall of many a royal house. Yet the experience of the last few decades would rather prompt us to exclaim: New dynasties arise! The very fact that the present and the immediate future are charged with the solution of the greatest and weightiest social problems, makes monarchs indispensable. The testimony of history assures us that the solution of such questions, the reform of institutions, and the removal of traditional abuses, are more easily and safely accomplished under a monarchy than under a republic. When the corruption of the Roman Commonwealth reached the lowest point, all intelligent judges admitted the incapacity of the republic for self-reform, and the inevitable necessity for the monarchy. So was it with the Polish Republic, and so, again, with the French Republic under the Directory. Had the United States of North America been under a monarchical head in 1862, rather than under a president erected for a few years, it would have been possible to conduct the problem of slavery, upon which the Union had split, to a peaceful solution, and to have avoided a bloody civil war, of which the wounds are still far from being healed, and which even yet threatens to give rise to fresh complications and intolerable grievances.

I have heard it said by Americans, with regard to the presidential election and the concomitant changes in all the public offices, that their national constitution is productive of evils for remedying which no one can suggest method or means.

There is a German play in which an imperious woman says to the man of her choice:

> O lass mich knien, vor dir im Staube liegen.
> Mich demuthsvoll zu deinen Füssen schmiegen.

Und schwelgen in der ungewohnten Lust,
Die Leben geusst in meine todte Brust,
Dass einen Herrn ich über mich erkenne,
Und doch nicht wider ihn in Hass entbrenne.[2]

To the German the sovereign of the land is the father of his people, and as such the object of reverence and love, to whom is willingly attributed the will and the power to remove every grievance if once it be brought to his knowledge, and his mind be not poisoned by the suggestions of evil counsellors. Even the manifest faults and errors of the monarch are often leniently overlooked by the people if they concern only his personal life. And how trustfully and with what hopes and homage are these people wont to welcome a new sovereign! The dynastic sentiment is too deeply rooted in the nature and history of mankind ever to become entirely obliterated. *Reges erunt in orbe ultimi.*[3]

[2] Oh, let me kneel, in dust before thee lie,
Whilst henceforth humbly at thy feet I sigh,
Revelling in happiness before unguessed,
Which fills with life renewed my deadened breast.
Since now a master's will my heart discerns
And yet no flame of hate against him burns.

[3] Adapted from the well-known motto: A. E. I. O. U., *Austria erit in orbe ultima.*

II

THE HOUSE OF WITTELSBACH AND ITS PLACE IN GERMAN HISTORY[1]

Very ancient is the race which, already famous 900 years ago, rose after the year 1180 to fresh importance upon Bavarian soil. Otto, hitherto Count Palatine of Wittelsbach, was a descendant of that Duke Luitpold who fell in combat with the Hungarians, and whose sons and grandsons had already worn the ducal cap of Bavaria. No princely race in Europe is of such ancient extraction; the Capets, the Guelphs, the Ascanians, the Hohenzollerns, the Habsburgs—all came later upon the world's theatre.

The gift which the Emperor Frederick bestowed upon the Count of Wittelsbach in return for long and devoted services, was not indeed one of the great hereditary dukedoms, which, governed by an imperial representative vested with full powers, only too often had disturbed or shattered the peace of Germany by their rebellion.

With the fall of Henry the Lion these dukedoms were broken up, and were presently replaced by a number of smaller territorial lordships. Even Otto received but a portion of the former dukedom; Tyrol, Styria, and Austria were severed from it; and meanwhile the bishops had risen to an equality with the secular princes and were possessed of the same rights of sovereignty. Bavaria was as yet destitute of towns: Landshut and Munich first rose

[1] Lecture delivered at the Festival of the Wittelsbach Jubilee upon the special meeting of the R. B. Academy, July 28, 1880, in the great hall of the University at Munich, and published by the Academy and by C. H. Beck.

into consideration in the course of the 13th century; Ratisbon, already a flourishing town, was regarded as the capital and residence of the Dukes of Bavaria, and the duke even pretended to the title of Burggraf. Beautifully situated upon the Danube, Ratisbon would have been peculiarly fitted to form the central point of an aspiring state and the residence of its princes, and would have afforded it additional strength and unity; but it was the seat of a bishopric, and in those days princes and bishops in Germany were unable to exist side by side. There was as little room for prince and bishop in one town as for emperor and pope in one kingdom.

Thus from the outset it was incumbent upon the dukes, and as time went on became still more so, to apply themselves to consolidating the influence of their house.

It was a fortunate circumstance that the powerful counts of the land soon died out. As many as thirty of them disappeared within 300 years. The crime committed by the Count Palatine, a nephew and namesake of Otto's, in the murder of King Philip also tended to increase the consideration of the Wittelsbachs, since the possessions of the outlawed murderer fell to his cousin, who by this time had become duke. A further accession of dignity and power awaited the family in 1214 in the acquisition of the Palatinate of the Rhine.

Duke Ludwig was now the most powerful prince of Southern Germany. His ambition seems to have prompted him to a further step when, unlike his father, he broke faith with Frederick II. and his son Henry VI., and put himself at the head of the hostile forces which the pope had incited against the Hohenstaufens. But the weapon of the assassin upon the bridge of Kelheim cut short his career. His son Otto the Illustrious, remaining on the contrary true to the imperial house, died excommunicate, and his dominions were placed for several years under an interdict.

The house of Wittelsbach was nevertheless in a fair way

towards becoming the most powerful house in Germany. It was already without a rival in the south. Upon the death of Otto a partition of the inheritance took place. This partition became to the family an hereditary evil, a fatal source of quarrel and of secret or open enmity. So long as the system of partition was persevered in—and as many as twenty lines were at last in existence—the wounds which the house inflicted upon itself were deeper and more serious in their effects than any which could have been dealt by an external foe.

The permanent acquisition of the German Kingdom and Empire would, indeed, during that time, from the middle of the thirteenth to the beginning of the fourteenth century, have been unattainable even for the united house; for the powers which had overthrown the Hohenstaufens, and had so utterly and entirely reduced the empire to subjection, would no longer permit any hereditary succession, nor allow a strong prince to ascend the throne. The emperors elected were mere phantoms, some of them foreigners who by means of lavish expenditure appropriated the glitter of the German crown, leaving the actual power in the hands of the electoral princes. The empire fell from predominance to impotence—looked upon with contempt from without; a prey to confusion and anarchy within.

In this dark and dreadful period of interregnum, when all men waited for the final dissolution of the empire, nothing appears concerning the Wittelsbach family. We seek in vain for any trace of influence exercised by the family upon the affairs of Germany in proportion with the position which it occupied.

It was strong in the Rhineland; stronger still in the south, where lay the centre of gravity of the empire. Just at the critical time, besides, the Wittelsbachs had command of two electoral votes, by which they might more than once have turned the scale. But they did nothing of the kind: the imperial election was decided principally by the votes of the ecclesiastical electors, who were guided by aims prescribed to them by Rome. The secular princes, numbering at first thirteen, and afterwards thirty-eight, against ninety-two ecclesiastical princes, had enough to do in consolidating and regulating their but lately acquired territorial sovereignty.

The Wittelsbachs, in common with all the other princes of the time, had come to look upon what had been originally *ex officio* authority, as an hereditary family possession; and whilst one of them, the Count Palatine of the Rhine, was engaged in the task of welding together and organising his scattered provinces, the other, Duke Henry, was taken up with repelling the aggressiveness of his powerful neighbour Ottocar, King of Bohemia.

Finally in 1273 Rudolf, the first of the Habsburgs, ascended the long-unoccupied throne. They elected him, an insignificant count, rather than Ottocar or one of the Wittelsbachs, with the expectation that he would confirm Rome and the princes in possession of all the rights and territories of which they had despoiled the empire during the last thirty years; which accordingly he did. A restorer of the empire, as he has been called, he certainly was not, but he created a certain amount of order in the German provinces and adhered so far as lay in his power to the peaceful policy which he had announced. He won over the Bavarian princes by bestowing his daughters upon them in marriage. Louis remained faithful and rendered him good service; but the turbulent Henry, who had already made war upon his brother for the possession of the electoral vote, deserted him, and for this Bavaria was punished by the loss of the vote, and of the territory above the Enns.

After Rudolf's death the electoral oligarchy again set up in turn monarchs of different houses, Nassau, Habsburg, and Luxemburg, with the result that claims to the succession were now raised by the three families of Habsburg, Luxemburg, and Wittelsbach. The half-French Count of Luxemburg, whose family until recently had been but insignificant princes, had now, thanks to his father Henry VII., become King of Bohemia. The Habsburgs possessed Austria. Ludwig the Bavarian owed his success to his being the weakest and the least to be feared; and to the fact, besides, that he was neither the son nor the descendant of a former emperor.

For three-and-thirty years did Ludwig rule as king and emperor in Germany and Italy. Of his predecessors, three only, Otto I. and the two Fredericks, had reigned as long. He found himself, as time went on, more and more surrounded by insuperable obstacles and inveterate hostility. Innumerable foes from within and from without opposed him, sometimes openly, sometimes in secret. The house of Luxemburg, and the princes who had favoured his election that he might become their tool, did not hesitate to betray him whenever it suited their convenience. Wearied and despondent, he was more than once tempted to abdicate. His life was passed in warfare and in travelling from place to place. For the empire had neither capital nor royal residence, nor was there even a permanent place of safety for the archives, whilst the revenues had been so reduced by each imperial election that they amounted to but an insignificant sum.

But Ludwig's most dangerous and enterprising foe was in Paris. The now powerful royal house of France had, since the beginning of the century, been intent, now upon winning the German crown for a French prince, now upon wresting the empire if not the German Kingdom for France; and, in the distracted state of affairs, was at the same time ever on the watch to lay hands upon some convenient portion of the imperial territories. The papal court, transferred to France, had become French both in the person of the pope and in its policy; and, with this mighty lever in his grasp, it was the object of the French King to acquire the sovereignty in Italy for the house of Anjou, and at the same time to compass the end in view with regard to Germany. A far-reaching scheme for the extension of

Latin influences at the cost of the German nation had been thus set on foot.

Ludwig must have been unaware of the toils that surrounded him when, at a summons from the Ghibelline party, undeterred by the misfortunes which had there befallen his predecessor Henry VII., he undertook the journey to Italy. Once more, and now for the last time, a struggle was to be made to restore the imperial power in Italy. On both sides of the Alps this effort was expected and demanded of Ludwig. Only by undertaking the gigantic enterprise could he hope to retain his hold upon Germany. In Italy, during the time of the interregnum, and afterwards through Rudolf's action, the greater part of the rights and possessions of the empire in Italy had been already lost, *i.e.* stolen, abdicated, or sold. Although sadly deficient in arms and means, it was now nevertheless expected that he should take up the contest against the formidable opponents leagued against him—the pope, the Guelphs, and King Robert; whilst his only support lay in the shattered forces of the Ghibellines, who deceived him even as they on their side had miscalculated concerning him. Yet he boldly ventured further than the Hohenstaufens had done, leaving no weapon untried in the struggle against the papacy in Avignon. He surrounded himself with learned theologians and jurists. Intellectual forces and ideas were at that time called forth and diffused, which only a century and a half later were to ripen and change the face of Europe. Failure, nevertheless, was inevitable, and so also was the formidable reaction which was to take place in Germany. Yet the electoral princes—a rare occurrence in the annals of Germany—unanimously and energetically ranged themselves, as the struggle proceeded, upon the side of their monarch. The proclamation of the electoral assembly at Rense, although assuredly laying more stress upon the rights of the electors than upon those of the empire or of the emperor, found an echo amongst the people, especially of the towns, which for the most part, despite many years of interdict, remained steadfastly devoted to their king. As a matter of fact Ludwig might justly lay claim to their gratitude, since his greatest merit consisted in having, so far as he had been able, raised the condition of the towns, protected them, and endowed them with manifold privileges. Emulating the example of the Luxemburgs and Habsburgs, he had also taken in hand the establishment of a great Bavarian power, and had added Brandenburg and Holland together with Hainault to his family possessions. Had these acquisitions been permanent, the fate of Germany might have taken a very different course. But Ludwig only added thereby to the number of his enemies, and to those of his house. The territory acquired in North Germany and the Netherlands was speedily forfeited, the Wittelsbachs being themselves not without blame for the loss.

After the death of Ludwig the empire fell into the hands of Charles IV. of Luxemburg, who even before that event had been elected by a disaffected portion of the electors; and proved himself able to split up the house of Wittelsbach by his unscrupulous policy, and so to deprive it permanently of any importance in the empire. Family discord, the evil genius of the house, coupled with a foolish partition of the inheritance made by the brothers in defiance of their imperial father's will, played into the emperor's hands. By a public breach of faith he deprived Duke Ludwig of the alternate right of the electoral vote, and bestowed it upon the Count Palatine alone, thus adding fresh fuel to the flames of hatred by which this house was now being consumed, which in 1343 had been the strongest in Germany. According to the saying of the Emperor Maximilian, Charles was a father to Bohemia and a step-father to the empire. He looked on with indifference whilst the imperial provinces were given over to violence, and to the excesses of the robber-bands in the pay of the territorial nobility. His pompous journey to Rome for coronation only revealed the utter contempt into which the empire had fallen in the peninsula; he returned home with the speed of a fugitive. Yet he succeeded where for a hundred years past every emperor had failed; for he obtained the election of his son Wenzel as his successor during his lifetime.

The deposition of Wenzel at Lahnstein in 1400 was the occasion for another member of the Wittelsbach family to ascend the throne. But the condition of the empire under Wenzel had become almost intolerable. Imperial authority was as if non-existent; a chaos of lawlessness and strife met the eye on all sides, whilst from his distant throne in the Slavonic country, the Bohemian King contemplated with stupid indifference the distractions of the empire. The electors had already, five years before, threatened to take the administration of imperial affairs into their own hands, and had then vainly solicited the appointment of a deputy charged with that office. They now set up Rupert III., of the Palatinate, against him, whose father and grandfather had both given proofs of earnest solicitude for the welfare of the empire. Now, at last, an election was carried without bribery; Rupert upon his elevation was not open to the reproach levelled against his predecessors, that 'florins had played a conspicuous part in it;' an event without parallel in the two previous centuries of German history.

Meanwhile Wenzel maintained his position; nor were there wanting princes and towns accustomed to rely upon themselves, and ready to support a sovereign who remained inactive and at a distance. Many, too, assumed a neutral, expectant attitude. Rupert was nowhere acknowledged in the north. Besides this it remained for a long while inevitable in Germany that each succeeding emperor should enter the lists with fewer resources, since in those days whoever, not content with the mere tinsel of royalty, resolved upon upholding the dignity of the empire, exposed himself to the unwearied assaults of a legion of enemies.

Rupert began his reign with the best will and the

noblest intentions, but he soon found his own cousin siding with his opponents. His journey to Italy resulted only in failure; the ecclesiastical princes who had acknowledged him hastened to disclaim their allegiance as soon as he required of them any sacrifice, or set his face against anarchy. The League of Marbach, formed to oppose him, obliged him to abandon his beneficent projects, such for instance as the destruction of the robber-nests and other pests of the land. Even his best enterprises were unrecognised and unsupported; only in his own domain, the Palatinate, did the wisdom of his administration cause his memory to be revered.

When the German crown again passed to a Habsburg, the situation, under Frederick III., became even worse than under Wenzel. The empire was out of course; the nation seemed in process of decomposition; whilst the emperor, indolent, phlegmatic, and insensible to anything but family ambition, looked on at the confusion, intent merely upon hindering every reform in church or state—as harmful in his own dominions as he was pernicious to the empire. The most prominent member at that moment of the Wittelsbach family was Prince Frederick the Victorious, Elector Palatine. Unacknowledged by the emperor, and finally outlawed, he not only understood how to assert his rights, but, being always ready to come to blows and a master in the art of acquisition and organisation, he bequeathed his patrimony to his successor with the addition of above sixty fortresses and towns.

The relations of the Wittelsbachs with their Austrian neighbours were often unfriendly. One hundred and fifty years previously the Bavarian house had been more powerful and more highly esteemed than that of Habsburg. But now under Maximilian I., 1493-1519, the fortunes of the Habsburgs rose, whilst those of the Wittelsbachs seemed to decline. The former had become possessed of Tyrol in 1363, and Maximilian availed himself of the family feud between the Palatinate and old-Bavarian lines to wrest the valleys of the Inn and the Ziller from the Bavarian prince. The Wittelsbachs had consequently well-founded reasons for dislike and mistrust; whilst as princes of the empire they shared in the general discontent against the monarch who allowed the reforms and institutions, which in 1495 had been hailed with delight, to fall again into abeyance, and treated the empire only as an instrument for the advance of his own hereditary power. Conscious of the danger which threatened them, they perceived the necessity for putting an end to the partitions of the inheritance. A new principality, that of Neuberg with Sulzbach, had even then just been erected for some member of the family; but the Statute of Primogeniture (1506) raised a barrier against these subdivisions, and Bavaria from that time forth remained an hereditary dukedom of which the succession devolved upon the eldest son.

And now a new, a third epoch begins; the middle ages have run their course and have bequeathed to the coming period a rich legacy of ideas and aspirations hitherto suppressed or not yet brought to light. Silently they had gathered strength, and their growth, joined to the new discoveries and inventions of the age, formed together a prodigious stream of new ideas, new needs, new claims, which, sweeping all before it, broke into every department of life, and most forcibly into that of religion. The German nation in travail brought forth the Reformation, which after a few years was destined, now victorious, now trodden under foot, to lay hold upon every state and nation of Europe.

The attitude assumed by the house of Wittelsbach towards this movement was destined to become a matter of historical importance.

Within twenty or thirty years the most prominent of the princely houses of Germany, besides most of the towns, had joined the Reformation and introduced it into their provinces. The princes of the Palatinate had been of the number. The majority of the nobles of the empire took the same side. About the year 1565 it was generally supposed that nine-tenths of the people had openly become Protestants or were secretly attached to the new doctrines. There was no difference between the north and the south in this respect. Setting aside the town of Jülich, which remained Catholic until 1609, only two of the dominant families of Germany persevered on the Catholic side, the Habsburgs and the ducal branch of Wittelsbach. Had even the latter of these followed the powerful impulse to which the rest had given way, the history of Germany, or even of Europe itself, might have taken an entirely different course.

The empire, 'the Holy Roman Empire of the German people,' as it had become in the middle ages, was the outcome of hierarchical conceptions, a half-priestly institution, as the emperor at his coronation, serving as deacon to the pope at the altar, showed. In the first place were his services due to the church; as her secular arm he must satisfy her needs, carry out her sentences, extend her jurisdiction. The dependence of the empire upon the pope and the ecclesiastical princes made it impossible that a Protestant emperor should be tolerated; a decree for his deposition would at once have been issued, and would have given the signal for invasion to foreign monarchs, above all to France. The half Spanish, half German Habsburger was well aware of this; Maximilian II. felt it, when he durst not avow his Protestant convictions; Frederick II. of Prussia acknowledged it, when upon the extinction of the Habsburgs in the eighteenth century he seemed upon the point of securing the imperial crown.

The Wittelsbachs, since the establishment of the Statute of Primogeniture, had found it expedient to provide for the younger princes of their family through the ecclesiastical principalities in Bavaria and the rest of Germany; and this circumstance constituted a strong tie to bind them to the old church, all the more so that in this way the power and influence of the house was heightened in Germany. The electoral prince-bishopric of Cologne remained from 1583 to 1761 uninterruptedly in the hands of the Wittelsbachs.

Thus it fell out that Wittelsbachs and Habsburgers were in accord upon church matters; and matrimony stepped in to strengthen the bond between them. The peasant insurrection, which blazed all around in 1525, had left Bavaria undisturbed; but neither Duke William IV. nor the Emperor Ferdinand I. was able to stop the spread of Protestant doctrines in their dominions. This much, however, they obtained: the whole framework of the old church system and forms of worship were preserved intact both in Austria and Bavaria.

Both Ferdinand and Duke Albert V. of Bavaria went indeed so far as to demand at Rome as well as at Trent a comprehensive and thorough reform in the church, not in doctrine, but in life, discipline, and ritual. This being refused, Albert first, and William likewise after him, applied themselves, with all the coercive means at their disposal and with the support of the holy see, to the extirpation of the new confession.

In the Palatinate meanwhile the Reformation had for thirty years been making steady but silent progress before the Elector Otto Henry gave it open and unrestricted admission, the two subordinate lines of Simmern and Zweibrücken having already done so. The next thing that happened was that the succeeding Elector Frederick III. declared for the Calvinistic in preference to the Lutheran doctrines which had hitherto been generally adopted in Germany. Here again the act of a Wittelsbacher made a decisive mark upon the course of events, for his example was presently imitated by two other princes. Thus the wedge of dissension was introduced into the compact mass of German Protestantism, which until then had remained firmly united by the league of the princes with the towns. Lutheran and Calvinist princes stood henceforth in active or passive opposition to one another, and even the dread of a common danger could not suffice to restore unanimity in their counsels; the wound which the Protestant cause received at that time has only been healed in our own day.

Frederick's great-grandson, the unfortunate Frederick V., paid a heavy penalty for the deed of his ancestor.

In Bavaria the counter-reformation was accomplished under William V.; herewith the restrictions imposed upon the ruler by the three estates had given way as they had also done in Austria; and the Elector Maximilian I. found himself free to dispose, even to exhaustion if he pleased, of the utmost resources of his country. Bavaria was now for the first time an independent state under the strong hand of a wise and energetic prince whose thought and will were steadily directed towards one object. She had now become a power with which the European powers had to reckon, a power which might even be called upon to decide the future of Germany.

And now, once again, it is remarkable how Wittelsbach stood opposed to Wittelsbach. This time the opposition was of wide historical import: Bavaria against the Rhenish Palatinate, the League against the Union. The princes of the Palatinate were now the support of advancing and aggressive Protestantism. They endeavoured to unite the Protestants at home and abroad for common defence. Whilst the electoral house of Saxony, which at first had stood at the head of the evangelical movement, now became more and more closely allied with the imperial house, the Electors Palatine brought armed support to the French Protestants, aided the people of the Netherlands in the struggle for religion and freedom against Spain, and placed themselves at the head of the Evangelical Union, whose members recognised that they must expect no quarter from the authorities of the empire, and that combination and self-reliance alone could save them from falling victims to the league for the extirpation of Protestantism. Opposed to them we find Maximilian at the head of the Catholic League, by joining which the ecclesiastical princes sought safety and help against the outward pressure which they dreaded from the wholesale conversion of their subjects to Protestantism. It was imagined by many, and above all by the most powerful and influential society of the time, that the moment had come, or at least was approaching, when all Germany would again be united under the rule of pope and emperor.

In 1619, the Emperor Matthias having died childless, the Duke of Bavaria was invited to become a candidate for the imperial throne. His friends put him in mind of his ancestor the Emperor Ludwig; the Elector of Cologne was his brother; his cousin the Elector Palatine came in person to persuade him; the ecclesiastical princes would gladly have seen the imperial power and their own claims in the hands of the leader of the League. Nevertheless, he declined, declaring himself in favour of Ferdinand of Habsburg.

And now followed those heavy blows which plunged Germany into the horrors of the Thirty Years' War, whereby the country was laid waste with fire and sword, and the people brought to the verge of ruin. Our fatherland, chiefly at the hands of her own sons under foreign leadership, was reduced to a wilderness and the people to barbarism. Two centuries were needed to raise them again from the depth to which they had fallen.

Whilst the election of Ferdinand was taking place at Frankfort, the Bohemians proclaimed the Count Palatine as their king. Thereupon Maximilian, having obtained from the emperor the promise of the electoral dignity as well as of any portion of territory which he might wrest from his cousin, marched against the Bohemians at the head of an army in the pay of the pope and of the ecclesiastical princes, defeated them at the White Hill, and took terrible vengeance upon them by the executions at Prague. Having caused himself to be entrusted with the execution of the ban of the empire against his cousin, Maximilian conquered the Upper and Rhenish Palatinates, and, by gaining possession of the electoral vote, destroyed the equal balance which had hitherto existed in the electoral college between the votes of the two confessions. A

Catholic majority was thus created amongst the princes in whose hands the government of Germany had rested during the reigns of the three preceding emperors.

The Union was dissolved; the evangelical doctrine was banished from the hereditary and crown lands of Austria; victory after victory was won by the armies of the empire and the League, and Ferdinand, finding himself more powerful in Germany than Charles V. had been, turned his mind to the hope of re-uniting Spain with Austria, and to the re-establishment of a universal empire. He made a Spanish settlement of the Lower Palatinate, and did all in his power to promote the establishment of these enemies of Germany in the Rhine lands.

Meanwhile he durst not put aside the remembrance that he owed to Maximilian the rescue of his house from the dangerous situation in which it had been placed. And how powerful the influence of that prince then was, is apparent in the Edict of Restitution and the release of Wallenstein, wrung from the emperor at the assembly of the Diet in 1630. Maximilian himself had perceived the necessity of winning the support of France if he wished to preserve the preponderance of his influence in the empire and to secure possession of the much-contested electoral dignity. He it was who set the precedent afterwards too freely followed by his successors, and, by a secret treaty with Richelieu, secured the electoral dignity together with territories which he had recently acquired.

What followed is well known: the defeat of the League and of the imperial forces; Gustavus Adolphus in Munich; Pope Urban VIII., irritated with the proceedings of the Habsburgs in Italy, siding with France and thus indirectly with Sweden. France after the death of Gustavus Adolphus began to take an active part in the war. Under the influence of a common danger the emperor and Maximilian were again drawn together, and each strained his resources to the utmost to continue the war, although victory had ceased to favour his standard. Once again in the last and most destructive years of this long war was Maximilian destined to see his country trodden under foot by hostile armies, and himself a fugitive in Braunau. Nothing then remained but to throw himself into the arms of France, making over Elsass to that country as the price of her intervention. It was a bitter destiny which brought Bavaria and Germany to utter destitution under the ablest of all the princes of the elder branch of Wittelsbach.

The Peace of Westphalia turned out favourably to the interests of the two cousins. The Bavarian house retained the electoral dignity and the Upper Palatinate, in consideration, however, of the payment of thirteen millions to the imperial house. Upon the Count Palatine was conferred, with the recovery of the Rhenish Palatinate, an eighth vote as well as the restoration of his family as Counts of Simmern. But Germany and the empire fared badly; the territory ceded to France and Sweden amounted in area to the extent of a kingdom. Ruin had at last overtaken the old empire; only a shadow of supremacy remained to the emperor; the princes had become totally independent, with the right of concluding alliances and treaties with foreign powers; whilst both France and Germany had acquired the power henceforth to interfere, as guarantors of the peace which had just been concluded, in the internal affairs of Germany, a power of which France especially was not backward in availing herself. As henceforth there existed no common policy for Germany—Austria, Brandenburg, Saxony, having each their own—Bavaria, consulting only her own interests, was forced by Austria to turn her eyes more and more persistently westwards.

When Karl Ludwig, the son of the unfortunate Frederick, returned, after fifteen years' exile spent in London, to the ancestral lands which he had quitted as a child, it was to find his country impoverished and depopulated; transformed from a garden to a wilderness. It was calculated that only a fiftieth part of the inhabitants remained. Yet the Palatinate, under the wise and beneficent government of this prince, speedily began again to flourish, the exiles or emigrants who had left it returned, and religious freedom attracted new and industrious settlers. But it is indicative of the situation, that even the emperor had not sufficient authority to induce the Spaniards whom his father had imported, and who had become the pests of the country, to evacuate the fortress of Frankenthal; they remained there for some years longer. This circumstance was a warning to the Palatinate that nothing could now be expected from the imperial court. The elector was soon obliged to recognise that, in all that concerned the political life and welfare of his dominions, nothing was to be hoped or feared from any one but his powerful French neighbour. Acting upon this view he gave his only daughter Charlotte Elisabeth in marriage to the dissipated brother of Louis XIV., 'a sacrificial lamb offered upon the altar of policy' as she described herself. All in vain; it was precisely she who, resembling her father in mind and character, furnished the pretext which led to the devastation of her native land by fire and sword in a manner that surpassed the cruelty and horror of the Thirty Years' War.

Bavaria, as compared with the Palatinate, which since 1679 had been a battle-field for the French legions, might almost be called happy. Under the gentle rule of Ferdinand Maria, the weak but well-meaning son of Maximilian, the country slowly but surely revived, the more so that, acting under the advice of his mother, who was a Habsburg, the duke had the tact to reject the specious gift of the imperial crown which after the death of Ferdinand III. Mazarin had designed for him, and at the same time to aid in preventing the choice from falling upon Louis XIV.

Very different were the counsels followed by his son Max Emanuel, the courageous, brilliant, but fickle and unprincipled pupil of the women at the court of Versailles. When scarcely twenty years of age he had assisted with his Bavarians at the siege of Vienna and in driving the Turks out of Hungary. He had then, in the service of the emperor upon the Rhine, turned his arms against Louis XIV. and had become the Spanish stadtholder in Brussels. Deceived in his brilliant hopes by the loss of his son, who was looked upon as heir to the Spanish throne, and embittered in his feelings against the imperial house; attracted also by the splendid promises of the French King, Max Emanuel joined Louis in the war of succession which was just breaking out, and with his connivance attempted to transfer the imperial crown from the Habsburg to the Wittelsbach line and to enrich himself by the annexation of some Austrian provinces. The contest ended in his speedy defeat, and the court of Vienna was unsparing in its revenge. With the combined consent of the other electors, both he and his brother were placed under the ban of the empire, for the latter, Joseph Clement, Prince Bishop of Cologne, had also been deeply implicated in the affair with Louis XIV.; the French had occupied the electoral state and were now proceeding to treat it as an incorporated part of the French dominions. Nothing remained to the prince but the appearance of authority, for he had become merely a tool in the hands of the French ministers and generals.

The whole of Bavaria was in the enemy's hands. According to the order of the Emperor Leopold to his generals (1703) the country was to be 'pressed and drained' to the utmost, for the benefit of the imperial exchequer. A popular rising which was excited by this intolerable oppression was put down by force.

In 1705 the emperor pronounced the final deposition of the house of Wittelsbach in Bavaria, which country had now been twice subdued. Portions of the country were allotted to the imperial favourites and ministers; the district of the Inn was absorbed into Upper Austria; the chapter-lands of Augsburg were enlarged. The whole of the Bavarian people—such was the state of frenzy reached in Vienna—was sentenced to capital punishment; but, as an act of clemency, the sentence was only to be enforced upon every fiftieth man in the towns, and every tenth man in the country. Fortunately the power required to carry out the wrathful edict was wanting. So completely forgotten were all the heavy sacrifices of blood and treasure which Bavaria during eighty years had made in the interests of the Habsburgs; it was even forgotten that but a few years had elapsed since 30,000 Bavarians had laid down their lives to win back Hungary for the house of Habsburg.

The partiality of the Wittelsbach princes for the French alliance appears to us now an almost inexplicable blunder. It had sprung up towards the end of the Thirty Years' War, and had now lasted fifty years. Yet it becomes more comprehensible, and at any rate seems less unnatural, if we carefully survey the political and ecclesiastical condition of Germany at that time.

The fast-decaying constitution of the empire was a tissue of contradictions and fundamental falsehoods. Its supremacy, now that it had neither revenues nor a central seat of government, had disappeared. Its hereditary states, even the German provinces, were becoming more and more disconnected in their relations with the rest of Germany. Institutions created for the benefit of the whole, whenever the court of Vienna had interfered, had been corrupted or paralysed. This was the case not only with the permanent Diet at Ratisbon—from which the princes now kept aloof—with its empty pomposity, its proverbial somnolence, and petty wrangling over titles and ceremonial; but also with the universally despised and abortive administration of justice in the imperial courts. The military system was pitiable: no German army existed, and the so-called imperial army had grown to be the laughing-stock of the people. On the most exposed frontier of the empire was established a long series of ecclesiastical princes who, being incapable of defending either themselves or the empire, naturally fell under French influence, and offered to the longing eyes of their too powerful, and now also too audacious neighbour, the tempting spectacle of German impotence. The Electorate of Cologne, which had become a dependency of the Wittelsbachs, was now together with Mainz a favourite object for French diplomatists, who possessed in this way a lever for their designs both upon the lower Rhine and the Isar.

National feeling no longer existed in Germany; self-reliance and public spirit amongst the people were wanting: the consideration that besides religion there might be other great interests common to all and for which every German should be answerable, was felt by few and expressed by fewer still. There was no public organ through which patriotic men might appeal to the ears of the people. The Germans, destitute of intellectual wealth, and with a language that had become harsh, awkward, and inharmonious, turned, in the absence of any popular literature of their own, to the study of French, which precisely at that time had reached the height of its classical bloom. To their eyes in consequence Louis appeared invested in the triple splendour of a bold conqueror and commander; a master in the art of government, and magnanimous patron of letters, art, and science; a fascinating ideal, to be gazed upon with reverence and amazement. Versailles was the school for German princes in their youth and the pattern diligently copied by the courts beyond the Rhine. With what enthusiasm does even Leibnitz, the most distinguished of German thinkers, write of the magnificence of Louis—what hopes does he found upon him! Yet none was more fully aware than Leibnitz of the danger which threatened Germany through the French Monarch, nor had expressed it more emphatically. In Bavaria there was moreover the highly important fact, that even at the papal court the prestige and influence of France was greater than that of the imperial court: for since the time of the Reformation the authority of the papal chair had in political matters usually been paramount in Munich. Each political question had its ecclesiastical side, and, owing to continual complications arising with the seven neighbouring bishops, who were all princes of the empire, the court of Munich had every reason for trying to act in accordance with the will of the papal court, a consideration that was well understood in Paris.

As to Austria herself, Louis, thanks to his excellent diplomatists, was often as powerful and lucky in policy at Vienna as at other courts. The Emperor Leopold in 1668 had, in a secret treaty with his arch-enemy the French King concerning the Spanish succession, come to an understanding about the elder branch of the Habsburgs; and statesmanship in Vienna was henceforth directed towards anxiously avoiding any step which might be displeasing to the French Monarch. French gold, besides, operated so efficaciously upon Leopold's counsellors and ministers that General Montecuculi complained that the orders transmitted to him by his imperial master were known in Paris before he received them. Leopold forwarded his congratulations to the king upon his victories over the heretics of the Netherlands at the very time that he was sending an army to protect them.

Since the imperial crown had become hereditary in the house of Habsburg the empire had been suffering continual losses, for which the Habsburgs themselves were chiefly responsible. The German Netherlands had been ceded to Spain; the separation from Switzerland had been occasioned under Maximilian I. by an unlucky war with the confederates of that country. Since then, by the Peace of Westphalia, Ferdinand III. had acknowledged the sovereignty of France over the three bishoprics of Lothringen, and had evacuated Elsass. Leopold I. consented to resign the countship of Burgundy, and to hand over Freiburg to Louis, who in 1697 was nevertheless forced to cede it again to the emperor when with the consent of the latter he retained the fortress of Strasburg. In 1713 the Emperor Charles VI. voluntarily abandoned the whole of Lothringen, the duke, his son-in-law, receiving Tuscany in exchange. The Dukedom of Milan, although still properly belonging to the empire, had long since ceased to be considered as such. Nothing under these circumstances could seem more natural than that Austria and Germany should regard one another as foreigners, and that any attempt on the part of Vienna to assert a right of supremacy or to interfere with German affairs, should be resented in most parts of Germany as an encroachment upon German freedom.

Max Emanuel and his brother were reinstated in their rank and possessions by the Peace of Rastatt in 1714, and it tends to the honour of the former that he sent his Bavarians to assist the emperor against the Turks and in the taking of Belgrade. Twenty-six years later the prospect of the imperial throne was again opened to the Wittelsbachs. The male line of the house of Habsburg had become extinct with the death of Charles VI., after having in a period of four hundred and sixty-seven years furnished sixteen emperors to the German throne. The Wittelsbachs, of all the families which had worn the imperial crown, now alone remained, and were moreover of purely German origin, whereas Maria Theresa's husband the Duke of Lorraine, to whom the throne was destined in Vienna, was a descendant of the French house of Vaudemont. Many of the electors agreed with the opinion expressed by Frederick that, under an emperor of another house, the reproaches abundantly levelled against the court of Vienna for oppression and persecution in matters of religion, and as to the administration of imperial justice, would cease; and that it was desirable for the empire to have at its head a sovereign who had no possessions abroad, and would not be perpetually involving the empire in foreign wars as the Austrian house had done.

Upon this last question of succession to the imperial crown Bavaria and the Palatinate had at last laid aside their old differences and entered into close alliance together. The unanimous election of Charles Albert by the electoral princes followed—an event which was chiefly due to the political activity of Frederick II. of Prussia. This prince was equally rejoiced to see Bavaria strengthened and Austria weakened by the transfer of the imperial crown.

Charles VII. thus suddenly found himself the head of three hundred and seventy sovereign princes and estates; emperor of a realm without a soldier and with only a few thousand florins of revenue. Munich, it was to be expected, would take the place of Vienna as the capital and as the seat of the imperial council. The imperial dignity, although carrying with it no direct accession of power, afforded facilities for laying the foundation of a family power beyond any which Bavaria at that time could offer. Charles Albert's first step was to put in claims to the succession of the Bohemian Kingdom and the Austrian Archduchy; but to support these it was necessary to have recourse to arms.

A magic influence, powerful if not outwardly perceptible, still lay in the imperial crown, identified as that crown still was with the ancient royal crown of Germany. In the north this influence seemed to have died out, for the Habsburg emperor was there only known as a persecutor of the religion of the land and a traitor to the border provinces; but it was potent still in the ecclesiastical principalities, and especially in the south, divided as it was among a number of small and very small potentates. An emperor sprung from the oldest German house, possessed of a German crown province, supported by a vigorous army, and surrounded by experienced statesmen, might soon have awakened the long-slumbering hopes of a resuscitated empire, and have found a joyful welcome in millions of German hearts.

But how far was the sad reality from this ideal of imperial revival! Charles Albert possessed no counsellor and general, as the last emperor had possessed in Prince Eugene; his only adviser was Count Törring. Feeble as the empire had become, it was, notwithstanding, the pivot of European politics, to hold the tangled threads of which, the ministers and diplomatists of an emperor had need of strong and skilful hands. But the condition of education in Bavaria at that time was not such as to offer a choice of useful men trained in the conduct of public affairs, neither could the impoverished country supply the necessary funds for any enterprise. Charles therefore found himself entirely thrown back upon France and Prussia for assistance. Therein he stood opposed to a remarkable woman, Maria Theresa, who in activity, foresight, and manly courage surpassed all former sovereigns of the Habsburg family who had sat on either throne since the days of Charles V. Albert was quickly deprived of the Bohemian crown which he had placed upon his own head in Prague, and proved himself moreover to be utterly incapable of holding the reins of government in Germany. After his early death in 1745 nothing remained for his son Max Joseph III. but to renounce by the Treaty of Füssen all claims to the inheritance, and to give his vote for the election of the husband of Maria Theresa in exchange for his own conquered Bavaria. The direct line of Ludwig of Wittelsbach, which had reigned in Bavaria for nearly five centuries, became extinct December 30, 1777, by the death of Maximilian III., a well-meaning prince, beloved and regretted by his subjects. Bavaria and the Palatinate, after a separation of four hundred and eighty-eight years, now once more became united under Charles Theodore.

The new prince, like his predecessor, had no legitimate descendants. He quitted with reluctance his territories of the Rhine to take up his residence in Munich, and readily entered into a plan of exchange, by which he contemplated ceding Bavaria, or at any rate the most considerable part of it, to Austria.

Maria Theresa had set her heart upon the acquisition of Bavaria. Lord Stair, an English statesman, had suggested to her some time before that Elsass and Lothringen, reconquered and erected into a kingdom, might form an exchange for Bavaria. Her thoughts, at a later period, turned towards Naples and Sicily. Bavaria, Prince Kaunitz also suggested, would be a fitting compensation for Silesia which she had lost; a foot of Bavarian soil was, he remarked, worth more than whole districts elsewhere; the house of Wittelsbach, always dangerous from its central position, would be better removed from the middle of Europe to a distance, and established in the south of Italy. Kaunitz insisted that Austria ought to retain the Netherlands, a far richer country—as the opposition of the maritime powers might be assumed—and yet appropriate a good slice of Bavaria to form a 'satisfactory boundary for the archducal domains.' The Upper Palatinate must also be taken, to interpose a good barrier against the Margraviates of Bayreuth and Anspach belonging to Brandenburg.

Upon the death of Maximilian III., Maria Theresa opposed at first the resolution of her son Joseph to proceed at once with the military occupation of Bavaria, but soon afterwards acceded to his desire, and the Austrian troops were put in motion. Charles Theodore had actually signed the treaty by which, without the consent of the estates of the country, or of the Duke of Zweibrücken, who was the rightful heir, the best part of Bavaria was made over to Austria. The mysterious behaviour of Charles Albert has never yet been explained; he remained a passive spectator of the rapid advance of the Austrians from Straubing upon the surrounding country. The phantom Diet dared not offer a remonstrance. Frederick II., however, flew to arms. Even Russia, to whom this first occasion for meddling in the affairs of Germany was welcome, interfered; France raised her voice; Saxony and Mecklenburg-Schwerin put forth claims to the inheritance, which were at least as valid as the feeble pretensions of Austria. Lectures were delivered in the universities upon the question, which had grown to be of European interest. Frederick's army marched into Bohemia, and a war was commenced, poor in feats of arms but destructive enough, which ended in the Peace of Teschen. Austria was repulsed, and contented herself with the spoils of the district of the Inn.

In 1785 Charles Theodore, to whom the possession of Bohemia seemed to have become a burden, again negotiated with Joseph II. for an exchange of countries. It was agreed that he should receive the Netherlands as a Burgundian Kingdom in place of Bavaria. But Frederick II. again frustrated this design with the help of the confederate princes.

During the first years of the French Revolution, when the possession of Belgium had become uncertain and dangerous for Austria, the court of Vienna once more attempted to acquire Bavaria in exchange for Belgium. Prussia, as the price of her consent, was to be allowed to take part of Poland; but the affair miscarried upon Austria raising a further claim upon Anspach and Bayreuth. It is true that Francis Joseph, who had the acquisition of Bavaria much at heart, hastened to drop the claim to the Franconian provinces; but Belgium had meanwhile fallen into the hands of the French. Charles Theodore, whose constant dread was the sudden occupation of his dominions by a military *coup-de-main* on the part of Austria, allowed himself to be drawn on into negotiations with the holders of power in Paris, a proceeding which was characterised in Vienna as an act of treason against the empire.

In the complicated state of European affairs this desire upon the part of Austria to gain possession of Bavaria was for ever breaking out. England pointed out in vain that when they were in arms against the French Revolution was not the time to incur the blame, themselves, of revolutionary acts of violence. The acquisition of Bavaria by Austria was again inserted as a secret article in a treaty concluded with Russia in 1795, containing an offensive and defensive alliance between the two imperial courts against Prussia. The Minister Thugut thought and acted upon this point as Kaunitz had done. Even in the Peace of Campo Formio, concluded with France in 1797, the fifth secret article runs thus: 'The French Republic shall provide that a portion of Bavaria with Salzburg be given to the Emperor Francis.'

These facts doubtless throw some light upon the subsequent policy of Bavaria with regard to the Confederation of the Rhine.

The relations of Austria with France having again become hostile in 1798, Max Joseph of the Zweibrücken-Birkenfeld line was able, in spite of the secret clause in the Treaty of Campo Formio, to enter into peaceable possession of the Bavarian inheritance when by the death of Charles Theodore the Sulzbach line became extinct. The Zweibrücken-Birkenfeld house had already given three remarkable kings to Sweden, and Bavaria now was destined to be beholden to it for a line of excellent princes.

We have now arrived at an important turning-point. The events with which the century closed introduced a new period for Germany as well as for the rest of mankind. Not least so for Bavaria. The accession of Maximilian as Prince Elector of the Palatinate and Bavaria is the mark which divides the old Bavaria from the new. By no gradual and imperceptible process of development were country and people transformed; it was with sore travail that the new birth was ushered in—that the old ducal stem of Bavaria assumed the shape of a stately kingdom, three times as large, of a nation compacted of the various territories of old Bavaria, Franconia, Swabia, and the Rhine and Upper Palatinates. In the opinion of an English statesman living in Munich in 1774, 'to describe the condition of this country it is necessary to go back two generations in the progress of human society.' These conditions have already almost faded from the memory of the present generation. So great are the changes which have since come about.

To King Max Joseph is the honour due of having raised Bavaria, after a century and a half of separation and estrangement, to a position once more of equality and complete fellowship with the rest of the German States.

To effect this, and to support the almost intolerable burdens which general warfare and ruin and foreign pressure had laid upon our land, a complete transformation of the political and social organisation of the nation was needful. It was necessary almost simultaneously to take in hand reforms in the schools, the church, the civil and military departments, the system of taxation, feudal customs and serfdom, the administration of justice, and offices of the state. That in these things many mistakes, and some of them serious ones, should for many years be committed, was inevitable. The king, the government, and the people had to pass through years of trial and to buy their experience dearly. Nor could it be expected that a state built up of incongruous elements, still under the pressure of a foreign yoke, and with a standing deficit, should at once rise into a healthy political existence in which government and people should co-operate in constitutional harmony. The old estates with their rights had already been crippled under the hands of Dukes William IV., Albert V., and William V., who looked upon them as a hindrance in the suppression of the new doctrines, and reduced to a very small amount of competence. The accession of so many newly acquired provinces, and the necessity of the times, seemed to point to the advisability of abolishing all local constitutions and privileges. A new constitution to be granted by the king was also promised, but, under the pressure of the catastrophe which shortly followed, the project fell to the ground.

Here we must not allow our estimate of a king like Maximilian I., of unsurpassed nobility and benevolence, to be disturbed by the remembrance of the Confederation of the Rhine, which a highly gifted historian has made the occasion for the bitterest censures. No doubt we can find therein, partly a dark fatality, partly a grievous fault, and who would not, if he could, efface July 12, 1806, with his blood? But how many must share the blame for that fault, and how far back must it be traced? The Confederation of the Rhine was the bitter and inevitable fruit of the sins and errors of our fathers; but it was also the immediate result of the envy and discord which subsisted between the two great powers of Germany, who, even in the face of a common enemy and despoiler, would neither trust nor help one another. Bavaria, so long as the existence of the moribund empire was prolonged, was debarred from creating any independent line of conduct for herself; for who, within sight of the events of the past century, could have advised the king to ally himself with Austria, with the certain prospect of being first betrayed by her ally, and afterwards crushed by Napoleon? What then? Should the king abdicate, fly, abandon his people to see them presently constituted into a second Kingdom of Westphalia under a creature of Napoleon or one of his marshals? A public opinion which might serve as a warning, guide, or encouragement to monarchs, did not as yet exist in Germany, and patriotism was accounted narrow-mindedness by the leading spirits of the day. Even a Baron von Stein could give his approval to the Treaty of Schönbrunn, by which Prussia accepted alliance with Napoleon and received the equivocal gift of Hanover.

When at last the moment arrived for casting off the foreign yoke, the king was not backward in seizing the occasion—albeit not without the sacrifice, by the Treaty of Rieder, of a considerable district—of taking an honourable part with the Bavarian army in the war for emancipation. King and people found themselves, however, in the sorrowful necessity of acquiescing in the federal constitution which the powers of Europe had designed for Germany with the express purpose of maintaining her in weakness and disunion. The Confederation contained the germs of decay from the first, and engendered in the whole nation a profound and ever-growing discontent, manifested sometimes in derision and sometimes in wrath, which hastened its dissolution. How the attempts to reform it and to give to Germany a better form of organisation failed or were rendered fruitless, and how this led to the events of 1866 and 1871, is still fresh in our minds.

The most pressing task for Bavaria now was the organisation of her internal affairs. Setting Weimar aside, the King of Bavaria was the foremost among the German princes to whom were given a constitution by Art. 13 of the Act of Confederation. We look back over sixty years of constitutional life chequered with conflicts and changes; a period of political education for government and people during which much has been learnt on both sides: principally, that the highest welfare of Bavaria lies in a strong monarchy raised above party bias, and that the preservation of the rights of the crown is the sacred duty of all from the ministers downwards. We Bavarians may at least claim this testimony, that, unlike most of the other states of Germany, we have never been guilty of a breach of the constitution. Every conflict, however sharp, has found a constitutional solution.

Honours and gratitude are due to the house of Birkenfeld for the great service it has rendered in obliterating the feeling of estrangement between Bavaria and the rest of Germany, so carefully fomented in former times, and exaggerated by the presence of foreigners, but the revival of which has now happily been rendered impossible. Under the guidance of our kings, intellectual barriers one after another have fallen. By word and deed, by precept and example, they have taught Bavaria to feel herself, through the constant interchange of mutual services, a member of a great national body, an integral portion of a nation to whom one of the highest missions of the world is committed.

In the Diet of the Confederation of the Rhine Ludwig I. as Crown Prince had headed the opposition against the 'French system' as it was called. In those troublous times he had already conceived the project of assisting through his Walhalla in the promotion of a German national sentiment. When under his patronage the School of Art at Munich rose to a height of brilliancy surpassing that of similar institutions in Europe, and when he set before the artists whom he had attracted to his capital, the noblest tasks for their performance, he was guided by the thought that Munich, both by teaching and example, should become a school for the fine arts to the rest of Germany. King Maximilian II. rightly perceived that Bavaria had a special mission of her own, for the advancement of German culture. It was his ardent wish to lead his people in preparing the way for and promoting the welfare of Bavaria as well as the greatness of Germany. An historical commission was also founded with this aim, and its labours restricted to the field of German history. Had his life been spared it had been the intention of the king to establish similar bodies for the investigation of other branches of science. His present Majesty has shown on every occasion his intention to tread in the footsteps of his father and grandfather in the promotion of German sentiments, as, for instance, in the liberal endowment of the high schools of this place upon the occasion of the Jubilee Festival.

Our kings of the Birkenfeld line have excelled many of the former dukes and electors by the assiduity with which they have sought greatness for themselves in promoting the mental and physical well-being of their people and in the prosperity of the state. Consequently, since the beginning of the century we find prince and people working harmoniously together. The fusion of races is not as yet complete; human power cannot control the forces which oppose it. Thus much nevertheless is accomplished, viz. that king and country are united in the conception of the Bavarian people, that is to say, the benefits which they have received or yet desire for their country they await only at the hand of their king.

Harmony betwixt king and people, the mutual confidence which characterises family life, reverence for the majesty of the throne, have with rare exceptions marked the history of the Wittelsbachs and their subjects. It is now our boast before the world, and we trust it may long continue so, that we approach our princes, not with slavish fear, but with feelings of love and veneration, which have been handed down from father to son for many generations; that we look up to them, and trustfully expect the best from them in spite of some sad experiences; and that this inherited loyalty forms a mutual bond of union between us and them. With the single exception, in 1208, of the crime committed at the commencement of our dynasty, and not on Bavarian soil, Bavaria has been guiltless of the death of any of her princes. The assassin of Ludwig Kelheim (1231) was a German, not a Bavarian. Our annals have no insurrections, no dethronements, no conspiracies or treasonable plots, and no political executions to show; but they tell of abundant examples of self-denying devotion, of sacrifices of wealth and life, and of loyalty of the people towards their princes which the most grievous sufferings and temptations could not shake. We yield the palm in this respect to no other German race.

It is the yearly custom of the Academy to celebrate the birthday of the king upon this day; and to-day the day has become to us a double festival. The foundation of our society by the last descendant of the elder line of the Wittelsbachs excited general sympathy and approbation in Germany and was hailed in Bavaria as an event full of promise. Each prince of the house of Birkenfeld has since that time exerted himself to improve its organisation, to widen the field of its labours, and to contribute to its resources; in a word, to prove himself a vigilant patron and sympathising benefactor. With grateful homage the Academy to-day presents its thanks to its gracious patron on the throne. It unites at the same time with the entire nation in the wish that God may bless and preserve the house of Wittelsbach-Birkenfeld; may it flourish and increase in inseparable association with the people from whom it sprang!

III

THE RELATION OF THE CITY OF ROME TO GERMANY IN THE MIDDLE AGES[1]

Two prerogatives, otherwise denied to the works of man, were ascribed by the ancient Romans to their city: permanence and the supremacy of the world. Rome is the *urbs aeterna*, Rome is the Queen of the Universe, was re-echoed from heathen into Christian times. Not only in the eyes of her inhabitants was Rome a divinity; other cities raised her worship above that of their own tutelary gods; in every province of the empire she had her temples and her priests.

But a complete revolution took place with the triumph of Christianity. The confident hopes of permanence gave way to a conviction of a terrible fate and of a sudden destruction destined for the Mistress of the World. In one day—so the Christians believed—the doom of requital would annihilate the great Babylon, the city upon the seven hills drunk with the blood of the saints. That the catastrophe foretold in the Apocalypse of John would be literally fulfilled—although perhaps not until a much later time close to the end of the world—was the interpretation to which most of the ecclesiastical commentators firmly adhered.

From the commencement of the fifth century, with the confusion brought about by the barbarian invasion and the dissolution of the Western Empire, Rome had

[1] Address delivered at the public sitting of the Academy of Science in Munich, July 29, 1882, printed here for the first time.

entered upon a long period of suffering and depopulation. The city, sacked by Alaric's Ostrogoths, was again not long afterwards plundered by the still more ferocious Vandals who crossed from Africa. It was conquered by the Suevi under Ricimer, and during the death-struggle of the Visigoths was besieged and occupied several times alternately by that people and by the Byzantine forces. In the year 543 the population had been so reduced that not more than 500 inhabitants, it was said, remained within the deserted walls. Yet it still possessed sufficient powers of attraction for a rapid increase in numbers under the protecting hand of the papacy, which, since the time of Gregory the Great, had been steadily gathering strength. It became once more an imperial city, belonging to the Eastern Empire but dependent immediately upon the Exarchate of Ravenna, and principally occupied in warding off the threatening encroachments of the Lombard power.

But Rome was, moreover, inspired with the longing to cast off the Byzantine sovereignty. Hatred of the Lombards and of the iconoclast Greek Emperors, led to an alliance with the Frankish Empire. Ties of mutual interest contributed to strengthen the bond. The popes prudently helped to bring about the deposition of the last of the Merovingians and the erection of a new dynasty, and Rome conferred upon Pepin the title of Patrician or Protector of the City. The Anglo-Saxon Winfrid (Boniface), who became the apostle of the Germans and the reformer of the Frankish Church, was at that moment extending his wonderful influence throughout the Frankish territories. He gave to the Germans, what in their disjointed condition had been wanting to them before, a sense of common nationality and an ecclesiastical organisation; they became more definitely included in the political jurisdiction of the Frankish Empire, and in the many-membered bodies of Western Christendom of which Rome was becoming the centre.

What Pepin and Winfrid had begun, Charles the Great

completed. Whilst Boniface did all that was possible to train the youthful Church of Germany into entire submission to Rome, and to impress upon her Roman forms and ordinances, Charles pursued the same end throughout the whole extent of his realm. But he was resolved that at least within this realm he would himself be the leader and guardian of the church—would, as the bishops demanded and expected of him, govern her internally whilst protecting and extending her externally. Rome, which had called and crowned him to be the first emperor of the resuscitated Western Empire, had now become the first city of his dominions and herself subject to his authority.

Endless conjectures may be hazarded as to the different courses history might have taken, and what a different form the destiny of Germany would have assumed, if that older branch, the Eastern Church of the Greek tongue, which in many respects had remained more faithful to the organisation and customs of primitive Christianity, had become the mother of the German Church. I shall presently have occasion to notice the contrast between the Roman and Greek use.

In the acclamations with which the Romans greeted Charles in the church at his coronation, they believed themselves to be exercising an ancient and unforfeited right of election, and this idea seems actually to have been present to the mind of Charles himself when he dated the preamble of the Capitularies for Italy from the first year of his consulate. It was upon this that Charles and his successors founded their hereditary right. Neither Ludwig, Charles's son, nor Lothar, nor Ludwig II. was elected or crowned at Rome, but upon the question of his right to the title of Emperor, Ludwig II. declares to the Byzantine Emperor, 'I received my title and dignity from the Romans; they were theirs from the first.' However, four years later an occurrence took place decisive in its effect upon the centuries to come, and of the highest significance to Germany. At the invitation of

Pope John VIII. the west-Frankish King, Charles the Bald, went to Rome, where, setting aside the rightful heir, his uncle Ludwig, and bribing the Romans with large presents, he received the imperial crown from the pope, who declared himself to be acting in the matter under the inspiration of Heaven. Thus the disposal of the empire passed into the hands of the pope, and future emperors found themselves under the necessity of undertaking the journey to Rome in order to be anointed and crowned by the pope, who could grant or refuse the service. Thereon hung the fate of Germany.

After the death of Arnulf, the first sovereign of purely German race who wore the imperial crown, Rome and the papacy entered upon a period of shameful degradation, during which the papal chair was disgraced by a succession of criminals and the favourites of designing women, whose elevation was not unfrequently brought about by the murder of their predecessors. It is a question how far the proceedings in Rome during those sixty years from 900 to 960 were known at the time in Germany. German sources of information, even the Chronicles, are silent as to the accession of one vicious pope after another, and as to the fact that Rome had become a centre of murder and vice where there was no longer any question of conducting the succession to the papal chair in the manner prescribed by the teaching of the church. Records relative to any action of these popes with regard to Germany are few. The German Church stood alone at that period, and only in exceptional instances applied to the pope for the bestowal or confirmation of certain privileges. Papal records referring to Germany only begin to be less scanty with Agapetus II. after 947.

Otto the Great undertook to raise Rome and the Roman Church out of their degradation. The union of the imperial dignity with the German Kingdom which began with him, a union destined to last for 800 years, brought the German nation and church into still closer connection with the papacy. But it was of evil portent that John XII., who officiated at Otto's coronation, was so utterly worthless that the emperor himself was obliged to depose him shortly afterwards.

Germany was now more firmly linked to Rome than it had been under Pepin and Charles the Great. The empire, during the whole of the middle ages, possessed neither capital nor imperial residence to the north of the Alps; Rome alone could be fitly called the metropolis of the Holy Roman Empire of the German people. Yet in Rome the emperor had no palace, and when he sojourned there it was necessarily as the guest of the pope or of some great noble, whilst entrance into the city was accorded to him only after lengthened parleys, backed by the presence of a large armed force. Every German felt himself to be looked upon with suspicion as an unwelcome stranger. At a later period, when the Curia sought to strengthen itself by the election of foreign, and especially of French, cardinals, and by closer alliance with France, the cardinal's hat was scarcely ever bestowed upon a native of Germany. From the time of the Concordat of Worms until the end of the middle ages, no German attained to any post of eminence at the Roman court. In the seventeenth century a proverb was still current in Rome to the effect that a German cardinal was a phenomenon as rare as a white raven.

Yet the German Church excelled not only the French but all other churches in submissiveness to Rome. At the Synod of Trebur in 895, German bishops had already declared, 'The Roman chair is our master in church discipline, therefore let us patiently endure the yoke laid upon us, although it be scarcely tolerable.' How often later on did Rome quote these words to their successors, and give a wider interpretation to the promise of submission than those bishops—albeit even then dominated by the false Decretals of Isidore—had any conception of.

It had not been within the power of the Emperor Otto I. to establish a permanent reformation in Rome. There was there an utter lack of men who could have been the supporters and guarantees of reform. The previous scandalous scenes were renewed, and a slight amelioration of things under the Popes Gregory V. and Silvester II., whom Otto III. placed on the papal throne, was but transitory. When the papal chair came into the power of the Counts of Tusculum, the old anarchy and shameless corruption again prevailed. For the third time it became necessary for an emperor, in this instance Henry III., to constitute himself the preserver and purifier of the papacy, first at Sutri and afterwards at Rome. At that period the papal chair was occupied within twelve years by five German popes, since amongst the Roman clergy no fitting candidate could be found. These popes, with one exception, died almost immediately, poisoned by the unhealthy atmosphere of Rome; one only, Leo IX., under Hildebrand's guidance, left any lasting trace of his pontificate, and laid the foundation of that Gregorian system which resulted in papal supremacy.

It is significant that, although the wretched condition of Rome, both of the city and of the church, and its palpable causes, were manifest to the Gregorian party, yet they should even as early as 1057 have sought to throw the whole blame upon the Germans and their emperor. According to Cardinal Humbert, it was the action of the Ottos and their successors, coupled with the cowardice and stupidity of former popes, that had brought misery and degradation upon the church. Thus the very men who had raised the papacy out of the lowest depths, and had afforded it strength and protection, were held up to reprobation as foes and despoilers. At any rate the Gregorian party was not scrupulous in taking revenge for the encroachments of which it complained, for through its machinations Germany was laid waste by nearly fifty years of civil war.

Let us now consider more closely how the influence of Rome made itself felt throughout Germany, and what results this produced.

The term 'Roman Catholic Church' is expressive of a very real distinction; it denotes that, besides the bond of communion and unity of doctrine, Rome has her own traditions, her ritual and use, whilst other portions of the universal church, the Græco-Byzantine, the African, the Hispano-Gothic, each in the course of equally free development, have created a diversity of forms. Such could not be the case in Germany, since the church of that nation had been strictly bound to the Roman ritual from the beginning.

Rome was assuming more and more the character of a sacerdotal city; the old wealthy patrician families had either disappeared or migrated to Constantinople; and as the seat of government was either at Constantinople or Ravenna, there was no class of state officials in Rome. But the clergy had become rich upon the revenues of the vast possessions of St. Peter, which included lands in all parts of Italy continually increasing in number and extent. Surrounded by the waste or hardly cultivable lands of the Campagna, without manufactures, trade, or industry of their own, the people of Rome were induced to rely upon exactions levied upon the foreigner, and upon profits derived from ecclesiastical institutions, the expenditure of the popes, and the receipts of the Curia. Hence the unvarying sameness in the political history of Rome from the fifth to the fifteenth century. At no period can the gradual development of organised civil life be discerned, nothing is visible but the wearisome spectacle of perpetually recurring scenes of uproar and revolution. The Romans strove for freedom, and long retained the right of self-government, until Boniface IX. by means of repeated executions made himself absolute master of the city. Their seething tumults and republican risings most frequently resulted in nothing but a change of masters. The emperor could rule only so long as he was personally present. Hence the possession of power long oscillated between the priesthood and the warlike nobility; there was, properly speaking, no middle class, and always too large a proletariat. Of all the popular leaders, Arnold of Brescia was the wisest and most disinterested; but even his ideas of reform, like those of Cola di Rienzi, were partly impracticable, partly too grandiloquent and fantastic.

No city has such a history as that of Rome from the seventh to the end of the fifteenth century: constant tumults, bitter party strife, violent changes in the constitution; deposition, banishment, assassination of those in power; quarrels of the powerful families among themselves, with the people, or with the priesthood; now siding with the emperor against the pope, now with the clergy and pope against the emperor. If for a moment internal discord was lulled, war was sure to burst out again with the neighbouring cities, Tusculum, Viterbo, or Palestrina. Turbulent, quarrelsome, covetous, ever ready to fly to arms, to engage in street combats, to besiege the strongholds of the wealthy, to plunder the houses of their opponents, and often even the churches—such was the herd of human beings which called itself the Roman people.

The red thread, however, which runs through the whole tangle, is the attitude of the people and the priesthood to one another.

The history of the city of Rome may be said chiefly to be a record of the continual struggles of the secular world against priestly government. The struggle is carried on now openly, now secretly; it assumes various forms; but of genuine peace, of harmonious co-operation, there is scarcely an interlude; if a pause occurs, it is but a temporary truce or a transient alliance against a common foe. The laity generally had the worst of it, either when the whole clerical body, firmly organised under its spiritual head, was arrayed against it, or when the pope found support in the emperor or the Italian princes. But it was frequently victorious upon occasions when the clergy were divided amongst themselves, or when the interests of the lower ecclesiastical orders coincided with that of the laity.

The effects of this state of things show themselves even in the early times of Roman Christianity.

Dissensions in the Roman community had begun even in the third century, arising in the first instance out of controversies on doctrine or discipline. Hippolytus was set up as antipope against Callistus, and Novatian soon afterwards against Cornelius. Directly after the persecution under Diocletian, the severity of Marcellus aroused a dispute which led to a tumult and to bloodshed in the streets, and resulted in the banishment of the pope from Rome. During the distractions arising out of the Arian controversy we find two hostile Roman bishops, Felix and Liberius, in arms against each other. The populace took part with one, the clergy with the other. The death of Liberius was the provocation of a fresh schism; fighting went on in the streets and churches with such fury that in a single day 137 bodies of murdered persons were found in one of the basilicas. Some years later, in 419, the disputed election of Eulalius and Boniface again brought on the customary acts of tumult and violence, and the Emperor Honorius was obliged to interfere. Thus things went on throughout the whole of the middle ages; twenty-four such papal wars or schisms may be enumerated during that period, of which only a few originated in disputes between the empire and the papacy. The schism which took place under Urban VI. lasted seventy years, and rent the whole of Christendom. The question which of the two rivals was the rightful pope was generally left in uncertainty.

By far the greater number of these schisms were the fruit of the factious spirit of the Romans. We find in Rome and nowhere else in the world at that time a state of tension and warfare between clergy and laity, which had lasted for centuries and had produced the greatest vicissitudes of fortune.

The clergy is a many-headed, hierarchical body, composed of many grades and organised, whose theory of government is absolute monarchy; it has large revenues at its disposal, derived from the many donations to St. Peter. Some part of the laity, also, which is dependent on the clergy, is almost invariably upon its side. Meanwhile the gulf between the priesthood and the people becomes ever wider and deeper. Even the earliest fictions which found their way into the papal chronicles give evidence to the endeavour to exclude the laity from interfering with matters reserved for consecrated hands. It was decreed that the heads of the church might not permit themselves to be served by laymen. Not a bell-rope, not a church-door key, says Cardinal Humbert, should be touched by a layman; and Gregory VII. affirms that even an exorcist in the church stood higher than a layman, even than the monarch himself, since as an imperator of the spiritual world he subdued demons.

Boniface VIII. finally went so far as to issue a bull affirming that the laity had always fostered a hatred for the church, to which even antiquity bore evidence. This statement became henceforth an axiom of canon law, and a basis on which to regulate the relations between clergy and laity, church and state.

This rigorous separation between clergy and laity, added to the unceasing antagonism dating from the fifth century between the two classes in Rome, inevitably produced a marked effect upon ecclesiastical life. The *esprit de corps* with its good and evil characteristics became more strongly and consciously developed amongst the clergy of that place than elsewhere. Whereas in earlier times even the clergy of Rome might frequently split into hostile parties, or take sides amongst the factions of the people or nobles, we see nothing of the kind occurring after the dispute upon investitures; even the violent contests of Guelph and Ghibelline, which rent the whole of Italy and threw the families of the nobles into a permanent state of collision, only transiently disturbed the ecclesiastical circles of Rome. With the sentiment of unity there grew up amongst the clergy the desire and the need to govern. No choice, in fact, was left them. Rome during the middle ages never experienced the benefit of a stable government founded upon long tradition and secured by hereditary succession: the clergy must either rule the laity or be forced to obey and serve them. Their thoughts and aspirations were naturally directed towards domination, though in securing it they succeeded better for several centuries in Germany than in their own city.

When the popes of the middle ages affirmed, in direct contradiction to the words of the Bible, that whereas the spiritual power was from God, the secular power was from the Devil, or, as Innocent III. expressed it, the kingdoms of the world were produced by the tyranny of man, they spoke under the impression of local circumstances by which they were surrounded and threatened. They had the barbarous violence and rude despotism of the imperial and patrician families of Rome and its neighbourhood before their eyes. It has been a point too little heeded, that the popes and their counsellors and officials possessed as a rule none of the exact acquaintance with distant nations and the ecclesiastical state of other countries which is only to be won by long personal study—that, on the contrary, they were governed by impressions gathered from the daily events of Roman society. To them the city of Rome was a microcosm, whose air they breathed, whose images they beheld, and whose social and intellectual atmosphere became for them the standard by which to test the motives and requirements of the rest of the world.

To the Germans, Rome was simultaneously an object of desire and of fear, pre-eminently attractive on the one hand, repulsive and odious on the other. The climate was deadly to them: many had journeyed to Rome and had never returned; whole armies had been carried off by sickness. Add to this the reputation of the Romans as the most covetous people in the world, and the dread of being caught in the snares of the Roman money-brokers, or at best of returning home laden with debt. Nevertheless the longing to behold the sacred relics, to worship before them and become partakers of the treasures of grace to be thus secured, outweighed with numbers the drawbacks of the journey. The most powerful attraction in early times had been the grave of the two Apostles (*limina Apostolorum*); crowds of pilgrims went to Rome that they might offer up their prayers before it. But objects of veneration soon increased: so many thousands of Christians had died for the witness of the faith in Rome that the soil of the city had been saturated down to the very sewers by the blood of martyrs, and at every step the pilgrim trod upon hallowed ground. The number and costliness of the relics had also been greatly augmented, particularly since the Crusades. Rome had become a second Jerusalem; almost every object mentioned in the Gospels that the Lord or His mother had touched or worn was there to be found—vessels, utensils, stones, garments, the instruments of His Passion, and even, in strange contradiction with dogmatic truth, portions of His body. Of the mother of Jesus Rome possessed everything which the worshipper of Mary could desire. Each nation had its guides who pointed out these treasures and proclaimed the indulgences for a thousand years attached to them; these guides held the place of the Roman publications of the *Mirabilia* and *Graphia*. One has only to read the conclusion of the description of Rome by the merchant prince of Nuremberg, Nicholas Muffel, to understand the magnetic power exercised by Rome at that period. To the German the lot of the Romans seemed enviable and highly favoured: even should he die there he was sure of a grave amongst the holy martyrs, and of immediate participation in the joys of Heaven!

If we turn to consider the special effect upon religion and worship in Germany produced by the influence of

Rome, we shall speedily recognise features strongly suggestive of old paganism.

Christians held it to be right and good that heathen customs and religious rites should be retained and christianised; Pope Gregory the Great approved and recommended it. A work by Marangoni, composed and sanctioned in Rome, pointed out a host of adaptations of that kind. It lies also in the nature of religious symbolism that, representing as it does general ideas and sentiments, it may equally be turned to the service of Christianity or paganism. Paganism in Rome was deeply rooted, and offered a tough resistance. At the end of the fifth century the popes were still wrestling with some of the surviving forms of pagan worship—the Lupercalia for instance. Christianity in Rome remained strongly impregnated with the genuine Latin and Etruscan belief in the magic power of forms and ceremonies. When popes caused the fields to be strewn with bits of consecrated tapers as a protection against fieldmice and caterpillars, and sprinkled the walls of the city with holy water to ward off the sudden attacks of her enemies, we recognise the survival of the old Roman beliefs.

The intellectual barbarism, the absence of all refinement of taste, which meets us in all the monuments of Rome of the middle ages, accounts for much. Every great city is wont to collect, at any rate from the country in the midst of which it lies, the materials for intellectual and scientific development, and to work them up, in order to pour forth to all both near and far the treasures thus won and enhanced in her keeping. But this does not apply to Rome; in this respect, as in many others, the history of the town is unique. For a thousand years after the fall of the Western Empire, Rome possessed no school of importance, nor any seat of learning whose influence was widely spread. A famous singing school existed, and that was all. Nor did Rome during the middle ages produce any literature of the higher sort, if we except the works of Gregory the Great, which were widely diffused, and formed the favourite study of the cloister. The few historical works are principally productions compiled for some particular purpose.

Nothing existed in Rome worthy of the name of theology until the time of the later scholasticism, when a theologian, the subsequent *magister palatii*, was appointed to the papal court. Pope Agathos even as early as the year 680 had caused it to be announced at the council in Constantinople that, owing to the prevailing poverty, obliging all to live by the labour of their hands, men of theological learning were not to be found either in Rome or Italy. No improvement was shown during the next three centuries, and when in 998 Gerbert taunted the Romans with their ignorance, the legate Leo could only reply that Peter himself had been an unlearned fisherman. The Germans could indeed buy MSS. in Rome, but scientific culture and theological learning could only be received from England and France.

The exorcising of evil spirits was made an act of ecclesiastical authority first in Rome, and as early as the third century an order of Exorcists was added to the ranks of the clergy. A further step was soon afterwards taken, and a law made that any one wishing to dedicate himself to the priestly office must first have received ordination as an exorcist, and have performed for a time the duties of that employment. This was one of the fictions which, to lend the matter a semblance of antiquity, were inserted in the Papal Chronicle. The Eastern Church remained a stranger to this rule, and reckons no such order amongst her clergy. But in the West all the nations and churches which were dependent upon Rome were obliged to accept, and have retained to the present day, an institution, the consequences of which may be measured by the fact that, throughout the middle ages, mental derangements of all kinds were considered and treated as demoniacal possession, and the cure of the sufferer entrusted, not to the physician, but to the exorcist.

The entire system of trial by ordeal was partly prompted, partly fostered and sanctioned, by the practice introduced into Rome in the sixth century of causing persons accused of crime to testify their innocence by an oath before the sacred relics or the graves of the martyrs; or, in the case of priests, by receiving the Holy Eucharist. Pope Eugenius II. even instituted trial by water: several councils sanctioned or decreed ordeals of a like description; churches and monasteries caused claims to be decided by single combat, the issue of which was likewise reckoned to depend upon divine judgment. Such proceedings were surrounded by all the pomp of religious ceremonies. In the twelfth and thirteenth centuries, however, we find the popes expressing disapprobation of some of the means employed in the trial by ordeal.

A people like the populace of Rome, perpetually struggling and fighting to free itself from sacerdotal rule, was not to be treated according to the canons of the older and purer church. These had taken for granted the harmonious relations between clergy and laity, and could be applied with success only so long as such harmony subsisted.

Under the conditions of constant anarchy which prevailed in Rome, it was found impossible to keep in force the ancient system of penance. By heightening the severity of so effectual a means of government, the Roman priesthood strove to secure to themselves the right of criminal jurisdiction, proof of which is to be found in the directions to the bishops contained in the Sacramentary of Gelasius enjoining the imprisonment of penitents during the whole time from Ash Wednesday to Maundy Thursday. This severity was exchanged for an opposite system of indulgent leniency as soon as the custom of commuting penances arose, and penalties could be bought off with money or with lands to be ceded to churches or monasteries.

During the first centuries the possessions of the church were considered to be equally the property of the poor, and indeed they had mainly sprung out of gifts and foundations which for the most part had been destined for the benefit of the poor. In the customary partition of the revenue into four portions, one portion was set aside for the poor. But during the constant confusion and anarchy to which Rome with but exceptional intervals was subject, the Xenodochia and Diaconia founded in better times fell to the ground. The right of the poor to participate in the goods of the church was forgotten; the clergy monopolised all. The worst of it was that through the distribution of common church property into separate benefices, and through the legislation which as time went on the Roman Church built up upon it, the idea of any claim possessed by the poor or of any corresponding duty incumbent upon the holders of benefices vanished almost entirely from the minds of the clergy.

Ever since the fifth or sixth centuries the popes had been obliged by custom to distribute in Rome, at stated intervals and upon particular occasions, large sums of money. The number and amount of these distributions to both clergy and laity—as described in the work of Moreto—is astonishing. It proves at how early a period, or at all events how by the ninth century, the whole system of religion and of divine worship had assumed a financial character. The Roman clergy expected payment for every service performed. Thus, in defiance of all the laws of the early church, the whole system of perquisites, fees, and priests' dues arose; the world's complaint that at Rome everything was a matter of traffic, and that without payment not the smallest favour could be granted, echoed there unheard.

The Germans in common with the Latin nations found themselves obliged by Rome to submit to the use of the Latin tongue in their church services. Had the German Church become affiliated to the Eastern Church, divine worship would now be conducted in Germany in the mother tongue. But the opinion early prevailed in Rome that it was not only unnecessary for the people to understand the liturgical forms and prayers, but even pernicious. It was forbidden to translate the Liturgy; eventually the pope declared that to do so would be to throw pearls before swine, and holy things to the dogs. From the moment that Gregory VII., overruling the opinion of his predecessor John VIII., declared the use of the popular language in divine service to be foolish and presumptuous, none had ventured to continue the custom in Germany. The consequences are now almost incalculable. In the first place the sense of fellowship between priest and people before God has been weakened and stifled, participation in the meaning of the prayers and their personal application restricted, and a belief in the magical power and sufficiency of forms apart from their sense strengthened. In the next place the teaching contained in the Liturgy was entirely lost to the people; German literature, moreover, was deprived of a most powerful aid towards development.

Another very significant change also originated in Rome, which, as it affected the celebration of the Lord's supper, the altar, and the oblations, had the result of transfiguring the life of the church in many particulars. In primitive times it had been the rule that each church should have but *one* altar; a plurality of altars would have been looked upon with abhorrence, the altar being the symbol of the one undivided church. But with Gregory I., or even earlier, altars began to be multiplied in the churches of Rome, partly on account of the relics to be consigned to them, partly to increase the offerings of the pilgrims. In connection with this innovation came an increase of the number of masses, and the appointment of special priests for saying them. Transported into Germany this custom resulted in a church in a small town possessing perhaps as many as twenty or thirty altars, with a priest belonging to each altar. That such a host of idle ecclesiastics should have rendered all moral discipline and reform impossible, and should have become an intolerable burden to the nation and the state, is a matter of historical evidence.

The ancient church custom of bringing offerings in

bread and wine was abolished first in Rome in favour of offerings made in money. This is accounted for by the fact that the ever-increasing numbers of pilgrims who visited Rome naturally brought pieces of money with them as offerings. At the end of the thirteenth century, these gifts from the pilgrims amounted yearly to thirty thousand gold florins in St. Peter's Church alone. The institution of the jubilee by Boniface VIII. was designed for the purpose of attracting to Rome in certain years at least ten times the usual number of pilgrims from the whole Western world.

It is perhaps hardly surprising that the city of Rome should, even down to the sixteenth century, have patronised slavery, and it was only natural that the rest of Italy should follow the example of the metropolis of Christianity. The popes were wont to issue edicts of slavery against whole towns and provinces: thus for instance did Boniface VIII. against the retainers of the Colonnas; Clement V. against the Venetians; Sixtus IV. against the Florentines; Julius II. against the Bolognese and Venetians; and the meaning of it was, that any one who could succeed in capturing any of the persons of the condemned was required to make slaves of them. The example of Rome encouraged the whole of Italy, and especially Venice, to carry on a brisk trade in foreign, and especially female slaves. The privilege which had sprung up in Rome and lasted for some years, by virtue of which a slave taking refuge on the Capitol became free, was abolished in 1548 by Paul III. upon the representation of the senate. Rome, of all the great powers of Europe, was the last to retain slavery. Scholasticism having undertaken in the thirteenth century to justify the existing state of things, a theological sanction was discovered for slavery; Ægidius of Rome, taking Thomas Aquinas as his authority, declared that it was a Christian institution, since original sin had deprived man of any right to freedom.

History, in the form in which Germany received it from Rome, had been crammed with myths and legends.

The order of succession of the bishops before the time of Constantine had become confused, and the error by which Clement instead of Linus became the first bishop appointed by Peter, was adopted in the German books of history, as it had been in Rome.

Genuine history has nothing to impart concerning the acts and fate of the popes before Constantine. Only in the case of three of them does the information supplied by Eusebius, Hippolytus, and Cyprian, dispel the darkness. Roman fictions filled the papal chronicles with martyrdoms and with the decrees which these popes were supposed to have issued, and these were the sources from which the German chroniclers drew when they made the earliest popes appear in the light of general lawgivers for the whole church. Later, that is after the eleventh century, a further fiction was introduced to the effect that every pope during the first three centuries had died a martyr. This was done with reference especially to the Decretals of Isidore, the authority of which was to be raised thereby.

The history of the Apostles, especially of St. Peter and St. Paul, was received by the Germans from Rome garnished with the fables of Abdias, Marcellus, Linus, and the Acts of Thecla. The legend of Simon Magus had a very practical effect in Germany. Having, so ran the legend, caused himself to be carried upward in a fiery chariot, before the eyes of the Emperor Nero, he was, at the prayer of the Apostle Peter, precipitated from it and killed by the fall. This fable, which laid deep hold upon ecclesiastical literature and thought, opened the way to a superstitious credulity as regards the black arts. After the end of the fourth century this credulity found fresh nourishment in the forged Acts of Cyprian and of Justina, which appeared first in Rome, where the relics of these legendary saints were said to repose, and which present a striking picture of the survival of the magic and theurgy invented by later heathenism, mingled with the growth of Christian demonology. The influence exercised by the

'Romance of the Recognitions,' which took the Roman Clement as its hero, when translated into Latin by Rufinus, tended in the same direction, and was all the more powerful to disfigure early Christian history in that the legend found its way even into the Liturgy. We may finally notice the 'Legend of Theophilus,' translated into Latin by a Neapolitan priest, which became exceedingly popular in a poetical form, quickly spreading throughout Western Europe and contributing in great measure to rouse and establish in the minds of the people those noxious and murderous delusions which prompted the trials for witchcraft to which we owe the darkest page of German history.

It had become impossible for Germans to form for themselves an idea in the slightest degree corresponding to the reality of either ecclesiastical or secular history. They were everywhere environed by fictions, which they dared not meddle with, lest they should incur a suspicion of heresy, or which confronted them with such weighty names and authorities that every doubt seemed to be sinful. Every attempt at critical examination became complicated with inexplicable contradictions; history had become a labyrinth, in which no guide, and from which no escape, could be found. So it happened that precisely during the period when the Germans stood most in need of the equipment and weapons of history for the defence of their rights and the protection of their throne, the deepest ignorance prevailed. They sank defenceless under the burden of the fables and fabrications which had been forged for them on the other side of the Alps. In Rome a flourishing literature of fictions and forgeries had sprung up, which, in consequence of the general absence of the historical and critical sense, obtained credence everywhere. The fabricators felt themselves secure; they had no need to fear being convicted. In any other case most of these falsehoods, clumsily constructed as they were by the coarse, illiterate minds of their authors, would have been easy enough to expose. But people lived in those days in a visionary world in which there were no limits as to what was possible or conceivable.

The period of the Roman fictions and forgeries—the date of their commencement is easier to point out than that of their end—began with the first ten years of the sixth century, when the long schism between Symmachus and Laurentius gave occasion for setting up and establishing a new doctrine respecting papal prerogatives.

A series of such inventions sprang up, intended to prove that the pope was not amenable to human judgment, and that consequently no accusation could be brought against him. Others have reference to the history of various popes, as of Felix and his opponent Liberius: one fiction represented the latter as a heretic and a persecutor of the orthodox faith who died unconverted; another, as a penitent, reconciled to God and the church.

The 'Donation of Constantine' was a document composed in Rome during the eighth century for the benefit of the Roman hierarchy. It furnished an inexhaustible pretext for claims of a manifold description: it helped towards the erection of the church into a state, and became the most effectual weapon in the long struggle which led to the ruin of the German Empire. Palpable as the imposition was, nobody in Germany ventured to question its genuineness seriously, any more than the truth of the fable with which it was combined, of the baptism of Constantine in Rome, or the absurd story of the healing of his leprosy, notwithstanding the contradiction of it which might be read in the Chronicle of Jerome, of which earlier chroniclers had made use.

The light of history is given us to the end that, according to the old Roman saying, we may neither grieve nor mock at things human, but understand them; that, looking before and after, we may consider impartially the causes and effects of every great epoch and violent catastrophe by which a new era is ushered in; content, as concerns the future of the world, to await calmly the course of events; not permitting ourselves to be deceived by visionary expectations as though the stream could all at once be made to run uphill. For my own part I must confess that what took place in Germany from 1517 to 1552 was to me for a long period an inexplicable riddle and a subject of sorrow and pain. I could only perceive the separation that was produced, only the fact that the two halves of the nation, rudely smitten asunder as by the blow of a sword, had been condemned to perpetual strife and enmity. Since I have searched into and studied the history of Rome and Germany in the middle ages, and now that the occurrences of late years have so strikingly confirmed to me the result of my researches, I think that I understand that which was formerly enigmatical to me, and I adore the ways of Providence in whose almighty hand the German nation has been an instrument, a vessel in the House of God, and not an ignoble one.

Rome once more has become what for 1,400 years she had ceased to be, the capital of a united Kingdom of Italy, and at the same time the centre-point of the church as the residence of the pope. The genius of Rome must complain, 'Two souls now dwell within my breast; two hostile souls burning with rancour and enmity one against the other.' They seem able neither to live together nor yet far apart; Vatican and Quirinal resemble two hostile fortresses within the same boundary. Meanwhile, the process of secularisation advances with great strides; from north and south a generation is growing up, which, less susceptible to spiritual influences, seems destined by degrees to absorb the elder generation which is gradually dying out. Ecclesiastical Rome is more powerful for the present in Germany than in Italy. This was also the case in the fourteenth and fifteenth centuries, and then happened—what we all know.

IV

DANTE AS A PROPHET [1]

The prophets of the Old Testament unmistakably served as guides and types to the poet of the 'Divina Commedia.' Confident in their mission, and impelled by the Spirit which dwelt within them, these men assumed the right or recognised the duty of speaking the truth before kings and princes, rich and poor, and of taking the poor under their protection against oppression and the arbitrary perversion of their rights. They held up to the whole nation the mirror of its sins, and testified to the judgments that would inevitably follow. Again and again they set before their contemporaries the ideal of God's people under theocratic rule, the realisation of which was to be looked for in the future. Yet they did not rest content with preaching, rebuking, and admonishing; they took an active share in the life of the people; they set the example of what they demanded. Men of the present, and of immediate action where such was necessary, they occupied themselves, not only with the future, but also with the past history of the people, in order to draw from it examples, sometimes of encouragement and sometimes of warning. They understood withal the art of clothing their thoughts in beautiful language, and of conveying them in the rhythm of poetry.

A prophet, in the sense and spirit of those Old Testament seers and poets, Dante aspired to be. The task which falls to his lot is fourfold. In the first place he is to be a

[1] Address delivered at the public sitting of the Academy of Science in Munich, November 15, 1887 - printed hitherto only in the *Allgem. Ztg.*

preacher of righteousness, of peace, and of love, and he has a doctrine to inculcate which has hitherto lain hidden, but without which these three blessings cannot subsist upon earth. Next it is his wish and duty to hold up to the people of his generation the mirror of their errors, their crimes, and their vices, and to lead them thereby to self-conviction and penitence. In connection with this comes the third part of his calling, which is, to rebuke the faults and abuses in church and state, and to point out the corresponding remedies. Lastly, he is to give intimation of a brighter future, and to awaken and encourage the hope of deliverance, not far distant, out of the abyss of sin and misery into which the Christian world has fallen.

Dante is filled and uplifted by the thought that he is charged with a mission from on high. It is a matter of conscience for him not to shun this mission; and he has been peculiarly fitted and educated for it by heavy strokes of fortune and by the lessons of his own life. He regards himself as an instrument chosen of God, to whom has been entrusted a not insignificant place in the Divine Counsels respecting the whole of Christendom, and Italy in particular, and an influence unique in its kind. His great poem, the work of his life and of his love, upon which of years he has concentrated the whole force of his genius, will in God's hands, he is confident, become a means of making mankind, and above all his own countrymen, ripe for the reception of the new order of things, and of pioneering the way for the great reformation in society, in church, and state, which is now impending, and of influencing men's minds and wills in its behalf. In his eyes the poem is a sacred one—

> that hath made
> Both heaven and earth co-partners in its toil,
> And with lean abstinence, through many a year,
> Faded my brow.'[2]

Of the three Christian virtues, Hope is that to which

[2] *Parad.* xxv. 1. (Cary's Trans.)

the poet feels himself called upon to give especial prominence. Beatrice assures him that the Church Militant possesses no son so gifted with hope as himself.[3] Part of the mission for which he is specially gifted is to be the prophet of Hope. By his description of Paradise and of the way of purification leading thereunto, he strives to kindle in men the consciousness that they likewise are called to the enjoyment of these glories, and to awaken in them the longing for them and the conviction that on themselves alone depends the attainment of these good things.

Hope begets love to God and man. Only through the revival of hope in the soul will covetousness, the root of all evil, be cast out of the hearts of men, and the regeneration or reformation be by that means made possible, to which Dante looks forward with the ardent longing of his whole being, and to the heralds and pioneers of which he deems himself to belong. Above all, therefore, he aspires to be the prophet and teacher of Hope to his contemporaries and countrymen. God, says St. James to him, has given thee grace to see these things in order that

> thou mayest therewith
> Thyself, and all who hear, invigorate
> With hope, that leads to blissful end.[4]

St. Peter, when the poet had made his confession of faith to him, had already

> benediction uttering with song,
> . . . compass'd *him* thrice,[5]

ordaining him to his prophetic mission. Beatrice, St. Peter, and his ancestor Cacciaguida repeatedly charge him to make public what he has been shown, boldly and unreservedly revealing the 'whole vision'[6] to his contemporaries.

It is indispensable, in order to comprehend rightly the great poem, and to appreciate the author and his views,

[3] *Parad.* xxv. 54.
[4] *Parad.* xxv. 46.
[5] *Parad.* xxiv. 148.
[6] *Parad.* xvii. 127; *Purg.* xxxii. 104.

that this preconception in Dante's mind and his consequent bent of character should be constantly kept in view. He styles himself a son of grace. Cacciaguida breaks out into exclamations of wonder that this his grandson should be selected for so great a favour.[7] He is filled with apprehension upon Virgil's being summoned to accompany him through the realm of the departed; he feels that so rare a favour, so extraordinary a privilege, can only fall to the lot of one who is entrusted with an office requiring proportionate strength and enlightenment. Only two living men before him, Æneas and St. Paul, have penetrated into the world beyond: the former, because he had been appointed to lay the foundations of the city which was destined to become not only the seat of the empire, but the residence of the head of the church, the depository of the supreme spiritual power; whilst the latter, St. Paul, shared this favour as the messenger of Faith and the co-founder of the Roman Church. But Dante?

> Not Æneas I, nor Paul,
> Myself I deem not worthy, and none else
> Will deem me.[8]

Can it be that to him is to be entrusted a work and a mission similar and akin to that of Æneas or of Paul? Yet he obeys, and in the course of his wanderings the certainty comes upon him that such is really the case; he recognises that, like Daniel or Isaiah, he is called through the poetic gift to be a teacher and censor of mankind, to foretell and to promote the healing and restoration of the institutions, of some of which Æneas had prepared the foundation, whilst others had been realised by St. Paul. Virgil for the present inspires courage and confidence into his soul by the assurance that three blessed women in heaven are concerning themselves with his safety.[9] Therefore it can be no less a one than St. Peter, the first founder and occupant of the holy chair, the bearer of the keys for binding and loosing—Peter, and none else can it be, who solemnly

[7] *Parad.* xv. 26. [8] *Inf.* ii. 31. [9] *Inf.* ii. 124.

consecrates Dante to his prophetic office.[1] Again, at the close of his lofty song, the bold poet confidently cherishes the hope that it may be recognised as a 'sacred poem,' and, operating with salutary effect upon the minds of his fellow-citizens who had banished him from the paternal city, may reconcile them with him and convince them of the high worth and value of their countryman. 'With other voice,' not as a political partisan, but as one called by heaven and consecrated to be a witness and teacher of truth and righteousness—

> I shall forthwith return; and, standing up
> At my baptismal font, shall claim the wreath
> Due to the poet's brows.[2]

Hence it appears that Dante had no intention that the publication of the completed poem should be postponed until after his death, because, as Foscolo thought, he shrank from the consequences, dreading the vengeance of those amongst the Guelphs and the clergy whom he had exposed or offended; he trusted, on the contrary, that he might enjoy the effect of it during his lifetime, and that it might be the stepping-stone for his return from banishment, and procure for him honour and fame amongst his fellow-citizens and throughout Italy. He does not hide from himself that the work, with its harsh reproofs and unsparing disclosures, which, 'as the wind, doth smite the proudest summits,'[3] must arouse many powerful and dangerous enemies against him. It would be more worldly wise to

> forecast, that, driven from the place
> Most dear to me, I may not lose myself
> All other by my song.[4]

Yet his ancestor reassures and encourages him; regardless of consequences, he is to reveal the whole truth; 'although at first unwelcome, his word, when digested, will turn to vital nourishment.'[5]

The founder of Islam of old appealed to his Arabian

[1] *Inf.* xxv. 14. [2] *Parad.* xxv. 8. [3] *Parad.* xvii. 28.
[4] *Parad.* xvii. 106. [5] *Parad.* xvii. 125.

followers on the strength of the literary beauty and symmetrical harmony of the passages in his Koran; he conceived that in such poetic strains they would recognise the surest testimony to his prophetic mission; and he was not deceived. Dante gave to the people of Italy more than did Mohammed to his followers. He raised the poetic language of his country, as with one giant stride, out of timorous straitened beginnings to classical perfection; he created a work in this respect unrivalled, much less excelled. But such an authentication of his mission could not suffice a Dante. He knew that whosoever would appear before Christendom as a teacher and prophet must enjoy a spotless reputation in moral relations, or at least have given proofs of purification by conversion and repentance. For this reason he assigns a prominent place in the poem to his own repentance and amendment.

Hence the poem is secondarily the history of a human soul—its aberrations, conversion, purification, and confirmation. It recounts in images and allegories how Dante's will, formerly perverted and enslaved, and his spirit, obscured by sin, had gradually attained to enlightenment, health, and freedom, whilst it uses a poetic licence in compressing the work of years into the space of a few days. But the individual is typical of the whole species, and mankind is called upon to recognise its own reflection in the mirror placed before it by the record of Dante's fate and conduct. Yet the scope of the poem is still wider; it aspires to an even higher flight. In the picture which he paints of the three classes of mankind, viz. those who are hardened in vice, those who are in process of purification, and those whose blessed souls are perfected, Dante develops his work into a theodicy representing the divine economy of the world's story, within the bounds, naturally, of contemporary knowledge, and in accordance with the poet's own views. This theodicy necessarily at once becomes a weighty and serious indictment against his times, and the poem is the boldest, most unsparing, most incisive, denunciatory song which has ever been composed. Lamentation, anger, and satire alternate with one another. Dante wages war against the follies and vices of his times and surroundings with the sharpest weapons; he deals around him deadly blows, and it is nevertheless peace, peace with God and man, which is the goal of his highest aspirations. The poet is himself meanwhile an exile, perpetually driven from one asylum to another; a fugitive wrestling with care and poverty, and under the burden of the sentence of death. On this account his work at the same time becomes a defence of himself, although he does not flinch from appropriating his own share of the general blame. Like a long gleam of light the image of Beatrice, the glorification of his youthful love, illuminates the whole poem. In compliance with a 'wondrous vision' Dante had vowed soon after her death to raise a worthy monument to her with all the powers of his poetic genius, and the manner and the skill with which the vow was accomplished will remain for the admiration of all time a phenomenon unique in the literature of the world. Lastly, the work is a Temple of Fame erected to perpetuate the memory of the friends and foes of the poet, or of individuals whom he held to be representative of any definite paths of life, whether of vice or virtue.

The disputes of modern commentators begin over the very opening of the poem, and interpretations become at once widely divergent, in a manner which exercises a decisive influence upon the signification of the whole work. Aroused from a confused slumber, Dante finds himself in the midst of a gloomy wood. In the wearisome endeavour to find an exit, he arrives at the foot of an eminence of which the summit is radiant in the morning sun. Attempting to make the ascent, he is set upon by three animals, a panther, a lion, and a she-wolf, who obstruct the path before him. He is pressed most sorely by the she-wolf; whereupon a help in need appears in the form of his teacher Virgil, who informs him that in course of time a greyhound (*veltro*) will appear and drive this beast, the tormentress and misleader of mankind, back into hell from whence she came, and will thus become the deliverer of Italy.

The question now arises, What do these animals signify? Are they moral delinquencies to which Dante here makes confession? Or is it an intellectual aberration, a conflict of doubt and scepticism with faith, which is indicated here at the outset, and with which his mistress later on reproaches him? How do they stand in relation to the chief personages by whom Dante is accompanied throughout his pilgrimage—Beatrice, Virgil, Matilda? And moreover, who is the *veltro*?

The animals are symbolical of the three vices by whose temptations at one period of his life Dante had been so fiercely assailed that he had more or less succumbed to them. They represent Pleasure (the panther), Pride (the lion), and Avarice (the she-wolf). Upon this point the older commentators, as well as those who were personally acquainted with the poet, are agreed. But it has recently been discovered in Germany and Italy that the three animals signify the three powers whom Dante looked upon as hostile to him — Florence, France, and the Papacy. This interpretation, in support of which there is not a single other passage in the whole poem, becomes a disturbing element in the whole fabric of the work, and necessitates the adoption of other interpretations equally untenable; yet the number of its advocates is at the present time considerable.

That Dante, although married, did not abstain from sensual errors is acknowledged by himself, and attested by his *canzoni* and letters—those to Morello Malaspina in particular—as well as by his contemporaries, amongst them his own son Pietro. Any one weighing the evidence collected by Scheffer-Boichorst[6] must acknowledge that the attempt

[6] *Aus Dante's Verbannung* (Strassburg. 1882), pp. 211–212. The evidence of Bastiano of Gubbio, one of Dante's pupils, which had previously escaped notice, is of special importance.

to deny the culpability of the poet upon this point is vain.

We must not be misled by his endeavour to invest some of his love-songs in the 'Convito' with an allegorical meaning, and to substitute Philosophy—how worthy soever to be considered as a gentle lady whose favour must be sought by earnest study—for those women and maidens for whose love he sued. Dante himself soon tires of the unnatural constraint which this conventional style imposes on him, and in the course of the piece drops the mannerism which had sunk to mere pedantic fooling. The custom, universal at that day, of interpreting the Old Testament, and above all the Song of Songs, allegorically, had momentarily misled him. This process, in which fancy and caprice played their part utterly uncontrolled, must have been familiar to him from his Biblical studies. It was a favourite occupation of the time, and even two centuries later Tasso allegorised his epic poem after a similar fashion.

Dante confesses that, partly through his *Canzoni*, and the love adventures which prompted them, partly through the life of dissipation which he led in Florence in company with Forese, he had given grievous scandal, and had obtained a bad reputation. The thought that he has in consequence forfeited the esteem and consideration which are indispensable for a poet-prophet, if his work is to produce the intended effect—this thought everywhere accompanies him and forms the bitterest drop in his cup of sorrow. This is the motive of the 'Convito,' which is designed to bear witness to the serious studies and scientific attainments of a man who hitherto has been only known through his love-songs. In his principal work no further attempts at palliation are made, but Dante at once sets himself forth as a man who has sinned much, but who has also loved much, and who through repentance and purified love has merited forgiveness. Beatrice represents to him that, having fallen so low, but one means of rescue remains possible for him, namely the sight of hell and of the punishments of the condemned. She reproaches him also with having lent himself to the allurements of a maiden.[7] At the entrance of Purgatory seven *P*'s (the seven deadly sins) are inscribed upon his forehead, which afterwards, as he pursues his way through the different terraces of the Mount of Purification, one by one disappear. Dante, in the course of his pilgrimage through Purgatory, is aware for which sins he himself will have to do penance. He will undergo the punishment of the envious for a short time only; heavier will be the penance imposed upon him for pride; still heavier that for his most cherished sins; even now, whilst only beholding the expiation for the other kinds of sin, he must, though only momentarily, yet in full measure, experience the pain of fire, the punishment for sensual sin; this is the price at which he must purchase the sight of Beatrice, and conscience convinces him of having deserved the punishment.

The attempt to exonerate Dante from the stain of sensual excesses and matrimonial unfaithfulness has led to another misinterpretation. It has been assumed that the reproaches of Beatrice and Dante's avowal refer to an intellectual aberration. He must, it is asserted, have at one time imperilled the steadfastness of his faith through his philosophic studies, and fallen into doubt and disbelief.

In the whole of Dante's writings there is not a trace of his having at any period of his life strayed from the faith. One passage only in the 'Commedia' lends itself with some degree of plausibility to the theory, and has consequently been constantly brought forward in proof of it. Beatrice says to Dante, who has failed to understand the lesson she would convey to him in figures, 'Know then that the school that thou hast followed cannot with all its learning follow my discourse, and see how thy way from God's way is far as the poles asunder.'[8] Now the lesson of which there is here question is certainly addressed to the poet in particular, and is one that was unknown in the philosophical and theo-

[7] *Purg.* xxxi. 58.

[8] *Purg.* xxxiii. 85.

logical schools. It is connected with his favourite doctrine of the divine foundation of the empire, of which the first beginning was to be traced back to the earthly Paradise. This means that the prohibition to eat of the fruit of the tree of knowledge was the beginning of law and ordinance, and of the corresponding duty of obedience. This was the foundation, in principle, of the highest earthly power, the empire, as the source of legislation and the protector of right. The tree also is thus made the symbol of the imperial rule of the Roman Empire. In the vision which is introduced, the Griffin (Christ) binds the pole of His chariot (the church) to this tree (the empire), and abstains at the same time from eating of the fruit of the tree. 'Thus is the seed of all rights preserved' is echoed around; and therewith Christ inculcates upon the church the lesson that she should appropriate none of the possessions and rights of the empire. Beatrice consequently reproaches Dante with a want of knowledge, not with error.

This, then, is the unsound foundation upon which a whole edifice of conjectures has been raised in the past and present, touching the internal struggles of Dante's mind and his supposed temporary infidelity. It is high time that these German fancies should be dismissed; they disturb and obscure the entire purpose of the poem. Philosophy in Dante's eyes is not the equal of Theology, but its helpful and indispensable sister; they do not contradict, but supplement and correct each other. Dante invariably speaks with fervent love and admiration of Philosophy, of the services she has rendered to him, and of the benefits and enjoyments for which he is indebted to her. Although unacquainted with the old Greek Fathers, Justin, Clement of Alexandria, and others, he shared their opinion upon this point. He goes so far therein as to deem the love of God the highest good—to be the combined result of philosophical principles derived from physics and metaphysics, and from divine revelation. Aristotle, the great master of human science, is invested in the poet's eyes with infallible power and authority which should rank next to the empire, directing and advising as the third in the sovereign band.

Virgil, in Dante's opinion, is a witness to the greatness and rightful supremacy of Rome, an unconscious prophet of Christianity, and above all the representative of the science and moral philosophy of heathendom. The latter, in Dante's eyes, is a preparation for and introduction to the Christian faith. It is Beatrice, therefore, the light of divine revelation, his heavenly protectress, who sends Virgil to be his guide and to assist him in the path of moral amendment. In this image Dante has clothed the thought —we might well say the fact—that the study of heathen literature and science turned his mind from earthly passions, illuminating and preparing it for the reception of the true Christian doctrine. For in Dante's conception the science and literature, and above all the moral philosophy and political teaching, of Greece and Rome, were interpenetrated with rays of divine light, and contained a fulness of eternal truth which Christianity, by its dogmatic teaching upon the Trinity, the Atonement, and the Church, afterwards supplemented whilst in a measure correcting it. It is significant that before the outset of the journey over the Mount of Purification, Virgil is recommended by Cato to cleanse Dante's face from all traces of uncleanliness, since it would be unseemly to appear before the Angel of Paradise with eyes dimmed by infernal mists. Thus, before the actual penance began, natural and ethical science had had a purifying influence upon his soul.

It is Virgil, furthermore, who protects Dante in hell from the petrifying glance of Medusa. For, if not maintained and nourished by classical learning and science, the light in the human soul, when forced to sojourn with the condemned in this world of hatred, lying, and slander, would be utterly quenched by the overpowering and benumbing spectacle of infernal terrors and bestial passions.

Once more it is Virgil who renders it possible for his charge to recognise the universal power of fraud, and to turn it into his service. The symbol of this is the monster Geryon, half man, half serpent, by whom the two poets were together transported into the infernal regions, where this many-shaped vice is punished. Dante has certainly no suspicion that he himself as well as all his contemporaries are lying buried under a mountain of impostures, fictions, and fabrications which it will only be given to much later ages to remove. Neither does he divine that many a truth once recognised by the ancients was now lying hidden under a rubbish heap of error and misrepresentation.

Dante's relation to Beatrice, to this combination of the earthly and the heavenly, of abstract symbolism with the most living personality, is something quite unique, unexperienced in any other human life. To him she is womanhood in its purity, loveliness, and ideal perfection, and with the remembrance of her earthly beauty is coupled the conviction, founded upon experiences or visions, that she is his protecting intercessory genius in heaven, as, without knowing it, she had on earth been the guardian angel of his youth. Admitted now into the unveiled presence of God, she floats before the poet, and, as a partaker of God's glory, her spirit, so far as it is possible for a finite, created being, has become radiant with the divine light. Meanwhile, by continually directing his thoughts and will towards his glorified love, Dante has entered, so to speak, into a kind of magic intercourse with her, in such a way that she has become his teacher, the source of his insight into things divine, his guide in the paths of theology. In his religious studies he is always accompanied by the thought, 'She already beholds and enjoys in blessed peace all that thou here below, slowly and step by step through weary exertions of discursive thought and wide research, mayst win for thyself. In her spirit now is neither darkness nor doubt, nought save transparent light. There before the throne of God she intercedes for thee, her faithful one; and thus to her thou art indebted for whatever from above has fallen to thy lot of light and knowledge of things divine, or of insight into the nature of the doctrine of Christ.' If Beatrice is commonly called the symbol of theology, the term is correct only under condition that the scholasticism of the day, against which Dante had much to object, be excluded, and theology, as he tells us himself in his 'Treatise upon Monarchy,' be understood to mean the teaching which is to be drawn from the Bible and the traditions of the church.

And now the much-disputed question arises, Who and what is Matilda? Historians no longer pretend that she was the Tuscan Countess, the benefactress of Gregory VII., who founded the States of the Church. Our colleague Preger has found the key to the mystery.[9]

To understand Dante thoroughly, it must be borne in mind that everything with him is connected with his inner experience. Many things have been shown to him in visions of which he sometimes makes mention; we perceive in him traces of his ecstatic moments. He himself relates how, in moments of intense contemplation, he had fallen into such a state of complete abstraction as to become entirely unconscious of things and persons around him. Once he had been rapt into a state of such fervent thanksgiving and devotion to God for the grace of salvation which had been granted to him, that he even forgot Beatrice (the evangelical doctrine of salvation). In this he refers to the condition described by all mystics when the soul feels itself as it were dissolved in God, and the consciousness of the separate divine attributes and benefits disappears. As the symbol of ecstatic conditions of this kind, and the visions appertaining to them, Dante has made choice of the nun Mechtilde or Matilda. Virgil, the personification of mere human unassisted knowledge, has just left him; he is now his own king and bishop, but the moment has not yet arrived when Beatrice will reveal herself to him and when the highest intuitive perception attainable by man of things divine will be disclosed to him.

[9] *Dante's Matilda*, an academical address. Munich, 1873.

Matilda, therefore, is for Dante that personification of the perception of holiness which is attainable through visions, and which beholds religious truths in images and allegories. The beautiful flowers which the poet sees her plucking[1] are images and allegorical visions of the same kind that are to be found in the book of the blessed Matilda, and so unmistakably affected was Dante's imagination thereby that many of her images and visions became incorporated with his poem, or at any rate left their trace upon his mind. It thus becomes intelligible that she should have dipped him in the stream of Lethe, that is, that she should have elevated him into a higher spiritual condition, in which the remembrance of the torment of sin was lost, and that he should extol her for having reinvigorated the halting power of his mind by vouchsafing to him the sweet draught from the river Eunoe (a serene disposition of mind at peace with itself).

The question whom does Dante signify by the *veltro* has been acknowledged to be the most difficult in all the poem; in fact, to be incapable of solution. Even his contemporaries and earliest commentators were at a loss what to say on the subject, and fell into fanciful and unfounded suggestions. His son, Pietro di Dante, knew nothing positively, and contented himself with asserting that it was a mistake to apply ''twixt either Feltro' to two towns between which the birthplace of the deliverer was situated. Yet this is precisely what has now been generally accepted in Germany, Italy, and England. The earlier commentators down to the sixteenth century are unanimous in the interpretation 'His land shall be 'twixt either *feltro*,'[2] *i.e.* he will be of lowly origin, or, he will belong to one of the monastic orders who are clothed in coarse cloth or felt. But modern critics are so sure of their opinion, that, in new editions of the text, and in translations, they take good care through the printed capital beginning the word that the reader should be left no choice but to receive it as the name of a town,

[1] *Purg.* xxviii. 40. [2] *Inf.* i. 105.

and therefore inevitably to understand none other than the Prince of Verona to be the promised apostle of poverty and frugality. The poet evidently carried his secret to the grave, and Rambaldi, about the year 1375, speaks of the thousands of different interpretations that had already been put forward. However, in 1450 a commentator of the 'Inferno,' Guiniforte delli Bargigi, seems to approach the truth. He conjectures that the *veltro* will be a holy man, who will awaken in the hearts of the avaricious sorrow and penitence for their sins.

All attempts to decide upon any historical personage in particular to whom the poet referred and of whom he expected such wonderful things would now be vain. The poet himself neither personally nor by reputation knew upon whom his hopes were set. Nevertheless he confidently awaited him; in accordance with his Joachimistic views Dante thought the epoch was at hand when a new brotherhood would, under its founder, effect a moral and religious revival in Central Italy.

The belief in the Empire and the Papacy as two health-giving institutions of which the one would be restored and the other purified and reformed, formed the groundwork of Dante's teaching and that which lay nearest his heart. But reform was impossible so long as the people of Rome and of the Latin Tuscan lands, the lowlands [3] of the peninsula, were not fitted to receive it, so long as the old she-wolf, low, blind Avarice, governed the mass of mankind. Yet this country is the place where God has ordained that emperor and pope should dwell and from whence their rule should proceed. When the *veltro* shall have finished his work here, and prepared the way for another of God's instruments, then will appear the 'Dux' and will complete the work of requital, of liberation, and purification. Thanks to the regenerative and salutary influence of the *veltro* the

[3] *Umile Italia* Dante calls it, borrowing the expression from Virgil (*Æneid.* iii. 522–523). The translation *gebeugtes oder demüthiges Italien* misses the sense.

'Dux' will compass this end without having recourse to desolating war.[4]

The *veltro* will subdue the she-wolf, that old national sin of the Italians, insatiable Avarice, the root and cause of all evil and depravity; he will drive her out of every town and hunt her back into hell from whence she came. It is therefore a purely moral reform which is in question, and in those days this could naturally be looked for only through religious means and influences by means of persuasion and of zealous pastoral rule. A *capitano* with his pillaging troops of mercenaries was surely the personage least fitted for such a task.

Dante was a Joachimist, but after his own eclectic fashion, with the reservation which his favourite doctrine of the divine right and calling of the empire rendered indispensable. Wonderful to relate, he knows of but one prophet in the whole course of Christian times since the Apostles, and that one the Abbot Joachim, to whom he assigns a high place in Paradise, near the Mother of the Lord and next to Bonaventura. The works ascribed to Joachim—the commentaries on Jeremiah and Isaiah which bear his name were then supposed to be genuine—set forth that the whole course of human history falls into three great periods, the era of the Father, followed (since the birth of Christ) by that of the Son, and finally by that of the Holy Ghost. Within these three periods seven other periods (*status*) are distinguishable. In the sixth period,

[4] A remarkable passage is to be found in a printed work of Armannino of Bologna, dedicated to Bossone da Gubbio and belonging to the year 1325, four years, therefore, after Dante's death. The wickedness of Tuscany was the cause of there being so much sin in the world. For the Tuscans were more popular amongst mankind than any other nation. *Ma quel gran veltro che caccerà la lupa della quale disse Dante, farà ancora scoprire tutti i loro difetti chiari.* Elsewhere he calls to mind the dissensions of the church, and adds: *Ma come dice Merlino, tutte finiranno poi per la caccia di quel forte veltro, che caccerà quell' affannata lupa, onde sorge tanta crudeltade.* Thus a prediction of Merlin appropriating the *veltro* of Dante had already found popular expression. See Bongiovanni, *Prolegomeni del nuovo Comento.* Forlì, 1858, p. 257.

which was reckoned to have begun or to be immediately impending, heavy judgments would befall the corrupt churches of the West, but a new spiritual power would at the same time be introduced in the shape of an order, the *parvuli* of the Latin Church, which would abstain from all worldly possessions. This is to be a society living under a severe rule of discipline and self-denial, and by preaching and example it is to bring about a widely extended conversion and regeneration.

It seems as if Dante may be alluding by the *veltro* to the future founder of this order, or perhaps to the order itself.[5] The image of the greyhound was the more familiar to him that the Dominicans had already chosen for the device of their order a dog with a burning torch in his mouth; this represented a dream which the mother of Dominic was supposed to have had before his birth.

With what warmth, animation, and rapture does Dante describe the bride espoused by St. Francis, his beloved Poverty, who for eleven hundred years had been without a suitor![6] No one else in the time immediately preceding his own does he extol so highly. Yet despite the emphatic expressions of admiration for the order, he does not omit to portray the terrible falling away of the greater portion of its members from the teaching and example of their founder. 'There are a few, in truth, who cleave to their shepherd; but these are so few, a little stuff may furnish out their cloaks.'[7]

Thus he, like the pseudo-Joachim, reckons none but the Mystics as the genuine disciples of St. Francis. Dante must certainly have heard the elders of his generation describe the powerful movement which the Minorites had stirred up in Italy between 1230 and 1260. He must have heard and even himself had opportunity of observing what a power lay in the preaching of these men, who could influence and

[5] *Sive solus appareat sive cum sociis, habebit magnam potestatem in loquendo verbum Dei*, are the words of Joachim's *Commentary on the Apocalypse*, 198 b.

[6] *Parad.* xi. 61.

[7] *Parad.* xi. 123.

reform the life even of the people in the towns. He who recognised in the old she-wolf the prevailing sin of avarice, the crying vice of the times, and who in a letter to the cardinals wrote 'All have taken Avarice to wife, who can never, like Christian Love, be the mother of piety and justice, but is the mother of profligacy and injustice,' was not likely to expect the remedy for the evil to come from a pope, nor from a warlike prince or *capitano* whose thoughts were continually bent on fresh conquests.

Dante certainly never contemplated that the task of the *veltro*, the vanquishing of the she-wolf, would be accomplished by a pope. History told him of no pope who had really brought about any permanent reform in religion or morals. He meets with two cardinals in Paradise, but not a single pope, not one at least who appears to him worthy of mention or whom he could have selected as a mouthpiece for instruction, warning, or prophecy. A pope like Gregory VII., supposing Dante to be acquainted with his history, must have been displeasing to him, as having been the opponent, not only of the emperor, but of the empire itself, and as having been the cause of its decay. Every pope since then as a matter of fact had followed more or less in the footsteps of Gregory with regard to the empire.

The opinion now almost generally adopted is that by the *veltro*, Can Grande della Scala, Prince of Verona, is intended, at whose hospitable court Dante for several years found a refuge. The poet certainly esteemed him highly. But the very manner in which the poet celebrates and praises him makes it impossible that he could have contemplated his acting the part of the *veltro*, and becoming the author of a moral reformation in Central Italy. His deeds are to be worthy of remark; he will care neither for gold nor hardship; through him kingdoms will become poor, and the poor rich. But of any higher vocation pointing to a great moral reformation – to the overcoming, that is to say, of the she-wolf – there is not a hint. Can Grande remained entirely aloof from the events of Central Italy. His successes were confined to conquests in the north-eastern corner of the peninsula. Dante, besides, had plenty of cause to extol his generosity and energy, and to remain silent about other qualities which would have been indispensable for the *veltro*. The eye-witness Ferreto of Vicenza[8] leaves no room for doubt that Can Grande was a heartless insolent tyrant, who gave over towns which he had won through perfidy to be plundered by his rapacious mercenaries, broke up their civil administration, set the villages far and wide in flames, and caused the peasants to be dragged into the towns, where they pined in confinement until they found the means of ransom. Dante's *veltro* is to be maintained by power, wisdom, and love, that is to say, by the substance of the Triune Deity. Is it conceivable that the poet could have stooped to such vile flattery, and thus branded his work with infamy?[9]

We are acquainted with the fragment of a work, *De semine scripturarum*,[1] composed in 1205, in which there is a prophecy that in a hundred years, beginning from 1215 (exactly at the time therefore that Dante was writing his poem), the Holy Land would be reconquered and the church cleansed from simony. Until then the cunning malicious Dragon would hold the people of God in captivity in the Roman land. But the cleansing of the Temple (the church), by driving out the buyers and sellers, would be accomplished amid fearful convulsions and national wars, resulting in general desolation by fire and sword until universal distress and poverty would perforce put an end to high-handed simony. Dante indubitably had this prophecy in his mind. From it he has borrowed the puzzle of the numerical signification of the letters, and the

[8] Muratori, *S.S. rer. Ital.* ix. p. 1060 ff.

[9] Neither is it conceivable that the poet who exalted the Latin races so far above the people of Lombard origin, and who wrote *Pone sanguis Longobardorum, coadductam barbariem, et si quid de Trojanorum Latinorumque sanguine superest, illis cede*, could have assigned to a Lombard capitano the office of converting this high and noble race from avarice to frugality.

[1] Karajan, *Zur Geschichte des Concils von Lyon*, p. 104.

symbol of the Dragon as Simony. But he amends it. He cannot bring himself to believe that Italy, already desolated and impoverished by eighty years of warfare, will incur so terrible a penalty simply through the fault of the hierarchy; for this would also be opposed to the expectation he has formed of the coming of an emperor who should liberate Italy without damage to flock or field.[2]

The prospect of an emperor coming from the North and fulfilling the judgments against France and the venal church of the papacy is also unfolded in the Joachimist works composed by the Mystics, only that the latter, being Guelphs, foresee in him a tyrant and destroyer, like the Assyrian or Chaldean Monarchs.[3]

I have styled Dante's epic fiction a theodicy, *i.e.* an exposition of the divine plan with respect to the universe, as Dante conceived that plan to be. Had he, in the actual state of things and their reflection in his own mind, confined his attention to the immediate past or present, he might have been driven to take refuge in a gloomy pessimism, or in blank despair. But his anticipations concerning the future preserved him from this, and enabled him to fulfil his mission for the enlightenment and improvement of the world.

Prophecy thrives especially in times and under circumstances where incongruities have sprung up between the truth and the ideas and expectations of mankind; where the national conscience comes into conflict with the actual

[2] *Purg.* xxxiii. 51.

[3] As an example of the Joachimistic vaticinations which find an echo in Dante's work, one may cite the following passage from the *Commentary on Jeremiah* attributed to Joachim: *Futurum est prorsus ut, orta discordia inter principes, non tantum ab imperio ecclesia corruat, sed etiam a Gallicano regno diffidatur, et unde fuit erecta et provecta in gloriam, inde dejecta et despecta veniat in rapinam.* Then a terrible prediction is repeated against the church (the papacy) concerning the punishment which would be received at the hands of an emperor proceeding from the North. It is also foretold in the same place (f. 46) that the nobility as well as the clergy in France would at one time declare themselves against the pope. Dante saw the fulfilment of this prophecy in 1303.

situation, or where the religious ideas of the time or of the nation demand a state of things in flagrant opposition to existing conditions. Dante was forced into becoming a prophet because, convinced as he was that the empire and the papacy were the two pillars ordained by God to support law and order upon earth, he yet saw the world in those days corrupted by their having become the very opposite to what they should have been. But Dante, whose poem gives marvellous proofs of a mind formed for cool deliberation, was not the man to shape his predictions of the future merely after the dictates of his own fancy. He cannot be charged with having merely invested his own individual wishes and needs with the garb of prophecy. He did that which was so constantly done at that time; he appropriated predictions which were partly already current, partly drawn from Biblical interpretations, and clothed them in the beautiful imagery of his poetic fancy, veiling them occasionally in designedly enigmatical form. The comprehension of them is facilitated if the facts are approached partly in the spirit of the poet, partly with a mind attuned to the conceptions of the time. In the first place, Dante was desirous of combating a prophecy which the Guelphs had set afloat within the last fifty years, and which, sometimes under Merlin's name, sometimes under the name of a Sibyl, set forth that at the death of Frederick II. the Roman Empire had become extinct, nevermore to be revived. Next we must consider Dante's belief in the influence exercised by the heavenly bodies and constellations, and the intelligent beings (the angels) who direct them, over earthly things. The revolution of the stars exercises over mankind a direction and impulse that generally predetermines or turns the scale, but in such a manner that the individual, as a free agent, can by the strength of his will oppose this influence of the stars. Dante consequently arrives at the conclusion that a universal transformation might at any moment take place if, he remarks, when foretelling the appearance of 'the Dux,' 'the stars be e'en now approaching.'[1]

Furthermore, it must be observed that Dante goes upon the accepted opinion that the end of the world was at hand. He gives vent to this idea by saying that he found almost all the places destined for the blessed in Paradise already occupied, so that only a small number could yet gain admission. That universal changes and mighty proofs of divine power and justice would be manifested more and more in proportion as the end of time drew near, had at all times been the general belief of the church—an expectation naturally shared by Dante himself.

Dante possessed a rare cultivation of mind, and his learning was so comprehensive and various that, if we except Roger Bacon, who belonged to an earlier period, very few can be found who came up to him, and none who surpassed him. We behold with wonder the wealth of classical and scholastic knowledge displayed in the 'Convito.' Aristotle was his chief master, although he was acquainted with him only through Latin translations. Boethius, Cicero, Seneca, ranked next as his favourites. He was familiar with the literature of physics, jurisprudence, and theology. One important gap in his knowledge, however, of which he himself seems to have been little aware, makes itself felt; the historical sense and acquaintance with past events is wanting. This defect he shared without doubt with his contemporaries; but it becomes only too manifest as a disturbing influence in a work, which, in its scheme for judging the world, divides the whole of mankind into the saved or eternally lost, and with audacious confidence undertakes to determine the future. As he knows nothing of a boundary line between myth, legend, and history, Æneas, Dido, the giant Cacus, and the Trojan Ripheus are to him historical persons as genuine as Cæsar or Augustus. He, as every one else at that time, takes the Donation of Constantine for a fact, however much of a stumbling-block it may seem

[1] *Purg.* xxxiii. 41.

to him; and he thus betrays the fact that the whole history of the period from the fourth to the eighth centuries was either unknown or incomprehensible to him. Dante gives credence to the Guelphic fable by which the mother of Frederick II. was said to have been a nun; and makes Hugh Capet, the founder of the royal dynasty of France, to have been the son of a Paris butcher. His ignorance leads to place Justinian, Gratian, and Fulk of Marseilles in Paradise. He draws his information, too, from an impure source when he assigns the place of a heretic in hell to the blameless Pope Anastasius. Again, when he sharply reprimands the two first Habsburg monarchs, Rudolf and Albert, and almost anathematises the latter, for forgetting their duty as emperors in not undertaking the journey to Italy, it is because he does not know that it was the pope who had rendered the journey impossible for the two princes.

It is by no means to be wondered at that Dante, in accordance with the character and spirit of the times, should have been misled in historical matters, or that he should have mistaken stories of heroes for genuine history. The laws of historical progress were as good as unknown to him, and he was therefore ready to attribute slowly developing conditions to the enterprise of an individual or even to an isolated act. Owing to his Joachimist views, and belief in the power of the stars over human things, Dante's predictions outstripped actual occurrences in the church. Whether or how far ecstasies, and possibly dreams which he deemed to be inspired, contributed thereunto, must remain uncertain, as the poem supplies only hints, and no safe basis for an opinion. It should be borne in mind that seers of both sexes, who predict the future whilst in a condition of ecstasy, were both then and afterwards highly honoured, and occasionally received the sanction of the church; witness St. Hildegard and Dante's contemporary, the Dominican prophet Robert of Uzes, who in the year 1293 was examined at a conference of the order in Carcassonne and received permission to come forward publicly as a prophet; whereupon he travelled throughout Italy, France, and Germany, preaching and prophesying, and threatened Boniface VIII. with divine chastisement.

In numerous passages scattered over the three parts of the 'Commedia,' and sometimes in a trenchant tone of profound indignation and with words that scorch like fire, Dante depicts the prevailing corruption of the times, of which he considers the popes to be the chief authors. It is they who, through their evil example and constant misuse of religion as a means to serve their own cupidity and ambition, have utterly corrupted both clergy and laity and led them to a like destruction. The papacy has become a power continually exciting to war, and itself carrying on war; it wields the secular sword together with the spiritual weapons of the Ban and the Interdict; it places the spiritual symbol of the keys upon its war banners. Of the members of one and the same church it treats one half (the Guelphs) as the saved, and the other half (the Ghibellines) as foes predestined to be lost. The Papal Curia has been turned into a market where everything is for sale, and Christ is daily put up for auction. Bishops and priests have taken pattern by the papacy and given themselves up like servers in idol-temples to the worship of mammon. Ecclesiastical ordinances, the administration of justice, the empire and the imperial power, all alike have been ruined by these successors of the Apostle Peter; even the rites of religion have been made of none effect through their false and lying privileges, and ravening wolves are everywhere to be seen in the garb of shepherds. 'My place of burial,' says the Apostle, 'is full of the stench of blood.'[5] For the popes 'write but to cancel.'[6] All that stands in their way—oaths, vows, treaties, obligations, the enactments of the early church,

[5] Comp. *Inf.* xix. 101; *Purg.* xvi. 103; *Parad.* xviii. 121-132; xxvii. 20-25 and 40-55.

[6] *Parad.* xviii. 126.

the decrees of their predecessors—all that it would profit them to sweep away, they cancel.

The majority of readers find it difficult to understand that Dante should so exalt the papacy and nevertheless pour such obloquy upon it as it then was—obloquy mingled with the heaviest accusations and reproaches. Where the dignity and power of religious matters is concerned, he is a son of his time, the disciple of Thomas Aquinas and the theologians of his day generally. He does homage to the sacred keys which Peter transmitted to the pope; the pope is the chief shepherd whom all are bound to follow. But the sublime power committed to him has been abused and misapplied until it has been turned to a curse, and weighs like an intolerable yoke upon the Christian world. The office nevertheless must be held in reverence. Dante describes the attack upon Boniface VIII. in Anagni, and the indignities heaped upon him, with expressions of the deepest abhorrence, although himself regarding Boniface as no rightful pope, but a usurper.

The ill-will felt by Dante against the papacy and the clergy takes a fourfold shape. He is wroth with them as a Christian, as an Italian, as a partisan of the empire, and as a professor of the rule of poverty. For two centuries accusations had been levelled from all sides against the church, that through the example of Rome and the Curia everything had become a matter of sale, and the whole of ecclesiastical life tainted with simony. The complaint was raised by all nations and classes, and not least by the clergy themselves, and we find scarcely an attempt to gloze the matter over, much less to deny it, although according to the church's tenets it involved the most fearful consequences. Hence upon this point the poet merely echoed the opinion of the time, and the observations of the older commentators prove that no one thought it at all extraordinary.

As an Italian Dante cherished a grudge against the popes, because their policy, the wars they had carried on, and the foreigners by whom the country had consequently been overrun, had caused the ruin of the peninsula and had divided its inhabitants for an indefinite period into two hostile parties, which, so long as they existed, forbade any hope of peace, and who had produced civil war in every town. A series of French popes had already managed to make the Roman chair subservient to the interests of the Angevin princes. And now the Curia under Clement V. had taken up its abode upon Gallic soil and from Avignon continued its customary policy in Italy entirely to the advantage of the French. 'Cahorsines and Gascons,' says Dante, 'prepare to quaff our blood.' [7]

As a warm partisan of the monarchy, as he terms the empire, Dante felt both sorrow and wrath at seeing that the popes had ruined an institution which was of all things one of the most indispensable for Italy. 'One sun,' he remarks, 'has extinguished the other, and now the sword is grafted on the crook.' [8] So was it in very deed. Within sixty years the popes, by preventing hereditary succession to the throne, and through the astute policy by which they fostered an interregnum, as well as by tampering with the elections by means of their dependants, the ecclesiastical electors, had reduced the old genuine imperial power to the merest phantom and had deprived the empire for ever of all vitality and power.

Thus far Dante's thoughts and words were in accordance with those of his contemporaries. German poets such as Walter von der Vogelweide, Freidank, and others, had a century before perceived the course things were taking, lamenting and denouncing them. And now an additional fatality had occurred, which, in the eyes of Dante and very many of his contemporaries, filled up the measure of Rome's iniquity. In the East all was lost. The Latino-Byzantine Empire had crumbled to pieces. The possession of the Holy Places, the Christian principalities in Palestine, all that, by untold sacrifices, had been fought for

[7] *Parad.* xxvii. 55. [8] *Purg.* xvi. 112.

and won during the last two hundred years, had now been forfeited and destroyed, and it was only too apparent that the chief blame for this annihilation of Christian hopes rested upon the popes. The wars which they had perpetually carried on or instigated, the squandering upon alien objects of the funds collected for the Crusades, the yielding to the dynastic and territorial interests of the two Capet lines, the want of military organisation, and the perversion to other purposes of the forces destined for the war in the East, had led to results which to the feelings of that generation were equally painful and humiliating. God's judgment was perceived in these things; the prolonged struggle between Christ and Mohammed seemed to have terminated in favour of the Arabian prophet. For the sake of annihilating the house of Hohenstaufen, of breaking the German power in Italy, and bringing the peninsula into bondage partly to France and partly to the papacy, the Mohammedans had been permitted to conquer, and to establish their rule in the Holy Land. Dante only casually alludes to this in his poem, but he knew the general opinion and feeling, and knew also how deeply shaken the old feeling of reverence for the papal chair had been.[9]

The attitude which our poet assumes towards Boniface VIII. requires particular explanation. Gregorovius,[1] borrowing an illustration from the Roman priest Tosti, says that Dante bound the soul of Boniface to the triumphal car of his wrath as a Ghibelline, and dragged him nine times round the crater of hell. Serious exception, however, might be taken against this representation, although it has met with the approval of many other writers. First, it was inevitable that the man under whose reign the journey described in the poem took place, and upon whose words and acts the fate of Italy and Germany at that moment hung, should be frequently in

[9] *Inf.* xxvii. 87, where Pope Boniface is charged with making war, not against the Saracens, but only against Christians.

[1] *Geschichte der Stadt Rom*, 2 Aufl., 1856.

Dante's mind. Secondly, Dante does not assign to Boniface a place in hell as the head of the Guelphs and because of his political conduct, but purely on account of his crimes against religion, and for simony; and he treats other popes in the same way. Thirdly, in the poet's eyes, Boniface was not a legitimate pope, but a usurper who had forced his way to the throne by cunning and violence. Dante, in common with many purists and theologians, regarded the bull of Celestine V., confirming the popes in the hitherto unrecognised and unexercised right of resignation, as null and void, and he was logically right. For the popes themselves had declared the bond which unites a bishop or pope to his church to be indissoluble by the law of God, and least of all could it befit the Vicegerent of God upon earth arbitrarily to sever that bond, and to emancipate himself from the sacred duties upon which he had once voluntarily entered. This is the reason why the Apostle Peter charges the poet to announce upon earth that in God's sight the papal chair is now vacant, and its occupant only an interloper. Finally, Dante had witnessed the unprecedented spectacle of proceedings opened with much pomp, and evidence taken, against the late pope by his successor; he knew that in Avignon witnesses of high standing, amongst them men of rank, both Italian and French, who had been in immediate attendance on the pope, had sworn to worse things than any that are recorded in the 'Divina Commedia.' It ought rather to be said that Dante out of reverence for the office had passed over much in silence.

Many reflections have been made even recently upon Dante's verdict upon the predecessor of Boniface, Celestine V. It has seemed scarcely possible that the poet should have treated the humble, pious man who resigned the papacy from the feeling of incapacity, with such severity. *Viltà*, cowardice, is the reproach which he casts upon him when he sets him among the throng of shame-beladen souls, hateful alike to God and His enemies—

wretches who have never truly lived;[2] and this in direct opposition to the opinion of Celestine's contemporaries, who honoured him as a saint, a proof of which Dante himself lived to see in his canonisation by Clement V.

Celestine, in Dante's eyes, had received a high mission from God; it had seemed like a miracle that the poor hermit monk should suddenly be raised to the chair of St. Peter, and placed in possession of the greatest earthly power. He ought to have been foremost in putting his hand to the great reformation; he should have dedicated the order, which he had founded, to that purpose, and then verily he would have become the true *veltro*. Out of cowardice he had rejected the sacred mission, and betrayed himself and the church to a man whose equal in wickedness could scarcely be found. A well-known contemporary of Dante, the poet Ubertino da Casale, the most gifted amongst the Mystics of those days, has passed a judgment upon Celestine exactly similar to that of Dante, excepting that he throws no doubt upon the personal holiness of the man, and expresses his blame in the mildest terms.[3]

It is historically incorrect, and prevents a just appreciation of the poem, to portray Dante as an ardent partisan of the Ghibellines. In the current acceptation of the term he was not so. In his youth he had borne arms as a citizen of Florence upon the side of the Guelphs, and had been sent into banishment as a moderate, white Guelph by the black Guelphs, who were in favour of the French. Henceforth he determined, in so far as this was possible for a man with neither home nor resources, and who was driven from place to place seeking protection and favour, to attach himself to no party. Unwearied in the desire to bring about his own recall to Florence, he was driven occasionally to take part with the Ghibellines, and was

[2] *Inf.* iii. 60.

[3] *Arbor vitæ Crucifixæ* (Venetiis), i. 4, c. 36. He says that he prays Christ daily *ut educat sponsam de manu adulteri.* His work was written in 1305.

frequently galled by the discovery that such an alliance might throw him into worthless and vile company.[1] In the Guelphs he saw the adversaries of the imperial power, who carried out their own selfish ends with the aid of the pope and the Franco-Angevin party, and combined with the enemies of Italy to convert that country into a bloody battlefield. To the Ghibellines Dante must often have appeared as a Guelph, whilst the Guelphs, as often as he declared against them, must have accounted him a Ghibelline. The last years of his life were spent in Ravenna under the protection and in the service of a prince of Guelphic leanings, Count Guido Novello da Polenta. Upon the whole it may be said of Dante that whilst intellectually he excelled most, perhaps all, of his contemporaries, he was emphatically a man of his day. Certain Joachimistic views he shared with only a small minority, and from these again he differed as to the empire.

His opinions upon ecclesiastical affairs were essentially the echo of the public sentiments, and they are confirmed by the writings of even cardinals and bishops, as well as by the memorials drawn up for the Councils of 1274 and 1311, by Bishops Bruno of Olmütz, Durando of Mende, and Le Maire of Angers. A commentary in confirmation of Dante's descriptions and denunciations might easily be compiled out of these and from the memoirs of Petrus Dubois, the writings of Roger Bacon, Bonaventura, and Alvaro Pelayo. Dante indeed is silent upon much that these ecclesiastical witnesses put forward, often with forcible colouring. For the fact must not be overlooked—Dante was a layman, besides being an exile without office or dignity, dependent upon the protection afforded him by strangers. He wrote at a time when laity and clergy were parted by a chasm broad and deep, when a pope had formally declared it to be an everlasting well-established fact that the laity were the foes of the clergy; whence it naturally followed that they must be treated as such. The

[1] *Parad.* xvii. 60.

laity were forbidden under pain of excommunication, even in private and amongst themselves, to speak upon matters of faith. In every town the inquisitor zealously exercised his office, and Dante was well aware that a mere suspicion sufficed to bring a man before the judge, and to condemn him to a painful death. Against this danger no princely asylum could ensure him permanent shelter; for he must be prepared for the possibility that his patron, under a threat of excommunication, would give him up, or that the authorities of a state, under similar pressure, would execute the sentence upon him. One need but to call to mind the fate of Dante's contemporary Cecco d'Ascoli—likewise a poet and scholar—who was condemned by the Inquisition to suffer death at the stake on account of his astrological theories. The dread of sharing such a fate is amply sufficient to explain Dante's silence upon certain matters, which must nevertheless have revolted his feelings of justice and humanity.

I turn now to the prophetic vision of the chariot.

In the earthly Paradise, the cradle of the human race—reached by Dante after his pilgrimage through Purgatory and before entering the regions of the blessed, and where the prophetess Matilda receives and leads him from one vision to another—the triumphal procession of the church is made to pass before him. It appeared in the form of a chariot drawn by a griffin (Christ), and accompanied by Prophets, Apostles, and Evangelists. In allegorical pictures their destiny is unfolded before him: persecution, expiation, victory, apostasy. Four catastrophes or transformations occur. Out of the earth a dragon arises who strikes his tail through the chariot and tears part of it away. Meanwhile the rest of the chariot is clothed with the feathers of the imperial eagle, and out of it grow seven horned heads. Hitherto Beatrice has sat in the chariot, but now in her place appears 'a shameless whore, whose ken roves loosely round her,'[1] and who bestows kisses

[1] *Purg.* xxxii. 147.

upon her lover, the giant who stands near her; but when she raises her eyes towards Dante, the giant scourges her, and, loosing the chariot from the tree to which the griffin has bound it, drags it off into the wood.

The chariot of the church has thus been doubly ruined, through the plumes torn from the imperial eagle and in the injury done to it by the dragon; the first is the cause of the second. The fatal Donation of Constantine awoke in the popes the desire, and furnished them with a pretext, for coveting the lands and subjects, the rights and revenues of the empire, and for appropriating them with the assistance of the spiritual weapons which lay in their power. Hence arose the long series of disputes between the emperors and the popes, which led both to the decay of the empire and the corruption of the church. In Italy and Germany the popes had so reduced the power of the empire, and had laid hands on so much of its territory, that it could scarcely any longer maintain itself; whilst under the stimulating example and with the connivance of the head of the church, the whole clerical body had become steeped in the vice of insatiable avarice. This passion, combined with the costliness of the wars waged by the popes during the past ninety years for no better purpose than securing their own territorial supremacy, had brought the Roman Curia into the habit of subordinating the whole conduct of affairs to considerations of gain, and of making everything a matter of traffic so that the whole church was infected with the disease. That is the dragon who has made a breach in the chariot: simony nurtured in Rome.

As this interpretation of the signification of the dragon differs from those which have been hitherto given, I must proceed to justify it.[6] No sooner has the dragon struck

[6] The variety of interpretations quoted in Scartazzini's *Commentary* II. 756, shows how widely opinions have differed as to the meaning of the dragon or serpent. The wildest significations have been put forward. Most modern critics, taking the cue from some of their predecessors, have decided in favour of Mohammed: thus Kannegiesser, Streckfuss, Blanc, Hoflinger, Bär, Göschel, Ruth, Philalethes, Longfellow, and a number of Italian writers.

through the chariot with his sting, than the latter is turned into a hideous seven-headed monster, upon whom sits the whore. Now even before this, when Dante meets Pope Nicolas in hell suffering punishment for simony, he upbraids him with the observation that in him, and in popes such as he, is fulfilled the apocalyptic prophecy of the Babylonian woman who sits upon the beast with the seven heads and the ten horns, holding in her hand the cup of abominations. Therefore both here and there is the same picture. The mystic chariot, the vessel, or sacred edifice, as Dante in one place describes it, turns into the apocalyptic beast with the whore. The vision of the chariot must besides be intended in Dante's opinion to be the allegorical representation of most weighty and decisive circumstances in connection with the church. Now there is nothing in regard to the church which Dante so repeatedly and so pointedly alludes to as the predominance of simony; so that it is inconceivable that he should overlook it in the vision. Dante well knew the danger of applying the apocalyptic prophecies to the papacy and to the simony of its acts; he knew that this interpretation had been regarded in the Waldenses as heresy and capital crime. Still he had high authority to fall back upon. Cardinal Bonaventura, the greatest theologian of the Minorite Order, and highly revered throughout Western Christendom, had forty years previously pointed out the apocalyptic image of the whore and the beast as symbolical of the Roman chair, and had repeatedly and in the most pointed terms accused the latter of simony.[7] Dante was thus led to the conclusion that the holy vessel the church, with her hierarchical orders and constitution, had ceased to be, having been destroyed by the serpent Simony. She must shortly therefore be reconstructed. He certainly did not mean

The most learned of English Dantists, E. H. Plumptre, now (1866) supposes that the dragon has reference to the controversy upon images, or to Satan working through schismatics in general.

[7] *Commentarius in Apocalypsin*, in vol. 2 of the *Operum Supplementum* (Tridenti), 1773, fol. p. 815 and elsewhere. The earlier editions have been tampered with.

that there was no longer a church upon earth, no common fold for Christian believers. Just as Bishop Otto of Freising had admitted that at the darkest hour of the church's corruption, 7,000 elect souls, known only to God, would yet remain, so was Dante doubtless convinced that in this, the church's eclipse, a numerous band of earnest believers had kept themselves in piety and moral purity. Long ago councils and popes had not only declared simony to be the most noxious of all heresies, but decided all consecrations and priestly offices performed by a simonist to be null and void. The people had been informed that their mere presence at the masses and prayers offered up by a simonist counted as deadly sin, and nevertheless since then simony had spread far and wide like a deluge over the church. Dante felt himself impelled to proclaim that, as there was no longer before God any true pope, so neither was there any true church, any life and health giving institution; the chair was vacant, the vessel broken. As he elsewhere says,[8] the vine which St. Peter planted has become a briar. And forthwith he makes Beatrice, the symbol of pure and primitive evangelical teaching, announce that she must for a time disappear. She is driven away by the shameless woman, by a false flattering theology of which the source is to be found in the false Decretals. The principles comprised in these statutes touching state and church, papacy and empire, were in Dante's eyes erroneous and mischievous, as he shows in his work upon the monarchy. But to have charged the papal bulls themselves directly with containing false doctrine would have been too dangerous. Dante declares them to be worthy of reverence, but that it was lamentable, as well as mischievous for the world, that the Gospels and the Fathers should be set aside in favour of their exclusive study as the surest road to preferment and riches.[9]

[8] *Parad.* xxiv. 100. [9] *Parad.* ix. 133.

A future emperor, the 'Dux,'[1] is to slay the giant and the woman. In what way can Dante have imagined that this would come to pass? Not through bloodshed and war; it would, he says, come to pass without injury to the fruits of the field, and we know that he detested any act of violence against an acknowledged, even though illegitimate, pope. But whenever the favourable juncture of the planets is accomplished, and the *veltro* with their aid has freed the Italians from the she-wolf (Avarice and Mammon-worship), Guelphs and Ghibellines will be reconciled and united, the mastery of the Neri in Florence will come to an end, and all will voluntarily submit to the emperor. This then is the death of the Gallic giant, for the ground will thus be cut from under his feet. This once accomplished, the emperor will seal the fate of the whore after the same peaceable fashion. Her abode is in Avignon, situated in the territory which still formed part of the Kingdom of Arles. Dante is aware that the emperors, the Ottos and the Henrys, formerly by peaceable means with the aid of councils succeeded in healing the corruption of the Roman Curia. An emperor might with the best right undertake to do the same again. For just at that time—between 1314 and 1316—owing to dissensions between the French and Italian cardinals, the papal chair had remained vacant for more than two years; at the Conclave in Carpentras a band of Gascon soldiers in the pay of the French had made a murderous onslaught upon the Italian cardinals, and forced them to seek safety in flight. The pitiable condition of the papal

[1] That the numbers indicating letters signify the word 'Dux' is certain. Dante borrowed this cipher for the expected deliverer and avenger from the Joachimists. William of Saint-Amour (in Martene, *Ampl. Coll.* ix. 1334), who incorrectly assigns the authorship to Oreme, quotes the following from the *Concordia* of Joachim: *Diligenter purgato tritico ab universis zizaniis assurget quasi dux novus de Babylone.* Joachim signifies thereby a pope, but Dante's views would make it refer to an emperor. It is also apparent that Dante distinguishes the *veltro* from the 'Dux,' making the former forerun the latter. The cleansing of the wheat from the tares is the office of the *veltro*. Only after that will the emperor appear.

court, its want of freedom and security, was thus conspicuous to all the world. Dante, therefore, expected that the first act of the new emperor would be the release of the Italian cardinals from their captivity upon French soil, which would bring about the return of the Curia to Rome. By this means, he says, the Vatican and the other places sanctified by the blood of the martyrs 'shall be delivered from the adulterous bond;'[2] whilst the great moral reform which will meanwhile have taken place in Rome will turn to the advantage of the papacy, and Beatrice will be reinstated in the place of the whore. Then also will follow Dante's own longed-for return to his native town—that town so severely inveighed against, and yet so ardently loved.[3]

History took a different course from that which Dante anticipated. The papal chair was absent from Rome for seventy years upon Gallic soil, its occupants well content with the wages to be earned by doing service to the giant. Both before and afterwards Gascons and Cahorsines drank of Italian blood, afterwards even more than before. The dragon with the sting became yet mightier in Avignon than he had been before in Rome. The supremacy acquired through the Decretals enabled the papacy to shine with undiminished splendour for centuries longer, exacting sacrifices innumerable. From time to time, but with continually decreasing power, German Emperors appeared in Italy soliciting coronation in Rome; but the imperial progress sank by degrees to the level of an idle pageant raising the scorn rather than the reverence of the people.

[2] *Parad.* ix. 137.

[3] We may here in passing draw attention to a prediction of Dante's which might be said to have been fulfilled. He affirms that God would not allow the Guelphs to attain their object of substituting the lilies for the eagle, *i.e.* French rule would never be established in the place of the empire. The question as to whether the prediction has been verified might be answered either way: in the affirmative if one thinks of the results of the battle of Pavia in 1525; in the negative if the Italian Kingdom set up by Napoleon 300 years later be taken into consideration.

The life of the poet passed away betwixt hope and disappointment, amid the cares and sorrows of ceaseless wandering, wrestling with want and poverty, and embittered by many vexations. Well might he say of himself that he was steeled against Fortune's blows.[4] He died in exile at Ravenna, at the age of fifty-six.

The reconciliation and fusion of the Guelph and Ghibelline parties, his greatest longing and dearest hope in life, was so far from being realised, that during the three centuries through which the struggle was prolonged 7,200 revolutions and over 700 massacres in the towns have been enumerated.[5] Full-blown despotism, side by side with anarchical republicanism; civil war breaking out at intervals of five or six years, and ceaseless quarrels between neighbouring towns, are the characteristics which mark these centuries. The Italian was born to a heritage of hate and a thirst for vengeance. He grew up to feel that the vocation of his life was to fight and hate with his party. Machiavelli's book 'The Prince' was the product of such conditions, and the theory which shaped the practice of nearly 300 years.

Yet Dante is still now as ever not only the martyr, but the prophet, teacher, and guide of his countrymen. Well may the statesmen of that country, when the serious questions of life crop up, take counsel from his works, even as the ancient Romans consulted their Sibylline books. They seem to feel this, for a separate chair has recently been endowed for the first time in Rome for the study of Dante, to which the most famous of living poets, Carducci, has been nominated.[6] Naturally the question presents itself: If Dante could now return among the living, how would he

[4] *Parad.* xvii. 25.

[5] Ferrari, *Histoire des Révolutions d'Italie, ou Guelfes et Gibelins* (Paris, 1858, 4 vols.), gives this reckoning.

[6] Carducci has since refused the offer, and up to the present time (Jan 1883) the post has not been filled up.

regard the present relations between Germany and Italy? Any one who has read the soul of the poet may answer for him: May both countries, to the benefit of the world and themselves, long remain united in friendly alliance, but dynastically and politically separate, independent one from the other!

V

THE STRUGGLE OF GERMANY WITH THE PAPACY UNDER THE EMPEROR LUDWIG THE BAVARIAN[1]

We are still under the impression of the mighty events which have changed the condition and form of Germany; we stand expectant before the gates of the future, and the profound differences of opinion which divide the public mind are represented by two great parties each of which confidently awaits for Germany the realisation of its own wishes. The one looks forward to a period of material and intellectual bloom, ascendency of power, and leadership in Europe; believing that Germany will again become, as she was from the tenth to the thirteenth century, the sustainer and director of the forms which mould the world: the other, on the contrary, predicts the speedy downfall of the empire and the rushing in of chaos. Yet as regards the future of Germany he alone can conjecture an approximation to the truth, who, after serious study of the history of the German people and their neighbours, like a prophet glancing backward, draws his conclusions from the past as to what the future has in store.

It will be well for us therefore to spend some time to-day in considering how Bavaria and Germany have arrived at what they now are, and we are at once easily led back to the epoch when Bavaria was called upon for the first time to play an active part in the history of Europe. This happened under that Ludwig who, if we except the transi-

[1] Address delivered at the Festival of the Academy of Munich, July 28, 1875, hitherto printed only in the *Allgemeine Zeitung*.

tory and shadowy appearance of the Emperor Charles VII., was the only Bavarian prince who wore the royal and imperial crowns. Sixty or seventy years ago our Academy was greatly occupied with the Emperor Ludwig; a prize was offered for a good history of the emperor and his reign, and was awarded to Mammert, whilst the rival work of Zirngibl was printed at the cost of the Academy. Both works have become antiquated and inadequate, and have been surpassed by Buchner in his 'History of Bavaria.' Still one may say that the period from 1314 to 1347 yet remains one of the most obscure in German history. Since the above-mentioned works were published in 1812, fresh material has come to light, and we now possess excellent preparatory works and studies of particular parts, but as yet no comprehensive work upon Ludwig the Bavarian, such as would meet the requirements of the present day, and such as we possess upon the earlier emperors—Henry II., III., IV., and Frederick I. and II.—and I would fain from this place incite one amongst our younger men of literary ability here in Munich, or in Göttingen, to undertake so worthy and useful a task—a task which would certainly demand some years of serious and persevering study.[2]

The empire of Ludwig and the empire of William—the Holy Roman Empire of the German people under the Bavarian prince, and the empire of 1871—how essentially do they differ, and what a world of changes and new formations lies between them! The former an empire collapsing into irremediable decay, the famous order of things which had endured for centuries passing away; the latter the pledge of resurrection and new birth, a Hercules vigorous enough even in the cradle to strangle the serpents that threaten his life. Yet, wide and deep as the gulf may be which separates the old empire from the new, we cannot move a step amongst the débris of the past without en-

[2] Since this was written the excellent literary contributions of Riezler, Preger, Karl Müller, and others have appeared, and have considerably widened our knowledge and appreciation of this interval of time.

countering figures and parallels which bring it into relationship with the present day.

The entire reign of the Emperor Ludwig, which lasted thirty-three years, puts one in mind of the painful task of Sisyphus, the heaving and turning of the stone, which, laboriously brought to the summit, rebounds away down to the valley, so that the weary toil must be begun again. It was not destitute of brilliant victories or splendid successes, but every gain was followed by loss, every victory in the field by defeat in the cabinet. The whole life of this gentle and philanthropic, but weak and fickle prince, was absorbed in the struggle with the two hereditary foes of imperial and German greatness—the German princes and the papacy—backed by the lurking malevolence of France, which was always on the watch to seize upon German territory or to appropriate the imperial title. We see Ludwig coming boldly forward to grapple with the difficulties that oppose him, but of his two mighty foes one has an ally in the bosom of the emperor himself. He trembles in his inmost soul before the spiritual weapons of his adversary, and he would fain purchase peace with him at any cost.

Like all his predecessors, Ludwig succumbed in the end; like them, too, not without fault of his own, and not without having fallen into many errors in the greedy attempt to increase his own family power.

It was through the elections both of bishops and emperors that the Roman Curia undermined the German Empire and brought on its ruin. The emperors of the Saxon and the Salic house had made the bishops, especially the Rhenish archbishops, rich and powerful, thinking that in them they should find the most trustworthy support of their own power and their most faithful assistants and instruments in government. These prelates, nominated by the emperors, became their chancellors or ministers, and helped towards the unity of the mighty empire. The struggle about investitures, and its conclusion in the Concordat of Worms, first loosened the tie which had bound the emperors to the spiritual princes, and step by step the popes found a way to wrest from the emperors the influence over the elections which at first had remained with the latter. Rome so contrived these elections that they became a source of revenue for the papacy, at the same time that they corrupted the church and nullified the policy of the empire. The primitive form of elections ratified by the combined acclamations of clergy and people was abolished, the original right of the metropolitans to interfere in the elections of their diocese, having become odious to the popes, was cancelled, and the privilege of voting confined exclusively to the cathedral chapter, a close and independent body that had become entirely estranged from its original organisation and purpose, having degenerated into an institution for providing for the younger sons of the nobles, and having been moreover recently withdrawn by the popes from the jurisdiction of the bishops. The chapter had consequently become a corporation in rivalry with the bishops, and intent solely upon its own interests, besides wittingly or unwittingly being made to serve constantly the interests of the papal court. In the hands of the chapter the election of a bishop was almost always either open to dispute, or simoniacal, or in some way at variance with appointed forms; giving occasion to suits which had to be carried to Rome for decision. It was about this time that, with the aid of the new text-book for dogma and statute—viz., the Decretal of Gratian—the new canon law of the church came into force, which, founded entirely upon the fictions and forgeries of the preceding centuries, made the bishops altogether dependent upon Rome, and obliged every disputed question of election to be referred to Rome for decision. An elected candidate thus frequently found himself under the ruinous necessity of carrying on for years a costly suit in Rome either personally or through his agents. When unable to raise the sum of money required in fees for the pallium, suspension and excommunication were employed to extort from him the payment of the debts. The popes had more than one screw in their hands which they needed only to turn to render the electoral prince bishops, bound by the pallium oath, compliant instruments of their commands and designs. After the thirteenth century the popes not infrequently interfered directly in the nomination of the spiritual prince-electors.

In this way it also came to pass that the election to the German crown was henceforth entirely governed by four considerations.

First, a son might not succeed his father, so that, whereas it had formerly been the rule that the son or the next-of-kin should inherit the throne, exclusion now became the rule. Two turning points are here to be noticed: (1) when at Forchheim, on March 13, 1077, the German princes, inspired by the suggestions of the papal legate, passed a resolution to the effect that the throne was no longer hereditary, and that in any case when the son of an emperor seemed unworthy or unpopular some one else should be elected in his stead; (2) when in the thirteenth century the electoral vote was restricted to the seven prince-electors, to the exclusion of all the others. To support this the Curia caused the fable to be circulated through one of its officials, Tolommeo of Lucca, attributing the appointment of the prince-electors to Gregory V., who obtained a written document from Otto of Brandenburg stating his conviction that the right of the prince-electors was derived from the pope. As a natural consequence this right could be exercised only under papal control.

Secondly, a weak prince from an uninfluential family was to be selected in preference to some member of a powerful house.

Thirdly, any candidate must be excluded, or if need be deposed, who was displeasing either to the pope or to the court of France, by which at that period the Curia was guided.

Fourthly, every election was made a matter of traffic.

No candidate was elected who had not given or promised to the spiritual princes either large sums or else the right of levying important taxes, and to the secular princes lands and vassals.

Thus every emperor commenced his reign shackled by the endless gifts and favours he had promised, and crippled by the alienation of a part of his imperial rights. The fruits of the Roman policy in the German elections are patent in the quarter-century between 1250 and 1275, when Germany received either foreign or feeble kings, under whose nominal sway violence and family feuds, general confusion and wild lawlessness prevailed.

The popes had artfully contrived during fifteen years to dispose of every fresh election, and it was not until that of Rudolf of Habsburg that a more orderly state of things was introduced. Yet Rudolf even was not destined to be succeeded by his son. Adolphus of Nassau was raised to the throne through the now customary means of bribery. Albert, although a victor in the open field, had none the less to purchase his election by concessions and widely distributed favours. The election (1308) of Henry VII. of Luxemburg, the possessor of an insignificant countship, was entirely the doing of the spiritual princes in reward for his readiness to satisfy their covetous desires; and they accordingly obtained the lion's share in the first distribution of favours.

Things stood thus with the empire when, after the death of Henry, Ludwig had the boldness to step into the fateful legacy. He had for opponents the two powerful houses of Luxemburg and Habsburg, both of whom, through the deadly use which the electors made of their privileges, had been despoiled of the crown which their fathers had worn, and each of whom was occupied with alternately grasping at the throne and undermining the power of the empire by enlarging their own borders at its expense. A struggle of several years sufficed to overcome the resistance of Frederick of Habsburg, but Pope John in Avignon was neither to be overcome nor conciliated. He claimed both the administration of the empire during the vacancy of the throne, and the right of decision in every disputed election, and treated the new king with haughty contempt. In this he was supported by Ludwig's most dangerous enemy, the French King; for since the election of the French Pope Urban IV. in 1261, followed by that of Clement IV. and Martin IV., the papacy had become French, besides which the transference of the Southern Italian Kingdom to a branch of the Capet family had so firmly established the preponderance of French interests and despotism in the Curia that even the Italians, whose reigns alternated with and followed upon those of the French popes, voluntarily or involuntarily submitted to this bondage.

The victory of Philip the Fair over Boniface VIII. was quickly followed by the removal of the papal court to the south of France. We find the proportion of French cardinals at once rising to seventeen in twenty, amongst whom seven had been ministers or chancellors at the court of France.

What was it at that time that France desired from Germany? First and foremost nothing less than the German imperial crown! Deliberations upon this matter had already been held in 1273; the ambassadors of Philip the Bold had, it was said, solicited and obtained from Gregory X. in Florence the assurance that the pope would, above all things, prefer to see the French King seated upon the imperial throne. The fact seems to tally with this, that Rudolf, despite immense exertions and lavish expenditure of the imperial possessions in Italy for the benefit of the Curia, could never succeed in obtaining the imperial crown from the hands of the pope. Philip next sought to procure, in 1308, but in vain, the imperial crown for his brother, Charles of Anjou. Had this endeavour been successful, the permanent vicegerency of the empire in Italy would have fallen on Robert of Naples, and that universal sway which jurists and theologians fancifully connected with the idea of the empire would have been partially realised in the form of an imperium extending over France, Germany, and Italy. In 1324 an assembly of German princes was really summoned for the deposition of Ludwig, but the project failed, because only Leopold of Habsburg presented himself.

The efforts of the French King to enlarge his own dominions at the expense of the empire were more successful. Philip the Fair had already annexed Lyons, the emperor had suffered the loss of Provence, and only a few fragments remained to him of the Kingdom of Arles. In Paris it was given out that at a meeting with Philip in 1299 King Albert with the German barons and prelates had given their consent to the French frontier being advanced from the Maas to the Rhine in Lothringen.

Upon his own part the pope had two objects in view: (1) the humiliation of the Ghibellines combined with the annihilation of all that remained of imperial government in Italy, which he counted upon dividing between himself and Robert of Naples; (2) the transference of the imperial dignity to the French nation. The latter is reported by Raynald,[3] the annalist of the Roman court, who alone had access to the records of the papal archives, as being expressed in a document addressed by the pope to the French King.

Raynald's words leave it uncertain whether this was to be accomplished in the ordinary way by the election of the French King to the German throne, or whether the pope, in pursuance of the theory of translation set up by Innocent III., had in view a permanent severance of the imperial dignity from the German Kingdom and the investiture with it of the French nation.

All the theologians and jurists who were partial to Rome, both at that time and down to the sixteenth century, contended that the popes had first wrested the empire from the Greeks to confer it upon the Franks, then upon the Italians, and after that upon the Germans. Thus it stood also now

[3] Raynald, a. 1324, § 25.

in the orthodox chronicles and annals, and it was with good reason that Pope John asserted that the 'approved' historical records needed only to be read to convince people of the legitimacy of the papal claims. Theoretically it was taken for granted that it was within the power of the popes to withdraw from the Germans what had been conferred upon them. Now every Italian pope would have reckoned that the connection of the empire with the carefully undermined and rapidly decaying Kingdom of Germany corresponded far better with the interests and aspirations of the Curia than would an empire erected upon the solid foundations of the French Monarchy, which would inevitably imperil the papal ascendency in Italy. But the national patriotism of Jacob of Cahors and many of his cardinals appears to have troubled the political vision of the Curia upon this point. If no open attempt was made to transfer the empire to France, the explanation lies with the cunning legists of the French court, who held that the more politic and practical way was to obtain the German Kingdom for France by means of a German election to the imperial power. Why should the hope not be entertained in Paris that the German prince-electors, who shortly before had sold their votes to an Englishman and to a Spaniard, would next be willing to elect a King of France who was ready to pay handsomely?

It is a known fact that Ludwig, excommunicated and deposed by the pope, entered into relations with a fragment of the great Order of Franciscans, those very Mystics whom the pope had condemned as heretical on account of the doctrine of poverty. Threatened with imprisonment or death, they found most of them (Italians) a refuge with him in Munich, and became his spiritual directors and court theologians, and induced him to make common cause with them. The controversy was indeed of deep importance. Wherein, it was asked, does the highest perfection consist, to which in religious things a man can attain in the sight of God? What is that gospel, that ideal of the devout life, which Christ and His Apostles proclaimed and recommended both by preaching and personal example? The greatest poverty, said the Minorites, the voluntary abandonment of every kind of possession, not only by the individual but by the whole social and monastic community; and upon the observance of this principle they rested the precedence of their order before all other associations of the kind. Neither storehouses nor barns, neither rents nor any other permanent revenues, might their houses own; the only proprietor of the things they used should be the pope. Thus they sought to establish a community upon earth in which the purest ideal of a life of renunciation entirely consecrated to God might be realised. The order had been solemnly recognised and confirmed by Popes Nicolas III. and Clement V.

A question of faith was undeniably involved here. If this form of poverty was indeed the highest perfection, sanctified by the counsel and example of Christ, then not only the Minorites, but every Christian, must be instructed in it, and strive, if only approximately, to carry it out. The papal bulls upon the matter must be entirely unimpeachable, *i.e.* if one proceeded from the idea of an infallible authority upon Christian dogma. It was precisely these new orders, the Minorites and Dominicans, who had developed and endeavoured to transfer to the minds of the people the idea first distinctly enunciated by Innocent III., that God has appointed a vicegerent upon earth, and that this vicegerent is the pope.

If this be accepted it must certainly follow that the pope, and he alone, is the infallible organ of divine dogma. The Minorites presumed themselves therefore to be perfectly secure in the possession of their rule, and in their high prerogative before the rest of the Christian world which did not aim at this *altissima paupertas*. Thereupon they and their favourite doctrine were assailed by John XXII., and in five constitutions of cumulative emphasis he proceeded to demolish the teaching of his predecessors until he altogether condemned it as heresy. The public contradiction of the bull of Nicolas III. he excused with the pretext that the pope had framed the bull alone in his chamber without the concurrence of his cardinals.

The irresistible logic of their principles at once drove the Minorites to extremes; a pope, they said, who contradicts his infallible predecessors is necessarily a false pope and a usurper of the highest dignity. John retaliated by giving them over to the Inquisition; his successors did the same, and within the space of about eighty years 114 martyrs to the doctrine of papal infallibility and the rule of poverty perished at the stake in Italy and the south of France, whilst a still larger number were tortured to death in the fearful dungeons of their order or in those of the Inquisition. Even in 1449 Nicolas V., during his stay at Fabriano, caused several of these martyrs to be condemned to death and burnt by the inquisitor Giacomo della Marca. The document in which Giacomo recounts the disputations which he held with them proves that the subjects in dispute continued to be the two questions of papal infallibility and of absolute poverty. Giacomo represented to them that a pope certainly might publish false doctrine and become a heretic; only Providence had so ordained it that a good Catholic was always sure to follow upon an heretical pope. Even in the Papal Curia this was the official dogma of the time. But—such are the fluctuations of human nature and human opinions—200 years later, whilst the Franciscans were urging on the canonisation of this very Giacomo, the Jesuits, in common accord with the Dominicans and the Curia, had in Southern Europe established the supremacy of the very doctrine for which, even as late as the middle of the fifteenth century, Italian priests and laymen had been sent to the stake. Henceforth any one who should repeat the assertion made by the papal inquisitor of 1449 would be liable to be dealt with by the Inquisition. It seemed difficult to get over such a stumbling-block when in Rome in 1654 spotless orthodoxy had become a primary condition of sanctity; for Giacomo's canonisation would at once have admitted the denial of papal infallibility to be in accordance with the orthodox faith. The canonisation was therefore postponed. But the order would not let the matter rest, and seventy years later, in 1726, Giacomo found a place in the calendar of saints, former scruples having been allayed by the argument that there was no absolute certainty whether the offensive book, which at that time still remained unprinted, was really written by his own hand. So, as one might say, by the irony of history it came to pass that in the Emperor Ludwig's time the rôles of emperor and pope were reversed. The emperor, firmly believing the doctrines instilled into him by the Mystics who had taken refuge with him, came forward as the champion of papal infallibility, little aware that in so doing he was sanctioning the emphatic declarations of Popes Innocent III. and IV., and the more recent assertions of Boniface VIII., to the effect that all worldly powers were under the jurisdiction and at the disposal of the papacy, and that he was thus placing himself at the mercy of his opponents, besides giving the lie to his apologists, Marsiglio and Occam. The pope meanwhile had issued a bull in which he solemnly condemned the teaching of his predecessor Nicolas III. as heretical—no doubt with many excuses and palliations for him personally—but dealing all the more pitilessly with the partisans of his teaching, whom he handed over to the courts of the Inquisition for having seriously advocated papal infallibility. Ludwig, by taking upon himself as emperor to declare that Jacob of Cahors, being a false teacher, was incapable of reigning as pope, constituted himself, though a layman, the judge over faith and doctrine. He had been prompted to take this step by his Italian counsellors, who had held up before him the example of the early Christian emperors. He conceived himself to be acting merely as Constantine, Justinian, and even Charles the Great had done; but such a measure had come to be strange and intolerable in his day; one in which the world would not follow him. Marsiglio, moreover, his apologist, had boldly gone back to primitive Christian times in his work upon the development of the church system, now almost a thousand years old, and had denied any inherent supremacy to the pope.

The pope gladly welcomed an opportunity of decrying Ludwig as a harbourer of heretics, as the protector of the Ghibelline leaders in Upper Italy—whom he had condemned as heretics—and the patron of such men as Marsiglio, John of Jandun, and the Mystics. Through the interdict which the pope launched upon the Germans—a spiritual weapon to which they were far more sensitive than the Romans—and through the indifferent attitude of the princes, especially of the Luxemburg princes who served the policy of France, confusion in Germany now reached its highest point, and the position of Ludwig was rendered desperate. It afforded him no comfort that some of the towns of Southern Germany, for whom he had done more than any previous emperor, endured the interdict for ten years with exemplary patience. To Ludwig excommunication and the dread of the consequences beyond the grave were intolerable. This accounts for the extraordinary treaty of the year 1333, by which, for the sake of obtaining absolution, he promised to abdicate the German throne in favour of his cousin, Duke Henry of Bavaria; Henry, upon his part, undertaking to surrender to the French King not only all disputed frontier lands, but all the Italian lands stretching from the Alps to the Mediterranean, together with the wide district appertaining to the see of Cambrai, until a German King should choose to redeem them at the price of 300,000 silver marks. Such was the height to which the power of the French King's word of command had risen by that time in Avignon. However, this was too much for the most clear-sighted prince of the day, Baldwin of Treves. The treaty was never signed, and the death of the pope took place shortly afterwards.

At length, in the year 1338, the electoral princes began to bestir themselves, and under the presidency of the archbishop, Henry of Mainz, who for pecuniary reasons had been excommunicated ten years previously, they unanimously drew up the famous Declaration of Rense, withdrawing from the pope any right of interference or decision upon the election of an emperor by a majority of votes. This was a defensive act equally directed against France and the Curia, to which no parallel can be found before or since in German history.

Yet to the Emperor Ludwig it brought no relief. From Avignon none could be obtained, since John's successors, Benedict XII. and Clement VI., both of them truckled to the French court. The knowledge that the irreconcilable attitude of the Papal Curia was entirely owing to the suggestions of the French King, drove the emperor in 1341 into a humiliating submission towards the latter. He threw over his alliance with the English King, gave his word to the French King that the territories which had been torn from the empire should not be reclaimed, and received in return a promise as hypocritical as insulting, that Philip would befriend him and, out of consideration for his wife and children, would intercede for him with the pope. But, notwithstanding all the sacrifices he had made and the humiliations he had suffered, the unlucky prince died excommunicate, after having been deposed by the electors. For the spiritual prince-electors—the worst foes of the empire upon German soil—had again given way before the inducements of bribery, and had relapsed into subserviency to the will of the Curia. Charles of Luxemburg had given and promised in Avignon, Paris, and on the Rhine, more than the exhausted Ludwig was either able or willing to afford. In Avignon Charles had consented to confirm all the nominations in the German Church which the popes had made in defiance of the rights of election; to permit all disputes between Germany and France to be decided by the French pope; and had at once hastened in person to assist the King of France in the impending attack from England.

Never assuredly did an emperor experience so fully as Ludwig what it means to become the representative of an empire with high-sounding titles and extensive claims, which nevertheless, through the carelessness of its sovereigns, through the want of able statesmen, through perpetual changes of dynasty, might, from the defenceless way in which it lay at the mercy of the Curia, be compared to a whale stranded helplessly upon the shore. Nothing had been achieved in the way of a written constitutional code; no authentic textbook of law existed; no trustworthy record of the resolutions of the Diet. Opposed to it stood the hierarchy, protected on every side by the bulwarks of its canonical law fashioned during the last 150 years by assiduous codification, not unaided by fraud and cunning artifice. The Germans of that time, in comparing their own country and people with the people and country of France, had every cause to look upon the latter as the land of culture, intellect, and science, whilst amongst themselves they could only mark a certain amount of warlike prowess and ambition.

The German Church was undoubtedly the richest and most powerful in the world, and the clergy with its excellent organisation—its episcopate and cathedral chapters, its abbeys and spiritual orders—ranked as the foremost and by far the most influential body in the nation. The state of things which we have been considering had been rendered possible only through the partly indifferent, partly hostile manner in which the church regarded the empire and the interests of the German people. How is this to be explained?

In 1288 a German Minorite monk, whose name has not been preserved, wrote that in his opinion the empire could not sink lower than it had done without being utterly destroyed, nor could the high-priesthood (the papacy) rise higher unless, stripped of its apostolic character, it were entirely transformed into a secular power. He was vastly mistaken as to the depth to which the German Kingdom and Empire could fall; but he made a remarkable conjecture in supposing it possible that the Roman chair might annihilate the German Empire with the assistance of France; whereupon, to be sure, he adds, in accordance with current prophecy, Antichrist with all attendant evils would immediately appear. Further on he directly points to the clergy in common with the French as the enemies who would bring about the ruin of the German Kingdom. With this it must be borne in mind that the empire still continued to be looked upon as the greatest ornament of the lay world, and the highest secular dignity. The ceaseless enmity betwixt clergy and laity was at that time accepted as a kind of natural necessity, owing to the feeling—in itself right enough—that a priestly kingdom like that of the papacy would be endured by the whole lay world, but always only with reluctance, as a heavy yoke and a hard bondage. Boniface VIII., in the famous bull *clericis laicos*, points out as a fact admitted in early times, that the laity are hostile to the clergy. In 1328, and therefore just when the struggle between emperor and pope was at its height, Bishop Alvarus Pelagius, employed in the service of the papal court, speaks of the hatred of the laity for the clergy as an understood thing, cites the canon law in proof of it, and draws the conclusion that the clergy ought necessarily on that account to be independent of any secular power, although he presently admits that the laity in general are better, more moral, and more devout than the clergy, who had been utterly corrupted by the doctrine, precept, and example of their superiors from the popes downwards.

Fully a century and a half before this, a Bavarian theologian, Gerhoch of Reichersberg, had with strange simplicity accounted for the hostile feelings of the clergy for the empire. It was in the divine counsels, he considered, that the great empire should be broken up into weak principalities, so that the clergy should be entirely safe from oppression under the sole sheltering power of the great and divinely appointed priest who filled the Roman chair, sitting supreme above all the kingdoms of the earth. Shortly before the Emperor Ludwig's time, the French King Philip the Fair had engaged in a dispute with Pope Boniface VIII. similar to that which it now fell to the lot of Ludwig to carry on with the popes in Avignon. But whereas Ludwig, and with him the German Empire, were overcome in the contest, victory remained with the monarch of the Seine, and the papacy suffered a hitherto unexampled defeat. If we compare the position of the combatants, the means and the methods which were brought to bear in the one struggle and the other, it is not difficult to perceive wherein the chief cause of the weakness of Germany lay.

King Philip was the representative of a slowly but steadily growing power. Whilst the law of France forbade any alienation of the crown lands in Germany, Ludwig upon his accession came into but a fraction of the former imperial power and resources of government, and witnessed the disappearance during his own reign of part of these. The empire was almost without revenues. Without statesmen or useful advisers, Ludwig had to fall back upon foreigners, chiefly Italians, who flocked to Munich, and belonged almost entirely to the party of the Mystics. Men of ability were wanting at that time in Germany in almost every department of knowledge; there were neither theologians nor jurists, nor did there then exist a single famous school. Bavaria in particular, in spite of the number of her monastic establishments, could boast of no celebrated theological writer since the death of Gerhoch of Reichersberg, that is to say during the last 150 years.

France, on the contrary, in the University of Paris possessed the oracle of all Europe. Her theologians were numerous, and she had a number of legal professors, men like Flotte, Nogaret, William of Plasian, the brothers Marigni, who, well versed in the Roman as well as the canon law, had gathered round the king, and were ready to meet every attack of the popes with a counter attack. The influence of the political and religious pamphlet was first made sensible in Europe through their writings.

Clever and skilful, Philip and his advisers knew how to stimulate the national feeling in France against the pope. Boniface, copying the precedent of Innocent III., had declared that the king in matters of conscience owed allegiance to him, *i.e.* that the pope could if it pleased him punish the king, reverse his decisions, and cancel any act either of his public or private life. Thereupon the king and his advisers suggested to the people that the pope had pronounced the French crown to be held in fief, and the king to be a vassal of the papal throne. In point of fact the papal claims went much further, arrogating to the pope, according to his pleasure, and for the advantage of the Curia, an authoritative right of interference in all things—even in the affairs of family life. To the popular mind, however, the thought that the kingdom could be held in fee from a foreigner was still more incomprehensible and repulsive. The whole nation rose against the idea, for the pride of the Frenchman was that his king was independent, and not the vassal of the pope. Boniface now desisted from the assertion that he was the liege lord of the king, but he maintained—against 'French arrogance,' as he expressed it—that the German Emperor, who since the transfer by the papal see of the empire from the Greeks to the Germans, partook of the pope's power through the coronation, was the suzerain of the French. Upon this, bishops and nobles, priesthood and laity, lawyers and theologians, nay even the monastic orders, the most faithful and unquestioning servants of the papacy, with the exception of the Cistercians, rallied like one man to the side of the king against the pope.

How different now was the situation of Ludwig and the behaviour of the Germans! Philip no doubt had done precisely what Ludwig now did; he had raised the accusation of heresy against the pope. But he had gone much more circumspectly to work, and had been more considerate of dominant ideas. He avoided charging the pope with any distinct accusation of heresy; only, as the hereditary champion and defender of the faith, he demanded that the pope should answer for his faith and doctrine before a general council of the church, to which at the same time he appealed.

The popes in Avignon were beyond the reach of Ludwig's power, but Philip had had his adherents and partisans in the immediate circle of Boniface, universally detested as he was amongst the cardinals, amongst the members of the powerful family of Colonnas and their dependants, and amongst the Mystics and all who held Boniface to be unlawfully pope on account of Celestine V. having had no right to resign. It was the Colonnas and their allies who committed the outrage upon Boniface at Anagni. The part played by Nogaret in this affair was so insignificant that his name is not even mentioned in the report of an eye-witness which has recently come to light; he did no more than lay before the pope, in the name of his master the king and the French nation, a citation to appear before a general council. Philip and his advisers were too clever to be the movers in a deed which could only bring odium upon them, and by which they had nothing to gain.

It may be affirmed with truth that the genuine ancient empire which contained a German kingdom, came to an end with the Emperor Ludwig the Bavarian. None strove again after his death to restore the imperial power. The golden bull of his successor Charles IV. sealed the fate of the old empire. Through it, and indeed through the entire conduct of Charles IV., King of Bohemia as he really was, and emperor scarcely more than in name, the imperial government passed more and more into the hands of the prince-electors, who came to regard the emperor no longer as their master, but as the president of an assembly in which he shared the power with themselves.

The aim and object of the two allied powers, France and the papacy, had been attained. Henceforth the German crown might become hereditary, for the popes deemed that they had done enough in undermining the strength of the empire and weakening German nationality, and that it would be carrying this policy too far to allow the princes to become the prey of France. With an interval of ten years during which Rupert of the Palatinate reigned, the house of Luxemburg ruled for ninety years, and when the race became extinct with Sigismund, the Habsburgs once more filled the throne until the empire came to an end.

From the time of Charles IV. the main object and chief occupation of the emperors was not the empire, but the aggrandisement and security of their own house. The empire served only as the means and instrument of their purpose.

The empire of the Habsburgs certainly rested from the seventeenth century upon the broad and stable foundation of extensive hereditary possessions. But their hereditary estates were chiefly non-German, in speech, nationality, and interests, and in every instance of collision the rights and possessions of the empire were sacrificed to dynastic interests.

We have now entered upon a new phase; a dynasty, whose members are the heirs of a great, united, and purely German kingdom, itself comprising the half of Germany, has become the bearer of the imperial sceptre. By this means most of those troubles and drawbacks which once checked the growth of Germany and prevented the attainment of that strength and prosperity to which, had it been united, it would have been entitled, have been removed. One hindrance indeed, and that one of the worst, has again become active.

Nevertheless we may say without being over-presumptuous: *Novus ab integro sæclorum nascitur ordo.*

VI

AVENTIN AND HIS TIMES[1]

A festival was lately held in Abensburg in memory of a native of that town, a man to whom I would upon this occasion seek to draw the attention of this distinguished assembly.[2] Breyer, speaking in behalf of our Academy at the first public meeting after its revival in 1807, described the merit of this man, and his importance as the 'father of the history of his fatherland.' But Aventin has such a striking personality, he occupies such an honourable position in Bavaria, almost unique (one may say), and unrivalled during the course of several centuries; his writings too are of such value, even to the present generation, that the Academy is but discharging a debt in again, after seventy years, bringing him into notice. Not with regard to the circumstances of his life; so far as they can be known they have been fully investigated. We shall be better repaid by contemplating him in the light of his times, depicting how he stood in relation to his own epoch, and it to him; the mental atmosphere in which he lived, the inspirations he inhaled from it, and the opposing forces of love and hate in which he moved. For his were times teeming with complex aims and aspirations; the mission was imposed upon them of solving problems which are amongst the highest and most difficult that concern mankind, and the ground of religious faith trembled, so to speak, under the

[1] Address delivered at the public sitting of the Academy of Munich, August 25, 1877; printed also by the Academy.

[2] The Academy and its guests.

feet of that generation. Yet the man who is engaging our attention showed himself equal to his times, took his share in the wrestling, strife, and suffering that distinguished them, and, even in the last decade of his life when things went badly in Bavaria, stoutly resolved not to give way to faint-hearted despondency. At an epoch when the history of nations was decided less upon the battle-field and in the cabinets of princes and diplomatists than in the closet of the student, Aventin took his place as a pioneer in thoughtful research. Opinions originating in such minds are those which by degrees subjugated the leaders of states, and drove them into new paths, or at least compelled them in their own interests to work with them and not oppose them.

The works of Aventin are not merely tokens of learned industry and calm objective research; they are monuments of the mode of thought and the bent of men's minds which prevailed in Germany at the period when these works were composed. The impression of the great occurrences which had either just before taken place, or of which the successive scenes were at that moment following one another with dramatic rapidity upon the theatre of the world, is traceable throughout his writings, and is perceptible to the acute observer even where it is not actually expressed in words. The historian obliges us therefore to follow him not only through the past which he sets before us, but through the contemporaneous history of his day. Since Aventin neither could nor would stoop to being a mere dry copyist or annalist, he becomes, even where he keeps strictly to the source from which he draws, an original author; present experience and the story of the past are united in his mind to form a theory upon the course of the universe; a theodicy. By the light of his theory he selects, arranges, and explains the events which he relates, and with overflowing feeling he throws into his narrative, wherever the slightest opening presents itself, an exposition of his own opinion upon passing occurrences. The situation, therefore, of Europe, especially of Germany, between 1477 and

1534, furnishes the key by which to understand and appreciate Aventin's writings; and these writings in their turn are an instructive source of information upon a time in which the ferment of new forces and fresh interests was so marked that even after prolonged study new and striking points of view continually present themselves to the seeker.

The period of fifty-seven years which covers Aventin's lifetime falls distinctly into two sections: (1) the first, including the last years of the middle ages; (2) the second, marking the commencement of a new era. In the intellectual world the former is the period of Humanism, the latter of the Reformation, the latter being the outcome of the former. The course of Aventin's life and the texture of his mind are what might be expected from this. To the humanists he owes his classical culture and his critical and historical ability; amongst them some were his teachers, and several his personal friends; at a more advanced stage of his career he lives and moves among the thoughts and hopes of the Reformation.

In the ancient history of Greece and Rome the humanists possessed a province in which, undisturbed by the suspicions and threats of the ecclesiastical authorities, they were free to dispose of things as they liked and to ripen their faculties for criticism and historical investigation. Humanism thus served the Germans as a preparatory school for the great religious struggle which, long approaching, and now wanting only a spark to set it ablaze, burst out when the signal was simultaneously given from Wittenberg and Zurich. It is a matter of great importance that German humanism, although engendered and fostered under Italian influences, had speedily made itself independent and beaten out a path of its own. Whilst Italian philologians and rhetoricians were only restrained by fear of the coercive power of the church from giving open expression to their infidelity and contempt for Christianity, or at any rate studiously avoided and silently shifted their ground from the subject of religion, the

German humanists, on the contrary, showed signs of a deepening seriousness in religious faith, often joined with a desire for church reform. If an aversion to the Roman court was betrayed by most of them, it was prompted as much by German patriotism as by religious feelings, for German humanism was thoroughly national in character, equally ready to turn against the Curia or against France, which was even then casting covetous eyes towards the Rhine frontier. The humanists by that time had extended themselves like a great brotherhood over the whole of Europe; Erasmus indeed was the recognised head of the movement, and was everywhere received with homage like a king in the realm of intellect. But it is precisely in him that we become aware of the difference referred to above; the tone of his mind is emphatically religious and so to speak polemical. The Germans took life and learning more seriously than did their brethren on the other side of the Alps, and were in consequence free alike from courtly arrogance and vanity, and from the proneness to petty squabbling which disfigured the Italian character. In this as in all the other relations of life, Aventin's feelings were those of a German. In his history, when he sums up the epoch in which he lived —and which he had otherwise depicted in the gloomiest colours—as a period peculiarly blessed, it is because Erasmus has brought to light the original text of the New Testament, and had for the first time given to the world a genuine version of it. Thus imbued with the learning and spirit of the humanists, Aventin—as an instructor of princes—takes up the pen of the historian; but this only after years of wandering spent in visiting many countries and towns. He had seen, as he himself relates, fifteen universities, amongst others Vienna, Paris, and Cracow; and he knew Switzerland, Poland, Italy, and France from personal observation. This taste for travel he shared with many of his contemporaries; it grew out of that cosmopolitan impulse which to this day is implanted in the breast of the German, and now drives him far from his home over land and sea, but which at that time was strengthened by the thirst for knowledge, and the insufficiency of the means of education at home. When neither daily publications nor periodicals existed, no other way was open but travel whereby to gain acquaintance with the world and a knowledge of the features of the time and of contemporary history; in this way only was it possible for a thoughtful man to compare the circumstances of his own land with those of foreign countries in order to arrive at an independent judgment.

When Aventin received from his princely patrons the commission to write a history of Bavaria, he travelled through the whole of Bavaria and the neighbouring provinces, and carried on his studies and researches in ninety different places—towns, castles, and cloisters. Besides intellectual profit, he acquired by this means such an accurate knowledge of his fatherland in the narrower and wider sense, *i.e.* of both Bavaria and Germany—their legal, economic, and ethical conditions—as far exceeded that of any of his contemporaries. But besides the comprehensive views which distinguish his works, we are struck by another feature which pervades them more or less openly from first to last: the pathos of the ardent patriot, of the prophet anxious and apprehensive for his people and country, who, having read in the past the inevitable future, holds up the mirror of history by way of warning to his countrymen, reminds them of the possessions and privileges which they have already lost, and points out the peril of a yet deeper fall, whilst bringing to their notice ways and means for renovation and recovery. Broad and full is the stream of instruction and admonition which flows from the reservoir of his historical knowledge to fertilise the thirsty fields of his country's intellectual barrenness. But he often yields to the impulse to relieve his over-burdened heart of the sorrows he has seen and experienced; it is the irrepressible outbreak of a deep and painful conviction, and his wrathful rebukes strike home, at one moment cutting and pointed as a dagger, at another heavy as the blow of a club.

The result of all this is the production of a work widely different from the adulatory, superficial historiography penned by writers like the Italian humanists, whom princes entertained at their courts that they might celebrate the deeds of their patrons. To this end had Henry VII. of England sent for and engaged the services of Polidoro Vergilio—just as Louis XII. had summoned Paolo Emilio; Matthias Corvinus of Hungary, Bonfini; and Casimir of Poland, Buonaccorsi or Callimachus—and commissioned him to become the historian of his country. They composed fluent readable books filled with fables, in which elegance of style was principally aimed at, and criticism or investigation into the accuracy of the sources from which the author drew, was ignored.

If we now inquire what impression was produced upon Aventin himself by surrounding circumstances and his own researches into them, in what light they must have appeared to him, we must remember, to begin with, that Aventin was a zealous patriot devoted to the princes of his race, and heart and soul attached to the German Kingdom and Empire. Patriotism was a sentiment common to the humanists of that period—Wimpfeling, Celtes, Bebel, Peutinger, Hutten are amongst those whom I call to mind—but with Aventin it had been developed by his studies, and so pervades the whole man and animates his works. Yet as regards his views upon the importance and dignity of the empire he belongs entirely to the middle ages. Germany to him is the Roman Empire of the German nation, the fourth and last monarchy of Daniel's prophecy, with the duration of which the existence of the world is bound up. It is, he considers, a great favour and the highest earthly honour to the Germans that God should have appointed them to be the upholders and representatives of the Roman name; only let them see to it that they never forfeit this name.

The empire was still, according to the social and religious views of the time, held to be an indispensable and divinely appointed institution; without the empire the great Christian republic, which in face of the encroaching power of the Turks was much alive to the sense of unity, would have seemed but a mutilated and helpless trunk. To the princes the emperor was indispensable, for it was he who gave legal embodiment to their demands and pretensions; to the towns he was needful as a protection against the princes; the peasantry, when it enrolled itself in brotherhoods or revolted against its oppressors, inscribed the name of the emperor upon its banners, and would fain have cast off the yoke of intermediate powers to obey the emperor alone, who certainly bid fair to be an easier master. The emperors themselves ended by valuing the imperial dignity and the power that remained with it merely as a means of founding a dynasty and of establishing and extending their family power.

Aventin, who had been absorbed in the study of the Saxon, Salic, and Hohenstaufen emperors, naturally perceived in this state of things tokens of deep and merited degradation, increasing weakness abroad, and a continual loosening of the old forms which constituted the strength of the empire at home. In his youth he had seen the end of the long inglorious reign of Frederick III., and seen too that the empire had not so much as afforded 4,000 men to help the emperor, despised even by his own hereditary subjects, against the Turks. Then followed the humiliating reverses of Germany during the Swiss war and the separation of Switzerland from the German Empire. Prussia had already been lost to Poland after a desperate struggle, Milan soon fell into the hands of France, and the loss of the Burgundian countries, Belgium, and the Netherlands was already threatened.

Although Frederick III., who for twenty-five years had never set foot in Germany, had done all that was possible to estrange the affections of the people, his son Maximilian was personally much beloved, was exalted by the humanists as a patron of literature and science, and as a prince who by inclination and interest was devoted to the cause of German nationality and to the preservation of ancient ways. But misfortune attended all his undertakings, and not undeservedly so, from the short-sighted unstable policy by which he forfeited the confidence of those around him. The well-meaning attempts of two of the electoral princes, Berthold of Mainz and Frederick of Saxony, to renovate the strength of the German Empire-Kingdom by the introduction of fresh institutions, had almost failed And when, after Maximilian's death, three youthful and powerful kings came forward as rival candidates for the succession, the electors made a shameless traffic of their votes, and it is scarcely too much to say that the empire was put up to the highest bidder.

It was just at that moment that Aventin was engaged upon the first book of his 'Chronicle,' and he observes, 'I know not the cause of the imperial election being so long delayed; but even if I knew, it would not be lawful to say.' Such a manner of breaking off, with a hint of imposed silence, is frequent in Aventin's writings. Out of consideration for his patron Duke William, who had commissioned him to write, he had very sufficient reason for not being too communicative on a subject of contemporary history. In the course of his narrative, continued down to the time of his death fifteen years later, it becomes more and more perceptible that Charles, upon whom the hopes of the Germans had at first been confidently centred, but who had coveted the imperial crown for the sole purpose of adding to the territories of his own house, had no intention of fulfilling any of their hopes, but had different ends in view, and, although endeavouring to restore the empire to its ancient might and grandeur, had neither understanding nor sympathy for the wants of Germany, or for her spiritual or intellectual advancement.

The hopes which had brightened the beginning of the

new emperor's reign, and their subsequent overthrow, are patent in Aventin's works. The 'Annals' give an account of the coronation in Rome of Charles the Great as emperor, representing the occurrence as brought about through election by the Roman Senate and people in combination with the pope, and observing in addition how the glorious empire has fallen into decay and decrepitude in consequence of the feebleness of the emperors, the cowardice of the princes, and the intrigues of the popes. Yet they conclude with the hope that under the younger and greater Charles the empire will rise to new strength. Thus he wrote in the year 1519. Eleven years later in a corresponding passage in the 'Chronicle' this hope, together with the mention of the decay of the empire and its causes, has entirely disappeared.

It was under influences and experiences of this kind that Aventin composed his historical work, the first which set before the German people a fuller and more correct account of their former greatness and of the causes of their decay than they had hitherto seen. The Bavarian history which he was commissioned to write soon developed in his hands into a history of Germany; indeed it would have been scarcely possible at that time to write a separate history of Bavaria—it would have been hardly more than a collection of disjointed notices. He himself intended his work for the instruction not only of all Germans but of all Christian nations; for he pointedly remarks that ignorance of history had been a great cause of loss and disadvantage to the empire and to the whole of Christendom. Any one writing history, like Aventin, for the use and edification of his contemporaries, must at that time have cast equally anxious glances towards the west, south, and east. Towards the west—because, however strong the antipathy of the nation already was to France, the submissiveness of the princes of the empire to French policy had become an understood thing; towards the south—because the fate of the German nation always hung more upon the decisions of the pope than upon the will of the princes or even of the emperor; towards the east—because the Turks were pressing onwards with increasing fury over the frontier of the empire, and in 1529 they already stood before the gates of Vienna.

In the preface to his work, where he holds before his people the mirror of their errors, Aventin, in conformity with predictions universally credited at the time, describes the Turks as the instruments of divine judgment employed for the chastisement of the Germans.

The judgment which Aventin passes upon the French nation in one passage of his history brings me to a peculiarity in his composition which, objectionable as it might now seem, was not then without example, although he may be accused of carrying it further than any of his contemporaries. He allows himself to put his own feelings, lamentations and reproaches, wishes and opinions, into the mouths of prominent personages of the time of which he writes, that under this transparent cloak he may set them safely yet forcibly before his readers.

An instance of this is in the speech of Bishop Conrad of Utrecht at the meeting at Gerstungen; another, in the speech of Archbishop Eberhard of Salzburg, so often quoted and printed; again, in the severe lecture addressed by Pope Alexander to the German clergy; and lastly, in the document in which Henry V., in the year 1107, not only sharply rebukes the French—'that wanton and superstitious people'—for meddling with German affairs in taking part with Paschal II. during the war of Investitures, but throws the blame of his own rebellion against his father upon the priests, who, he complains, had deluded him and led him astray when a youth. So far as I can make out, Aventin has spun this whole tirade out of the short notice in Ekkehard, where the emperor is said to have declared that he would accept no decisions made in foreign countries concerning his rights. These fictions, the tone and purport of which were not a little influenced by the violent pamphlet issued by Ulrich von Hutten, are certainly, although brilliant in style, no embellishment to Aventin's works; they are anachronisms; for fear of the consequences if he should put forward such things as his own views, he puts the language of the Reformation into the mouths of people of the eleventh, twelfth, and thirteenth centuries.

However, such blemishes in style ought not to hinder us from admiring Aventin's healthy views and excellent appreciation of history. Fables and falsehoods, which had been hitherto generally accepted, he was in some instances the first to see through—*e.g.* the delusion as to the female Pope Joan. He rejected the fable invented in Rome of the institution of the college of prince-electors by Pope Gregory V., to which even his contemporary the learned Bebel of Tübingen still firmly adhered. It may therefore appear all the more strange that he should introduce into his work such a fantastic picture as he gives us of German primitive history, including a mythical period in which illustrious rulers, flourishing communities, and the heroes of great deeds abounded. The primeval German Kingdom existed fully a thousand years before the fall of Troy; Aventin rejects the myth, dating from the seventh century, of the descent of the Franks from the Trojans, simply because it would have made the rise of German greatness and power much too recent. He furnishes us with detailed accounts of the primeval German 'kings' Schwab, Bayer, and Gambrinus, and imagines that with further research many old sources of information and ancient monuments might be brought to light which would prove the Germans 'in their past deeds and history not to have been outdone by the Greeks and Romans.' Upon this point he often appeals to the ballads current amongst the people and to old songs and poems. It must be allowed in his favour that, according to the received opinion of our own day, the old heroic legends originated amongst the ancestors of the Bavarian people. But as he also quotes the Meisterlieder of the fifteenth century as his authorities he may have borrowed a good deal out of these now forgotten rhymes. The principal source, however, upon which he draws for this mythical history is the false Berosus of the Dominican Annius of Viterbo. Twenty years before, Nauclerus or Vergenhans of Wurtemberg had made this Annius the basis of primitive German history in his chronicle which was afterwards revised by Melancthon; but that Aventin, otherwise so clear-sighted, should have nevertheless failed to recognise imposture in this instance can only be explained by his patriotic blindness and his desire to set before the world a genealogical tree which should carry the origin of the German race far back into the brilliant but undefined ages of the primitive world. He allows himself also to be duped by a pretended Chancellor and Secretary of Duke Thassilo named Kranz. The Bavarian chroniclers shortly before and in Aventin's time had made out a plausible list of the mythical kings. Without considering the genuine German nationality of the Bavarian people, Aventin, for the sake of giving them a more remote origin, turns the Celtic Boii into Germans, and makes them into the ancestors of the later Bajuvarians. This leads him to maintain that all the Celts who had lived in times of yore upon German soil and on the borders, were of true German stock, that is, German by descent, language, customs, and laws; even the Celtic Galatians of Asia Minor were in his eyes German, or rather Bavarian, so that according to this view St. Paul had addressed his epistle to the Germans, and the Galatian bishops who had appeared at the Councils of the fourth century were German bishops. Even the Sarmatians, Getæ, and Thracians are said by Aventin to have been Germans. This resembles the transposition with a contrary aim, on the other side of the Rhine, of the terms Franks and French, first made current in Germany by the Chronicler of Strasburg, Fritzsche Closener, who adds the Carlovingians to his list of the Roman and Byzantine Emperors, with the observation that the empire passed to the French.

Now this and everything else which appears strange to us in Aventin's writings must be attributed to the views which he entertained of the double ruin, political and moral, into which the German nation had fallen. He and other humanists regarded with anxiety the rapidity with which the power of France had lately been increased and her monarchy consolidated. They saw the weakness and defenceless condition of the western frontier of the empire, the greater portion of which was under the rule of the spiritual princes. Supposing, too—and in those times it seemed far from improbable—that her two hereditary foes, the French and Ottoman powers, were to join hands for a simultaneous advance upon Germany, who could then avert the ruin of the empire?

Even in his preface Aventin reminds his readers that each war which had as yet broken out between Christians and Turks had terminated unfavourably to the former; and for this the crimes and impiety of the princes and their followers, as well as of the clergy, that is to say the two ruling classes, were to blame.

In 1519 the danger that the German crown should fall into the possession of France was imminent. Aventin knew of but two means of averting it. The first was that Germany should be renovated religiously as well as morally, that the church should be reformed, and the clergy, who, according to Aventin, had poisoned the morals of the people and were chiefly answerable for the prevalence of vice, should be made to amend themselves, or somehow be rendered innocuous. The second alternative, which, however, presupposed the first, appeared to him to lie in the political elevation of the Germans, only to be attained on condition of their being brought to a consciousness of the latent power within them, and to a recollection of their former national greatness, such as would inspire them to set about and carry through a reform of the constitution of the empire. Whoever would comprehend Aventin must often read between the lines, and study contemporaneous writings, especially those of Eberlin and Ulrich von Hutten. In fervent patriotism Aventin stood not a whit behind the Franciscan knight, but he was not, like him, a restless adventurer, and less given to exaggerated rhetoric.

Aventin, like Hutten and the rest of the humanists, was always zealous for the maintenance of the national honour, which, owing at that time to the relations with France, Italy, and more recently with Spain, was peculiarly sensitive. The discrepancy between the vast pretensions of an *imperium mundi* and the actual resources of an empire with neither revenues, landed possessions, nor military power, and unable even to put down the highway robbery systematically carried on in some parts of the country, often drew down the contempt of the neighbouring nations upon the Germans, especially since the misfortunes that had almost invariably attended Maximilian's undertakings, and since German weakness had been exposed by the result of the Swiss war.

All the more zealously did writers endeavour to represent the former dignity and splendour of the nation in glowing colours, to magnify the number of its victorious campaigns and its superiority over the most renowned and powerful nations of antiquity; and, as the limits of historical time appeared insufficient, a period of fabulous antiquity was added. Thus fictions, such as shortly before Aventin's time the Abbot Trithemius had invented about Hunibald and his fabulous primitive history of the Franks, were not repudiated, and were treated as harmless.

The great and excellent work of Dlugoss, a history of Poland, written forty years before Aventin, largely partakes of the merits and defects of Aventin's work. Dlugoss also had put together with marvellous industry all that he had managed to collect out of the chronicles and records of libraries and archives. With equal conscientiousness he too, like Aventin, was bent upon setting before his countrymen a glowing picture of their past, filled with heroic figures and deeds, and was skilful in weaving together a consecutive but idealised history out of the fragments of popular ballads. The object of his work is to prove that the countries which had become in course of time estranged from the Polish crown and people, including a considerable part of Germany, would some day be reunited to Poland.[3]

It is remarkable that in 1531, three years therefore before Aventin's death, a work upon the commencement of German history appeared in the three volumes by Beatus Rhenanus of Elsass, in which the weak and untrustworthy portions of Aventin's works—as to the false Berosus and the transformation of Celts and Gauls into Germans—are picked out for scathing criticism and fundamentally disproved. Germany, remarks Rhenanus, has military fame enough of her own, and can leave the French theirs.

It must be understood that in this he was not aiming at Aventin, whose writings could not have been known to him, but at the precursors of Aventin: the credulous Wimpfeling, who sought to raise a temple of fame for Germany out of the fables and exaggerations which his patriotic enthusiasm led him to adopt; Konrad Peutinger of Augsburg, the friend of the Emperor Maximilian, who, only for the sake of proving that the Franks had never ruled over the Germans, would not reject the wonders of Berosus; and Heinrich Bebel of Swabia, whose patriotism rose to the point of inducing him to assert that the German crusades were undertaken solely for the sake of God and the faith, and for the spread of Christianity. Unfortunately we are ignorant whether Aventin saw the work of Rhenanus, and, if he did so, whether he was hindered from making use of it by sickness, by the failure of his faculties, or by the dislike of sacrificing a considerable portion of his own work.

The keynote of Aventin's work is to be found in the maxim that the freedom or servitude, greatness or degradation, happiness or tribulation, of the German people depend

[3] Geissberg, *Die polnische Geschichtsschreibung*, p. 331.

upon their moral worth. They have always fared according to their deserts, and prospered in proportion as they possessed the virtues of temperance, truth, and justice. Formerly, he thinks, when national life was simpler and purer, God suffered the Germans from time to time to be chastised by foreign foes; but for the last 400 years judgments had come upon them through internal discord and the covetousness of their princes. This opinion, viz. that the dissensions of the princes and the want of a strong imperial government are the cruellest scourge upon the backs of the people, was the spoken or tacit opinion of every German of average cultivation. Aventin was so penetrated with it, that in the preface to his 'Chronicle' he expressly points out, as the task of the historian, the exposition of the true causes which lead to unity or discord between the different classes and estates in the country. Seeing that he himself was convinced that the dissensions at imperial elections, the civil wars, the insubordination of the princes to the emperor, had been always incited or fostered by the popes, and that it was the latter who still were perpetually spreading confusion and discord in Germany, it is not surprising that, religious motives apart, his works should have received so anti-Roman a colouring.

Aventin evidently bestows especial care and attention upon the history of Henry IV., Henry V., Frederick II., and of Ludwig of Bavaria, for the very reason that they mark the period of the great struggle of the emperors with the papacy. Like Cato he takes the beaten side, that of the Germans and their emperor; and not only this, it is clear also, in spite of all the prudence and reticence which he observes, that he sees in the popes the most dangerous and irreconcilable enemies of the empire and of the German nation. Since the death of Frederick II., says Aventin, the German nation has accomplished nothing really great or noble. When he characterises the struggle of the popes with the last emperor of the house of Hohenstaufen as a war of which the true motive was the humiliation of the German Kingdom, already over powerful and over prosperous, later research corroborates his judgment upon the facts. He knew at whose door the chief blame rested for the terrible times of imperial interregnum, and what irreparable losses the Germans had then undergone. The two speeches which we have already mentioned are those in which he especially gives vent to his opinion upon the papacy and its behaviour towards Germany. He recurs again and again in many places to the corrupting and ruinous effects of the influence of Rome upon Germany. Far from recognising in the strife about investitures and in the conduct of Gregory and his adherents a genuine movement of reform, Aventin totally condemns them, and we cannot but acknowledge that in his times and circumstances it was perfectly natural that he should do so. Once aware that the rule of succession in the empire had been broken by papal influence, and arbitrary election set up as a principle in its place, as a preliminary step towards that downfall of the empire which could now no longer be prevented, he was justly indignant that the struggle should have begun and be carried on with the cry of 'Down with the simony of the laity!' when all the while the ultimate result was the surer establishment of that simony which flourished without restraint in the ranks of the clergy from the highest to the lowest. Finally he could not fail to perceive that the rule of celibacy which Hildebrand and his successors had ruthlessly forced upon an over-numerous and wealthy class, living for the most part in luxurious idleness, had been conducive to a shameless immorality patent to all the world. The difference between the echo of the public opinion of the time and the conclusions which Aventin's studies had led him to must here be marked. During the years in which Aventin was composing his work it is certain that a feeling hostile to Rome was widely diffused amongst all classes, chiefly the burgher and learned classes, but also even amongst the clergy. Erasmus gives utterance to it in 1518, and King Ferdinand does the same in a memorial dedicated to his brother the emperor in 1524; besides which the papal legate, Cardinal Cervino (afterwards Pope Marcellus II.), writing a few years after Aventin's death, says that he is filled with horror at perceiving the extent to which the Germans have swerved from their allegiance to the papal chair.[4]

The personal impressions which Aventin received in Italy must also be taken into account; as the companion of a prince who himself belonged to the ecclesiastical class, he was favourably placed for gaining a deeper insight into the condition of things in that country. That which the very names of the popes from Paul II. to Clement VII. suggest to us, Aventin saw and understood from observation on the spot. In Paris again he had the opportunity of acquainting himself with the views of the French upon the papal court, and the nature of them it is easy to discover from the utterances of one witness only—Bishop Duchatel of Orleans.[5]

Now and then Aventin's aversion to the papacy leads him into unfair statements, for instance when, not in the 'Annals' as some one has foolishly supposed, but in the later 'Chronicle,' he charges the papal party with the murder of Duke Ludwig of Kelheim in 1231, a crime which, judging from the relations of the duke to the pope and the emperor at the time, it is impossible to believe in.

Our opinion on the subject, however, is somewhat modified by the reflection that Aventin, and indeed he only, had read and made extracts from the memorandum book of Albert of Possemünster, and had taken his impression from that, for, in a note amongst the papers that he left at his death, he remarks, 'It grieves me to read what

[4] *Relatio legationis Cardinalis de Nicastro*, in the *Anecdota Litteraria*, Romae, 1773, i. 143 ff. The popes, says Cervino, formerly made use of the people to extort obedience from the princes, but the mass of the nation has now become hostile to Rome, and, with the exception of a few right-minded individuals, the minority, who outwardly stand firm, are only kept so by the fear of their princes. This was the condition of affairs in 1540.

[5] *Petri Castellani Vita*, auctore Petro Gallandio, ed. Baluzius, Paris 1674, pp. 67, 88, 89.

these foxes and ravening beasts were not afraid to accomplish.'

Aventin dimly foreboded much more than he clearly perceived. He inevitably overlooked many essential items in the process by which abuses had grown up in the church, for many facts belonging to it were as yet unknown, and most of the sources from which we now draw our knowledge of these things were then closed. Touching the revolution which had begun in the church under Hildebrand, he says that Christian modesty forbade him to reveal the forgeries upon which it had been founded. This observation could not be meant to refer to the Isidorean Decretals, for their spuriousness had not been brought to light in his time, but was more likely occasioned by certain assertions contained in the letters of Gregory VII. and in the writings of the Gregorians, concerning the falsity of which his acquaintance with older documents and his critical insight would have convinced him. That the old order of the church should be superseded by a new creation of cunning and fallacious canon law, and that the system now become dominant was bound up with a concatenation of inventions and forgeries reaching over a thousand years, were matters of which he proves himself, by various isolated utterances, to have been dimly conscious, without being able, however, to grasp the true connection of facts. Of Gratian's Decretal, a work which partly effected and partly confirmed the complete transformation of the church to an absolute monarchy, he certainly says that it 'reduced' the canon law 'to a tangle of shreds'—an expression falling very far short of the truth. Finally, when he asserts that the example of Charles IV. in purchasing the imperial dignity from the electoral princes, for himself first and then for his son Wenceslaus, was very evil and quite unprecedented, he could not have been aware that the venality of the electors had regulated the elections ever since the middle of the thirteenth century.

Aventin has been severely blamed by one of his biographers for the bitterness of his expressions against the clergy. He has been accused of vindictiveness and blind anger, and even of malice and falsehood.* It is true that he not seldom breaks out into bitter expressions, and chooses the strongest terms which language can afford him. He calls the princes, for example, in one place selfish money-grabbers, intent only upon hunting and gambling. But his utterances with regard to the clergy are not more severe than are those of most of his contemporaries both in and out of Germany, and every word is corroborated a hundred times over by the testimony of other writers of the period. The identical accusations raised by Aventin against the clergy, now in jest and scorn, now in anger and indignation, were then universally brought against them. He only clothes them in terms grown, as he assures us, proverbial in the mouth of the people. Above all, Aventin's descriptions receive abundant justification from members of that class itself, especially the clergy of Bavaria. The German language, too, it must be observed, was extraordinarily rich at that period in terms of satire and invective, manifestly because the tendency of the day lay in that direction. The writings of Sebastian Brant, Geiler of Kaisersberg, Pauli, Hutten, and Eberlin testify to this.

Aventin was by no means alone in the opinion, to which he now and then gives energetic expression, that the Papal Curia was chiefly answerable for the miserable condition of the church and for the corruption of the clergy. Just at the moment when he was composing the last book of the 'Annals,' Pope Hadrian VI. had publicly confessed to the Germans that the corruption of the church had been principally brought about by the papal chair. His neighbour, Bishop Berthold, of Chiemsee, the author of the book 'The Burden of the Church'—*Die Last der Kirche*—and Aytinger, the priest of Augsburg, in 1496, give the same testimony. There was not to be found at that time, even amongst the most zealous partisans of the church, a single

* Wiedemann, p. 192.

voice of any weight which would have questioned the notorious fact that Rome itself was the head-quarters of all abuses and religious corruption. What most contributed to embitter public opinion and to kindle the longing for the reformation of ecclesiastical institutions, was that whilst the Roman Church still continued to set herself forth as the only perfect pattern of the Christian Church, she was everywhere through her influence and tyrannical action carrying irremediable corruption into ecclesiastical life. Had Aventin lived a year longer he would have read an official confirmation of his charges against Rome in the report drawn up by the cardinals whom Paul III. had commissioned to inquire into the matter.

How did matters stand, then, as regards Aventin's religious convictions? Was he at heart a Protestant, or did he hold fast to the old church? Any one who would profit by his works must form an opinion upon the subject.

To any clear perception or definite logical views upon the differences between the Catholic and Protestant doctrines, Aventin certainly never attained. We come upon passages in his writings composed from the standpoint of the church of the middle ages, which it is hardly fair to accept as mere efforts at accommodation. Thousands found themselves in that transition period in the same predicament, uncertain whom or what to believe; and whilst many made comparatively light of this fact, comforting themselves with the thought that the fundamental Christian doctrines comprised in the two oldest creeds still constituted a common bond of faith, others suffered poignant anxiety, tormented by the feeling of having lost all certainty of belief. We stumble upon a numerous class of so-called expectants, who, mindful of the great reforming council of the previous century, are content to wait and live on in doubt in the hope, never to be realised, that all points of dispute would one day be decided in a free council. There were about that time in Passau two ecclesiastics, the dean of the cathedral, Rupert of Mosham, and Philonius Dugo, a companion of the Bishop of Passau, whose writings bear a certain relationship to Aventin's, and who both strove to take up a position between the adherents of the old and those of the new doctrines.

Aventin, who all his youth had been a pious and faithful son of the church, became, when in Paris, a pupil of the famous Lefèvre of Etaples, who introduced him to the study of the New Testament. Lefèvre himself remained until his death a member of the old church, but several of the reformers were disciples of his school. In Germany Aventin reckoned amongst his friends several leaders of the Reformation, such as Urban Rhegius, Althamer, Spalatin, Osiander, and he himself inclined more and more towards the doctrines proclaimed in Wittenberg, upon which side the majority of the thinking and educated people of the day amongst the laity also stood. The mainspring of the movement, in point of fact, was in the inner life and consciousness of the German people. Thus it came to pass that with irresistible power it turned all existing forces in Germany at once into its service, availing itself of all the learning and intellectual resources of the country for the one great task of church reform—a circumstance that in course of time led to a too exclusive predominance of theology and an unhealthy preponderance of dogmatic questions. Aventin himself points out the influence which his historical studies exercised upon his religious convictions; in the animated descriptions that he gives of the advantages to be gained from the study of history he reckons 'the restoration of faith to the unbeliever,' because those who have been led astray by the caricature of Christianity presented before their eyes by the present state of religion and of the church, will, when they see what the noble primitive form of the church was during the first centuries, perceive their present stumbling-blocks to be only the result of later corruptions. Throughout his 'Chronicle' he is evidently taking pains to make manifest and glaring the contrast between the customs and ordinances of the primitive church, and the conditions and abuses of recent times.

But this he could not do without danger. Not later than 1523 the pope had commended Duke William of Bavaria greatly, and thought fit to confer various privileges upon him, for his zeal in the extirpation of the new doctrines, even by means of capital punishment. Not long afterwards, when the teaching of the Anabaptists had spread with astonishing rapidity throughout the whole of Southern Germany so that the people of both the country and the towns were converted in crowds, the same Duke William issued the terrible mandate that 'whoever recanted should be beheaded; whoever did not recant should be burnt,' and the thing was done. Aventin was thrown into prison,[7] 'for the gospel's sake,' as he says himself; but was shortly afterwards liberated by his protector, the Chancellor Eck. In 1529 he applied to Melancthon to find him, if possible, some situation in Wittenberg; but the application was rejected. If this migration to Saxony had taken place we may be sure that much would have appeared in Aventin's works which is not to be found there, and much more which is merely hinted at, or insinuated, would have been stated plainly. He has avoided, for instance, any expression of opinion upon Huss and Jerome of Prague, although in a later passage he reports the burning at the stake of two German priests, Ratgeb and Grünsleder, in Ratisbon, for their Hussite teaching, but puts his own opinion into their mouth, viz. that the two Bohemian theologians suffered death in Constance not on account of real errors, but because of their denunciations of the corruption of the church. So also as to the question on which the existence of the papacy depends he discusses the

[7] Letter to Dr. Eck in Rome. See Wiedemann's *Joh. Eck*, s. 666.

pros and *cons* as to whether St. Peter was ever in Rome, with knowledge of the subject, but he shirks disclosing his own view with the hypocritical words 'I will wrangle with no man upon this point—it is all one to me.' Thus his last years were passed in Bavaria in prudent obscurity. In his writings he has avoided any mention of the names of Luther, Melancthon, and other reformers, even of Hutten; Erasmus alone he singles out to exalt him as one of the greatest benefactors of Christianity. With Erasmus, in fact, he has much in common, sharing his opinions possibly upon most questions. Any suspicion that the Reformation would lead to a complete and permanent separation into two hostile churches doubtless never entered his head. At the time of his death, and for some time afterwards, this thought was, even to the heads and leaders of the movement, strange and scarcely conceivable, as one sees by the utterances of Melancthon and Camerarius. Like most of his contemporaries, he carried with him to the grave the hope that the Reformation would be general, and his beloved Germany be spared the misfortune of a lasting schism. Things have turned out otherwise. Least of all could he have foreseen the destiny of his more immediate fatherland, Bavaria.

In Aventin's day Bavaria was intellectually on a par with the rest of Germany. After his death, persecution drove the men who were his equals in education and thought out of the country, or forced them to keep silence; and after 1550 Bavaria for two centuries ceased to take her part in the life and aspirations of the German people.

Aventin's two principal works have been imperfectly preserved to us in two partially incorrect editions. Even in the Gundling edition several passages are missing. The case is still more unfortunate with the 'Chronicle,' which is such a remarkable monument of the language. The full value of Aventin's work and its importance in our literature, together with the services which he rendered to the language and history of Germany, will never be recognised until we have before us a correct edition of the 'Chronicle' from the original manuscript. It is a point of honour for Bavaria that a good edition should be produced, and it is with much satisfaction that I can state that the Academy has already taken the matter in hand by the appointment of a committee to prepare the work.[a]

[a] The new edition, prepared by the Royal Academy of Munich, has since appeared in 5 vols. (*Christian Kaiser*, Munich, 1881-86).

VII

ON THE INFLUENCE OF GREEK LITERATURE AND CULTURE UPON THE WESTERN WORLD IN THE MIDDLE AGES[1]

The culture and literature of Rome, which, together with Christianity, have served as the means of education for modern nations, had their origin in the far richer civilisation of Greece. It is well known that from the sixth century after the building of the city, Greek men and Greek books in rapidly increasing numbers flowed into Rome, which was enlarging itself to become the metropolis of the world. Numerous Greek slaves and freedmen spread the knowledge of their tongue as well as of their literature amongst the households and families of Rome. Roman students began to undertake the journey to Greece for the sake of visiting the famous Hellenic centres of education. To this may be added the influence of trade, and of diplomatic exigencies in the intercourse with the countries and courts of the East.

In the Augustan period of Rome's intellectual bloom it was the recognised rule that in all the kinds of literature adopted by the Romans, Greek forms and models should be studied and imitated. The noble language of Rome only attained to perfection through the formative and enriching influence of the Greek tongue. Early in the period

[1] Address delivered in the new hall upon the celebration of the 128th anniversary of the foundation of the Academy of Munich. The introductory congratulatory phrases have been omitted. This and the following five addresses have already appeared in a more or less complete form in the *Allgemeine Zeitung*.

of the empire the old hatred and antagonism against foreign speech and literature had given way to general admiration, to enthusiastic appropriation, and imitation faithful but often far too servile. The anxiety lest the genuine ancient Roman character in morals and politics should thereby be disintegrated and given over to irretrievable dissolution had not yet disappeared, but was powerless to resist the increasing force of the new current. The entire education and culture of the Roman youth was Greek. No education was considered complete which did not include a smattering, if not a knowledge, of Greek literature. In an empire where Greek was the language of the majority, ignorance of it implied inability to fill any office or to carry on any business.

From the time of Alexander's conquest, Greek had become a universal language, or rather, the language of the known world. Three centuries had elapsed since universal history had entered the Hellenic period. Under Macedonian rule the Greek intellect had become the leading intellectual power of the world. The great Greek-speaking towns of the East were alike the strongholds of intellectual power, the battlefields of opinions and systems, and the laboratories of scientific research, where discoveries were made and literary undertakings requiring a combination of forces were carried out. Such was Antioch on the Orontes, the meeting point of Syrian and Greek intellect; such, above all, was Alexandria. Under the lavish care of the Ptolemies the Museum, the first learned association resembling a modern academy, was formed, with free access to the greatest library of antiquity. There the critical study of language first came into fashion, and care was taken to discover the correct text of the classical authors, more especially of Homer. Antiquarian research and general education were there first established upon a wider basis. The foundation of the sciences was laid, which to this day continue to furnish our intellectual food, and upon that basis we continue to build. Scholars and students from every nation flocked to the city of splendour and delight, and all alike prostrated themselves before the genius of Greece. What Paris became in the eighteenth century, Alexandria was in those days.

During the period from the third century before Christ to the close of the second century after Christ, when the Egyptian capital was at the zenith of her renown, the fame of ancient Athens seemed well-nigh to have sunk below the horizon. But it dawned again in the time of the empire under the protection of Roman governors and patrons, and the city continued for yet five centuries to be the chief nursery of philosophy which no educated Roman left unvisited. Yet from the time of the fall of the republic and in the early times of the empire the true centre-point of the universe, not only politically but intellectually, was Rome. Here lay the heart of the great empire, the centre towards which all intellectual energy was attracted and from which again it flowed. Greek immigration was continually on the increase. The ties which bound the two nationalities together grew ever closer and stronger till the whole became gradually fused and inseparable. It was a contest, an intellectual struggle, from which the Greeks issued victorious, but in such wise that the vanquished themselves rejoiced ungrudgingly over the issue. For the gain was mutual; the Greeks could not help admiring, as Polybius did, the vigorous union of the universal empire, contrasted with the political incapacity and anarchy of their former small republics; nor could the Romans fail to acknowledge that the empire, composed of an agglomeration of different nationalities united only through conquest, was in need of a soul, a common intellectual life, to animate and complete it. For this neither was their own language suitable nor did their literature suffice, but it was a need which the culture of Greece, now universally diffused, was alone able to supply.

In Rome itself, far from resembling the Jews in national exclusiveness or in the tenacity of the ties which only drew them more strongly together in exile, the Greeks were soon to be found filling every situation in life. Active, clever, and versatile they well understood how to make themselves useful and indispensable. Greek slaves abounded in the Roman households, and if educated fetched extraordinarily high prices. Although these smooth-tongued adventurers, who, under the stress of circumstances, turned their hands to any employment, sometimes became the laughing-stock of their Roman masters, Greek influence, upon the whole, was beneficial. It was advantageous in moderating Roman hardness, in curbing Roman insolence, and in giving a higher tone to the lives of the wealthy upper classes. Intercourse with the Greeks in Rome inevitably awakened new ideas and new interests which the former people were alone capable of instilling and satisfying. An instance of this was in the science of medicine, which for five centuries had remained unknown in Rome. There nostrums and incantations were the remedies resorted to, whereas Greece had long ago possessed the school of Hippocrates. Celsus was the first Roman who, in the time of Tiberius, attempted to write a treatise upon medicine, founded, it is needless to say, entirely upon Greek models.

It was Greek influence that first roused the Romans to an interest in the primitive history of their race and the nature and history of their own language. But when Ennius, the father of Roman poetry, whose education had been entirely Greek and his style formed by making translations from the Greek, interwove the Pythagorean and Stoic doctrines about the soul of the universe and the dæmons into his great national work of the 'Annals,' thoughtful Romans felt themselves constrained to inquire into these systems, notwithstanding the slight attraction which philosophical speculation possessed for so practical and unimaginative a people. But the progressive decay of the state religion, which indeed would have set in even irrespective of any contact with philosophy, left the Romans no choice in the matter. If the system of the Stoics could give them compensation and be a moral support in life, they must familiarise themselves with the physical side of the doctrine, even though, as it often turned out, they were sceptically to thrust it aside in the end. Thus all the philosophical schools had their representatives in the city. Soon even the emperors were imbued with Greek philosophy. Hadrian himself, who, by wearing a beard, affected the outward appearance of a philosopher, sought to embody in the practice of his life the views which his contemporary Plutarch had unfolded in theory; namely, to set up the Platonic monotheism as a higher knowledge and a purifying principle by the side of the popular religions; while these were to be preserved and reconciled, their short-comings supplied, and their differences, in part at all events, adjusted, and finally to be welded into a whole.

But the rightful heiress of the truths preserved in these religious yearnings had already been born, and, however lowly and little accounted of hitherto, was already fully equipped to fulfil her destiny as a ruling power in the world.

Up to this point we have had in view only the old classical speech and literature of Greece. But in the second century before Christ a new element had arisen which shortly became of immeasurable importance, and more potent year by year to influence the course of history.

The Jews, partly through their political reverses, partly through their commercial spirit and the desire to quit their own narrow boundaries, which no longer sufficed for the numbers of the population, spread themselves over the whole Roman as well as over the Parthian Empire. They soon became settled in their new homes and readily adopted the universal language, which had by that time made its way triumphantly even as far as Bactria and the borders of the Indus. Compared with the scanty, awkward, Syro-Chaldaic dialect of Palestine, the rich refined idioms of Greece were the most perfect instruments of thought which the human mind had ever forged for itself. Out of this a Greco-Jewish literature was now formed, peculiar in itself and somewhat obscure in origin. Its head-quarters were in Alexandria, but its works were spread as widely as the language of Greece was spoken. The object of its professors was to magnify the Jewish religion, to propagate its doctrines, and to aid in implanting and promoting the continual growth of monotheism. The Alexandrian translation of the Old Testament; the writings of the Neo-Platonist Jew Philo; the books of the New Testament—these three volumes, closely related to each other, form the foundation of this Hellenistic literature. Every Jew considered it his vocation to be a light to the Gentiles and to denounce the heathen manners and customs which he abhorred. This was the origin of a peculiar species of anonymous compositions and fragmentary writings of which the authorship was falsely ascribed to the most famous Greek poets, and occasionally even to the Roman prophetesses, the sibyls. Their purport was to proclaim the unity of God, the nullity of idolatry, and approaching judgment.

Forgeries and interpolations of this kind excited no scruples of conscience in those days; men were satisfied with their own good motives, believing that the end justified the means. The Neo-Pythagoreans did the same—witness, amongst others, the Orphic poems.

The Jews of the Dispersion on their side were powerfully influenced by the religious and philosophical movements of the times; they aspired to partake in the universal citizenship, superseding national limitations, taught by the thinkers of Greece. To this end they did not hesitate to affirm the Mosaic law to be the source of all the religious and moral truth comprised in the Greek systems; Pythagoras, Plato, and other wise men had drawn inspiration for their best thoughts from the books of the Jewish religion. The fact that many proselytes were attracted to them from heathenism fortified them in the endeavour to induce the educated classes to join them by adorning and enriching the Mosaic teaching with the results of Greek speculation. They themselves were willing to acknowledge that the Greek thinkers had developed a wealth of fundamental truth in the sphere of morals, which was vainly to be looked for in their own religious books.

In the midst of this atmosphere Christianity arose. In the course of a few decades, Christian communities sprang up in all the considerable towns of the East—in Asia Minor, Greece, Egypt—and extended even to Rome. In all of them the Greek language prevailed. Their liturgies and sermons, and their own early writings, all were exclusively Greek. Even in Rome this continued to be the case until far on in the third century. Whatever compositions there saw the light were written in Greek. The first Latin composition that appeared in Rome was by the Presbyter Novatian in A.D. 250. Yet even in the commencement of the fourth century the Roman Bishop Sylvester wrote a polemical treatise against the Jews in Greek. To this day the Roman Liturgy betrays its Greek origin in some well-known formulæ.

At the end of the second century the African Tertullian first began to wrestle with the difficulties of the Latin language in the endeavour to make it a vehicle for the expression of Christian ideas. In reading his dogmatic writings the struggle is so apparent that it seems as though we beheld a rider endeavouring to discipline an unbroken steed. Tertullian's doctrine is, however, still wholly Greek in substance, and this continued to be the case in the church of the Latin tongue until the end of the fourth century. Hilary, Ambrose, even Jerome, are essentially interpreters of Greek philosophy and theology to the Latin West. With Augustine learning begins to assume a Latin form, partly original and independent—partly, I say, for even later compositions are abundantly interwoven with Greek elements and materials. Very gradually from the writings of the African fathers of the church does the specific Latin element come to occupy that dominant position in Western Christendom, which soon, partly from self-sufficient indifference, partly from ignorance, so completely severed itself from Greek influences that the old unity and harmony could never be restored.

Still, the Biblical study of the Latins is, as a whole, a mere echo and copy of Greek predecessors. Origen is the father of exegesis in the West as well as in the East. The later Biblical interpretation, which after long silence awoke again in the eighth and ninth centuries, and appears in the writings of Bede, Rhabanus, Walafrid, Strabo, and others after them, is likewise only borrowed from the works of the earlier commentators, so that in the most important department of learned inquiry the whole of the middle ages still derived intellectual nourishment from the Greeks, scanty and obscure as the source had become.

And here we stand in the presence of a fact of immense historical importance, which even in these days it is worth while to weigh and place in its proper light. The whole of modern civilisation and culture is derived from Greek sources. Intellectually we are the offspring of the union of the ancient Greek classics with Hellenised Judaism. Greeks and Israelites: a sharper contrast, greater mutual repulsion, could (it appears at first sight) be scarcely imagined. Yet similarities of feature were not wanting. Both pretended, so to speak, to dominion over the world. Aristotle had impressed upon his pupil Alexander that the Greeks were called to rule over all the nations of the earth. The hope of a Messiah led the Jews to expect that the man would soon appear who would lead Israel to victory over the Romans and to supremacy over the pagan world. In Christianity these pretensions were to find their correction and the realisation that was to reconcile them. The two nations had yet another point in common in that the whole national character of each was penetrated with religious ideas and intimately bound up with religious interests. In the case of the Jews this is evident; that it was also true with regard to the Greeks will be allowed if the great national importance of the mysteries as institutions be taken into account, and if we consider the fact that the conflict and controversy between philosophy and popular religion, resulting in the progressive dissolution of idolatry, and of faith in the false gods and in the worship devoted to them, forms the staple of Grecian history since the time of Alexander.

Let us now turn to the period of religious fusion and of fluctuating contest betwixt pagan and Christian Hellenism in order to gain a clear appreciation of the nature of the Greek influences which affected the Western world.

It is well to observe that conversion to Christianity was brought about by free choice only in the smallest degree, chiefly by compulsion and by the assistance of those means of intimidation and favour with which despotic rulers are able to enforce the triumph of a religious faith. The proportion of Christians to the population at the accession of Constantine amounted according to the most probable calculations to a twelfth in the East and a fifteenth in the West. The coercive and penal statutes of the Christian emperors succeeded one another with ever-increasing severity during two centuries. That a mass of heathen conceptions and customs came thus to be imported into the Christian church was a natural consequence of such legislation. Although the divinities, many of whom were mere abstractions and personified ideas, might be eliminated or placed in the category of evil spirits, men's minds only clung the closer to the belief in the magic effect of words, forms, and ceremonies.

In the year 161 Marcus Aurelius, who may be characterised as an embodiment of the Greek philosophy and the best of all the emperors, ascended the imperial throne. In the whole texture and bent of his mind Marcus Aurelius was far more of a Greek than a Roman, of a philosopher than a ruler. In his campaigns he was surrounded by a train of philosophers; in the camp he composed his 'Meditations,' one of the most remarkable books in the Greek language, the mature fruit of a mind strengthened and ennobled by severe self-discipline. These were the latter days of Greek literature, brilliant indeed, but brief, for afterwards, under the soldier emperors and amid civil war and repeated strokes of ill-fortune, neither state nor individual could recognise any other interest but that of self-preservation. Greek ascendency, which could only have been maintained under conditions of peace and personal security guaranteed by settled government, disappeared. The beautiful richness of the language became a superfluous, even burdensome, luxury; whilst Latin, adapted to the present time of want, poverty, and distress, again took the lead. By the beginning of the fifth century the Bishop of Rome could find no one in the whole city who was capable of producing a Greek composition.

Within the space of fifty years Rome was thrice plundered and laid waste. Of the twenty-nine libraries still in existence at the beginning of the fourth century, not a single one remained in A.D. 450. Subsequently when inquiry was made for Greek works in Rome it was almost always affirmed that none existed. Thus, therefore, the bridge of communication was broken down over which Greek literature had hitherto found its way to the West and North-west. Things remained so for fully a thousand years. Even the temporary supremacy of the Greek emperors, Justinian and his successors, brought no change in this respect. It was thought in Rome that knowledge of Greek might well be altogether dispensed with. It would probably any time have been easy to find an educated Greek at hand to act as secretary. Here and there such a case may actually have occurred. Yet it seems to have been looked upon in Rome as a point of honour to write only in Latin, for the great collection of papal writings from the fifth down to the fifteenth century is exclusively Latin.

And here it may also be observed that, in the metropolis of the Christian world, not only Greek but all scientific culture and enterprise had died out, and was not resuscitated before A.D. 1500. Not a single school of learning nor public library existed. 'We have a library,' wrote Martin I. in the year 649 to Bishop Amandus, 'but no manuscripts.' In 787 there were still a few isolated grammarians and arithmeticians in Rome, some of whom Charles the Great took with him to France, and classical study in Italy had been pared down to the meagre idea of grammar. But complete barbarism soon regained the upper hand, and in education Roman society stood far below France or Germany. We do indeed towards the end of the ninth century meet with a Roman librarian, Anastasius, who had learned Greek in Byzantium, and his translations gained importance in the church, although, as was to be expected, in the height of the period of hierarchical forgeries, they were designedly untrue. Again, at the end of the tenth century, the most learned man of his time appeared in Rome, Gerbert, or—as pope—Sylvester II., but his learning had been acquired in France and North Italy; he himself declared that there was no one in Rome of literary acquirements (*qui literas didicerit*), so that one may say he stood alone in Rome. Fifty years later we learn from the mouth of a devoted partisan of the papacy, Bishop Bonizo, that among the Roman clerical body there could not be found one man who was not either ignorant, or a simonist, or *concubinarius*. The blame was thrown upon the poverty which prevented the clergy from visiting foreign schools. Poverty soon afterwards disappeared once for all, but with easy circumstances, which speedily grew into riches, no schools appeared. For 900 years not a single literary work of any importance was composed in Rome.

During the stormy period of barbarian immigration in the fifth century, Greek erudition had likewise entirely died out of the towns of Southern Gaul, such as Marseilles, Arles, and Lyons. Intellectual culture seems gradually and entirely to have withered away in the course of the three centuries which cover the transition from the old age of the Roman Empire to the early youth of the Germano-Roman countries and states, or down to the year 750. In the Frankish Empire Latin had ceased to be the speech of the people, and had to be learnt as a dead language. That in spite of this it maintained its ascendency, and that whilst the new mixed languages were yet in process of formation books could still be written, was entirely due to the church, which had taken the Latin language under its care and protection as the idiom of divine worship and clerical usage. Of Greek there could of course be no longer, or not as yet, any question.

Here we encounter another fact which, however easily accounted for, is none the less astonishing. After the time of Jerome,—*i.e.* from the year 420—the Western Latin-speaking world entirely laid aside the use and study of the New Testament in the original. For 800 years, that is to say until Roger Bacon (1260), no one felt the necessity of having recourse to comparison with the original text, which, in the opinion of the present day, is the indispensable means of clearing up the obscurities of the Latin version. Not a single Greek copy of the New Testament could then be seen in a monastic or cathedral library. The same might be said to be the case at the present day in Roman Catholic countries, but we all know the reason of *this* phenomenon, whereas in the middle ages, as the heaps of commentaries show, a fervent zeal for Biblical study prevailed.

I will show by one or two examples how replete with consequences, both positive and negative, was the long estrangement between Greece and the West.

Ever since the seventh or eighth century a dogmatic passage, probably first introduced in Italy, has been interpolated in the Latin text of the first Epistle of John (v. 7). It is entirely unknown to the Greek Church, and is not to be found in any Greek MS. nor indeed in the older MSS. of the Latin version. Since the beginning of Biblical criticism the spuriousness of the passage has been generally recognised; yet for hundreds of years the interpolation has disfigured the text of the Latin version of the Bible, and the Western Church cannot avoid the reproach that whilst the Eastern Church has preserved its Bible intact, carelessness and ignorance on the part of the Westerns have allowed such an interpolation to stand in the text.

Another example of this kind is afforded by the ecclesiastical prohibition against taking interest for money. Misled by the erroneous translation of the passage in Luke vi. 35—*nihil inde sperantes*, instead of *nihil desperantes*—the Western Church imagined these words to convey a prohibition of usury by Christ; the heads of the church, and foremost amongst them Clement V. and the Council of Vienne in 1311, made it out to be a divinely revealed dogma. Inconceivable perplexity and disturbance of social as well as mercantile intercourse arose in consequence; the laity, especially the merchant class, found itself under a yoke so terrible and oppressive that nothing like it is known in all antiquity.

Few names can be cited as upholders of what in those days passed for learning—Gregory of Tours in France, Isidore in Spain, Aldhelm and Bede in England, Boniface in Germany. Of these Isidore and Bede enjoyed the highest reputation, and their writings were the most sought after. Still they were mere compilers destitute of original thought, transcribers, or abridgers. Meanwhile, it was for this very reason that they were so popular. Italy could boast of no other than Pope Gregory I. who made a principle of rejecting all other than Biblical and patristic knowlege. None of the above-mentioned writers (with the exception of Bede) understood Greek. Only in England had Theodore of Tarsus, whom Pope Vitalian made Archbishop of Canterbury (660-669), diffused some knowledge of his native language; but it was a light which was very shortly extinguished.

With Charles the Great came a revival of all that in that age was considered worth knowing. The two most learned men of his court—Paulus Diaconus and the marvellous Alcuin, a phenomenon in his time for acumen and refined culture—knew Greek, and made use of it in the Byzantine iconoclast controversy. Charles's theologians were apparently superior to the Greek theologians of the time, who could only take refuge in fictitious testimony and perversions of the Biblical text. The supposition, however, that a Greek school existed at Osnabrück rests upon spurious records. Soon after the death of Charles the dismemberment of the Carolingian monarchy began amidst bloody wars and fratricidal contests. Nations were divided, new kingdoms arose, and in the confusion and bewilderment of the time the greater part of the schools, and the cultivation of learning introduced and fostered by Charles, died out. Not until the twelfth century did a fresh impulse spring up, more vigorous, comprehensive, and durable than that which education had received from Charles the Great.

The most trustworthy informant as to the condition of learning during those stirring and restless times is the Englishman John of Salisbury, who died in 1180. He was the best of Abelard's pupils, and outstripped all his contemporaries in encyclopædic learning and knowledge of the Roman classics. The school of Paris, which gradually was to become the queen and mother of the European universities, was then in its first modest beginnings. The school of Chartres meanwhile was flourishing under the leadership of the famous Bernard of Chartres. There the ancient authors were commented on and imitated. The 'Timæus' of Plato was known and studied through the incomplete translation of Chalcidius: this was, perhaps, the most influential of all Greek writings during the whole of the middle ages; all other writings of Plato remained entirely unknown. Besides the 'Timæus,' the philosophic writings of Apuleius were used as a favourite source of knowledge of Platonism. Aristotle was only known through his works on logic. John of Salisbury was acquainted neither with the 'Metaphysics' nor the 'Ethics.' He and the other theologians of the time must have gleaned all they knew of Greek philosophy, in the first place from Cicero, and in the next from Macrobius and Seneca. They adorned their writings with a few Greek phrases, but it is evident that none of them, not even Abelard, had read the whole of any Greek work.

It was not entirely obtuseness of intellect and mental inertness which led the world of the middle ages to forego any attempt at gaining an insight into Greek philosophy. It was, at the same time, fear. Some knowledge of the Greek systems could be obtained through Cicero and Augustine, and it was also known from Jerome that the influence of that most dangerous heretic, Origen, had contaminated the whole literature of the Greek Church. The Western mind, conscious of its own weakness and insufficiency, quailed before the dangerous task of recognising and sifting the good and the true from the mass of false doctrine, real or imaginary. What could the sword of Scanderbeg effect without the arm of Scanderbeg? Even the works of pagan Rome were not to be meddled with except with the greatest caution and with ever-increasing suspicion. The Romans themselves had already adopted, with few exceptions, the prescription of Ennius, only to sip from the fountains of philosophy, never to plunge into them.

The highest authorities, Jerome, Augustine, Gregory the Great, and most of the monastic fathers, had expressed themselves in terms of warning against immoderate indulgence in such doubtful intellectual sustenance. Even Alcuin forbade to his monks the study of Virgil, although he had formerly enjoyed it himself. Frightful examples served as warnings. In Italy some learned linguists of the tenth century—the most esteemed of them was Bilgard—had given to the Roman classics the preference before the Bible. They were all executed.

In the whole course of the middle ages only one man recognised clearly the great value and need of an acquaintance with Greek literature even for the church, and advocated earnestly the filling up of this enormous deficiency in the intellectual knowledge of the time. This man was Roger Bacon, who lived in the middle of the thirteenth century. He deserves to be called the most original, independent, far-sighted intellect of his age. But he was a preacher in the wilderness. His own order showed itself hostile to him; he had to suffer imprisonment and other torments. It is from him that we learn the effect produced upon Western literature by the Crusades. Greek MSS. were nowhere to be found in the West. They had formerly been easily obtainable in Constantinople, but between the Greeks and the Latins hatred and repulsion had now risen to their greatest height. The taking and sack of the Greek capital, the erection of a Latin empire, and the despotic ill-treatment and oppression of the population left no possibility of reconciliation or of a renewal of peaceful intercourse.

Bacon, who also looked upon the Greeks as schismatics, and as consequently enemies to the faith, likewise declared that the difficulty of obtaining MSS. from them was increased by their suspicion that they would be falsified in translation. He himself laments the wanton manner in which translations were made without adequate knowledge of the language; they were altogether faulty and misleading. Through the whole of Christendom there were not five men who had thoroughly mastered the Greek, Hebrew, or Latin grammars, although some few could speak either Greek or Arabic. Translation was consequently accounted so difficult that most of those who applied themselves to it were reputed to deal in magic, all the more so that among the number were Jews and Saracens. General curiosity was turned towards Aristotle, for although some of the writings of the Stagirite were known through their Arabic translations, it was clear that these were very imperfect; and costly treasures, it was thought, lay hidden in the yet unknown writings. Attention, at the same time, was drawn towards the pseudo-sciences of the time, which were likewise amongst the questionable gifts which the Oriental Greeks had lavished upon the West—alchemy, or the transmutation of metals, astrology, the casting of horoscopes, and magic in every conceivable form.

What the short-sighted apathy of the Western intellect could conceive no use for the East appropriated with a youthful ardour for research. The Arabs, who hitherto had remained entirely shut out from the civilised world, roused by the inspiration of their new religion, had now made themselves masters of all the Greek centres of civilisation. They had conquered the Byzantine Monarchy, the guardian of Greek culture; the Oriental Greeks had submitted to their yoke. Like the Romans they had become the pupils of the conquered, yet in quite a different and more restricted sense. Poetical, historical, rhetorical literature they left quite untouched; their interest was centred in philosophy and the natural sciences, astronomy and mathematics, and, above all, in the art of medicine. Just as in the Christian world philosophy and theology, so in the Mohammedan world philosophy and medicine, were inseparable. The Arabian philosopher invariably studied medicine; the physician was a philosopher. The movement began from above; the impulse to it was given by the Khaliph Al Mamum (813–833 A.D.) of the house of the Abassides, who, dissatisfied with narrow Moslem orthodoxy, turned his attention, like the Emperor Hadrian, to the investigation of foreign religions and systems, and, in pursuance of his end, caused Greek MSS. to be searched for throughout the East, and translations to be made either by Syrian Christians or by Arabs. The teaching of the Stagirite and the immense extent of his knowledge filled even the Mohammedans with admiration, and an Aristotelian school flourished for nearly three centuries in the dominions of the Kaliph.

Under the dynasty of the Ommiades, Græco-Arabian science and literature were carried from the East into

Moslem Spain, where, from the ninth century onwards, institutions for instruction and learning reached a period of prosperity such as only long afterwards, and then but partially, was to be seen in Western Christendom. Latin Christendom, when seeking to become acquainted with Greek works, had first to sit at the feet of Spanish Mohammedan teachers; then to translate those works from Arabic into Latin, and finally to listen to instruction on Aristotle from the mouths of his Greek commentators. The Greek classical works on the art of medicine, especially Hippocrates, took the same circuitous route to reach the Romano-Germanic peoples in an intelligible form, before they could be studied in the schools of Salerno and Montpellier.

Guizot has observed that during the whole of the middle ages the legends of the martyrs, whether in prose or verse, furnished the literature most welcome and most in request, not only amongst the clergy but amongst the laity. The text of by far the greater number of these legends was derived from the Greek.

Now it can hardly surprise us that such legends should have afforded such welcome and attractive subjects for perusal, and should have been so diligently collected, and versified and adorned by the poets. They were needed in an age of violence, when liberty and life were insecure, and when existence was so full of fear and anxiety. The martyrs, witnessing with heroic constancy and steadfast faith to the truth, served as patterns of encouragement, and also as intercessors. In addition to this came the longing after types of female heroism. Classical antiquity only knew one poetical figure of magnanimous self-sacrifice in woman—Antigone; Christian legends celebrated the unconquerable devotion and fortitude of multitudes of women and virgins. The preference of a credulous age for miraculous stories, and the tendency of the uneducated to delight in descriptions of cruel martyrdoms, must also be taken into account.

The attraction of legend-lore was heightened by contrast with the courtly and knightly poesy of the time imitated by both Germans and Italians from the French; the poesy of chivalric woman-worship, of the struggle with the infidels, with heathens and Mohammedans, abounding in endless descriptions of the pursuit of aimless adventures and the insatiable love of fighting for fighting's sake. We can understand that the religiously minded amongst the poets and readers of the triumphant stories of the martyrs, should give the preference to these simple, plain narratives of touching deeds and sufferings.

It was a Byzantine statesman, Simeon Metaphrastes in Constantinople, who first put together a great collection of somewhat fanciful stories of martyrs and saints; a selection of these were translated into Latin, probably by the monks of Southern Italy. One might almost affirm it to be the richest collection of fables in the world. Much of it is pure invention, whilst in some of the biographies a grain of truth lies hidden beneath a mass of extravagant fiction and hyperbolical phrases. Simeon's collection was surpassed in the thirteenth century by an Italian, Jacobus de Voragine, in his 'Golden Legend;' his biographies are nearly all of them insipid and ridiculous tales. Nevertheless, or perhaps upon that very account, the 'Golden Legend' became one of the most popular of books, and furnished material for innumerable discourses from the pulpit. It is obvious that this could only happen in an age when the mass of the clergy and the laity moved in a thick atmosphere of illusion and deceit; lacking entirely the faculty of distinguishing the historically possible and conceivable from simple impossibilities.

It was inevitable that these legends should become interwoven with the historical works of the time, irretrievably confusing them, and entailing the introduction of a multitude of other fables. The German imperial chronicle was principally drawn from legends. To what a pitch of bewilderment historians were brought through the mingling and interchange of fiction and well-founded fact, may be fully seen in the writings of Godfrey of Viterbo, Helinand, Gervase of Tilbury, Vincent of Beauvais, and others. As a coping-stone to this crushing edifice of falsehood and fable, there arose in the course of the ninth century a series of fictions and forgeries even more confusing and misleading than the ancient fables of Greece, affecting the religious and politico-religious province of life, and the spuriousness of which was recognised by no one.

The belief in demons, systematised by the Neo-Platonists, combined with pagan conceptions of possession and the power of exorcism, as well as the delusion that the souls of the dead took possession of the living—all of this, when transferred to the popular consciousness amongst Christians, was tolerated or encouraged by the Greek fathers of the church, and had, amongst others, this effect, that all mental diseases were looked upon and treated as cases of possession. The teaching of Origen, that madness was only a form of demoniacal possession to which human nature was subject, was readily accepted in the West, with the consequence that for more than a thousand years the majority of mental disorders were regarded as demoniacal possession, and the supposed energumens treated, or rather maltreated, according to the practice laid down by the church. This is a dark page in the annals of Europe.

This state of things involved a retrogressive step for which a parallel can scarcely be found. For even 400 years before Christ, Hippocrates, and later Galens, and in Rome Cælius Aurelianus, had already recognised that mental diseases were identical with diseases of the brain.

Yet another fatal gift of Greek delusion must here be mentioned. This was the invention of legends, such as those of Cyprian and Justina, or of Anthemius and Theophilus, in which heathen demonology appeared in a Christian garb. The tale of Anthemius and Theophilus is the first instance of an imaginary picture so dark, so profoundly unchristian, and so fraught with the direst mischief, that one feels almost tempted to characterise as suicidal the avidity with which it was forthwith seized upon and systematically enlarged by the West. Moved by the desire to regain a lost office, Theophilus enters into a contract with Satan, whom he has summoned to his aid, and signs a document in which he denies Christ and the Virgin. No sooner has he regained his office, than he does penance, invokes the Virgin, and prays that the contract may be laid upon his breast during sleep. Thereupon it is publicly burnt, but he himself soon afterwards dies a pardoned sinner. This legend, translated into every language, has been related in every form which prose narrative or epic poem or drama could admit of; hardly any other has been so popular. I can in no way account for the hold it took upon the public mind. It shows, however, in what manner the idea, entirely unknown to the early Christians, of a compact with Satan arrived at such predominance, and what deep root the belief in witchcraft, formally adopted by the church, and solemnly erected by her authority into a dogma, could take.

Let us turn to a more wholesome style of literature. One of the legends for which the West is indebted to the Greeks, and which achieved the greatest popularity, finding its way, both in prose and verse, into all languages, was the religious romance of Balaam and Jehosaphat. It was supposed to have been composed by John of Damascus, the most famous theologian of his time. It exhibits a fusion of Buddhism with Christianity, Buddha himself being properly the hero of the romance. Of this, however, nobody in the West could at that time have had any suspicion.

One favourite romance of the middle ages, derived from a Greek source, that of Apollonius of Tyre, assumed many forms both in prose and verse. Æsop's fables had a share in the origin of the satirical stories about animals, a bold clever style of fiction to which there is nothing to be compared either in Greek or Roman literature. Since there was no direct knowledge of Homer in the middle ages, the source from which the numerous poetic narratives of the Trojan myth were drawn by such writers as Henry of Veldeke, and Herbort of Fritzlar in Germany, and Benoit de Saint More in France, was the Latin version of which the original was attributed to the fictitious Greek authors Diktys and Dares. In these narratives the Greek heroes are transformed into knights errant, love adventures are made the centre of interest, and Homer, whose most beautiful scenes are naturally ignored, is condemned for representing the gods as carrying on war with mankind—probably a reminiscence of a Latin quotation from Plato. In the middle ages there was no such thing as a Latin translation of Homer. The effect of the void which ignorance of the greatest of ancient poets caused in the education and culture of those times, is very perceptible through the whole course of Western literature and culture. It certainly mainly accounts for the fact that the best efforts of the most aspiring spirits fail to rise above mediocrity, or sink after a momentary rise. Virgil, though generally and diligently studied, and almost idolised, could be no substitute for Homer, even though the 'Odyssey' might be the foundation of the first half of the 'Æneid,' and the 'Iliad' of the second. Virgil, however, has worked up together Greek and Latin material, mixing and confusing different periods and stages of civilisation, and moreover has admitted utterly alien religious matter out of the philosophy and the mysteries of his own time. He has no doubt imitated the phraseology of Homer; but of the Homeric spirit there is absolutely nothing in the 'Æneid.

To the poets of the middle ages, Alexander of Macedon was a more attractive theme than the tale of Troy. No more appropriate material in fact for the poetic fancy could be found than this hero of Asiatic and African conquest. The Greek romance attributed to Callisthenes, composed at the end of the fourth century and forthwith translated into Latin, a tissue of the most marvellous adventures and extraordinary wonders, served as the source from which to draw. The French poet De Berney represents the king and his Macedonian generals as modern knights, sallying forth to tournaments and falcon hunts. The fancy of the German Lamprecht is less extravagant; but altogether these poets are hardly to be surpassed in fabulous absurdities.

I hasten to a conclusion. Within the period extending over more than a thousand years, over which we have taken a rapid flight, we have passed over many a dreary tract of gloom and confusion. Involuntarily we ask if such a state of things could be necessary. Could it be necessary that mankind should follow such circuitous and misleading paths, amid so much sorrow and misdoing, in order to arrive at the measure of civilisation which we now enjoy? Why should an advance in knowledge, which is now accomplished in a decade, have formerly cost a century?

I might reply with Dante—

> What then,
> And who art thou, that on the stool would'st sit
> To judge at distance of a thousand miles,
> With the short-sighted vision of a span?
>
> (*Parad.* xix. 79.)

Still I emphatically assert that the benefit which mankind has derived from Greek influences, the earlier as well as the later, far outweighs the mischief they caused.

It is a general law of universal history, to which every age and every people however highly gifted must submit, that all intellectual and moral progress must be purchased by heavy sacrifices; that no truth can be wrestled for and secured without the throes of martyrdom. The story of Galileo repeats itself again and again in various forms. I also think that in the future the results brought about by the study of the great examples and teachers of antiquity will prove still more beneficial than they have been in the past.

When we glance back to the condition of delusion and bondage in which nations were formerly held, we rejoice to welcome and contrast with it our own enjoyment of intellectual freedom. And wherein does this freedom consist? Surely, as Goethe says, in being able to do at all times and in every place whatever reason dictates as the best to be done. Our Academy is a conservative body. Amongst its responsibilities is that of ensuring the preservation whilst preventing the abuse of so high a privilege.

VIII

THE ORIGIN OF THE EASTERN QUESTION[1]

AMONGST the great problems of our age, none is more fitted to occupy the thoughts, not only of the professional statesman but of every keen-sighted individual who takes an interest in politics, than the so-called Eastern Question. It is the pivot upon which the general politics of the century now drawing to a close are turning—and it will be so for the coming century also. More than any other it will furnish the standard by which later generations will measure the tact and ability of the statesmen to whose guidance the world's history is now committed.

It is not a question which has disturbed the peace of Europe only yesterday; it is not even a production of this century. It has exercised a powerful influence upon the course of the world's history for above 500 years. Proteus-like it has assumed various shapes, experienced and engendered many changes. Men in Europe have often behaved as though it had been settled or had ceased to exist; it has been underrated, or grossly misunderstood, or people have wilfully shut their eyes to its magnitude and closed their hearts and ears to its warnings; but the consequences have invariably been serious—the fate of Europe is bound up with the Eastern Question.

It is well worth while to go back in history and to

[1] Address delivered at the festive meeting of the Academy of Munich, July 25, 1879. This address, besides being printed in the *Allgemeine Zeitung*, appeared as a separate pamphlet amongst the publications of the *Alma Mater*, Vienna, 1879.

consider the beginning—the first stage of the Eastern Question; and to try to explain how it came to pass that at that time, seven centuries ago, under exceptionally favourable circumstances, the object upon which the desire of the whole of Christian Europe was set, failed to be attained; and now, in spite of immense sacrifices willingly offered, a heritage pregnant with mischief was left to the generations that were to follow.

I have singled out the period of the Crusades—the two centuries from the beginning of the eleventh to the end of the thirteenth century—as the first stage of the Eastern Question.

It was in the latter half of the eleventh century that this question first presented itself as a problem demanding immediate solution at the hands of the Western world. The Asiatic countries bordering on the Mediterranean, the Anatolian peninsula, and Syria, are geographically, historically, and commercially nearer to Europe and more intimately connected with that continent than with the interior of Asia. Syria, which had fallen under Moslem rule as early as the seventh century, still possessed a very numerous Christian population. Along the coast indeed the Christians formed the majority. In Asia Minor the Byzantines and the Seljuk Turks were still fighting for the mastery. After the fall of the Kaliphate of Damascus, the situation of the Christians in Syria and Jerusalem had become worse; they were exposed to the oppression and rapacity of the wild Turkish hordes, and had to bear the brunt of the war which had burst out between the Egyptians and Seljuks. The ever-increasing bands of pilgrims were frequently ill-treated and despoiled. Their appeals for help had repeatedly reached the West, and to many it appeared both shameful and intolerable that the church, which at that very moment was rising to the height of worldly power, should remain in helpless servitude in the very place of her birth. The popes bethought themselves of sending assistance. They saw that no greater increase of dignity and power could accrue to the Roman chair, than if Syria and the universal mother church of Jerusalem were brought under its sway.

The letter which in 986 Gerbert wrote in the name of the Church of Jerusalem only appealed for assistance in money. A more serious, bolder appeal was made by Pope Sergius IV. in 1010, when news was received of the destruction of the Church of the Holy Sepulchre by Kaliph Hakem. Issuing an order for a general peace, Sergius proclaimed that a great fleet was to be got ready by Genoa, Venice, and the rest of Italy, to convey the army, of which he himself would take command, to Syria for the purpose of recovering the grave of Christ. But of any result of this proclamation, to which was not yet appended any offer of absolution or indulgence, there is no record. A proclamation by Gregory VII. remained equally ineffectual; he also was ready to place himself at the head of an army destined for the East, not however with a view to the conquest of Syria or Palestine although the rescue of the Holy Sepulchre entered incidentally into his design, but with the object of freeing Asia Minor from the yoke of the Seljukian Turks, securing the safety of Constantinople, and—most important of all—reducing the Byzantine Church to entire submission to the papacy; of attaining, in fact, the purpose for which Innocent III. caused the Crusade of 1204 to be proclaimed.

True it is that the first Crusade, with its brilliant results, was an undertaking mainly due to French enterprise; as, therefore, it has been asserted, frequently in former times, and quite recently again in Paris, that the fame and honours of the Crusade must be assigned to the French nation, the contention must on the whole be allowed; but obviously on condition that that nation should also share with the authors of the movement the blame for the endless disasters of the expedition. It was a French pope, Urban II., who issued the summons for it; a French synod, that of Clermont in Auvergne, which gave the final assent to it.

From France first proceeded the cry, which then and later became the general watchword : 'Dieu le veult.' The chivalry of France, impatient of idleness, eagerly grasping at an occasion which promised gain and glory both here and hereafter, flocked to join the ranks, and formed the nucleus and main strength of the army. They were joined by the Normans from Lower Italy, and even Lorraine, Burgundy, and the Rhineland were carried away by the movement. Germany, however, wasted by thirty years of civil war, and the purely Slavonic countries, as well as England and Scandinavia, held aloof from the enterprise, although a certain number of English, Danish, and Norwegian knights took part in it. In the firm belief that as the chosen instruments of God they were under His guidance for the accomplishment of His will, amid constant signs, visions, and miracles, hundreds of thousands flocked to join the Crusade. Most of the pilgrims perished, and but a small remnant ever found its way home. Nevertheless Jerusalem was taken, the Holy Places passed once more into Christian hands, and a Christian kingdom, with a German prince as the first king, was established. Four principalities in nominal dependence upon it, Antioch, Tripoli, Edessa, and Tiberias, were formed at the same time. The foundation of the kingdom was rendered possible only by the discord which prevailed amongst the Moslem princes ; it wanted the towns and fortresses which might have given it solidity, for they had either remained in the possession of the enemy or speedily fell again into his hands. Incapable of standing by its own strength, surrounded by powerful Moslem princes and warlike peoples, it could only be maintained by the continual reinforcement of fresh Crusaders.

Yet the brilliant expectations of the West, justified by the first victorious results of the expedition, seemed about to be realised ; fresh victories were gained over the terrified Moslems, whose strength was continually wasted by internal dissensions, and soon the whole of Syria, from El-

Arisch upon the Egyptian frontier as far as Mesopotamia, had submitted to Christian rule.

But reaction speedily set in. Not later than 1101 three pilgrim armies, French, German, and Italian respectively, in all 300,000 men, which Pope Paschal had assembled through the heralds whom he had sent to preach the Crusade, perished in Asia Minor.

The warning of these catastrophes remained unheeded, and when forty-five years later (1146) the news of the loss of Edessa called forth the third Crusade, the pilgrim armies followed the same route to destruction. The summons had again been issued and the preachers sent forth by the head of the church. Bernard, the most noted and popular saint of the age, at the command of Eugenius III., and by the promise of unfailing success, kindled an enthusiasm amongst both princes and peoples, far exceeding that which had first been roused under Urban II. Not only France, but all Germany with Conrad III. at its head, was drawn into the movement; but of the two powerful armies which set forth, only a feeble remnant returned from an expedition entirely destitute of success. It was calculated that Germany alone suffered the loss of over a million of her sons. When the news of Saladin's victory, the defeat of the Christians at Hattin, and consequent loss of Jerusalem, together with the greater part of Palestine and Syria, reached the West, all again flew to arms, and her three most powerful princes, Frederick of Germany, Philip Augustus of France, and Richard of England, set out for the Holy Land. But the death of the emperor, followed shortly by that of his son Frederick, maimed and scattered the German forces, which had already been sadly reduced in numbers during their passage through Asia Minor. Philip Augustus, after a short sojourn at Acre, returned to France, and Richard, in spite of the victory which he gained, was unable to subdue Jerusalem. Acre alone remained as a fortress and basis of operations for the Christians in the East; but it was a hotbed of pestilence, and continued for a hundred years to be the grave of innumerable pilgrims.

During the years that followed, fresh summonses were issued and fresh armies set in motion, but these were isolated efforts and without result; the largest expedition, upon which the most brilliant hopes were centred, the Crusade of 1203, was destined, not for Syria, but for Constantinople, there to lay the foundation of a Latin empire. The distress of the Syrian Christians was thereby aggravated, and the final destruction of both the Byzantine and Syrian Kingdoms rendered inevitable.

A bold naval expedition to Egypt in 1217, under the command of the papal legate Pelagius, began promisingly by the subjection of Damietta, hitherto considered impregnable and regarded as the key of Egypt. Nevertheless dissension and incapacity again led the war to a miserable and shameful termination.

At length, twenty-one years later, the moment of rescue seemed to have arrived, when the Christians might enter into peaceable possession of the much-coveted city. By means of negotiation and treaty, and without a stroke of the sword, the Emperor Frederick II. obtained from the Sultan Kameel the cession of Jerusalem, Nazareth, and other towns, with the intermediate country, as well as a ten years' truce—objects for which monarchs at the head of powerful armies had for fifty years vainly striven. But Gregory IX., who had previously excommunicated Frederick for dilatoriness in joining the Crusade, pursued the emperor, now become King of Jerusalem, with his anathema; an interdict was laid upon the holy places; a papal army marched into Frederick's hereditary dominions, and in Palestine all that lay in the pope's power was done to frustrate the carrying out of the treaty.

> Was mag ein König schaffen,
> Seit Christen, Heiden und Pfaffen,
> Streiten genug gegen ihn.
> Da verdürbe Salomon's Sinn—

sang Freidank, an eye-witness, in those days.

From that time forward Frederick, during his long contest with the pope and the Guelphs, could do but little to sustain the monarchy in the Holy Land, which rapidly sank to a mere empty title. Jerusalem, retaken and plundered by the Moslems, was again reduced to a heap of ruins. Louis IX., the most famous prince of his time, and the favourite of the church, invaded Syria in 1251, with a miserably weak force, after his reverse and imprisonment in Egypt; but he also was left entirely without support, and was unable, within the three years that he remained there, to accomplish anything of permanent importance.

After his time the history of the Holy Land becomes a mere series of reverses and losses; one town or fortress after another fell into the hands of the Moslems, and in 1291 the Frankish rule in Syria came to a fearful and bloody termination with the storming of Acre.

It has been calculated that during the two centuries of the Crusades, European Christendom suffered a loss of somewhere about six millions of men.

Thirty years before, the Latin empire in Constantinople, that darling offspring of the labour and travail of the papacy, had perished, and the last emperor, Baldwin, had become a wanderer throughout the countries of Western Europe, vainly soliciting help amongst them. To people in those days it seemed as if a special curse lay upon the undertakings of the popes. The events which took place between the years 1261 and 1291 could hardly create another impression.

A result so pitiful, so replete with evil consequences, such a complete frustration of the aims and expectations of the whole of Christendom, forces upon us the question: How did this happen? Who was to blame? How was the undertaking conducted? What manner of men were the pilgrims and colonists who composed the main body of the expedition?

The method which the popes employed to set the

Crusades in motion proved not only at first, but for hundreds of years, to be singularly effectual. The history of the world, we may say, has only one other phenomenon of a similar kind to show us. One of the greatest and most radical changes in the life and views of the Christian world was ushered in by it. For a long time previously, through the clerical invention of indulgences, the primitive institution of penance had been widely diverted from its original object. What formerly had been intended as a religious and moral gymnastic for strengthening the will and weakening the dominion of the senses, had since the ninth century degenerated into a traffic in sins, and served to enrich the church with money and lands. Subsequently Gregory VII. had taken upon himself to grant a general remission of sins to the adherents of the rival king Rudolf. But it was not thought prudent to continue in this course. Urban II., however, promised remission of all penances, as well as certain salvation, to all who would join the Crusade, allowing sins to be expiated by confession and absolution. In this way the ancient institution of penance received its deathblow, not all at once, but in the natural course of things. That which, when the Crusades ceased, was substituted for it, was of such a nature that, from an ecclesiastical standpoint, the year 1096 must be described as an ill-omened epoch, and the action of Pope Urban as an irreparable blow dealt against religion. At a later period, dogma was made to accommodate itself to predominating custom.

Men like Bernard and Innocent III. understood the summons to the Crusade as an exhortation to conversion and amendment of life. Often was the saying repeated that whoever went forth as a champion to fight for the faith must lead a life worthy of so high a calling. In occasional instances the endeavour was really made, but as a general rule the undisciplined crowds, which had flocked together from all quarters, gave themselves up to all kinds of excesses, and frequently brought ruin upon themselves in consequence. Powerful, indeed, was the attraction of these holy wars, which in the imagination of the time sanctified every participation in them, even the most humble. The cross, the badge of the crusader, was a talisman for his protection; so long as he carried it, even when the vow remained for years unfulfilled, he was exempt from the jurisdiction of secular tribunals; no creditor could force him to pay his debts, or even demand interest from him.

In the disordered condition of Germany, Italy, and France, each country was overrun by swarms of criminals, murderers, vagabonds, adventurers and banditti, outlaws and fugitives from justice. To all of these an asylum was now open in which they could not only find personal security and immunity from punishment, but upon their return home, honour and renown. Bernard had proclaimed that the very malefactors, the outcasts of society, were chosen by God to take part in His holy war, and the new and joyful message was repeated by every succeeding preacher of the Crusades. Otto of Freising saw in the hordes of robbers who hastened to take the cross an evident miracle of God's grace. Jacob de Vitry observes that, notwithstanding that in the Christian armies which left Acre for Egypt there were many thieves and robbers, God gave them victory. Defeat followed quickly upon the steps of victory, and we presently find him remarking that the vengeance of God had smitten the Christians on account of their crimes and robberies. Menco does not hesitate to say that in the Netherlands many murderers had obtained pardon by taking the cross, and contemporaries were compelled to acknowledge that not much improvement was to be traced in the warriors who returned.

Out of this rabble of criminals numbers settled from time to time upon the newly acquired territory in Syria, and from such seed there sprang the degraded mongrel race of the Pullani, which, uniting in itself the vices of both East and West, became the curse of the land and the ruin of the Christian cause. This alone was sufficient to hinder any growth or prosperity in the Christian kingdom upon the Jordan.

To all this must be added the faults inherent in the constitution of the Christian principalities. These principalities were examples of the purely feudal state transplanted from its Frankish home. In itself it was well adapted to a country surrounded upon three sides by aggressive foes, and depending for its very existence upon constant preparedness for war, and upon unremitting discipline continually placing a well-trained body of faithful vassals at the disposal of the sovereign prince. Yet even amid this dangerously explosive atmosphere feudalism produced its usual bitter fruit; self-seeking dissensions, the want of a spirit of co-operation in undertakings in which unanimity was indispensable, and even open mutual hostility, were more frequent than any self-sacrificing devotion to the common good. During its brief existence the kingdom thrice suffered from the minority of its king in the persons of Baldwin III., IV., and V., aggravated by disputes about the regency; and as crown and fief descended through the female line also, the fate of the country at one time depended upon the caprices of a young woman.

In a kingdom which, like this, owed its origin to the popes, it was natural that the church with her hierarchical pretensions should stand on a level with the feudal state. The newly appointed Latin patriarchs considered the kings as their vassals, and as a matter of course carried on against them the war of hierarchical against secular power, with the traditional weapons of ban and interdict.

The Latin bishops, superfluous in number, and endowed with baronial rights, were able whenever they pleased to furnish mercenaries, in most cases an unruly contingent, to the army in the field. These troops disbanded themselves at once upon the lapse of the time of service agreed upon. The kingdom was altogether overrun by the clergy. The popes had taken pains by the offer of substantial privileges to induce a large number of ecclesiastics to take part in the march of the army and in the occupation of Syria. The consequence was that in a very short time every form of conflict between the hierarchy and the laity with which the length and breadth of Europe was then afflicted raged within the narrow borders of this kingdom. The churches, handsomely endowed from the first, soon became the richest landed proprietors, the bishops and monastic orders being continually enabled to add to their territories through the sums of money sent to them from Europe. This wealthy body of clergy and monks, severed by descent, by language, and now, since the schism of the churches, by religion, from the Syrian Christians, were despised for their immorality, but feared on account of their power. The breach between the Western immigrants and the old Syrian colonies became year by year wider.

The behaviour of the popes at this time with regard to the Eastern Church and the Latin kingdom was pregnant with momentous and decisive consequences.

The weal or woe of the Christian government in Syria was intimately bound up with the Byzantine Empire. The very existence of the little kingdom ultimately depended, it may be said, on the attitude assumed towards it in Constantinople. The religious question was of predominant importance. The numerous Christian population of Syria, descended from the old subjects of the empire, owned allegiance in ecclesiastical affairs to the Greek Church. Whether the new arrivals and masters from the West would be regarded by the Syrians as fellow-Christians, or treated as heretics and schismatics, depended entirely upon the attitude assumed by Greeks and Latins towards one another in Constantinople. The number of Latin clergy, monks, and laity upon the shores of the Bosphorus was considerable; if ecclesiastical matters there came to an open separation and quarrel, the stability of the newly founded Frankish principalities would be undermined.

When the era of the Crusades began, the relation of the two churches to one another was still fluctuating and ill-defined. At that time and even throughout the course of the twelfth century the Latins had no scruple in taking part in the services of the Greek Church. No impediment was placed in the way of marriage between Latins and Greeks. Simultaneously with the cry for the liberation of the Holy Sepulchre arose another: 'Let us succour our brethren the Christians of the East!' The Western nations as yet knew nothing of the heresy of the Eastern Church. No great council had as yet by its anathemas raised a wall of separation between East and West. Even theologians were constrained to acknowledge that the Greeks had remained truer to their traditions than the Latins to theirs. The dogmatic difference on the question of the double procession of the Holy Spirit and the addition to the article of the Creed might, with a little good will upon both sides, have been easily disposed of; but behind it stood the Roman claim of submission to papal authority in the guise which that demand had first assumed under Nicolas I. and Gregory VII. The series of forgeries and fictions upon which the popes founded their recent claims to unlimited and universal supremacy over things spiritual and temporal—the foundation stones upon which the system of Gregory and Innocent was erected—remained wholly unknown to the Byzantines, whose traditions and ecclesiastical law-books only bore witness to the old church system, recognising in the Roman bishop the first of the five patriarchs; a right of precedence without authority.

Then the conquest of Constantinople took place, and was followed by the erection of a Latin empire, and Innocent III., however sharply he had condemned the perversion of the Crusade from its first destination, resolved to support the usurpation and to make use of the sudden and violent establishment of Latin rule as an instrument for consolidating his own power and for reducing the Eastern Church into the same relation of servitude to Rome to which for the last 150 years the churches of the West had voluntarily resigned themselves. Ecclesiastics seeking for place, and greedy of gain, now flocked from the West to the Bosphorus, and spread themselves through the Balkan Peninsula and Greece. To the Greeks they behaved with the double arrogance of exacting conquerors and of intolerant orthodox bigots. Every peculiarity in the Greek Liturgy was looked upon with suspicion, and thus was hateful and repulsive to them; and there was no lack of persecution, imprisonment, and even capital punishment brought to bear upon the rebellious Greek clergy. The latter soon added contempt to hatred for their oppressors. The Latins—as even Humbert, the General of the Dominican Order, allows in his memorial to the pope—were, in respect to morals, far worse than the Greeks. Ecclesiastical relations now grew thoroughly hostile; the whole body of Greek clergy, and under their influence the laity, began to regard the Western nations in the light of heretics, and their popes and bishops as tyrants and persecutors of the church. To the 'Submit yourselves' of the Latins the Greeks retorted with 'Be converted.' The nationality of the Greeks which had been jeopardised was thereby saved, for clergy and people combined in steadfast and general resistance, and by the end of fifty years the Latin yoke was once more shaken off. But foremost amongst the ranks of those who were to blame for the ruin of the Christian colonists and their kingdom in the Holy Land stands the figure of Pope Innocent. For the Christians belonging to the Syrian and Byzantine Church formed the bulk of the population; according to Burkard, in the year 1280 the proportion of Christians to Mohammedans in Syria was still thirty to one, notwithstanding that by that time most of the Franks had been destroyed or had left the country. These easily submitted to the Moslem rule, deeming it on the whole preferable to Frankish tyranny with its double yoke, the feudal and the spiritual.

In those days it would seem a matter of course that the papal chair should assume the supreme direction and organisation of the Crusades; none other than the original author could carry the work through to its end. For the

German emperors, now daily becoming weaker in their own land, frequently, too, at enmity with and under the ban of the church, and hemmed in by the snares of Italian policy, it was no longer possible to take the lead. Their imperial dignity, as formerly and still nominally constituted, might have assigned the distinction of leadership to them, seeing that according to papal theory the emperor should be the protector of the church and the natural commander-in-chief of the armies of Christendom against the unbeliever. Any serious attempt, however, to exercise the powers inherent in such a position would on all sides have met with opposition and resistance—before all from the popes themselves, who would have perceived in it an assumption of the authority which they claimed for themselves alone. For it was the popes who had, as it were, sucked the lifeblood from the empire, shorn it of its highest prerogatives, or made any exercise of them impossible.

In 1274 Humbert de Romans aptly puts the question, 'Who could undertake the guidance of Eastern affairs?' and answers it, 'None but the pope.' Yet even by that time, 180 years full of disaster, of vain endeavour, and wasted sacrifice, showed that this partly actual, partly imaginary leadership of the Christians in the Holy Land had led to the brink of an abyss into which but a few years later they were destined to sink for ever.

What above all was wanting in Rome was a permanent body of officials charged with administering the affairs of the East according to fixed principles. Not one of the popes did anything towards this object, nor was a congregation of cardinals called together to consider the matter. The pope on his part possessed no regular representative to report to him from the East, nor had the Eastern kingdom any resident or envoy at the court of Rome. The poverty of the kings, and the universal conviction and experience that nothing could be obtained from the Curia without great pecuniary sacrifices, sufficed to render any regular business intercourse impossible. It happened, besides, that just at the moment of the most important crisis in the East, the Curia was itself unsettled and occupied in wandering from town to town. Everything that the popes undertook for this most costly and hard-won acquisition of Christendom, was carried out by fits and starts, without plan or concert, chiefly through the fortuitous assistance of individuals. The papal decrees teem with general admonitions, with exhortations to particular princes and nobles to take part in and promote the cause, and to give assistance in money, and they comprise moreover a heap of decisions upon petty details touching the sacristy, the cloister, clerical squabbles, questions of precedence, and so forth. But to the graver matters connected with the East, and when speedy help was needed, the Curia turned a deaf ear.

So we learn from Odo de Deuil, a monk of St. Denis, that the Germans on their return from Constantinople had lost 30,000 of their number simply from starvation caused by the helpless crowd which hung about them. The pope had indeed gone so far as to forbid them to take hounds and falcons, and had even prescribed to the knights the form of their clothing and arms,—but would to God, exclaims Odo, that the holy pontiff had also published directions for the people that the weakly should be ordered to their homes, and that to every strong man should be given a sword instead of a wallet, and a bow instead of a staff. The eloquent preacher of the Crusades, and zealous advocate for the Christians on the Jordan, Cardinal James de Vitry, wrote that when (under Honorius III.) he arrived at the Curia he found much that disappointed him; every one was so exclusively absorbed in politics, and immersed in lawsuits and litigious questions, that to spiritual affairs—and to this category the business of the Crusades belonged—none would give the slightest heed.

It was admitted upon all sides by those who knew anything of affairs in the East, that the presence of a fleet, however small, was indispensable for retaining possession of the Holy Land. The papal court alone refused to recognise this necessity, and papal policy, having first reduced the Kingdom of Sicily to a state of anarchy, and then taken advantage of its consequent dissensions to render it utterly powerless, negatived every attempt to organise a fleet destined for service in the East.

To the officials of the Curia the Christian colonies in the East had long since become a weariness; they brought little return, and were constantly needing assistance in money, which Rome, particularly since the struggle with the Hohenstaufens, was not in a position to afford. Innocent III. indeed had fitted out a ship at his own expense; but not long after his time the popes appropriated the funds collected for the Crusade to their own wants, or to the remuneration of armies raised by the promise of indulgences or the hope of booty, and destined to operate both in Germany and Italy for the overthrow of the imperial house. The vows of pilgrims on the way to Syria, where they yet hoped to make an effort for the recovery of the holy places, were converted into promises of participation in a crusade against the Hohenstaufens, or into payment of a sum of money towards it. Numbers had begun already to *uncross* (*décroiser*) themselves, that is to say, to be released from their Palestine vow by the payment of a sum of money. A period of general discouragement and despair set in, of which the memoirs of the time furnish many proofs in the shape of stern comments alternating with grievous reproaches against the avarice, selfishness, and faithless policy of the Roman see.

The discovery made by Urban II. and his successors, that the promise of spiritual benefits and favours sufficed to assemble a valiant army and to kindle the ardour for war and conquest, soon bore fruit in the announcement of fresh crusades, of which the object was neither Syria nor the Holy Sepulchre. None controverted the assertion of the Curia, that a war carried on in the service of the church or of the popes was as meritorious in those who took part in it as fighting in the Holy Land. The theory and practice of religious warfare in the service of the popes rapidly developed. An undertaking only needed to be declared a matter of faith (*negotium fidei*), or a prince pronounced heretical or an enemy of the church, for the head of the church to call a crusade, in which whosoever should take part would enjoy the same privileges and assurance of salvation as the combatants for the Holy Land. When Innocent III. proclaimed a crusade against Languedoc and the adjacent provinces because many of the inhabitants clung to the Catharist and Waldensian doctrines, no voice of disapprobation or opposition was raised from any quarter. The horrors of that campaign surpassed anything hitherto seen in the West, but we know of one man only, the Frenchman William Clerc de Normandie, who dared to assert that the Albigensian war was the most shameful event of the time.

In like manner in 1232 the Frisian house of Stedinger was extirpated by a crusade summoned against it by Gregory IX. on the plea of heresy, but in reality because it had refused to pay tithes to the Archbishop of Bremen. A few years later the same pope caused a crusade to be preached against the Emperor Frederick II. From 1250 to 1265 the popes outdid their predecessors in the proclamation of religious wars: the Lombards were to be extirpated as heretics; the last of the Hohenstaufens, the German Emperor Conrad IV. and his brother King Manfred, were overthrown by the crusading armies; whilst at the same time Rome declared war against Duke Boleslaus of Liegnitz because he had imprisoned a bishop. Clement IV. ordered a crusade against the English barons because they defended their Magna Charta against his benefactor and *protégé* Henry III., and he proposed also that the Northern heathens, the yet unconverted Lithuanian and Finnish tribes, should be compelled by the sword to receive baptism.

Century after century had many a heathen people been rapidly and easily won over to the church by the gentle means of preaching and tender persuasion; thus had it been with Germans and Slavonians, and thus had the Greco-Byzantine Church converted the whole of Russia. The messengers of the faith had encountered as a rule but little opposition, and that little had been easily overcome. Only when they appeared as tools of a foreign conqueror, and when the spread of Christianity went hand in hand with political subjection, were people wont to offer any permanent resistance. The conversion of the Saxons may be called a turning point in missionary history, for it was the first of the conversions by fire and sword introduced by Charles the Great, which at first were merely consented to but afterwards were prescribed by the popes.

Meanwhile, throughout the middle ages, theologians continued to uphold the old doctrine that no unbaptized person, whether Pagan, Jew, or Mohammedan, ought to be compelled to receive baptism. But popes and bishops cared little for this; voluntary missionaries, of whom formerly there had been so many, were scarcely to be found after the eleventh century; it was too arduous an undertaking to learn the speech of these nations, and too dangerous to sojourn defenceless among them. So when the oracle of his time, Saint Bernard, declared that the Northern Christians instead of proceeding on their way to the Holy Land should make an onslaught upon the Wendish nations, and uproot them or convert them—*aut delendas penitus aut convertendas nationes illas*—his dictum brought fatal and far-reaching consequences. Bernard, in fact, was a child of his time, trained upon Hildebrand's system, a system which bore fruit after its kind. It was the self-same spirit which moved Innocent III. to inform the 400 bishops assembled at the Lateran Council that the papal authority delegated to them was a deadly weapon of which they should avail themselves for the extirpation of the ungodly. The exhortation was readily received and applied, and religious warfare, with the devastation and cruelty, the contempt and waste of human life, which especially mark it, may be regarded as having signalised the next four or five centuries. *Ubi solitudinem faciunt, fidem appellant*, might soon afterwards be quoted, when many a district had been depopulated rather than converted by endless crusades; whilst amongst those baptized under terrorism and compulsion, and forced into life-long hypocrisy, heathenism retained its held down into the sixteenth century.

If in those days the Germans in the North may be said to have fought under the banner of the Cross more for the sake of widening their own dominions and spreading their nationality than anything else, it may also be affirmed that whilst the French, outstripping other nations in this respect, were invariably foremost as the champions of the papacy and in fighting Rome's battles, it was always in such a way as to consolidate the power of the royal house of France, and to strengthen the kingdom, in spite of the heavy sacrifices in life and wealth which the nation was forced to make in support of the closely combined policy of the throne and the papacy.

A German priest in the year 1288 descants, not without expressions of surprise, upon the readiness with which the people of Gaul allowed themselves to be made use of for carrying on the papal wars, and expended their best blood upon the battlefields of Europe and Asia in the interests of the Roman Curia. Hundreds of thousands of Frenchmen, he exclaims, have forfeited their lives in recent times by hunger, pestilence, and the sword in Greece, Sicily, Calabria, Apulia, in Romagna, Catalonia, Aragon, and Hungary; by sea as well as by land. French popes, more than any others, were lavish of the lives of their countrymen, especially Martin IV. (then lately dead), who, out of zeal for his people, threw the whole church into confusion, desiring to govern the whole world in French fashion—that is, according to the wishes and interests of the French—but who, in point of fact, did more harm to both nation and dynasty than he would, perhaps, have done by persecution.[2]

It is apparent enough now, that the numerous crusades and religious wars in the North-East, in the South, and in the centre of Europe, sapped the strength of the Christian kingdom in Asia, which was incompetent to maintain or protect itself. When service in these wars, on either side of the sea, brought equal assurance of indulgence and salvation, nothing was more natural than that the majority should select the nearer, less dangerous, and less toilsome alternative, with a prospect at the same time of richer booty. That Jerusalem was not retaken after Saladin's death, in spite of the dissensions and weakness among the Moslems, was chiefly owing to the Albigensian war, which offered to the French nobles an easier and more lucrative employment for their arms. A similar cause, the prosecution of papal wars, afterwards deprived King Louis of the succour necessary for him in Palestine, and obliged him to return home without having achieved any result.

The fact could no longer be concealed by the close of the thirteenth century that the Crusades had ended in the complete discomfiture of Christendom. The princes and people of Europe, both clergy and laity, had been vanquished by their persistent and deadly enemy Islam. It has been observed that only one trial by ordeal of battle took place in the Frankish camp in Syria. But the series of Crusades, extending over 200 years, was for both sides one great ordeal. The Christians were the challengers and the aggressors, and they were defeated. Yet more: they laid the foundation at the same time of fresh losses in the future, and they paved the way for a yet worse foe to penetrate into the very heart of Europe.

The final verdict upon the Crusades can hardly be doubtful after what has been said. The goal towards which the Western world persistently and unanimously strove was not, as was supposed in the last century, a phantom

[2] See the *Notitia sæculi* in Karajan, *History of the Council of Lyons.*

pursued in blind enthusiasm. The task of winning back the Asiatic countries bordering on the Mediterranean, and of hindering the advance of an irreconcileable and aggressive foe, was inexorably imposed on Christian Europe at that time, though it was recognised by few. But the great undertaking was badly conducted from the beginning; the motives assigned for it, and the means and manner of preparation, all carried in themselves germs of dissolution and suicidal poison. The perverted theory of penance and indulgence adopted in those days by the church weighed like a mountain on the Frankish armies and their Syrian colonies.

The two dogmas which served as levers in the hands of the church—the theory of penance and indulgences and the doctrine of the divine right of the pope to direct the world—sufficed to set multitudes in motion towards Asia, and to enable them when there to win battles; but they were powerless to instil into the hearts of princes and people those virtues which alone could ensure permanent possession of that which had been won in the heat of contest; such qualities as moderation and discipline, self-abnegation and sacrifice, unanimous and steadfast striving after a common and clearly recognised end.

The downfall of the Christian kingdom in Asia was a just retribution for the vices and crimes of the Christians. This was said by contemporaries, and the historian may add that it was the inevitable consequence of the mistakes committed by the heads of the movement, and of the ruin and discord introduced into Europe by the struggle between the hierarchy and the secular states. In the very years when the Christian occupation of Syria was at its last gasp, at the end of the thirteenth century, there arose in the interior of Asia Minor the still small and nameless Turkish race of the Osmanli, destined first to inherit the decaying power of the Seljukian Turks, and afterwards to destroy and supplant the Byzantine Empire. It was long before the Christian governments of the West became aware how formidable an opponent had grown up against them in these new supporters of Islam. They themselves had, indeed, prepared the way for them, when by military conquest and devastation, as well as by religious dissension, they had broken down the Byzantine Empire, and had destroyed the power of the bulwark of Christendom. Christian Europe calmly allowed the city, which above all others conferred upon its possessor the position and means of erecting a universal monarchy, to pass into the hands of this Ottoman people. With the year 1453 closes the second act of one of the great dramas of the world. Its end was even more dishonourable to Christendom than that of the first act, which closed in 1291. The end of the third act is now drawing near—very near; will the issue be more conducive to the honour, security, and peace of Christian Europe? Will it bear more favourable testimony to the foresight and pure-mindedness of the princes and statesmen who guide our destiny? None amongst us can well venture to answer this question without hesitation. We all oscillate betwixt fears and hopes.

IX

THE JEWS IN EUROPE[1]

The Academy celebrates to-day, by anticipation, the birthday of its royal master and honoured patron. A festival of this kind appeals to the simplest, purest, most elevating feelings of the human heart—love, reverence, gratitude. It is an occasion besides upon which we feel ourselves drawn into immediate relation with the monarch as he surveys with thoughtful and critical eye the affairs of his people, weighing the condition of Germany and the important events of the day, as well as their bearing upon the future. Our thoughts turn involuntarily towards the latest occurrences and towards the serious problems which imperatively clamour for solution.

Amongst these, by no means the least is the Semitic question which has now for some years agitated Germany. Party feeling runs high upon the subject, and just as in the thirteenth century were heard the cries of Guelph and Ghibelline, *Hie Welf, Hie Waibling*, so there re-echoes to-day throughout the German provinces the rallying cry of the Semite and the Semite's friends against the anti-Semite. We have been not a little surprised to observe that this feeling is hottest in the metropolis of the empire, and amongst those too who belong to the aristocracy of intellect. If Southern Germany also has hitherto not been drawn into the movement to the same extent as the North, yet the inciting motives are not without force even in our own neighbourhood. Knowledge in our time can no longer afford to hold herself aloof, as formerly, from the region of

[1] Address delivered at the festal meeting of the Academy of Munich, July 25, 1881.

practical life. On the contrary she has the strongest reasons for devoting her best energies to the solution of the problems which beset our time and nation, so that she may take her part reciprocally in all those influences which contribute to enlighten and to elevate society.

Let then one offering which our Academy makes upon this occasion to its royal patron take the form of an endeavour to show how the skein was gradually twisted which none at the present day can hope to unravel, and how History, the guide of life, points to her mirror in which past errors are reflected as warnings against fresh mistakes which may be impending.

The fate of the Jewish people is perhaps the most moving drama in the history of the world.

Just as the Greek tragedians were wont to represent *Ὕβρις*, the insolent abuse of power, as the darkest destiny which doomed mankind to destruction, so in the fate of this people we may be said to be confronted by a *Ὕβρις* of the middle ages, weighing upon it like a curse—a *Ὕβρις* compounded of religious fanaticism, low avarice, and instinctive race hatred. It was produced by a moral and intellectual defect equally prevalent for many centuries amongst the rulers of mankind and amongst the masses, and still widely exists, although custom, fear, and public opinion have now outwardly suppressed it. This defect was and is, in a word, a want of the sense of justice.

We are well acquainted with these powers and their instruments, which even now repeat, under every imaginable form and disguise, one and the same thought: 'We alone are in possession of the full saving truth, and therefore everything which may be necessary or serviceable in spreading or enforcing this truth must be conceded to us.' Where this principle rules, as it did for the thousand years from 500 to 1500, and where it is represented as in these days by some who still cling to the views of the middle ages, the bare idea of justice must appear a damnable delusion—of that justice at least which is able to estimate man according to his education, tendencies, and prejudices, to penetrate into the circle of his thoughts and sympathies, to judge him and acquit him accordingly, to tolerate his deviations from our own line of thought, belief, and action, and to respect his right of independent action The Christian religion implies this justice in the commandment that a man should love his neighbour as himself; yet this highest commandment has been misunderstood, trampled upon, ignored, to an almost infinite extent, by rulers and by the masses, by teachers and pupils by learned and ignorant alike.

It is not my purpose to deal with the present condition of these matters.

It is easy enough to perceive that a nation stands high as a pillar of civilisation in proportion to the number of her citizens who are imbued with this high sense of justice, and according to the adequacy of the national institutions for the protection and encouragement of it. Wherever human intercourse touches upon the province of religion, men are apt to call the want of the virtue under discussion fanaticism; and there have been times when even the best men, men of the noblest character, have thought and acted fanatically, so that it is all the more necessary for us who pronounce the verdict of history to mete out that justice to those who themselves disowned it in their own lifetime and denied it to their fellow-creatures.

The Jews, even before the destruction of their city and of their national sanctuary, were the most widely dispersed of all nations. Strabo remarks that not a spot in the world could be found which did not afford shelter to Jews and which was not in their power; and the world which he referred to extended beyond the regions of the Mediterranean and included the countries of Asia, as far as the Perso-Parthian Empire. By innumerable pathways, by half voluntary, half compulsory colonisation, by wars and slave traffic, and little by little by their growing spirit of commercial enterprise, the Jews of the dispersion had become a community especially numerous in the maritime towns, a Greek-speaking community for the most part and impregnated with Greek learning, but invariably holding together and preserving their own traditions and customs. Like the rest of the inhabitants of the empire they enjoyed the benefit of Roman law. They were upon the whole rather protected and favoured than oppressed by the emperors; their elders even enjoyed particular privileges. Holding strictly together and mutually supporting and furthering each other's undertakings, they were successful competitors in every sphere of industry; and were hated accordingly. Much as their circumcision, their sabbath-keeping, their laws about meat and drink, their close exclusiveness might arouse derision and contempt, there lay in their worship of the one invisible and purely spiritual God a mighty element of attraction for the heathen with their overcrowded pantheon. Enemies of the gods and of men! —so rang the cry of the heathen populace against a nation whose springs of action were incomprehensible. About the time of the Roman conquest of Judæa the Jews were not infrequently sacrificed by thousands to the fury of the heathen populace.

They soon recovered a rallying-point and chief ruler; in the little town of Jamnia in Palestine a sanhedrin was established—the president of which became recognised and honoured as the patriarch of the whole nation—forming both a chief court of justice and a high school of instruction.

It was just at that period, and in consequence of the ascendency of the party of the Zealots, whose predominance had much increased during the late wars, that Judaism received a powerful impulse towards concentration. Pharisaic views became exclusively prevalent to the rejection of all other influences, such as Hellenism and Essenism; the Talmud, which, like a band of iron, held the nation in its grip, and kept all its limbs fast-bound, completed the separation of Jew from Gentile all the more surely, because

Roman law forbade the circumcision of those who were not of Jewish birth. Meanwhile the vital question was: What attitude would those to whom the future belonged, viz. the Christians, adopt towards the Jews? The primitive churches remained in this matter faithful to the example and word of their Master and to the teaching of the Apostles. Hence they believed and taught: first, that the death of Christ, of which the elders of the Jews and a part of the people of Jerusalem were guilty, was by no means a crime burdening the whole nation for ever; Christ, on the contrary, Himself prayed for the forgiveness of those who crucified Him, and this prayer was doubtless heard. Peter, like his Master, excused their offence by their ignorance. Secondly, the nation is by no means cast off by God, even though its dispersion, the destruction of its polity, of its temple and city, are to be looked upon as punishments. Israel remains the chosen people, for God does not recall His election and promises. When once the fulness of the Gentiles shall come in, then the fulness of believing Israel, with the believers from amongst the Gentiles, will go to form one united community. Starting from these views, gathered out of the New Testament, the wisest and most esteemed amongst the fathers of the church taught that the Jews are brethren who have temporarily gone astray, but will sooner or later return to their Father's house, and who still are, and will continue to be, the possessors of irrevocable promises. Christians, therefore, were enjoined, without separating themselves from the nation to whom Christ and His Apostles belonged, to treat its members with toleration and forbearing love. Origen, the best informed and most intellectual of the earlier fathers, declares, 'They are and will ever remain our brethren, who will in due time be united to us whenever we, through our faith and life, shall have roused them to emulation with us.' Even Augustine frequently expresses the opinion that in the hearts of Christians lives the conviction which is continually acted upon, that the descendants of the Jews of the present generation will be united to the Christians in one faith. These sentiments of the older church were obliterated, however, when Christianity became the religion of the state in Rome, and the heathen masses in Rome who hated and despised the Jews were half willingly, half compulsorily, converted to Christianity. Synods now began to forbid eating with a Jew, and Ambrose, who, whilst yet unbaptized, had been raised to the bishopric of Milan, pronounced the burning of a synagogue in Rome to be a deed well pleasing to God, and charged the Emperor Maximus with being a Jew because he commanded the synagogue to be rebuilt. With few exceptions the Christian writings now breathe a hostile tone ; the term brethren disappears ; alienation from the church is no longer ascribed to ignorance, but to culpable obstinacy. The hope of future union still survives, but is relegated to a remote period in the future, at the final catastrophe of the latter days before the last Judgment. Life in community with Israel, when Israel moreover, according to the teaching of Scripture, would be restored to his hereditary primacy, was such a burdensome and irksome prospect, that it was pleasanter to restrict it to a few days or months.

The Christian emperors had made no essential alterations in their legislation concerning the rights and privileges of the Jews, until Theodosius II., in the year 439, excluded them from all offices, even municipal ; and as the statute of Theodosius was embodied in the code of Justinian, this may be regarded as an indication of their position in the Eastern Roman Empire as well as in Europe.

In the West we come across the first attempt at compulsory conversion at the end of the sixth century in the Frankish Kingdom ; Avitus in Clermont, and the kings Chilperic and Dagobert set the example, which was quickly followed wholesale in the Gothic Kingdom of Spain. Here, where the bishops governed the state, King Sisebut, in the year 612, allowed the Jews no choice but to leave the country or to receive baptism. Many preferred the latter, but relapsed afterwards into Judaism, and a series of coercive laws was thereupon passed with the object of retaining in the church those who had been baptized by force, and of punishing apostasy—so runs the decree of the national synod of Toledo—a weighty determination, destined to cost more blood and tears than any of the ancient heathen statutes, for it served as the precedent for innumerable acts in subsequent times. Within the Frankish realm the decrees of the episcopal councils shaped themselves for a long time upon the lines of the imperial edicts. Jews were forbidden to marry Christians, to possess or to sell Christian slaves, or to sit in judgment upon Christians. Christians might not break bread with Jews; to call in a Jewish physician was declared unlawful. Bitter hostility against the Jewish people is first apparent in the Frankish Kingdom in the writings of the Archbishops Agobert and Amolo of Lyons, about the year 848; the latter commended Sisebut's proceeding as well-pleasing to God and worthy of imitation—an evil omen for times to come. These writings, however, show that, in the first place, there was as yet no question of the Christians being impoverished by the usury of the Jews, and in the next, that the emperor, the state officials, and even the peasantry were still well inclined towards the Jews, and that the governing power still protected them.

But with the close of the eleventh century things took a turn of portentous significance to Christians, as well as Jews and heathens. The highest authority in the Western world had proclaimed the principle of religious wars, and had discovered the means of nourishing them and continually provoking them afresh. It had come to be a purifying and saving work to make war upon nations that were not Christian, to compel heathens and unbelievers to embrace the faith, to plunder and root out those who resisted. This inevitably placed the Hebrew people in a much worse position than they had been in before, and although Europe far and wide was making great progress in the formation of regularly organised states, it brought no advantage to the Jews, but rather, with every century previous to the Reformation, a continual aggravation of misery. For in the eyes of the Christian of those days the Jew was worse than the infidel; in the official language of the church he was *perfidus*, that is to say a man deserving neither of truth nor trust. *Oremus et pro perfidis Judæis*, runs the Liturgy for Good Friday, and all the theologians and canonical writers of the time make use of the same expression. The Jew was to be avoided as one that is plague-stricken, whose breath is infectious; as a dangerous seducer, whose discourse is redolent of the poison of doubt and infidelity. The laity were forbidden to exchange a single word with him on religious subjects.

When the hosts of the Crusaders set out for the war against the Mohammedans in Asia, they first murdered the Jews in their homes and plundered their houses. The establishment of the Kingdom of Jerusalem was inaugurated by the burning of the Jewish inhabitants together with their synagogues.

These were the acts of fanatical, undisciplined bands. Yet, by princes also and people, by priests and laymen, it was only natural that the decisions of popes and councils should be taken as the standard for the behaviour of Christians towards Jews.

The Roman bishops had not at first concerned themselves about the Jews; their letters and enactments of the first six centuries contain no mention of them—the imperial statutes were considered sufficient. Gregory the Great was unwearied in his endeavours to protect the Jews of Lower Italy against the frequent acts of violence of which they were the victims, and forbade their being forced to embrace Christianity; but in purchasing their conversion by guaranteeing to them certain advantages, he set up the perilous principle so often appealed to afterwards whenever conversions were effected by force, that the church gained thereby, if not the very persons who were bought over, yet at any rate their children.

For the next three hundred years the popes were silent as to the Jewish people. The first great rise of the papacy, dating from the middle of the ninth century, was the work of the pseudo-Isidore, Nicolas I., and his immediate successors. When the long silence was broken by Stephen VI. (885–891), an exceedingly hostile tone had in Rome already taken the place of the old clemency. The intelligence, wrote the pope to the Archbishop of Narbonne, that the Jews, those enemies of God, were there by means of royal grants possessed of freehold estates (*allodium*), and that Christians lived in daily intercourse with, and did service to, those dogs from whom God Himself, in punishment for the death of Christ, had withdrawn all the favours and promises He had sworn to give them, filled him with deadly anxiety.

Thus the signal was given and the new pathway entered upon, along which still further advance was made. The Jews were certainly not seldom successful in obtaining letters of protection from the popes. The prohibition against baptizing them by force, robbing or murdering them, was frequently renewed; but whereas in other matters, even the most trifling, ban, interdict, inquisition, and other drastic measures were threatened and employed, bulls to protect the Jews never went beyond general exhortation; the penal sanction was wanting.[2] Kings and great nobles everywhere set the example of lawless oppression, ill-treatment, and robbery of Jews, and no instance is to be found of the popes rebuking these proceedings, or interfering to take the part of the oppressed. On the contrary, when Philip Augustus despoiled and banished the French Jews, Celestine III. pronounced that he had acted out of godly zeal.[3] So when an ecclesiastical prince, to make sure of his ground, petitioned the pope for permission to exile the

[2] The bull of Innocent IV., 1247 A.D., is an exception.

[3] *Revue des études Juives*, i. 118. Paris, 1880.

Jews, it was willingly accorded. The declaration of Innocent III. that the entire nation was destined by God on account of its sins to perpetual slavery, was the Magna Charta continually appealed to by those who coveted the possessions of the Jews and the earnings of their industry; both princes and people acted upon it. The impression which it made was not mitigated by the circumstance that the popes grounded their occasional letters of protection solely upon the prophecy that a remnant would remain who would be converted in the latter days. Such a fragment of Judaism would certainly, it was supposed, never fail to be found, if not in Europe, yet at any rate in Asia.

The succeeding popes took their stand upon the maxims and behests of Innocent III. If the Jews built themselves a synagogue, it was to be pulled down; they might only repair the old ones. No Jew might appear as a witness against a Christian. The bishops were charged to enforce the wearing of the distinctive badge, the hat or the yellow garment, by all the means in their power. The wearing of the badge was particularly cruel and oppressive, for in the frequent tumults and risings in the towns the Jews, being thus recognisable at a glance, fell all the more easily into the hands of the excited mob; and if a Jew undertook a journey he inevitably became a prey to the numerous bandits and adventurers, who naturally considered him as an outlaw. In Spain the Jews had consequently gained permission to dress as they pleased upon a journey, but the permission was very soon withdrawn.[1]

Foremost in heightening the severity of the already merciless legislation directed by the church against the Jews was Eugene IV., who overruled the more humane provisions made for them by Martin V. It is a matter of astonishment, if all these regulations were strictly enforced, how these people could have carried on their wretched existence.

Where popes failed to interfere, the councils of the

[1] Amador de los Rios, *Historia de los Judios de España*, iii. 412.

various countries made amends for the omission; they forbade, for instance, a Christian letting or selling a house to a Jew, or buying wine from him. Besides all this, the order was often renewed that all copies of the Talmud and commentaries upon it—consequently the greater part of the Jewish literature—should be burnt—on account of the passages hostile to Christianity contained in them; and this order was a fruitful pretext for intimidation, persecution, and imprisonment. It would appear as if the powers of the earth could offer only stones for bread to this persecuted people, and had no other answer to their petitions than that which their own ancestors had once given to their tyrant Herod when he asked what he should do for them, and they shouted to him that he should hang himself!

The new theory as to the Jews being in a state of slavery was now adopted and enlarged upon by theologians and canonists. Thomas Aquinas, whose teaching was received by the whole Roman Church as unassailable, pronounced that since the race was condemned to perpetual bondage princes could dispose of the possessions of the Jews just as they would of their own.[5] A long list of canonical writers maintained, upon the same ground, the right of princes and governors to seize upon the sons and daughters of Jews and have them baptized by force.[6] It was commonly taught, and the ecclesiastical claim still exists, that a Jewish child once baptized was not to be left to the father. Meanwhile princes had eagerly seized upon the papal doctrine that the perpetual slavery of the Jews was ordained by God, and on it the Emperor Frederick II. founded the claim that all Jews belonged to him as emperor, following the contention prevalent at the time that the right of lordship over them devolved upon him as the

[5] *De regimine Judæorum ad Ducissam Brabantiæ.* Opp. xvii. 192.

[6] The gloss upon *c. Judæorum*, c. 289. 1 (ed. Lugdun. 1584, p. 1545), disapproves of the compulsory baptism of Jewish children, but only when it happened *indistincte*, and in so far that if universally carried out there would soon be no Jews left, whereas a remnant must be allowed to remain for the fulfilment of the prophecy.

successor of the old Roman Emperors. We even find his son Conrad IV. making use of the expression 'bond-servants of our treasury,' and the 'Mirror of Swabia' professed to know that 'King Titus had made a present of them to the imperial treasury.' King Albert went so far as to claim from King Philip of France that the French Jews should be handed over to him; and certain Jews themselves, later on, stated, in a memorial addressed by them to the Council of Ratisbon, that they belonged to the emperor, in order that he might prevent their total extermination by the Christians and preserve them in remembrance of the passion of Christ.[7]

From the fourteenth century this 'servitude to the state' was understood to mean complete slavery. 'You yourselves, your bodies and your possessions, belong,' says the Emperor Charles IV. in a document addressed to the Jews, 'to us and to the empire; we may act, make, and do with you what we will and please.'[8] The Jews were, in fact, constantly handed about like merchandise from one to another; the emperor, now in this place, now in that, declared their claims for debts to be cancelled; and for this a heavy sum was paid into his treasury, usually 30 per cent.

The protection which emperor and empire were supposed to guarantee to the bond-servants of the treasury was often illusory, even when privileges were granted to them; they remained substantially without rights. The government in reality only interfered when self-interest demanded that men, who were so useful and profitable in many ways, should not be permitted to be entirely ruined. In other respects every man's hand, from the king downward through all classes even to the common people, was against them. Protection was frequently guaranteed to them for a certain period, upon the expiration of which they were as good as outlawed, unless they purchased the renewal of their writ of protection by the payment of an exorbitant sum. They

[7] Gemeiner, *Regensburger Chronik*, of the year 1477, iii. 602.

[8] Hegel, *Chroniken der deutschen Städte*, i. 26.

were treated as sponges which are allowed to suck up water that they may be squeezed out again. An occurrence which took place in 1390 ought for ever to be remembered by Germans as a warning. King, princes, nobles, and towns had all alike fallen into debt through continual civil war, and the precedent set by France was thereupon followed. The Diet of Nuremberg declared all debts owing to the Jews to be cancelled upon payment by the debtors of 15 per cent. into the royal treasury. The Duke of Bavaria, the Count of Oettingen, and the town of Ratisbon secured in this way 100,000 gold florins apiece.

If ever a prince chanced to show some favour towards the Jews of his land, or towards any individual, by the concession of a piece of ground or the appointment to an office, a papal brief of warning and rebuke forthwith appeared, with the reminder that the son of the bond-woman must never be preferred to the son of the free-woman. The papal cardinal-legates ordained at the councils—for instance, at that of Vienna in 1267—that no Jew was to be tolerated in a bath-house, tavern, or inn, and that no Christian should buy meat of a Jew, since the Jew might easily take occasion to poison him. In the year 1335 the Synod of Salamanca declared that physicians of the Mosaic faith only offered their services with the crafty design of exterminating the Christians—the whole population, that is to say, of Europe.

The hatred and abhorrence thus sown were reaped in a crop of massacre. Accustomed to the notion that every Jew was a born enemy and debtor to the Christian, the people of that time, which, to say the least of it, was a period of enthusiastic credulity, or rather eagerness to believe in, all that was horrible and unnatural, imagined the Jews to be capable of even the most impossible crimes. Since the twelfth century the fable had gained ground that the Jews needed Christian blood—by some it was supposed for their Paschal Feast, by others as a remedy against a secret hereditary evil—on which account they yearly murdered a boy. Others were convinced that a Christian was yearly crucified in mockery of the Redeemer.

If a corpse, showing traces of violence, or a dead child, was anywhere discovered, it was at once assumed that a Jew had been the murderer. The usual hypothesis was that of a crime committed by a number of Jews in concert, and torture was applied until it produced confessions. Horrible executions, and in many cases a general massacre of all the Jewish population in the town and district, were sure to follow. There was no thought of regular and impartial judicial proceedings. The judges and officials themselves trembled before the frenzy of the multitude, who were convinced beforehand of the guilt of the accused, for the presumption always was that every member of this murderous race was ready to commit the most abominable deeds. From time to time the report that a Jew had stabbed or mutilated an image of Christ was the signal for a general massacre. In 1290 rumours got afloat of the mishandling and miraculous bleeding of the sacred host. From Paris, where the first case was recorded, the marvellous tale spread through the neighbouring countries; the possession of such a sacred wonder was soon coveted in other places, until at length it appeared as if the Jews, seized by a demoniacal frenzy, at once believed and did not believe a dogma of the church, and withal cherished an irresistible craving for an excruciating death, so often was vengeance taken upon them for the supposed sacrilege.

In London the Jews were murdered because they were said to have intended to burn the whole city with Greek fire.

The great plague which passed over and depopulated all Europe in 1348 was attributed without hesitation to the Jews. The fact that so temperate and abstemious a people were visited far more lightly than the Christians raised suspicion to certainty. They had everywhere, in pursuance of a great conspiracy, to which even the lazar-house was a party, poisoned the wells and springs and even the rivers. In Zofingen poison was said to have been found in a well. A few Jews and lepers confessed, under torture, to have been guilty of the deed; and thereupon there broke out over the country a storm of fanaticism, of inhuman vengeance, and sordid avarice, such as Europe has never witnessed before or since. The victims in some towns were counted by thousands. Many forestalled the fury of the populace by committing suicide. Vainly in two bulls did Pope Clement VI. declare the Jews to be innocent. Only those who managed to take speedy flight found a refuge in distant Lithuania.

But the popular hatred against the Jews was not due solely to religious causes and to a belief in the crimes imputed to them; a third motive must be added, as strong as, or even stronger than, the rest. The Jews lent money upon interest—they were usurers; they carried on an industry, indispensable indeed, but at the same time sinful, and sucked the lifeblood, it was said, of the Christians. The accusation, without being untrue, was unjust.

Popes and councils, relying upon an incorrect interpretation of a passage in the Gospel,[9] had since the end of the eighth century unanimously and with increasing vehemence condemned and threatened with the punishments of the church any one who should lend capital at interest, in whatsoever form. In the early church only ecclesiastics had been forbidden to receive interest, but with the growing influence of the papal chair the prohibition was extended to laymen.

No distinction was made between interest and usury; every condition imposed or sum received, even to the smallest amount, over and above the amount of capital lent, was condemned by popes and councils; and Alexander III. in 1179 declared that the prohibition in this matter could never be suspended by dispensation. At the Council of Vienna, 1311, Clement V. pronounced in addition that to assert the taking of interest not to be sinful was heresy.

All trade and commerce were by this means intolerably

[9] Luke vi. 35.

shackled; the more so that Pope Gregory IX. further declared that even to advance the money upon interest which was necessary for maritime trade was damnable usury.

In this way the church had placed herself in opposition to natural laws, to the exigencies of civil life, and to the general intercourse of mankind. But it was one thing to prohibit; it was quite another to insist that her subjects should advance their money without interest. With the general deficiency of ready money at a time when no remedy existed for the steady decrease in the supply of gold and silver,[1] every one, from the highest to the lowest, was frequently in the predicament of being obliged to borrow money, and since money-dealing was strictly forbidden to Christians, and could only be carried on by them under cover of many formalities and in round-about ways, the Jews, who were debarred from all other lines of industry and situations in life, here stepped in.

The Jews had always been an industrious people. So long as they formed a polity of their own, agriculture, horticulture, and handicrafts had been their prevailing employments. Palestine had become under their hands one of the best cultivated and most fruitful countries of the earth. The Mosaic Law had been directed towards the cultivation of the ground—towards the production of corn and wine and oil. Even in the first century after Christ, and after the Dispersion, the people had remained true to the old custom. Josephus, in the beginning of the second century, extols the industry of his fellow-countrymen in handicrafts and agriculture.

In Roman literature and in the laws of the emperors there is no trace of the Jews devoting themselves to chaffering and petty trade, or of their becoming at all a mercantile people. The swarms of Jews living in Rome seem to have been poor. The violent and bloody revolts of the Jews in Egypt, Cyrene, and in the islands, also point

[1] As Peschel has showed.

to the fact that they were a population not addicted to trade or selling, for such people are not wont to rush to arms. Even down to the tenth century they formed no settled population in Spain, in the south of France, or in Germany, for settlement in those countries had, thanks to the hostility of the church and the people, been made impossible. After the rise of the commercial and maritime cities of Italy, with their fleets, the Jews had, moreover, been ousted from the occupation of carriers between the West and the East. The creation of guilds and the prohibition of intercourse prevented them from carrying on any handicraft. Still less could they gain a livelihood by agriculture, since they were forbidden in almost every place to own land.

Cardinal Jacob de Vitry, who was well acquainted with the East, observes, about the year 1244, that amongst the Mohammedans the Jews were enabled to carry on certain occupations, although of the lowest and most despised kind, but that amongst the Christians they lived by putting money out to interest. This cannot but force us to reflect of what benefit it would have been to the world, both Christian and Jewish, if a cardinal or a pope in those days could have taken to heart this contrast between the Jews under the Koran and the Jews under the Cross, and have drawn the practical conclusion which is obvious.

In the same way the Jews were debarred, as a rule, from the medical profession, although in Mohammedan countries it was in the art of medicine that they attained to great renown. But councils had forbidden the sick, under pain of excommunication, to receive remedies from a Jewish physician, since it was said to be better to die than to allow oneself to be cured by an unbeliever. From all schools, high and low, it is needless to say, they were excluded. Those who were ambitious of learning had to become Rabbis, and if by a rare exception a prince like Alphonso X. of Castile availed himself of the services of Jewish mathematicians and astronomers, the education of these men had been acquired in countries under the sway of the Koran.

The Jewish law allowed its people to take interest from strangers, and by neither side was it at first thought that Christ's supposed prohibition could be binding upon the Jews. But from the time of Innocent III. this too was changed. Theologians and canonists began at the end of the twelfth century to teach that to receive interest was forbidden, and as such made sinful, both by the Old and the New Testament. Innocent III. accordingly ordained that the Jews should be compelled to return the interest they had received, and in order to enforce the decree had recourse to means not hitherto employed, namely—that Christians, under pain of excommunication, should break off all communication with Jews who refused to refund the interest. This meant nothing less, if the order were strictly carried out, than that the latter should be given up to starvation. Desperate confusion and conflicts of every kind thereupon arose. The bishops, upon whom rested the responsibility of putting into effect the sentence of excommunication, were seriously in earnest with it, and synods (for instance, that of Avignon in 1209) exhorted them to be so. The princes, on the contrary, in whose interest and as whose liegemen the Jews carried on their money-dealing, shielded them, or in many instances cut the matter short by appropriating the whole wealth of the Jews, upon the plea of its having been acquired through interest, or else compelled the Christian debtors to pay the arrears of interest into the princely coffers.

The quagmire into which the hierarchy, with its prohibition of interest, had brought itself and the rest of the world, both clerical and lay, was bottomless. Canonical writers cudgelled their brains to invent distinctions and to discover a way out of the labyrinth. In innumerable cases men were either helpless in the presence of the actual circumstances, or else had to sacrifice the principle, which nevertheless in theory no one, on pain of death, dared to impugn. Christians, it would be naturally inferred, ought to be forbidden to borrow upon interest, since they were thus inducing the Jews to commit sin. Yet popes, bishops, and clergy were themselves constantly in the position of having to borrow, and consequently of having to pay interest; indeed, the whole organisation of the Curia, the administration of benefices, the taxation of the clergy by the popes, were so constituted that bishops, priests, monasteries, and ecclesiastical foundations had to borrow on interest from the Jewish capitalists. So the canonists taught that, the Jews being once for all lost, it mattered not whether the number of sins to be laid to their door were greater or less; the Christians who borrowed were excused by the necessity.

No doubt the interest demanded by the Jews was excessively high, and often such as was impossible to obtain; but this was necessitated by the high value of money at the time, the scarcity of coin, and above all by the oppressive duties which the Jews were forced to pay to the princes and to the municipal authorities. The Cahorsines and the Italian bankers put their rate of interest quite as high as the Jews, and whenever business fell into their hands, as happened in Paris in the beginning of the fourteenth century, people wished the Jews back again, for their skill as money-brokers, taken as a whole, was in many ways beneficial and at that time indispensable. In the northern countries and in Spain they performed the services that in Italy were rendered by the banking companies of the so-called Lombards,[2] the money-brokers of Asti, Sienna, Florence, and other towns, which were partly favoured by popes and bishops, partly silently tolerated, and often employed. In France and England it sometimes happened that Jews and Lombards acted in concert. In 1352 Ludwig the Brandenburger, son of the Emperor Ludwig, publicly invited the Jews to settle in the country, free of taxation, because 'since

[2] Compare Neumann, *Geschichte des Wuchers in Deutschland*, s. 202.

the time of the destruction of the Jews'—*i.e.* since the great massacre of 1348—'prevails a scarcity of money amongst rich and poor throughout our land.'[3]

A glance at the varying fortunes of the Jews in France, England, and Spain, brings before us in a clearer light the position in which they had been placed by the hierarchy.

In England, as well as in Germany, the Jews were the particular property of the king, and from time to time, being regarded as a valuable and profitable possession, were cared for and endowed with privileges, but at other times, especially under King John and King Henry III., were subjected to bloody oppression. Nominally they enjoyed the protection of royalty, but, upon occasions of sudden popular risings, assistance almost invariably came too late and only inflamed the hatred of the people against them. Henry III., after extorting much treasure from them, suddenly in 1230 seized upon a third of their possessions, and somewhat later pawned the whole of British Jewry to Earl Richard. The Jews, finding the situation intolerable, petitioned for leave to emigrate, which, the king's affection for them being so great, was denied them. Bishops, amongst them Grostête of Lincoln, demanded their banishment. Edward I., acting upon this demand in 1290, found himself deprived of the best instruments through which his predecessors had hitherto indirectly taxed their subjects. In the absence of any organisation or sufficiency in the revenues of the crown, which all states then suffered from, it became imperatively needful to find some substitute for the exiled Jews. Such a substitute was afforded by the companies of the Cahorsines and Italian money-changers, who had found their way to England through being employed by the Roman Curia as collectors. However, in 1345, the most considerable amongst them suddenly became bankrupt, and departed with debts unpaid. As usurers and

[3] MS. of the Royal Archives of Munich, *Privilegiorum* tom. xxv. fol. 22, 195.

financiers for the crown they were not less detested than the Jews.

In France the maltreatment and despoiling of the Jews was carried on with even more method and cunning. Philip Augustus began his reign of fifteen years (1182) by pillaging and banishing all the Jews. The rumour that a Christian was yearly sacrificed at the Passover was the pretext advanced, but the true motive was the load of debt under which his father had left him. In 1198 the Jews were recalled. Louis VIII. cancelled by proclamation all claims on the part of the Jews for interest, and ordered that the moneys owing to them should be paid in to their liege lords, the king and the barons. Louis IX., equally convinced that all taking of interest was grievous sin, and that all Jews in the land were his bond-servants, forced them several times to ransom themselves, and when he thought that he had extorted sufficient from them, banished them from the kingdom and confiscated what they still possessed. A petition by the Jews to the Governor of Narbonne for the restoration of the rights of which the king had deprived them was couched in these terms: 'The Jews are robbed of their money and nevertheless are compelled to pay their debts, whilst their debtors are relieved from the obligation of paying their Jewish creditors. We are forbidden to lend money at interest, and shut out from every other means of livelihood.' The royal mandate was not completely carried out: many remained; others gradually returned.

Louis's brother, Count Alfonso of Poitiers, devised a peculiarly clever policy with regard to the Jews in his state, which was frequently copied afterwards in Germany. He first obtained from the pope permission to appropriate all the interest due to the Jews under pretext of employing it for the Crusade, and then incontinently threw all the Jews, men, women, and children, into prison, from which the poorer after a time were liberated; but the wealthier with their wives were detained until they had fully satisfied the avarice of the count and his officials. Philip the Fair did not fail to follow the example of his grandfather in a yet more thorough and lucrative manner. In 1306 he suddenly banished all the Jews, seized all they possessed, sold their houses, synagogues, schools, and even burying-grounds, to the highest bidder, and compelled all their debtors to pay their debts into his treasury. He effected a compromise with the barons, who clamoured for their share of the booty.

The drama was finally closed in 1394, when Charles VI., upon the representation of his confessor and at the request of his wife, decreed the last expulsion of the Jews from the kingdom, because, it was said, many who carried on communication with them were observed to grow lukewarm (*tepidi*) in the faith.

Under the Moorish government in Spain the lot of this persecuted, tormented people was more tolerable than in any Christian country. Although not absolutely free, the synagogues nevertheless elected their own national judges or kings to represent them before the authorities; their schools flourished; medicine was practised by them with more success than by the Christians. Under the Christian kings of the twelfth and thirteenth centuries, they rose to still greater influence as financial advisers and treasurers, astronomers and physicans; in Toledo alone they numbered 12,000; their wealth allowed them at any rate to purchase the most indispensable human rights at exorbitant rates. Their condition in Spain from the time of the Moorish supremacy to the end of the thirteenth century was upon the whole more favourable than in any other country of Europe. Within the walls of the Jewish quarter (*aljamas*) they lived according to their own laws and customs. The fourteenth century brought disaster to the Jews of the Peninsula and elsewhere. Valuable and serviceable to the kings as farmers of the taxes and as financiers, they were detested by the people; first in one town and then in another they were attacked and murdered, and their synagogues were burned down: and at length, in 1391, the storm broke upon them in all its fury, and raged through the length and breadth of Spain. Priests like the Archdeacon of Ecija had contributed by their preaching to fan the flame of persecution. Many thousands were slain, whilst 200,000 saved themselves by receiving baptism, but it was discovered in a few years that 17,000 had lapsed into Judaism. A century later, in 1492, a royal edict commanded all Jews to quit the country leaving their goods behind them.[1]

As the Inquisition at the same time forbade the sale of victuals to the Jews, the majority, however much they wished it, were unable to quit the country, and were compelled to submit to baptism. Of those who withdrew into exile—the numbers are variously reckoned from 170,000 to 400,000—the greater part perished from pestilence, starvation, or shipwreck. The descendants of those who survived, the Sephardim, found refuge in Italy, and under Turkish rule in the East, and, for a short space, even in Portugal. Spain was overrun by a mixture of races, and the contentions on the subject of pure and impure blood, old and new Christians, poisoned the whole of social life.

In Portugal the Jews fared even worse than their brethren in Spain. Their position had for a long time been better than in the rest of the Peninsula; the deadly storm of 1391 had not touched them; they enjoyed certain privileges, possessed land, followed the pursuits of agriculture and commerce. But in 1495 under King Manuel, a sovereign otherwise remarkable for his mild and philanthropic disposition, a terrible blow overtook them: their children under fourteen years of age were torn from them

[1] In Spain the right to strip the outcast Jews of their possessions was proved -1, out of the teaching of Innocent III., supported by the divine ordinance to the effect that the Jews were in a state of slavery; 2, out of the decretals of Pope Alexander III., forbidding converted Jews to be despoiled, from whence it followed that the unconverted might be plundered by the Christians; 3, out of the decretals of Clement III., forbidding the confiscation of their property except by the permission of the governing powers, by whom the act was rendered legal. Paramo, *De orig. off. s. Inquisitionis*, 164 (Matriti, 1598).

and baptized; they themselves were permitted to remain in the land only upon condition of turning Christian. Thus this kingdom also was filled with pretended converts and those who had been baptized under compulsion. The consequences were fearful. In 1506, upon one of these new Christians in Lisbon expressing a doubt concerning a supposed miracle, 2,000 converts were massacred in three days. The Inquisition was soon afterwards introduced, as the approved means for handing over to the exchequer the wealth of the new Christians.

The existence of the Jews in the great mercantile cities of Italy was comparatively tolerable; for, the business of banking and exchange being already in the hands of the Christians, they were enabled to apply themselves more to trade. No massacres or popular outbreaks against them took place in that country.

All this becomes more comprehensible if we note that not a single word of pity or sign of reprobation is to be found in the writings of the historians who lived in the period when these outrages were committed. Ecclesiastical chroniclers frequently testify approval of them; the monk of Waverley, for example, relates in triumphant tones the massacre in London on the occasion of Richard I.'s coronation, which took place without the slightest provocation upon the part of the Jews, and he concludes with the exclamation: 'Praise be to God, who hath taken vengeance upon the ungodly' ('Annales Monast.' p. 246). The chroniclers do not fail, however, to observe, that avarice had been the principal motive for such misdeeds, and that the outcry against the Jews had been raised by nobles and citizens for the sake of getting rid at a blow of their Jewish creditors. Money in those days was indeed both the guardian angel and the avenging angel of the Jews; the wretched people were compelled to prosecute their debtors, in constant expectation that the next moment they would be prosecuted themselves.

Since the clergy had pronounced the very existence of

the Jews amongst the Christians to be an immense danger requiring the greatest vigilance and careful surveillance and segregation, it might be expected that the church would use every endeavour to induce the conversion of the Jews by persuasion. But nothing of the kind took place. There was an entire lack of men capable of undertaking such a work down to the beginning of the thirteenth century; and even after the rise of the mendicant orders, to whom missionary work amongst the Jews was committed as part of their calling, a theologian was seldom to be found who could pretend to the amount of education indispensable for such an enterprise. A commentary upon the prophetic books, calculated to make an impression upon educated Jews, was beyond the powers of that time. The great stream of allegorical meanings which overspread the Biblical literature of the Christians appeared to the Hebrew expositors like a foolish play upon words produced by an arbitrary and undisciplined imagination.

The early church had stood altogether nearer to the people of the Old Testament and their faith; the great changes and transformations of the middle ages had immeasurably widened the breach. The adoration of images, which according to Jewish conceptions was contrary to the decalogue; the entire system of authority and coercion introduced by Hildebrand; the religious wars, with the system of indulgences—were things which rendered the conversion of a Jew, from inward motives of conviction, next to impossible. The pictorial representation of the Trinity, which became the fashion in the latter half of the middle ages, necessarily appeared to the Jew like a confirmation of the Tritheism with which he reproached the Christian. In many places the Jews were compelled to listen to controversial sermons from monks whose practice was the direct contrary of what they preached. It is related of the preaching friar Vincent Ferrer that his eloquence effected 30,000 conversions in Spain. But the supposed conversions took place in conjunction with the terrorism created by the massacres of 1391, and how much they were worth quickly showed itself as we have said in the apostasy of 17,000 of the new converts.

In the event of a Jew voluntarily becoming a Christian he forfeited all the privileges that his intercourse with that steadfast and faithful people had hitherto afforded him, without gaining in return any favour from the Christians; on the contrary, he found himself in many ways in a worse situation with regard to them than he had been before. For the church regarded him with suspicion. In Rome it was proverbial that a baptized Jew almost invariably fell into apostasy.[5] If he was wealthy, it was made incumbent upon him to restore all the sums that he had received in interest, which often exceeded his whole income; and in France it was customary to confiscate the whole fortune of a converted Jew in compensation to the king or baron for the loss he had suffered in the person of his bondman and the income to be drawn from him. Two statutes of Charles VII. did, indeed, annul this custom; but the same king took from the Jews who saved themselves from exile by conversion two-thirds of their fortune, which contemporaries regarded as a great mitigation of the severity of the old statutes.

If the Christianised Jew happened to be poor, he stood in need of the bare necessaries of life; for he had learnt no trade, and might no longer carry on financial business; nothing remained to him except, perhaps, to become a hawker or pedlar.

But worst of all for the new convert was the supervision of the spiritual tribunals under which he found himself. Wherever there was an inquisitor the merest suspicion sufficed as the signal for him to be seized, tortured, and condemned to a fine or imprisonment. As early as 1330 the canonists had given out that the inquisitor was justified in imposing a fine upon mere suspicion, and certainly nothing was easier and more enticing than to find

[5] Petra, *Comment. in constitutiones apost.* iii. 261 (Venet. 1729).

out grounds for suspicion against a rich Jew, whether baptized or unbaptized.

Whilst the Spaniards were striving to rid the Peninsula of the Jews, they were preparing for themselves the most terrible scourge, and were destined for centuries to bleed under its stripes. For, when they compelled so many Jews to enter the church, and under fear of death to live a life of hypocrisy, they introduced into Spain the institution of the Holy Office, of which the immediate intention was the correction of secret Judaism. Most educated Spaniards in these days perceive in the Inquisition the greatest national misfortune, an institution which inflicted a stain upon the Spanish name, and became a source of misery to the Spanish people, besides being a school of hypocrisy. That the institution maintained itself in the country for so long a period, and for more than two hundred years continued to find victims for its 'acts of faith,' the events of 1328, 1391, and 1492 must be held to be responsible, combined with the distinction between absolute and relative compulsion in baptism which the church had created.

Many thousands of Jews were at that time forcibly baptized; they were left no choice but death or baptism. In many instances they preferred the former, and died by suicide or under the hands of their oppressors; the example of a few carried away whole multitudes after them. At the same time very considerable numbers were driven by the fear of death or banishment or loss of property into accepting baptism, and it was only natural that the moment that they could breathe more freely they should renounce Christianity and return to the religion of their fathers.

Certainly it had always been taught and received among the tenets of the church that baptism administered by force was null and void; and as a matter of course it would seem that the recipient would be free to return to the worship of his fathers. But even so early as 633 the Visigothic bishops in Spain had declared that the compulsorily baptized must be kept steadfast in the church. This proposition found its way into Gratian's book of doctrine and law, and henceforth no one who had been once baptized was allowed to abjure Christianity and return to Jewish worship. Once a Christian, he came as such under the jurisdiction of the tribunal of faith; if he recanted he suffered death at the stake like all apostates and heretics. Where no tribunal of the Inquisition was at hand, the princes were always ready to carry out the penalty. The Emperor Frederick III. possessed a valuable servant in a young man who from fear of death had allowed himself to be baptized. When he recanted he was condemned by the emperor to be burnt, and went to the stake singing psalms. In Spain and Portugal news that some Jewish rite had been performed amongst the new converts was sufficient to condemn them to imprisonment and the rack. No heed was given to the fact that in this way the church was filled with hypocrites, and the profanation of sacred things, otherwise so strictly guarded, made inevitable. In her better times the church had regarded entrance into her fold enforced by the fear of death and torments as a disgrace and an outrage; but now bishops, priests, and laymen all worked together in branding the church with this infamy. This was especially the case in Spain.

It is scarcely possible to imagine a more painful existence than that of a Jew in the middle ages; and had he possessed historical knowledge, with what longing might he not have looked back to the happier times of the Roman Empire! A Jew in the middle ages lived in daily expectation of being mulcted of the whole or part of his possessions and of being thrown into prison or exiled. Emigration was often impossible, permission to leave the country being refused so long as anything could be extorted from him. And even if it were granted the situation was hardly improved: it was generally a change from bad to worse, for permission to settle for even a few years in another district had to be purchased at a ruinous price. The public roads of a country were for him as unsafe as for an outlaw.

Thus during nearly a thousand years the outward history of the Jews is a concatenation of refined oppression, of degrading and demoralising torture, of coercion and persecution, of wholesale massacre, and of alternate banishment and recall. European nations seem to have emulated one another in seeking to verify the delusion that to the end of time the Jews were destined by the counsels of Heaven to endure the fate of Helots, and that the sons of the Gentiles were called upon to act the part of gaolers and executioners towards God's chosen people. They were felt to be indispensable, they were found useful in many ways, and yet none would tolerate them. The very sight of them was an irritation to the assured believer, to whom the persistence of the Jew in the creed of his fathers against the light of the Gospel seemed to proceed from malicious obduracy.

Yet as we turn over the tremendous mass of castigatory preaching, of denunciatory and hostile declamation against the detested race, with which the church literature of that period teems, amongst all its phraseology, stereotyped by repetition, one remarkable feature strikes us. So far as family life, purity, temperance, faith in contracts is concerned, their morality was unimpeachable. Besides the reproach of avarice and of usury, it is only their religious observances which furnish grounds for accusation—blasphemy is the constant cry against them, for which it was sufficient that they ignored the doctrines of the Trinity and the Incarnation. Doubtless it seldom really occurred that Christ and His Mother were insulted within Christian hearing, for too well they knew that a word of the kind might condemn them and even their whole family to death. To seek to turn a Christian to his faith would hardly enter into the mind of the Hebrew. The Talmud taught that proselytes were as injurious to Judaism as ulcers to a healthy body. If a Gentile was really determined to come over, the following discourse must be held to him: 'Canst thou then be ignorant that the life of a Jew is one of torment and oppression, of insult and expulsion, of torture and martyrdom?' He was put in mind at the same time of the burdensomeness of the laws and of the prescribed privations and sacrifices.

'The Christian has made the Jew what he is,' cries the history of thirteen centuries to us with a thousand tongues. When the Jews in Spain were to be uprooted and expelled, a Rabbi is reported to have said to the Christians, 'We are a blessed and an accursed race at the same time. You Christians now seek to exterminate us, but you will not succeed, for we are blessed; the time will come when you will endeavour to raise us up, but neither in that will you succeed, for we are accursed.' [6]

If these words were really uttered it is nevertheless uncertain whether the Rabbi referred only to the Spanish Jews—the Sephardim—or whether he supposed the whole people to be included in the curse. A backward glance over nine centuries of disgrace and misery might well have given rise to such a thought. However, since the Reformation the lot of the Jews has steadily improved, and no Rabbi of the present day could well feel a curse to be resting upon his race.

The number of the Jews throughout the world at present has been approximately calculated at twelve millions: should this be an exaggeration, it is yet certain that the number far exceeds that which was ever attained in ancient times, even at the period of political independence. The authoritative interpretation of prophecy in the middle ages, that this people was destined by persistent ill-treatment and persecution to be reduced to an insignificant remnant, has been disproved. Despite all the crushing blows struck on this anvil, despite numberless defections to Christianity and Islam, they have not decreased, but on the contrary

[6] Heinr. Thiersch, *Ueber den Christlichen Staat*, s. 69 (Basel, 1875).

continually increased in number. For hundreds of years Israel has striven after and finally succeeded in obtaining equal rights of citizenship in almost all the countries of Europe. Russia, Spain, and Portugal still withhold them. They are wanting also in the Mohammedan world. In Europe the Jews in general are in possession of all social and political rights. They sit in Parliaments and in Chambers, are admitted at most of the universities as teachers, and the numbers who flock to them for instruction yearly increase; posts of trust are already confided to them. Their skilfully organised society, the Israelitish Alliance, which holds its sittings in Paris, seems to be constantly gaining influence. The evidence of comparative statistics is favourable to them. In most states they furnish relatively the smallest number of crimes dealt with by the amenable law, and in point of prosperity, riches, and even longevity and increasing numbers, they hold the foremost place among the population. The old virtues of moderation and temperance, of orderly and affectionate family life, of respect from children for their parents, which so greatly contributed to preserve this people from destruction during the troublesome times of the middle ages, have not yet lost their hold. Family alliances with Christians and conversions to Christianity have become more frequent; in Berlin alone 2,000 proselytes were reckoned a few years ago.

This bright picture, however, has certainly some gloomy shadows. The better spokesmen of the people do not deny their grievous faults; they are forced to admit that there is abundant material for severe blame; they only contend that the faults lie more upon the surface than the good qualities. The heaviest accusations, the principal motives of the popular hatred against them, turn upon the economic injuries caused by wringing profits out of the peasantry in the Slavonic, and even in some of the German countries, through the still favourite occupation of bartering and usury. Further eastwards, in Galicia especially, these injuries are defined in still stronger terms; they are said to amount to absolute ruin for the peasantry. The guilt is undeniable —our Jewish fellow-citizens lament it as we do ourselves; but it would be unjust to make them bear the responsibility for a remote part of their community with whom they are not even in communication. The same may be said of the bubble companies and mischievous gambling in stocks, in which the Christians are quite as much to blame as the Jews. If of old alchemists, astrologers, and diggers for hidden treasure took advantage of the blind credulity of the upper classes, Jews and others are doing the same to-day with their speculations. Christian editors, again, must share with Jewish editors the sins of the daily press, when they do not enlighten public opinion, or attempt to remove prejudices, but pander to them.

The great internal movement of reform begun by Mendelssohn amongst the Jews has transformed them as a body in Germany, France, and England. Whilst the portion of the nation inhabiting the Slavonic countries has remained almost untouched, and still clings to the precepts of the Talmud, the Jews of Western Europe have cast aside many of their prejudices and customs, and conformed in a great degree to Christian views and habits.

Germany is at the present day the centre and foster-father of the intellectual life of Judaism, just as Spain, Northern and Southern France, and Holland, formerly were in turn. German Jews influence the rest of the world through the tongue which they speak; the German Jews alone possess a religious and theological literature of their own, from which instruction flows to their brethren in other lands. It may indeed be said with truth that German thought and German philosophy exercise the strongest influence amongst even the distant Jews of North America.

In civilised nations, whose intellectual culture has its peculiar characteristics, the Jew of the country shares the same views as the mass of the nation. The German Jew takes an essentially German view of all questions of intellectual and social life, which a century ago was certainly not the case; and since the culture and civilisation of our time have grown out of Christianity and have taken a Christian colouring, he cannot, however averse he may otherwise be to Christianity, avoid, wittingly or unwittingly, thinking and acting in many ways upon the lines of Christianity. Marriage, for instance, is no longer considered and treated amongst the Jews from the Eastern and Old Testament standpoint, but from that of the Christian and German. It is not otherwise with the British and French Jew; he thinks and feels in unison with the great nation in the midst of which he lives.

The false and repulsive precept that mankind is perpetually called upon to avenge the sins and errors of the forefathers upon the innocent descendants, has ruled the world far too long, and has blotted the countries of Europe with shameful and abominable deeds, from which we turn away in horror. Woe to us and to our children if ever the precept of retaliation should come to be applied to the descendants of the Germans, French, Spaniards, and English of the middle ages! There is one thing which the movers in the so-called anti-Semitic agitation of to-day should never forget, viz., that hatred and contempt are feelings sad and unprofitable for those who nourish them, torturing and embittering to the objects of them. Sad it is when, to use a Scriptural phrase, 'one deep calleth another.' Let our motto ever continue to be the saying of the Antigone of Sophocles:

Kindness, not hatred, am I here to match.

X

UPON THE POLITICAL AND INTELLECTUAL DEVELOPMENT OF SPAIN[1]

In seeking to direct the attention of this assembly to the past history of Spain, I am principally impelled by an obvious motive, viz., that no one can form a correct opinion upon the present condition and life of a nation, who has not studied and comprehended the history of that nation in the past. I am also prompted by the perception that Germans above all people, when brought into contact with Spain and the Spaniards, show a marked predilection for them, often amounting to admiration, and readily extol the attractive qualities of a people still vigorous and noble-minded in spite of its errors. Besides, it is only by the help of history that a solution can be found for the enigma that the Spaniards, averse to all innovations and revolutionary movements, and clinging tenaciously to all that is old and traditional, have nevertheless made or suffered more revolutions during the last century than even the excitable French.

A single disastrous battle sufficed to destroy the Gothic Kingdom. Whilst pagan Spain had not succumbed to the Romans till after a struggle of two centuries, the Christian kingdom yielded at a single blow before the first shock of the Moslem armies. They swept over the Peninsula as far as the Pyrenees, and penetrated even into France, in a tide of conquest which nothing could stop. Spain first became a province under the sway of the Kaliph of

[1] Address delivered at the festal meeting of the Academy of Sciences at Munich, July 25, 1884.

Damascus, but afterwards rose to be an independent kaliphate, which was soon parted into separate kingdoms. A state of anarchy supervened; the Mohammedans were constantly at feud with each other. The power of the Crescent declined. Meanwhile, in the Cantabrian and Asturian mountains Christian principalities had been formed. The scattered descendants of the Goths, combined with the native mountaineers of those regions who had maintained their independence, now broke from their fastnesses and, inured to hardship and poverty, and strong in religious faith, pressed resolutely forward, seizing upon new territories. Thus began seven centuries of continual warfare and reconquest, which, being as much a conflict of races as a war of religion, has left an indelible mark upon the Spanish people.

The mass of the Christian population of the Peninsula, the Mosarabians, learned indeed after a century to endure with patience the indulgent rule of the Moors, but they remained distinct in language and customs, as they already were by religion and descent. Conversions seldom took place from one side to the other; a real community of interests between conquerors and conquered could not arise even under the most favourable circumstances, and was impossible with a people whose manner of life and moral views were regulated by the Koran. Still it was inevitable that, after living so long together, some features of Moorish habits and sentiments should be transmitted to the conquered race, the echo of which reaches us through the rich treasures of Spanish romance.

The origin of the little Christian kingdom in the Asturias is wrapped in obscurity; its founder, Pelayo, only lives as the hero of the ballad in which his praises are sung; but about the year 765 we find the kingdom comprising the present provinces of Navarre, Biscay and Asturias, part of Castile, Leon, and Galicia.

The rule of the Franks was soon afterwards established in the Spanish Marches.

In the eleventh century the advance of the Christians towards the south became more rapid, and the resistance of the Moors, who were divided by internal quarrels, weaker. The three Christian kingdoms, of Leon with Castile, Aragon, and the County of Barcelona (Catalonia), already comprised the whole of Northern and a portion of Central Spain. When the time of the Crusades came, and Europe was penetrated with the idea that war with the infidel was as necessary as it was serviceable and salutary both for this life and the next, the Spaniards, after long seclusion, awoke to a strong consciousness of their fellowship with other Christian nations and their superiority amongst them. If to other nations warfare with the unbeliever was the temporary business of individuals, to the Spaniards it became a life-long vocation in which the entire nation had its share. In this way a fundamental trait of the Spanish character was developed—that national loftiness of mind which led each one to feel that he belonged to a race called to be the champion of the Christian world. It was their habit to look back upon a line of ancestors each one of whom had striven for the faith and won a share in Paradise; to which their grandsons following in the same path could not fail to attain. Trust in their own capacity, patient endurance and confidence under misfortune, tenacity of purpose and unrelaxing effort for this one object, stubborn adherence to inherited customs, traditions, and fables, and above all fervent zeal in the faith, such were the natural characteristics of this people. They did not prevent the various races of the Peninsula from being and continuing to be more sharply distinguished from one another in their peculiarities than was the case in other kingdoms. In reality, excepting religion, the contest with the Saracens was the only common motive that stirred them. This contest they everywhere carried on with the same weapons, the same contrivances and artifices, whilst the three semi-religious orders of knighthood of Alcantara, Calatrava, and Santiago imposed the necessary restraint upon the guerilla warfare of the masses, gave the necessary firmness of organisation to the whole military system, and, acting as its legitimate upholders, preserved and continued the martial traditions of the land. So Spain became the great battlefield upon which East and West, Mohammed and Christ, the Koran and the Bible, measured their strength. If the Moslems, although sometimes oppressed and reduced to bondage, from time to time gained fresh strength by the arrival of fanatical zealots from Africa, the knightly and warlike ardour of the time, and the hope of rich booty in land and goods, drew the French nobility over the Pyrenees to reinforce the Christian armies; and to this brotherhood in arms the Spaniards owed, amongst others, the brilliant victory of Navas de Tolosa. But of the Spaniards themselves it has been truly said that they were the first and the last Crusaders both in practice and in theory. We may gather what this meant from a story told in one of the Spanish chronicles, to the effect that kings, barons, and knights alike used during the height of the war with the Moors to keep their horses in their bedrooms, in order, when the alarm sounded, to be able to mount instantly. Even in our own days Martinez de la Rosa has gone so far as to say: 'Our fathers, roughly and hardily educated, always in harness and with sword in hand, for eight centuries did not sleep securely for a single night.'

We must now consider a curious characteristic of Spanish history. It might be thought that the annals of a people engaged in ceaseless combat with a superior foe, in unwearying self-assertion, and constant advance towards better political and ecclesiastical conditions, would afford rich and suitable materials for traditions which would be as beacons throwing light upon the path of the nation, and would serve as a means of education and discipline in the ways of patriotism. Yet it has happened otherwise; history, true or fanciful, became a *magistra vitæ* in Spain, but too often a perverted and perverting instructress.

The history of no other nation has been confused and

disfigured to such a degree by coarse and palpable falsehoods, by arbitrary fictions, by fantastic adornment, as that of Spain; nowhere has the practice of falsifying facts and of spreading fables known to be such been so methodically and persistently followed. Consequently the difficulties which this history presented to the inquirer were formerly so great as to be scarcely surmountable. It is a history which has only been recognised and understood during the last thirty or forty years, and even yet important parts of it remain too obscure for explanation. The early chronicles, down to the thirteenth century, were so scanty, colourless, and insufficient, that fancy, nourished by national pride, found free scope for fabulous additions. When King Ferdinand I. of Castile (c. A.D. 1063) is made by the chronicle to march with a Spanish army to Paris, where he subdues all the nations and powers in league against him, and compels the German Emperor humbly to do homage and pay tribute to him, the invention, for which there is not the slightest foundation, shows the arrogance of the people whose king in the seventeenth century could still say to his followers: *Nos contra todos, y todos contra nos*, a saying which even at that time had to be somewhat modified by another: *Con todo el mundo guerra y paz con Inglaterra.* (War with all the world but peace with England.)

Nowhere but on Spanish soil could a freebooter, faithless and cruel, although heroically brave, who fought alternately with his own people against the Moors and with the Moors against his own people, have been extolled and idealised in ballad and poem, and honoured as the flower of the Christian knighthood of Spain and as the ancestor of her kings; only in that land was it possible that Rodrigo Ruy Diaz, the Campeador or Cid, should be transformed into a national hero, such as no other civilised people could show, a hero in whom the nation complacently saw and admired its own reflection. Certainly it cannot be denied that in the fourteenth and fifteenth centuries the Spanish people only too truly resembled the genuine historical Cid. Nor was this enough; clergy and people turned him into a saint, who worked miraculous cures after his death, and whose canonisation Philip II. demanded in all seriousness from Rome.

In like fashion a Kingdom of Sobrarbe was invented which never existed; and Kings of Sobrarbe created who had never lived; all for the sake of adding to the splendour of Aragon in the olden times. The Spanish provinces have rivalled one another in tricking out their early history in the garb of fancy, borrowed, not even from the popular poetical ballads, but from the inventions of local patriotism, so that the Spanish annals are full of assertions of which the falsehood is patent, but which are allowed to remain as a valuable legacy only for lack of courage to discard them.

Still wider and greater influence was exercised in Spain by religious myths, originating not in the poetical fancy of the people, but in deliberate invention on the part of the hierarchy. That the Apostle James the elder came to Spain to preach the gospel, is indeed contrary both to the Bible and to history; but in Spain ever since the tenth century it has been received as an unassailable fact; he is the patron saint of the country, and every Spaniard to this day maintains it in the face of the world. Santiago, the Apostle, the fisherman, has become the knight and leader of battles; in thirty-eight combats he has been seen mounted upon his white charger putting the terrified foe to flight. The legend that his corpse, floating from Palestine round the whole of Spain, was brought to land, and preserved upon the Galician coast, is a somewhat later invention. Compostella, however, became for some centuries the most frequented place of pilgrimage in the West, and apocryphal literature was enriched by the book composed in recommendation of this pilgrimage by the Pseudo-Turpin as well as by the writings of Calixtus II.

Everywhere in the middle ages forgeries and inventions of records and facts were intimately connected with hierarchical pretensions, but nowhere was this the case to so great a degree as in Spain. We might name a long series of chronicles and other documents, either entirely fictitious or partly interpolated and falsified, which were prepared in the interests of the church, either for the sake of confirming or extending the papal power, or for the benefit of some bishopric or monastery.

A living historian of the Spanish Church, Vicente de la Fuente, in spite of his genuine Spanish orthodoxy,[2] says, when speaking of the eleventh century, 'We float in a sea of fables.' The pernicious practice was carried on a couple of hundred years longer. The Spanish mind was thereby filled with delusive images, and every Spaniard bred up in a credulity which laid him open to any deception that flattered his national pride and nourished his prejudices. The consequence was that in decisive moments he relied upon supernatural help more readily than upon the exertion of his own powers. A readiness and even a willingness to be deceived has frequently been noted as a prominent characteristic of this people, and I must confess that in reading Cervantes I have often felt a suspicion that the poet desired to portray this feature of the popular character in his description of the hero and his squire.

Even in the Augustan period of Spain, in the time of Cervantes and Antonio Agustin, that is to say in 1594, the whole nation, with its high schools, its colleges, and hosts of famous theologians, was the victim of a forgery—a forgery so comprehensive and enormous that its parallel is not to be found either in ancient or modern times—contrived by Jesuits simultaneously in Granada and Toledo. Ramon de la Higuera was the chief originator of this imposture, which was cleverly calculated to entrap the national vanity and the national ignorance—an imposture which would even in those days have been impossible in any other civilised country, and which could only have succeeded amongst a people already nurtured upon falsehoods and blinded with national pride and religious fanaticism. Inscribed leaden tablets which, as had been arranged, were to be dug up in

[2] *Historia eclesiástica de España* (Madrid, 1873), iv. 105.

Granada, and some fabulous historical books prepared by the Jesuits, were to gratify a longing wish of the Spaniards by supplying the hitherto missing tradition and historical authentication for certain cherished popular beliefs, more especially for the legend about St. James, and for the apostolic origin of the doctrine of the immaculate conception. For nearly a century and a half the whole of Spain from the king to the beggar believed in the genuineness of these most transparent inventions, the fraudulency of which would have been palpable to any fairly well-educated man. The Holy Office covered them with its shield. Hence not a soul in the Peninsula dared to attack them. It was reckoned a matter of honour and an affair of state to maintain the imposture. Many volumes were filled with arguments in its defence; lengthy although fruitless negotiations were carried on with Rome on the subject, and, as if Spain had not already had enough to bring her scholars to shame, a new production of Spanish fancy and excited religious feeling was added about the middle of the seventeenth century—the revelations of a nun, Maria of Agreda. This work, in the first instance a production of the peculiar theology of the Franciscan order, was a monument of the grossest superstition, amounting even to blasphemy. But the king frequently consulted this nun as a divine oracle, and she exercised a marked influence upon his political decisions. Her visions being in complete harmony with the cherished conceptions of the people, and sanctioning the previous frauds, there was not only a great desire on the part of the king to see this monkish abortion, 'The Mystical City of God,' incorporated amongst the sacred writings of the church, but it was regarded as a point of honour by both the nation and the church. The whole influence of Spain was brought to bear upon Rome to obtain the papal ratification of these revelations, and the conclave found in them sufficient matter to occupy them for a century and more. Even under Charles II. the Spanish ambassador in Paris was ordered to obtain from the Sorbonne a reversal of its judgment condemning the book. After this, it is not astonishing to find that this king, the last of the Habsburgs, feeble and epileptic as he was, should have been declared by his confessor and his twenty-four physicians to be possessed, and have been for a considerable time exorcised repeatedly.

Let us return to the course of our narrative. By the middle of the thirteenth century, Castilian valour had accomplished deeds which left only a shadow of Moorish rule remaining in the south of Spain. After the victories of Navas de Tolosa, Merida, and Xeres de la Guadiana, 1212–1233, the Moorish capital, Cordova, was taken, and, twelve years after that, Seville, the finest, richest, and most populous town in the Peninsula; Medina Sidonia, Xeres de la Frontera, and Cadiz fell soon afterwards, so that the power of Castile extended to the sea coast. It might have been expected with good reason that Granada, which had sunk into a small tributary town, would have quickly fallen into the hands of the Christians, and the great work of re-conquest have thus been accomplished before the close of the century. Certainly, when the Castilians contrasted the pitiful issue of the Crusades in Palestine with their own successful deeds, they might well have been filled with pride and confidence.

The question still remains why it was that, after such mighty successes crowning the efforts of five centuries, 300 years of hard fighting should still have been required to complete the work of re-conquest. The causes lay in the hereditary faults of the Spaniards; discord, jealousy, avarice, struggles of the kings with their insubordinate vassals, prevented them from striking decisive blows such as had formerly been dealt. Time after time the internal dissensions of Castile and Aragon, or war between the two, operated to the advantage of the Moslem foe. A union of the Christian forces in one kingdom embracing all Spain had been on the point of taking place in the twelfth century, and Alfonso VII. had had himself crowned King of Spain.

But a Spanish Kingdom based upon empty pretensions and without the means of enforcing them was soon effaced.

The Spanish chronicle of the fourteenth and fifteenth centuries is a sadly confused and dispiriting narrative. It is significant, to begin with, that one chronicler enumerates 179 revolutions in the Christian and 61 in the Moslem states during that period—revolutions which almost always had their cause in the disorderly conduct of a restless and haughty aristocracy, the *ricos hombres*. Now and then anarchical conditions are suspended by a reign of terror like that of Pedro the Cruel and of many others in his time and afterwards. These monarchical changes, class struggles, and revolts of the grandees against the crown, which too often rested on the heads of feeble princes or of women and children, gave a respite to the Saracens in Granada of which they knew how to take advantage. It is an infamous feature in the history of these uneasy times that the belligerent spirit of the nobles and citizens was more often exercised in quarrelling amongst themselves than in fighting against the common foe.

When at last, after long anarchy, the union of Spain was accomplished by the marriage of Ferdinand and Isabella, and the taking of Granada put an end to the Moorish power in the Peninsula, Spain, by a sudden and marvellous impulse, rose to be the most flourishing and powerful monarchy of Europe. The world had never yet seen a ruling pair so excellently suited to each other and working so harmoniously, though in distinct provinces; and both became, properly speaking, the creators of the modern Spanish Monarchy; they laid the foundation upon which Charles V. and Philip II. built.

Isabella was indubitably the greatest monarch, and the noblest and most pure-minded character, who ever reigned in Spain; when she erred—and she erred deeply and fatally—it was because her conscience was enthralled by human authority, sometimes that of her husband and sometimes that of her confessor. In history she ranks with Maria

Theresa, who, like her, surpassed all the other princes of the house from which she sprang. It is part of the contrast between France and Spain that in the former country, in spite of the Salic Law, the government and political influence of women—not of the wives, but of the widows, as regents, and of the mistresses of kings—has been as injurious as it has been frequent; whilst on the contrary, in Spain, besides the great Isabella, who reigned independently, the consorts of the kings, who, generally through the weakness and incapacity of their husbands, were forced to act as their substitutes, have often governed not ingloriously.

It has been continually asserted that Charles V. of Habsburg and his son Philip strove to establish a universal monarchy. The expression, however, needs definition and limitation. For if thereby we imagine an aim or policy analogous to that which the Corsican emperor upon the French throne deliberately sought to realise, the two Habsburg princes followed quite other paths and pursued other ends: their aims were above all religious. It must be allowed that they often made use of religion as an instrument of power—the favour they showed to the Inquisition and the direction they gave to it testify to this—and that they also occasionally made it serve as a pretext and excuse for the violation of sworn rights and for a breach of the constitution. Still the ultimate and highest aim which they set before them was in itself religious; the consciousness that it was such filled them with confidence and trust in God, and reassured them in the choice of immoral means. For with the thought that they were God's chosen instruments was naturally combined the assurance that they participated in the prerogatives of the Deity, and that for them a strictly binding law did not exist.

Charles V., though more occupied in defending and keeping together the states and countries unnaturally united under his sovereignty than in extending his power still further, yet always cherished the wish and hope of proceeding to the East at the head of a crusading army, to overthrow the Turkish supremacy and regain Constantinople. That this was never fulfilled, that not even a beginning of it was ever made, was the fault of his own blindness.

Ferdinand, Charles, Philip, raised Spain by regular steps to the level of a great power in the world. Castile was the centre from which Spain, Italy with the islands, and the Netherlands were to be ruled, and the fate of Germany was to be decided. To these a new world had been added, but, through the fault of both sovereign and people, so grievous a curse lay on the conquest of America from the very outset, that the gain in power and gold was outweighed ten times over by the mischief which it brought with it. Charles himself, after a few years' sojourn in Spain, had been transformed from a Netherlander into a Castilian, and just as the Castilians had influenced him, he in turn influenced them. He shared with them the opinion that Spain, under the guidance of Castile, was the chosen instrument for the defence of the Catholic religion in all lands, for the extension of the dominion of the church, and the uprooting of all opposed to her doctrines and societies. The whole of the proceedings at the coronation in Bologna testified to the fact that a Spanish, not a German king, was being crowned; and Charles's opinion was that the empire should be transmitted, not to Ferdinand and his son, but to his own son, Philip, a thorough Spaniard, and that Spain, instead of Germany, should henceforth become the support of the empire. King Ferdinand had more than once agreed to this, but he broke his word; Philip meanwhile held fast to his claims, and long occupied himself with plans for their realisation.

But he was not successful in these, nor indeed, in the long run, in any of the high-flown plans and projects which he formed; except in the subjugation of Portugal, which, after all, was only of short duration. Nevertheless Philip was by far the most powerful ruler of his time.

Philip was not a hypocrite, as has been asserted,[3] but

[3] *E.g.* by Motley in his work *The Rise of the Dutch Republic.*

on the contrary thoroughly upright, and, in his way, even conscientious; that is to say he acted continually in deference to his conscience, which had been formed by the clergy, nor would he ever lightly undertake any important matter without the approval of his spiritual advisers. Far inferior to his father in intellect and practical power, he nevertheless carried out Charles's system, and in the fifty years of his reign gave to the Spanish people and nation that impress which later occurrences and catastrophes, however much they might appear to alter actual circumstances, were never able to efface. He was, and is in the most emphatic sense, the 'Catholic' king, the shield and sword of the church, the leader and champion in the universal war which his father first began to wage against the Reformation in Germany, and which Philip carried on upon a wider scale in all directions. Intimate union with the papacy, and the fusion of his dynastic and Spanish international aims with those of the Roman Church, were his leading principles, and not even the ferocious hatred of Paul IV. could turn him away from them. He was well aware that under the circumstances of the time the Curia and the cardinals were devoted to Spanish interests, that his will would be law with them, and that the election of the succeeding pope would be guided by his suggestions. The bond which chained him to the papacy was four or even five fold. America he possessed through a papal deed of gift, and what one pope had given, another could take away. Navarre was his by the same title; Julius II. had bestowed it upon his grandfather, and thereby perpetuated the enmity between the houses of Habsburg and Bourbon. He depended for a considerable portion of his military expenses upon the religious taxes, which he could only raise from either clergy or laity with the concurrence of the pope; the *cruzada*, a considerable tax levied upon every Spaniard, had on each occasion to be solicited from the popes. He could neither hope to attain to the imperial dignity without the assistance of the papacy, nor could his designs upon England succeed without the support of Rome. Finally, as master of the Two Sicilies and the Milanese, he could, if only the pope stood by him, be dominant over the whole of Italy, making that country subservient to his ends, so that even the haughty Venetians must obey him. He, the king, as well as the Spanish Church, were at times even more papal than the papacy, at least as it was under Sixtus V.; and if a perfect sample of a Roman Catholic Church was to be found in those days, it had to be looked for in Spain rather than in Italy. As King of the Two Sicilies he was the vassal of the pope, pledged to pay him tribute. When, in violation of his oath, he trampled upon the popular liberties and class privileges in the Netherlands or in Aragon, it was not until he had obtained the papal release from that oath. Although he had far too much the upper hand with the Spanish clergy for any serious conflict to arise, yet he shared both the power and the profit of the situation with the Curia; the Spanish priest could without scruple combine his submission to the king with obedience to the pope; the nuncio himself could exercise a special jurisdiction under the eye of the king; the cardinals and the nephews of the pope were in Philip's pay; the theologians—at that time no country had so many or such influential theologians as Spain—worked for him, and wrote with an eye to the interests of Spain and the king; the bishops were foremost in setting an example of submission to him.

As a matter of fact there were at that time sufficient grounds for the fear generally expressed that Spain was on the way to become the political and intellectual centre of Europe. In most complete contrast to the early Monarchy of Castile and Aragon, which often had to succumb in the unequal struggle with haughty and undisciplined nobles and with sturdy townsmen jealous of their *fueros* (municipal rights), the son of Charles had developed his government into an absolute despotism. Bishops proclaimed that a King of Spain, instead of following the advice of others, would do better to follow the voice of God speaking within him.[1] The President of the Council of Castile, Don Manuel Arias, actually exhorted the young King Philip V. in these terms: 'Forget not that God has placed you at the head not merely of a monarchy, but of a despotic state; yes, of a state which is more despotic than any other in Christendom.'

But whilst Spain, partly of her own accord, partly compelled by her king, engaged in this tremendous struggle to which Philip's physical and mental powers were quite unequal, a period of decay had set in even before the king's death, which filled those who looked below the surface with gloomy forebodings. The expulsion of the Jews and Moriscos had been carried out with the utmost severity and cruelty, to the lasting injury of the country, which in the first place suffered the loss of its formerly flourishing trade, and then saw large tracts of cultivation disappear and whole provinces left desolate. Numerous districts became *despoblados*—desert. With agriculture trade also sank. Things soon went so far that hundreds of thousands made roadside begging their occupation, and only one class, the clergy, continued to flourish, and, to the detriment of all others, to increase in numbers and wealth, whilst the entire population in a short time was reduced from ten to eight millions and still continued to decrease. The blood of Spain was all the while being wasted in hopeless undertakings which did not admit of success; the Netherlands, England, and France were at all costs to be subdued, and in the effort, the fleet, the flower of the army, and the national welfare were sacrificed. We gaze in the seventeenth century upon a downfall unexampled in any civilised nation since the close of the middle ages. Philip III.—these Habsburg princes followed one another with continually decreasing powers

[1] Thus Miedes, Bishop of Albarrazin, *De vita et rebus gestis Jacobi regis*, written under Philip II.

both of mind and body—desired to carry out his father's policy, yet was forced to concede that which would have broken his father's heart.

The conclusion of the twelve years' truce with the Netherlanders, whom forty years of warfare had failed to subdue, was momentous alike for Spain and Europe: it proclaimed that the marrow of Spain was dried up, and that henceforth that country could no longer play the part of an aggressive power. For a hundred years Spain had struggled to force other nations to bow once more under the dominion of the Roman see. Only in Germany, thanks to a league with the Austrian branch of the house of Habsburg, had she partially succeeded in this; everywhere else the endeavour had failed, and now after enormous sacrifices of blood and treasure the bitter discovery had to be made that Rome, hitherto entirely submissive to Spanish policy, was beginning more and more to turn and pay homage to the rising sun of France.

Vainly in the year 1624 did the minister and favourite of Philip IV., Olivarez, set before the nuncio Sachetti that the king was now the only monarch in the world who, solely on account of religion, carried on war permanently with Turks and heretics; it would be more for the political advantage of Spain to make peace with her enemies; but the king would strip himself of his shirt rather than give in where religion was concerned. Urban VIII., in spite of protests raised even in the Consistory, attached himself to the French side, and thereby prepared for the house of Habsburg and for Spain the humiliation of the Peace of Westphalia.[5]

With the elevation of the house of Bourbon to the

[5] 'Olivarez mi rispose che lui solo [the king] in questo mondo manteneva guerra contro Turchi e contro eretici per il solo puntiglio della religione catolica; che per politico interesse gli sarebbe stato molto commodo di quietarsi con gli suoi nemici, il che saria sempre stato in sua mano, mentre avesse voluto rimettere il rigore della difesa e protezione di catolica religione. Ma che non avendo il suo rè altra politica che d' esser buon catolico, con determinazione e per mantener tale li suoi stati, di lasciar da parte, come aveva fatto, tutti gli altri interessi, avria più tosto voluto restar in camiscia e perdere il tutto, che rimettere una parte in questa materia di religione.' From the *Codex of the British Museum*, No. 8,693; Sachetti, *Nunziatura*

Spanish throne a new period began in the life of the Spanish people and state, a period in many respects quite unlike that of the Habsburgs. The political and intellectual life of Spain became more and more saturated by French influences, and I might characterise the whole period of nearly two centuries after the death of Charles II. as one of struggle between the old Spanish and the French natures; it is one of alternate appropriation and rejection; a national ferment, set up by the intermixture of antagonistic elements, traceable, like a red streak, throughout the modern history of Spain, and discernible as the active cause, now immediate, now distant and indirect, of all important events. Dynasty, court, and diplomacy were the media through which it worked; the statesmen under Philip V. belonged to the French school of Richelieu, Mazarin, and Colbert. The unlimited monarchy of Richelieu and Louis XIV., the 'l'état c'est moi,' according to the French pattern, was to take the place of the Habsburg absolutism. Whereas the kings of the sixteenth and seventeenth centuries had contented themselves with creating in the capital a mass of ministers and officials whose duties were not distinctly defined, and who contravened and paralysed each other's action, so that the more distant provinces were to a great extent left to themselves, efforts were now directed towards the introduction of an administrative machinery animated and guided by one supreme will. Spain at all events received by degrees the outward polish and semblance of a modern state.

The revolution in the province of intellect and literature was the most conclusive token that the Spain of former times was buried with the past. To most departments of human thought and knowledge, and especially those

di Spagna. With this it may be noted that Philip IV. surpassed even his grandfather in the excesses of his life; he had thirty-two illegitimate children. The irritation at that time in Spain against Pope Urban VIII. was so great that the same nuncio reported on Jan. 16, 1625: 'It is publicly said in Madrid that the pope ought, by poison or some other means, to be put out of the world.'

which are now practically indispensable, Spain, owing to the general suppression of all intellectual activity, had contributed nothing; Spanish literature, overflowing with romances, plays, collections of homilies, lives of saints, and scholastic ethics and dogmatics, had nothing to show in the way of antiquarian research, or mathematics, or natural and political science. To fill this void, foreign literature streamed in; and that, although to a Spaniard, born and bred in the mental atmosphere of old Spain, French literature, the only kind which offered itself, must at first have appeared monstrous and most objectionable. In poetry, and especially in that class of poetry in which Spain had excelled, the drama, death and sterility had taken the place of the redundant creative life which had been apparent but a few years before. The theatre was now supplied by translations from French poets, who themselves sought their inspiration from the rich storehouses of Spain, and on the Spanish stage were produced servile copies of French dramas which in some cases were themselves imitations of Spanish originals.

The nine and twenty years of the reign of Charles III. are now considered to have been the happiest period for Spain since the time of Isabella. The foreign policy of this monarch was indeed neither wise nor fortunate. By the family compact he bound Spain to France. He went to war with England in the interests of France. By supporting the North American Rebellion he prepared the way for the revolt of Spanish America. But under the guidance of the ministers who had advised him, Floridablanca, Aranda, Campomanes, Jovellanos, a series of reforms were begun and partly carried out, which, if they had been permanent, and had not for the most part fallen into decay or disappeared under Charles's incapable son, would have given to Spain a government resembling the rest of the European states. But these statesmen, and the group of authors who wrote under their inspiration, were so entirely governed by the political conceptions of France, so imbued with the

Gallican spirit, that their own productions might be mistaken for French translations. An irresistible destiny seemed to link Spain closer and closer to France, and to entangle it more deeply in this intellectual thraldom. It is well known how, when this vassalage had through Godoy become a grovelling servitude, and Napoleon imagined that by a bold stroke he had got possession of the whole of Spain, the nation woke from its lethargy, and by the help of the English broke the yoke from off its neck.

And now one word more upon the intellectual relations between Germany and Spain. It may be generally admitted that points of contact between the two countries are becoming more numerous, and relations closer than was ever the case at any former period. When Spain and Germany were united in the person of Charles V., they remained both inwardly and outwardly estranged. Not a single German was to be seen at the court of the emperor in Spain, and Spaniards only occasionally went to Germany when compelled by military duty in time of war, or in the retinue of their king. The league of kinship and policy between the two branches of the house of Habsburg, the German and the Spanish, only roused amongst the Germans fear and aversion. It brought a few Spaniards to Vienna, but only diplomatists. In the days of the Habsburgs, moreover, a Spaniard could not easily quit his own country; if he did so, suspicion was excited, and upon his return he fell a victim to the Holy Office. Since the commencement of the present century matters have altered. Spaniards and Germans have been comrades in fate and misfortune, and have fought in arms together against the common enemy and oppressor. Since then also the attentive and loving study of Spanish literature and history has led the Germans further and further towards a favourable judgment of the character of the people, of its great qualities and various endowments, as well as of its moral standard, although for the most part the lower classes, rather than the upper, the rich, and the educated, are credited with these characteristics. With what admiration and eloquence does Ernst Moritz Arndt, that stern, strict censor of national qualities, express himself with regard to this people! I will only remind you further of the friend of my youth, Victor Amadeus Huber, of William von Humbolt, von Hügel, Alex. Flegler, and more recently of Graf Schack, Lauser, Thienen-Adlerflycht, Willkom, Minutoli. I might almost assert that the Germans are inclined to look more readily upon the bright side of the Spanish character than the Spaniards themselves; at least it appears to me that the harsh judgments, half in commiseration, half in condemnation of this people, and the gloomy prognostications as to their future which we meet with in Spanish as well as in French and English publications, find no echo in German writings. And even where Germans, in face of the hopeless condition of the higher classes, incline towards a pessimist view, the hope can still be discerned that the latent energy contained within that part of the nation which has remained healthy and sound may sooner or later receive an impulse of revival and spring forth in new birth.

If we now ask what is the attitude of the Spaniards towards the Germans, we are forced to answer, *Ignoti nulla cupido*; the German people with its 50,000,000 as compared with 15,000,000 of Spaniards, with its literature, the richest in any language, remained until a few years ago far less known to the Spaniards than France, Italy, and England, in fact hardly more known to them than the people of Turkey or Persia.

Here then are materials and opportunities neither for hatred nor preference. The overpowering influence of French literature stands in the way of German ideas and intellectual productions; there is not room for them; it is only necessary to compare the numerous translations from the French with the rare translations of German works, to perceive this. That a great bond of intellectual union exists between the Romance or Latin nations, that intellectually France is the natural leader and guardian of these races, that Spain, failing a literature of her own suitable to meet the needs of the day, falls back upon the lighter and more original literature of France—this, so far as I can see, is at present the prevaling opinion amongst the educated classes beyond the Pyrenees. Castelar declared but very recently, without exciting contradiction, that Spain was morally a French province. Nevertheless for some few years past the attention of at least a few eminent men has been turned towards the intellectual life of Germany. The voice of the man who now stands at the head of the government, Cánovas del Castillo, above all deserves our attention.

Some years ago, in an address delivered at the Athenæum in Madrid, Cánovas observed that even in the time of Charles V., the Spaniard Avila, although he described the victory of the Spaniards over the Germans at Mühlberg, yet declared that humanly speaking the rest of Christendom together would not be capable of defending itself against the German power. He then showed how, above all in political life, the Germans are superior to the Latins, because freedom, a freedom strictly disciplined and curbed, and shielded by the law, is to be found only amongst the English and Germans, whereas the Latin races, slaves of arbitrary abstractions, exhaust themselves in the ceaseless pursuit of vain ideals. He then goes on to say:

'Sheltered by this fortunate combination of freedom and order, German science has flourished, so that if Charles V. could now rise up again, he would esteem not only his warriors of Mühlberg and his imperial sceptre, but also his sovereignty over the greatest thinkers of the human race, such as Francisco Vitoria and Domingo de Solo,* less highly than Kant or Fichte, Hegel or Krause. For not only are the Germans admitted to be the greatest metaphysicians of modern times, but even the latest growth of materialism is indebted for its apostles to Germany.'

* That two scholastic theologians can here be named as dominant intellects whose names are not known in Germany but to a few scholars, must be excused in Spaniards, who are not accustomed to our very different standard.

He who thus spoke is a Spanish Guizot, at once a learned historian, a professor, and a statesman; and he is not without sympathisers in his opinions, although republicans like Castelar and Garrido, relying upon France, and receiving their inspirations from thence, speak of the Germans with hatred and contempt, desire their ruin, and prophesy it accordingly.

We may at all events rejoice over the fact that the gates of Spain are at length open to German science and literature, and that our language is every year more widely studied. Besides this five times more space and attention in French books and periodicals is now devoted to German works than was the case ten years ago. Thus Spain will through this familiar channel be directed towards, and become acquainted with, the greater wealth of German learning and research, and we may therefore express the hope that, with the increasing fellowship of knowledge and ideas, firmer ties of mutual understanding and intellectual commerce may be formed.

XI

THE POLICY OF LOUIS XIV

When the two famous historians, Thiers and Ranke, met in Vienna in October 1870, the former asked, 'With whom are the Germans now fighting, since the fall of the emperor?'—'Against Louis XIV.,' answered the German scholar. The truth of these words lies in the fact that the king who died 167 years ago is still in our own time a more prominent figure than that of the first Napoleon; that, both in church and state, we still benefit and still suffer from the after effects of his administration and must still take them into account. The story, therefore, of his life is not that of a prince to whom we are strange and indifferent; the mark which he left in history, in the history of all Europe and especially in that of Germany, was too deep and significant for that; and whilst engaged in the consideration of what he strove after, and what he attained to, and how, and why he willed it, we are in reality studying a chapter of German and of European history.

Probably there are not five historical personages upon whom the world's judgment is so irreconcilably divided, so sharply at variance, as upon Louis XIV. So it was even in his own time—as we are reminded by the contradictory utterances of Leibnitz; so it remained throughout the eighteenth century; and now, although the nineteenth century has laid open to us a mine of wealth by the publication of records which place the most important portions of his history in a new light, and furnish the key to much besides, opinion is still irreconcilably divided upon him, in France even more than elsewhere. Whilst some see in him the type of a selfish tyrant who prepared the way for the Revolution—made it, in fact, inevitable—and who is responsible for the downfall of the monarchy, others regard him as the sovereign who, at the cost, it may be, of temporary distress, has left to the nation an enduring legacy of fame, splendour, and power, along with imperishable treasures of intellectual activity.

It is particularly difficult for Germans to arrive at a fair, unbiassed judgment concerning this king; their gloomiest, most humiliating recollections are connected with his name and with deeds done by his orders. I have myself keenly experienced this difficulty, for, when studying his history, I have had continually to avoid dwelling upon the images indelibly impressed upon the memory by Worms, Spires, Oppenheim, and Mannheim. However, I trust that I may escape the reproach of partiality, since I have endeavoured strenuously to distinguish the part which the king, through his personal inclinations and aversions, principles and passions, took in the events of the time, from the part to be attributed to existing political conditions, to opinions characteristic of the age, and, above all, to the temper of the people and the sentiments which prevailed amongst them.

We possess one excellent source of information in the memoirs of his reign dictated by himself partly for the instruction of his son and partly as an historical monument; they only cover some of the first years, yet they hold the key to the understanding of later events so far as these were determined by Louis. Louis here appears as a thinker who has learnt to know his rights and duties, not from books—he was never fond of reading—but emphatically from his conversations with Mazarin, from passing events, from the study of mankind, and from reflection upon himself and his position. Nobody who cares to understand the king's thoughts and the motives of his conduct should leave these records unread.

Goethe somewhere says, that in families of long descent, Nature occasionally produces an individual uniting in his person the characteristics of all his ancestors. The remark does not exactly apply to Louis, since the Bourbon family only came to the throne with his grandfather. But, taken in a somewhat wider sense, it may be said that from amongst Louis's ancestors Philip Augustus, Philip the Fair, Louis XI., Francis I., and Henry IV. appear to have been combined in him, and to have imparted to him a share in their character and aims. They and the two cardinals all helped to prepare the way, and did the hardest part of the work for him.

The reign of Louis XIV. afforded the most brilliant imposing spectacle of pure monarchy that the world had yet seen. The consciousness of royalty was developed in him to the highest degree ; he possessed, to the greatest perfection, the art of playing the king. The self-control demanded by this art, the capacity of mingling pleasure with abstinence, serious business with courtly amusements, besides unerring tact in ordering and organising matters great and small, grave and gay—all this he possessed at an early age. Lofty and pretentious in his dealings with foreign powers, he was a pattern of good-nature and dignified familiarity with his courtiers, officials, and subjects. He scarcely ever gave way to fits of anger. According to Saint-Simon, he would have been every inch a king even if he had been born under the roof of a beggar. He was reckoned the handsomest man in the kingdom. Thus his personal appearance contributed to rouse the enthusiastic admiration of the nation, and to beget a sort of religion of royalty, a worship of his person, which reacted upon himself with intoxicating effect, and obscured the natural clearness of his judgment.

The Fronde had acted as a warning upon both king and people. This frivolous and wanton assault of the upper classes of the land, of men and women of the highest rank, upon the foundations of political order—following upon the protracted rule of a heartless prelate, and of an avaricious and detested Italian—had left a sense of bitterness and humiliation which awoke in the French a longing for a strong unlimited monarchy. And now in the brilliant and attractive personality of Louis, in all points corresponding to the national ideal, the longing was to be realised. The tendencies and desires of the nation were embodied in royalty; each one saw himself reflected in the king; only infinitely magnified and embellished. The crown was sanctified by the holy anointing oil preserved at Rheims, which had descended from heaven, and through it the king was endowed with supernatural power. He must be absolute lord and master; any limitation would seem a diminution of the national power, of the greatness and magnificence of France. *Si veut le roi, si veut la loi.* The jurists constructed the theory of absolute government upon the Roman law, and pronounced the monarch to be unfettered by the law—his pleasure, in fact, to be law; the clergy, with Bossuet at their head, founded it upon the Bible; the nobles, upon tradition and the ancient custom (*coutumes*) of the provinces. Public opinion, so far as it existed in the country, may well be said to have consisted in admiration for the king and the worship of royalty.

This idolatry was by no means a new thing in France. Even under the disastrous rule of the last of the Valois, the Venetian ambassador Michiele reported to his senate in 1572, 'Frenchmen neither can nor will live out of France, since they know no other God but the king; when he passes the people go down upon their knees in adoration as though he were God.' 'It is certain,' said Leibnitz later, 'that no nation is so rejoiced at heart when their king is spoken of with honour as the French. They delight to see in the hands of their king that absolute power which others hate, and would add to it if possible. The reason of this is that the French are by nature courtiers, *gens aulica*, their bodily and mental vivacity tend toward outward show and pleasing manners, they are formed for oratory and easily persuaded by it : such a people is monarchical.'

In attempting to form a general opinion of the spirit and aims of the government of Louis XIV., and to mark in particular its relation to the political development of France before and after his day, we encounter a fact which appears to me not to have been hitherto sufficiently observed and appreciated even in France. France, from the fifteenth to the end of the eighteenth century, was, more than any other country, I may almost say continuously, under the rule of cardinals or men who aspired to that dignity ; the marks of priestly government are strongly imprinted upon the history of the country, and to the experienced observer afford the explanation of many an event and many a peculiarity of the time.

Strictly speaking, and if oaths of obedience are to be understood in their literal sense, the position of cardinal combined with that of minister or chancellor would be simply untenable. For the points of collision upon which the holder of this double office would be forced to swerve from his obligations either to the Tiara or the Crown must be innumerable. But the close connection between Rome and Paris, their common interests and enemies, the long period during which French popes willingly served the royal policy of France and the Gallic element predominated in the Curia, the fact that a strong French party continued to exist amongst the cardinals, and that that high dignity was compatible with holding an accumulation of lucrative benefices—all combined to induce leading statesmen, if not shackled by the bonds of matrimony, to scheme for obtaining the red hat, and led kings, and still more queens who were entrusted with the Regency, to assist them in their endeavours.

A cardinal, moreover, by the laws of the church, was as inviolable as the monarch himself; whoever conspired or even was privy to any meditated offence against him incurred the guilt of high treason, and was liable to the severest penalties of the church. *Je couvre tout de ma soutane rouge*, said Richelieu.

Louis, however, considered that France had had more than enough of cardinal ministers. He made use of cardinals, and with good success, where they could serve him better than others, but he kept them from meddling with the business of the state. Nevertheless it may be said that in a certain sense the reign of cardinals continued even under him, since he was guided in the main by the principles of Richelieu and Mazarin; and, though by imparting to his policy a strictly denominational stamp he appeared to differ from his two masters, he certainly believed that they would not have acted differently in view of the great changes in the situation of Europe and of France. At any rate in the latter years of his life he conformed his policy in ecclesiastical affairs entirely to that of the cardinals, and implicitly followed the counsels of the cardinals Rohan and Bissy. After his death the traditions of public administration on the same principles and in the interests of the cardinalate were still perpetuated by Dubois, Fleury, and Bernis, up to the time when royalty itself had begun to tremble at the outburst of the Revolution. Then, under Cardinal Loménie de Brienne, they were totally wrecked and lost.

In a country like France, where the church, with her vast wealth and landed possessions, her stability of organisation, and her *esprit de corps*, was so strong and influential amongst a people still preserving an emphatically religious bias, the monarchy could only reach unlimited power by ruling over the church and availing itself of her influence. Pope Leo X. had laid the foundation of this by the concordat, which conferred upon the kings the entire patronage of the higher offices in the church, including that of the abbeys, so that the whole clergy became dependent in its hopes and needs upon the royal power. One after another the cardinal ministers, and Richelieu especially, grasped the reins of government with powerful hands, and having combined the rights and privileges of the office of cardinal with the exercise of sovereign power, transmitted to an energetic monarch, educated in their own school, a heritage greatly augmented by mastery over the church.

Fénelon more than once remarked that the king, far more than the pope, was the ruler and master of the French Church. This he lamented, and sought to persuade the Roman court into more energetic interference; yet even he, when his own theological views were called in question, rested his hopes of carrying them into effect entirely upon the authority of the king over the church, and he demanded, as his correspondence shows, that the king should suppress, by wholesale deposition and banishment, the Augustinian and Thomist teaching which was hateful to him. Louis, being himself thoroughly ignorant on religious subjects, in his government of the church naturally followed the suggestions and counsels of the persons on whom, in this department, he bestowed his confidence. These, besides De Harlay, the Archbishop of Paris, were the king's confessors, more particularly Annat, La Chaise, and Tellier. Each of the numerous priests and theologians who became the object of the royal displeasure, and were subjected to imprisonment or banishment, knew pretty accurately, as a rule, to which of the directors of the king's conscience his disgrace was to be ascribed.

Unlimited sovereignty is a form of government of late development amongst the German states of Romanised Europe. In ecclesiastical states such as the States of the Church, and the German spiritual principalities, it was nurtured by the union of the spiritual with the secular power; the popes of the sixteenth century vigorously exercised it in their provinces. Wherever the movement of the Reformation commenced from above, the royal power was certainly strengthened and confirmed; but under the form given to it by Calvin, the impulse towards self-government and republican institutions was awakened or was gaining strength. Just at that period, however, a wave of absolutism passed over Europe. The great counter-reformation, which, in Austria, and in the spiritual principalities of Germany, had succeeded in suppressing Protestantism, and in many districts in entirely eradicating it, even where its adherents had been in the majority, had gone hand in hand with the destruction of class privileges and of municipal liberties. This increased the necessity, which had always been strongly felt, of finding shelter from the oppression of the nobles under the protection of the crown. It was at this very time, namely in 1660, that changes in the political constitution of Denmark were accomplished, by which the king, with the help of the clergy and burgesses, broke the power of the nobles and established an hereditary and at the same time unlimited monarchy.

A century and a half before this time, under Louis XI. and Francis I., the royal power in France had become practically unlimited. During the civil wars ,between 1562 and 1594, all self-governing institutions, especially those in the towns, had been undermined or destroyed, and in the uproar of the Fronde the work of destruction was carried still further. Besides, the municipal bodies in so large a kingdom were far too feeble to resist the central power, having no district or provincial organisation for their own defence. In some of the southern and western provinces, and in Burgundy—the *pays d'états*—assemblies of the estates possessing the right of taxation existed; but the clergy and nobles, who formed the majority in them, made it easy for the government to reduce the right to a mere formality. Meanwhile, in the time of Philippe the Fair, and still more effectually in that of Francis I., the principles of Roman law had, thanks to the jurists, penetrated into the veins of the body politic. According to those principles, the ruler is the sole arbitrator of the public welfare; he is above the law; his will is law, and opposition or criticism become high treason. Upon this foundation, and in accordance with these ideas,

Richelieu raised the stronghold of absolute monarchy, having previously crushed the despotism of the feudal lords. Mazarin's brilliant victory over the Fronde proved not only the weakness of his assailants, but also that the power of the monarchy had become invincible. When Louis XIV. undertook the government in person, he found nothing remaining in his way but the parliaments, and it cost but little trouble to deprive them of their political power. During his long reign no important attempt was made to assert the rights of the estates, of feudalism, or of the provinces, against the will of the crown. Even the clergy, who alone had preserved some slight measure of corporate independence, confined themselves, at least openly, to requests and petitions, it being, however, understood that the payment of their subsidies depended on these being granted. The king himself never doubted that the form of government, which he imagined to be founded upon divine right, must be in accordance with the mind and will of his people; the summoning of the States General (*états généraux*), which had met for the last time in the year 1614, never even came into question.

The disorders and unworthy intrigues of the Fronde had, from the indignities which they cast upon the crown, made a lasting impression upon Louis, although the flame which they kindled was speedily extinguished. He never forgot that as a boy, though already a king, he had been forced to fly in almost complete destitution from Paris. He resolved to rescue the monarchy from its condition of abasement or eclipse, and to raise it to the dignity and authority befitting it. He had determined, he said, to show the world for once a real king. In his memoirs he takes pleasure in describing the delights of governing. Despatches, calculations, tables of statistics—nothing of the kind was too dry for him. He worked regularly twice a day with his ministers in turn; he never did allow, nor could he have allowed, a chancellor or prime minister to superintend the whole. That, he considered, was his own business.

He seriously believed in a special illumination, a divine instinct in kings, leading them, if left to themselves, to decide aright in all important questions. He mentions the discerning of spirits, the bestowal of offices and distribution of favours, as things in which he, as God's vicegerent upon earth, was guided by inspiration from above. It is not the king who receives good advice, said Louis, but it is he whose wisdom trains good ministers, so that when he receives good counsel from them, he himself is properly the source of it. He acknowledges that he made mistakes, and that they gave him infinite trouble and vexation, but this had only happened when, in careless haste, he had followed the opinion of others.

Even his writing lessons when a boy had been made a vehicle for instilling into his mind that, as king, he might do whatever he pleased. The highest dignitaries of the church, such as Talon and Bossuet, declared that the intelligence of the monarch was a ray of the divine wisdom; that he governed under divine inspiration; by the special gift of God the king could discover even the most secret matters. 'Truly, kings are gods,' said the Bishop of Meaux; 'they carry upon their brows the stamp of divine authority.' The Bishop of Chartres, in 1626, set forth, in a political document composed in the name of the clergy and approved by the parliament of Paris, the orthodox doctrine concerning monarchical power. Kings, it is therein stated, are gods, not by nature, but by grace; the life and death of their subjects is committed into their hands; even when they despoil us of our property or of our freedom, and work all manner of mischief amongst the people, blind obedience remains a sacred duty.

It would, indeed, be hardly possible for a deeply religious monarch, penetrated with the consciousness of unlimited power, not to pass on to belief in his own infallibility, that is, in divine guidance upon all important questions affecting the public welfare. The Emperor Joseph II., in a letter to the pope, had made the same claim for himself. How could

Louis have thought otherwise, who, from his youth up, had been told that the thoughts and wills of kings were under the guidance of God; and how could he possibly distinguish the suggestions of his own political inclinations or passions from the promptings of a higher inspiration? In the last resort he could always appeal to the sacred mission with which he believed God had charged him, namely, the leadership of the Catholic world. The consciousness of his ascendency, and afterwards the first victories of his armies, were to him, as it were, the seal of this mission.

'A monarch,' writes Louis in his memoranda, 'must above all give increasing attention to the means of gaining or losing public applause. He is born to possess all, and to rule over all, but he must nevertheless exert himself indefatigably to secure public opinion.'

In these words is apparent one source of those fatal delusions and errors which brought misfortune upon France as well as upon his own latter years. He mistook for public opinion the flattery and homage which intriguers and courtiers heaped upon him, even after he had forfeited the good will and admiration of the people. His own action had made it impossible for the popular voice to reach him. The press was completely servile, governed entirely by the chancellor; the most rigid censorship suppressed any liberty of speech: no complaint, or intimation of abuse or wrong could make itself heard. Imprisonment or exile awaited the author, torture and the cord the publisher, of any document displeasing to the king. Towards the end of his life the prisons were filled with authors who had written either against the Bull 'Unigenitus,' issued at the request of Louis, or on the deeply disordered condition of the country. The governors of the provinces took good care to report nothing of the state of popular feeling; and how little impression was made by adverse criticism abroad, is shown by the fact that the French government scarcely ever deigned to notice it.

In his treatment of disobedience and mutiny, Louis followed the example of Richelieu rather than that of Mazarin. He made no show of imposing heavy penalties upon the higher nobility; the universal fear of incurring the royal displeasure was sufficient to ensure their obedience. He thought it necessary, however, by numerous executions, to put down the popular tumults caused by famine and excessive taxation. When in 1662 a revolt broke out in Gascony against the introduction of the Gabelle, the king ordered the commissioners whom he sent to the spot, before proceeding with their inquiry, to begin by executing at least 1,200 persons, and to select the strongest amongst the prisoners for the king's galleys. The Duke of Chaulnes received orders to extinguish with the utmost severity a rebellion, into which the people of Brittany had been driven by the burden of the stamp duty, and the events which then occurred may be reckoned amongst the most abominable of modern times. Since, moreover, the theory of absolutism naturally leads to the doctrine and practice of the end justifying the means, the king's cabinet condoned the most high-handed acts of violence against the law of nations; for instance, an Armenian patriarch was carried off from Turkey, brought by sea to France, and detained for years in prison, because he had made himself obnoxious to the Jesuit missionaries in the East.

Louis's literary education had certainly been neglected by Mazarin, and the oversight was never repaired, so that even the ladies of the court were sometimes astonished at the king's ignorance. Mazarin however had taught him the art of government and initiated him in the principles and artifices of Italian policy. There was, he pronounced, in Louis, the making of four kings and of one good man. The Duchess Elisabeth Charlotte says that it was the fashion at court to follow the king's example of laughing at learning. It is remarkable that Louis, in all that he dictated or wrote, never once appeals to the testimony of antiquity nor to any authority of the past. Yet he had a Racine for reader, a Molière in his personal service, a Pellison for secretary, a

Bossuet for his frequent adviser. The most eminent scientific and literary men of the country were called upon to assist in the organisation of three academies; distinguished foreign professors were gratified by pensions, naturally in the expectation that they would do battle for the king's rights, or at any rate magnify his deeds. But the University of Paris, the venerable mother of all universities, formerly the ornament and the pride of France, the cherished nursling of her kings, was treated by Louis as a step-child; it is not even mentioned in his memoranda; he never did anything for its benefit. It was, as was said by its rector in the year 1716, the oldest and poorest institution in the kingdom, and the long reign of Louis XIV. was the darkest period of its history. How things stood with regard to freedom of teaching is shown by the fact that a law made by his father forbidding, under pain of death, any deviation from the scholastic Aristotelian system, remained in force under Louis. The excuse for the royal displeasure lay chiefly in this: that, whereas the importance and fame of the university had of old rested upon the theological faculty, the king now suspected the majority of the theologians of Cartesian or Jansenist tendencies. The recollection of a time when the university, a little state within the state, played an energetic part in public affairs, could only injure it in the estimation of the king who had broken up and extinguished all corporate life in France.

Louis had received his moral and religious training from the Jesuits; they won and retained his full confidence. He compelled all the members of his family to choose Jesuits for their confessors; even statesmen and courtiers were more easily received into the royal favour and confidence if they surrendered their consciences to the guidance of this order. Richelieu indeed extorted from the king the dismissal of the royal confessor Caussin with whom he had quarrelled; but Louis himself never had a difference with the keepers of his conscience, and he never changed; it was only when a member of the order died that his place was filled by another. These confessors received papal instructions from Rome upon important cases, either through the general of the order or the papal nuncio in Paris. They were nearly all of them in succession exceedingly able, highly cultivated men, perfectly cognisant of the limits of their influence, and could be silent, if not consenting, when opposition would have been in accordance with the general practice of their order. In return for this they had the first, usually the decisive, vote in the council of Louis's conscience (*conseil de conscience*), manipulated the royal church patronage by the distribution of bishoprics and prebendary stalls, until compelled to share that privilege with Madame de Maintenon, if not to abdicate it in her favour, and, in fact, managed on the whole to achieve all that they set their hearts on, filling Louis with a detestation of Protestantism and Jansenism, and persuading him that his policy was to be more Catholic than his predecessors', and to use his power everywhere for the benefit of the church. The alliance between the king and the order was useful to both; all over the world, even in the most distant mission stations, the Jesuits found themselves favoured and protected by French influence; whilst they, for their part, helped to spread the interests of France everywhere and to establish the belief, even where appearances might be to the contrary, that the policy of France was essentially Catholic and bent on securing the welfare and extension of the church. A French Jesuit—Maimbourg— even went so far as to question the supremacy of the pope involved in the Romish system, whereupon Cardinal Sfondrati publicly uttered the reproach, that the genius of the Company of Jesus was now altogether wedded to the fortunes and power of France. James II. was warned from Rome not to put confidence in the Jesuits, since the order was entirely devoted to the French King, and only laboured for his advantage.

Magnificent and costly expenditure in an unceasing round of festivities and amusements, and in architectural improvements, were considered by Louis as indispensable aids to government; for admiration is a relief from that sense of entire subjection to the will of the monarch which the welfare of the state demands. He understood well that which Napoleon afterwards formulated into a principle of the art of government, namely, that both in speech and action it is necessary to work upon the imaginations of men.

Paris was too self-reliant for him, too habitually centred in its own objects, and had behaved ill at the time of the Fronde. For years he would not show himself in his capital. Six times he vainly attempted to check its growth; instinctively, it may be, he felt that Paris was on the way to become what *he* had determined that he alone should be: France. Versailles, formerly a hunting-lodge, he transformed into a royal town where every inhabitant was more or less employed about the court, and where all were blindly devoted to the service of the monarch. There he collected all the nobility, from the great feudal lords to the small nobles of the provinces. The great offices of state being withheld from them, they served in the military guard or held some post about the court. They were at once actors and spectators in the majestic display of royalty, reflecting its beams upon a brilliant multitude of worshippers; a spectacle splendid indeed, but darkened from time to time by the family misfortunes which successively snatched away two generations, leaving the royal house, in its desolation, to centre its hopes upon a single boy, Louis's great-grandson.

The reproach of an egotism, sinking everything and everybody in himself, has been levelled frequently against Louis, both by contemporary and later critics. This impression is produced, however, by the necessary consequences of his position. He must, as a boy, have already felt that he was the sun around which all else revolved. If we except the few years after his grandson the Duke of Burgundy had attained his majority, there was not a day during the fifty-four years of his reign that, from his own point of view, he would not have said to himself that his illness or death would be an immense misfortune for France, and even for the whole of Catholic Christendom. Louis's famous saying, '*L'état, c'est moi,*' was indeed merely the expression of a lifelong conviction, that with him the monarchy of France, the people, and the welfare of the state were morally identified. Self-love, self-admiration, meant with him love and admiration for France, and *vice versâ*. Just as the popes and their canonists were wont to limit the simile of the head and the members to its narrowest sense by making Rome and the person of the pope the seat and centre of all thought, will, and action in the church, so Louis made it the image of his relation to France. This may be seen in his writings. 'Everything through the king, everything for the king,' was his maxim. The king, he alone, surveys all things, holds in his hand the threads of internal administration as well as of external policy; he reflects, decides, commands, whilst all besides, from the highest to the lowest, are but instruments for carrying out his designs. Louis besides entertained a preference for mediocrity of intellect, and an aversion for distinguished men of talent, with whom he would not consent to work, and whom he could not endure to see about him. In his presence every one was required to extinguish his individuality, and to shine only by the reflected light of the monarch himself. It offended him that the merits of a man should be celebrated, even after death, by an inscription, or recognised by a monument. It seemed as though he expected to be magnified in the eyes of contemporaries and of posterity in proportion as all figures around him were diminished.

From the first dawn of conscious reflection, he had felt himself, as a king, the foremost and mightiest upon earth; to every word he uttered, his tutor Villeroi only responded '*Oui, Sire.*' Morning after morning, for seventy years, he woke with the thought that other kings envied him, and that the eyes, not only of his own but of other nations, were turned upon him with admiration. A consummate actor, he sustained the part of king to perfection, as

Napoleon sustained the part of soldier. If not the greatest of kings, says Bolingbroke from personal observation, he was at least the greatest actor of majesty that ever filled a throne. Louis experienced as a natural consequence the passionate desire that all actors feel for public and vociferous applause, and for every sort and kind of homage. He is said to have sung verses composed by himself in his own honour. Flattery little short of deification was not repulsive to him. When, as frequently happened, it fell from priestly lips, when the church exalted him as her truest son and foremost champion, it was doubly welcome to him. It could not be otherwise than a gratification both to him and to the nation to receive from the mouth of bishops the assurance that the wars that had been carried on were such only as had been imposed by necessity and duty. From the same source, in 1666, emanated the testimony, that 'the enlightened mind of our king has invested his ministers with wisdom; he is the most perfect man of his century, as well as, by right of birth, the greatest monarch of the world. His soul possesses such an abundance of the rarest qualities that, distributed amongst the monarchs of the earth, they would suffice to make of every one of them a perfect sovereign.' It might seem incredible, had not the speech been printed, that a representative ecclesiastic should have ventured to tell the king that, thanks to his majesty's solicitude and good example, piety and morality prevailed throughout the kingdom. The impression produced upon contemporaries may be seen from Bayle, and can be estimated by those who are acquainted with Fléchier's 'Great Assizes;' with the great poisoning case in Paris in which members of several of the most distinguished families figured as criminals: or with the mutually corroborative narratives and disclosures of the Duchess Charlotte Elisabeth and the Duke of Saint-Simon; and with the information recently brought to light by Ravaisson out of the archives of the Bastille. The annals of criminal law in France at that time disclose a terrible picture of lawless wickedness, moral obliquity, and refinement of crime, combined with judicial barbarism and cruelty.

A friend, in whom he could confide, such as his grandfather had possessed in Sully, Louis never had; his letters are mere business letters; he jealously checked any interference in affairs by the princes of his house. Unconsciously he allowed himself to be swayed by his ministers, by Colbert, and still more, far too much so, indeed, by the evil genius of his life, Louvois, and by his confessors Annat, La Chaise, and Tellier, but above all by that remarkable woman, the widow of the poet Scarron, who made herself completely mistress of his heart and mind. This woman, as great in her way as the king himself, superior to him in intellect, marvellously free from most of the weaknesses and faults of her sex, was for thirty years more completely queen of France than the Spanish princess who preceded her; her influence upon the destinies of the nation was more marked than that of any other woman in French history.

In a remarkable letter addressed to Madame de Maintenon in the year 1690, probably in answer to some previous communication or inquiry, Fénelon says that since the king now desires to be assisted and governed (*assiégé et gouverné*), she ought earnestly to devote herself to this work in the interests of the king and the people, and to strive to bring the best men to his notice and into his confidence. From this it may be conjectured that Louis himself, having a high opinion of her judgment and penetration, had expressed the wish to be guided and counselled by her; and Madame de Maintenon exercised marvellous tact and discretion in the use which she made of her influence. She submitted herself however, with unquestioning obedience and complete surrender of her own judgment, to priestly guidance. Unfortunately, it was not to the peace-loving Fénelon, the enemy of unjust and aggressive warfare and the ardent sympathiser with the griefs of the impoverished people, that she entrusted her conscience, but to priests like Gobelin and Godet des Marais, for the latter of whom she obtained the bishopric of Chartres, and both of whom were imbued with the idea prevalent amongst the clergy, that the king was called by God to minister to the extension of the church, to obtain by the sword the victory over schismatics, and to convert heretics by all the means of coercion which lie within the hand of an absolute monarch. Thus the predominance of those spiritual and secular influences was secured which encouraged the continuance of war; and Madame de Maintenon was compelled, much as she detested Louvois, to co-operate in maintaining him in his position, since his genius and capacity for work were indispensable to the king in time of war, and since he had deservedly earned the reputation of understanding better than any one else how to win a victory from his writing-desk.

Here it may well be asked whether this Louis, constantly yielding to the advice and guidance of a woman, could be the same monarch who had written these words to his son: 'In the position which you inherit from me, you cannot without shame allow yourself to be guided by the opinion of others.' But between this letter and that of Fénelon lies an interval of nearly thirty years, a period abounding in spent illusions, abortive undertakings, and disappointed projects; dreams of infallibility had been modified if not dispelled, and whereas formerly the vicinity of any man, whose judgment and ability he must have acknowledged to surpass his own, would not have been tolerated, he now willingly gave place to the moral and intellectual superiority of a woman whom he loved and who devoted her life to him. Under her guidance he anticipated temporal blessings and eternal salvation.

The magic word *gloire*—for which we have scarcely an equivalent—filled Louis's thoughts and formed the motive of his actions. He said himself that a high reputation in the world was dearer to him than life. He understood his people sufficiently to be aware that to retain their admiration and worship, the king must find continually at any cost fresh gratification for the national thirst for feats of arms and conquest. As the leaders of the national vote in France still tell us, the strongest passion of the people, possessed to an equal degree by no other nation since the times of the Romans, is the desire for conquest, and this was keenly felt and acknowledged by Louis. His feeling was the same as that which the first Napoleon afterwards expressed to Metternich : 'I must have honour and glory ; I cannot appear with diminished fame in the midst of my people ; I must remain great, glorious, admired.'

With ambition were combined the suggestions of policy. Even of old the maxim, of which foreign ambassadors to France had to take account, was that, to preserve peace internally and orderly government, the people from time to time must be occupied with foreign wars. This, said Count Zinzendorf, even for the most pious kings of France, must be an invariable rule. The king's belief that the wishes and aspirations of the nation must be identical with his own, could not be otherwise than strengthened and confirmed by witnessing the general and self-sacrificing submission with which he was obeyed. 'Property and life,' wrote Madame de Sévigné, 'are as nothing to the French when it is a question of pleasing the king.' The remark which she adds, 'We should be great saints did we but serve God as earnestly,' reminds one of the saying of Colbert upon his deathbed, that if he had done as much for God as he had done for one man—the king—he might feel assured of eternal salvation.

In Louis's memoirs we find the impression produced upon him by the extraordinary contempt of death with which, for the sake of meriting his praise, officers and men accomplished feats of arms before his eyes. He felt, he said, that to a nation which poured out its blood so willingly for him, he owed a return in the shape of fame, greatness, and conquest.

Never had a monarch possessed, in diplomacy, such

excellent auxiliaries as Louis. Everywhere in Europe his emissaries were well provided with money for bribery and for the payment of spies and informers. Like the Spanish King Philip II., he had his paid adherents and tools in every cabinet. He sometimes by such means succeeded in winning greater victories in diplomacy than through his generals in the field. A pattern of an ambassador after the king's heart was Gremonville in Vienna, of whom the king himself bore witness that he did all that satanic effrontery and subtlety could accomplish. An ambassador from Louis had usually two ends in view: one public and avowed; the other covert, and carefully concealed. No scruples were entertained as to the employment of bribery upon the most extensive scale and under various forms.

Money for this purpose was never wanting, since Louis held all the means of government at his disposal, and as his ministers well understood how to provide for his necessities by tightening the screw of taxation and by the sale of public offices. French gold consequently flowed in an unremitting stream towards all the capitals of Europe, where it was employed in purchasing the good will of the ministers, statesmen, and other influential personages. Kings, the two Stuarts for instance, Charles II. and James II., were pensioners of Louis. In England, Sweden, Poland, Italy, amongst the ecclesiastical prince-electors in the Palatinate and Saxony, at the imperial court of Vienna, and in Madrid, French gold was actively employed, and usually with good success, for his agents were generally able to outbid those of other princes. With golden chains, he intimates, much could be done amongst the emperor's ministers, and he relates in his notes that one of the ministers in Vienna allowed himself in some financial matter to be bribed by 100,000 thalers to act contrary to the emperor's interest. Leopold's two most able ministers, Auersperg and Lobkowitz, laboured energetically under the guidance of Louis's ambassador, Gremonville, for his objects: the former in the hope of obtaining a cardinal's hat through Louis's recommendation, the latter out of personal admiration for the king, and because he saw in the French Monarchy an ideal to be aimed at by Austria.

From the despatches of his ambassadors in Rome it may be seen how powerful the influence of French gold, and of other advantages and rewards which Louis held at his command, were amongst the cardinals and with all grades of officials in the Curia. Conversely, it is remarkable, and it is a matter which places Louis's personality in a very favourable light, that statesmen, diplomatists, and agents invariably remained true to him and inaccessible to foreign allurements. At a period when in political transactions the general custom was to receive and to give money, and when at every congress the ambassadors of the powers appeared furnished with the necessary sums, the incorruptibility which the French shared only with the Dutch, coupled with the inexhaustible resources of the French King's treasury, was the guarantee for a long series of diplomatic victories.

Next to the services of so excellent a diplomatic organisation came the advantage which Louis gained by the favour and confidence with which the clergy throughout Europe regarded him. These were by no means diminished by the quarrel, open or silent, which lasted for nearly thirty years between him and the two popes Alexander VII. and Innocent XI. He remained, notwithstanding, in the eyes of the church her faithful champion, her shield and sword, the enemy of her foes. With the popes who succeeded the implacable Innocent XI., friendly relations were restored, and under Alexander VIII., Innocent XII., and Clement XI., Rome readily learnt to revere in Louis the most Christian majesty, the eldest son of the church, and to bestow her favours upon him. At the time of the first war with Holland, Buonvisi, then papal nuncio in Cologne, and afterwards cardinal, had already laid much stress upon the advantage to be gained by the church from the complete humiliation of the Dutch, upon which account he had persuaded the emperor to render them no assistance. The French bishops therefore, in comparing what the king had done for the church to the acts of a Constantine or a Theodosius, were hardly guilty of exaggeration. It would have been more appropriate to liken him to Justinian, to whose reign that of Louis offers a striking resemblance. It would, however, be difficult to find any monarch in the early centuries of the Christian era who laboured as earnestly as Louis did by every means in his power, by arms, by influence, by diplomatic negotiation, and by the expenditure of money, to promote the advantage of the church in the form that was set before him by the advisers of his conscience. In the college of cardinals, and even amongst the Italians, Louis consequently had a number of adherents always ready to further his interests with the Curia. The choice at the papal elections generally fell upon the individual whom he had recommended and who obtained the support of his ambassador and of the French cardinals. More than one pope after his election declared that he owed his elevation to the French King. Even in the dispute with Innocent XI when Louis, through the councillor of state Denis Talon, publicly accused the pope of favouring the Jansenist heresy, the greater portion of the clergy, and above all the Jesuits, took part with the king. Clement XI. bestowed upon him a mark of confidence such as had never previously fallen to the lot of any monarch; he submitted to him, yet in the greatest secrecy, the scheme of his dogmatic bull *Vineam domini*, for criticism and approbation, in order that after its publication it might meet with no opposition in France. Innocent XII. also sought the approval of the king before nominating as cardinal the Abbot Sfondrati, who had written against the Gallican doctrine.

Any one who has made himself familiar with the behaviour in former times of the Roman see towards Germany, Italy, and Spain, may feel considerable surprise that the whole system of royal interference in church government, carried on by Louis, should have been so quietly accepted in Rome. It was not merely tolerated, it was sanctioned, and, moreover, supported by the whole apparatus of indulgences and dispensations of which the Curia disposed, and occasionally Louis even received special thanks after having inflicted some heavy punishment upon theologians whose writings had given offence in Rome. Clement XI. wrote to him to the effect that he distinguished himself by a wisdom in ecclesiastical matters that was quite remarkable.

The same pope in a speech before the cardinals publicly testified his admiration for the king in terms sufficiently glowing to satisfy even the monarch himself. 'He has,' said the pontiff, 'exhibited all the Catholic virtues; he has been the most powerful guardian and undaunted champion of the Catholic faith, full of justice, prudence, piety, religious zeal, and magnanimity. He has displayed his zeal for religion in the most signal manner by freeing France in the space of a few months from the errors of Protestantism, and by upholding and putting into effect for a number of years the papal decrees against Jansenism.'

Even Innocent XI. did not venture to formulate against such a monarch any general denunciation of his dealings with the church, notwithstanding that it went far beyond mere guardianship, and amounted in truth to complete dominion exercised under the eyes, and often with the connivance, of the nuncio. The pope contented himself with breaking one thread of the net, the right of the *Régale*, yet even in this matter he was obliged to yield, for the clergy, delighted with the edict of October 22, 1685, held fast to the king. The importance of the fact that king and clergy, inseparably allied, alternately swayed and governed one another, was duly appreciated in Rome. Alexander VIII. declared that in the affair of the declaration of 1682 he entirely sided with the king, because the bishops conformed their views and religion entirely to his wishes, and were equally ready, at his behest, to separate themselves from the Roman see, or to recognise its infallibility. Fénelon reported the same to Rome. Forcible language and authoritative decrees could alter nothing in a situation which the Curia had itself, step by step, formed and established. Louis, so far as his relation with the papal chair was concerned, was animated by two motives. His bitter hatred against all that he had been led to connect with Jansenism prompted him to extend the widest recognition to the principles and claims of Rome in doctrinal matters, for in the sphere of conscience he felt the insufficiency of his own discernment. Yet, at another time, either the idea occurred to himself, or was suggested by others, that the doctrine of the papal supremacy over states and monarchs, and the right to depose princes and absolve nations from their allegiance, which the popes had so pompously proclaimed and exercised, was inseparable from the theory of papal infallibility. Thus he was induced at one moment to call upon the clergy to renounce the defensive formulæ and reservations of the Gallican Church, and at another to command strict adherence to, and the public observance of, the Gallican system.

That Louis, despite his zeal for the church, should have fallen into prolonged disputes with the two popes Alexander VII. and Innocent XI., happened in each case from a different cause.

The difficulty with Alexander came to Louis as a legacy from Mazarin; the hatred borne by the two cardinals, Chigi and Mazarin, for one another, dated from the Peace of Westphalia; the latter had endeavoured to exclude the other from the papacy, and with that intent had caused the young king, then only seventeen years of age, to write a letter to Rome injurious to the interests of Chigi. Chigi, who had been elected notwithstanding, was the more inclined to favour the Spanish party just at the time, when, owing to the large amount of church patronage at the disposal of the Spanish government in Italy, that party was predominant in the Curia. It was an additional grievance to Rome when Mazarin concluded the Peace of the Pyrenees with Spain, without consulting the Roman see; and thus seriously damaged the position of the papacy in Europe, by depriving it of the influence it had hitherto exercised in politics. On the whole Louis came off victorious in this dispute.

More serious, and more fruitful of consequences, was the breach which followed between Louis and Innocent XI. It was curious that at that time Louis's two most determined and dangerous opponents should have been the men who stood, the one at the head of the Catholic and the other at the head of the Protestant world—Pope Innocent XI. and Prince William of Orange. Innocent deservedly enjoyed the reputation throughout Europe of a morally upright, pious, and moderate man, who fulfilled the duties of his high position with delicate conscientiousness. Protestants as well as Catholics honoured in him a pattern of priestly virtue; so much so that the French bishops, at the very time when the dispute between Innocent and the king was at its height, and they themselves had taken the part of the latter, declared, in a hortatory address to the Protestants of the country, that now, whilst the church was ruled by a pope who was an example of holiness before the eyes of the whole world, was the propitious moment for them to endeavour to return to unity. Innocent threw himself energetically upon the side of the emperor, who was just then engaged in a severe struggle with the Turks for the liberation of Hungary; in his eyes Louis appeared as the chief disturber of the peace of Europe at a time when all the Christian powers ought to have made common cause against the hereditary foe in the East. He was also annoyed that Louis should monopolise for himself the mastery over the clergy and over ecclesiastical affairs in France. The king, however, bitterly resented the fact that he, the champion of Christendom, who had turned every war to the profit of the church, should meet upon all sides with opposition from the pope—the same pope, too who but a few years before, at the outset of the quarrel in 1678, had borne witness that the great services rendered by Louis, and the reputation he had won in the cause of the Catholic Church, had placed him upon a level with the most glorious of his predecessors. Moreover he could not forget that his watchful zeal for church orthodoxy, and for the extirpation of Jansenism, for which the possession of his royal prerogative was indispensable, was just what had stirred the resentment of the pope against him. The revocation of the Edict of Nantes appeared likely to prove a means of reconciliation between the pope and the king, for Innocent professed himself highly delighted at the step, commended it in a speech to the cardinals, and was not stingy of his praises. But the pope did not think proper to tolerate the Gallican Declaration of 1682, and thirty episcopal sees remained vacant in consequence; Innocent refusing to ratify the nominations to them. Steps were thereupon taken in Paris to induce the pope to summon a general council. This threatened to create a situation which might have become dangerous and unpleasant for Louis. A trustworthy politician, residing at that time in Paris, asserts that this circumstance contributed to bring about the new attack on Germany, and the outbreak of an eight years' war which proved very disastrous for both countries, but of which the true motive has always remained a mystery. He says that Louvois had persuaded the king of the necessity of terrifying the pope into submission, and a desire for reconciliation, by the prospect of a great European war, and of the danger which would consequently accrue to the States of the Church. The object was not attained. It may account, however, for the war having been prosecuted in Germany by the French generals in the name of religion. Under this pretext churches and schools were wrested from the Protestants, and the Catholic counter-reformation everywhere enforced in the Palatinate.

None of his predecessors, certainly no monarch, had possessed such an amount of sovereign power as Louis had inherited. This he was constantly occupied in increasing. When he assumed the government the monarchy was the most compact and the most richly provided with money of any in existence. He knew that the nation expected him to perform deeds of which it might be proud. He was strongly imbued with the wish to put the means which he had in his hand to a use proportioned to the aspirations, and worthy of the greatness, of France. Germany and the Netherlands were the first arenas in which he tried his skill. It is important to examine into the views which he himself held with regard to his relations with the German Empire. He has himself described them to us.

Louis had formed his own conception as to the position which he occupied in relation to Germany and its empire. Our dynasty, he says, formerly reigned over France, the Netherlands, Germany, Italy, and the greater part of Spain; Charles the Great assumed in consequence the title of emperor. His courage and the victories which he gained raised him to this eminence. For—says Louis, thinking of the then existing Carlovingian monarch of France—where these divine gifts of courage and success are to be found, they are tokens that God has made choice of a sovereign to whom the other powers must submit. It is evident that he regards the empire as a sovereignty established for the benefit of the princes of his own house. The Capetians, in his eyes, are identical with the Carlovingians. The present emperors do not, he considers, merit that high-sounding title, being in reality no more than the subordinate and dependent captains-general of a German Republic of recent date. He is offended that at the papal and other courts the imperial ambassador takes precedence of the French ambassador. He thinks that there ought always to be in existence a genuine empire which, like the Roman and Carlovingian empires of old, should be the secular head of Christendom; and this dignity properly belongs to himself as the only true descendant of Charles and the only rightful representative of the Carlovingian house, and because he alone has sufficient power to uphold the empire, and to assert the authority which befits it.

This is true to a certain extent, but the assertion about the Carlovingian inheritance was a fiction dressed up to suit the requirements of the royal diplomacy. Hugh Capet was not of Carlovingian, but of Saxon origin. He had been elected through the interference of his friend Adalbert, Archbishop of Rheims, in open contempt of the right of inheritance, and by setting aside the lawful heir. Charles the Great, on the contrary, was by birth and breeding a German, wore the German costume, lived chiefly in Germany, held most of his public assemblies there, and during his long reign went only once to Paris, the royal residence of the Merovingians. A successor to Charles, therefore, if to be found at all, could only be sought for in Germany.

This subject was connected in Louis's mind with a double hope and a double claim. If he could succeed, whether by force of arms or through his right of succession to a part of Spain, in enlarging and transforming his kingdom of France into a great Carlovingian power, the imperial crown would devolve upon him as a matter of course. He was sure of the votes of the spiritual electors, and of the two Wittelsbach votes in the Palatinate and in Bavaria; the remaining two would easily be secured by money or other means. Once elected, he would abolish the electoral system and re-establish hereditary succession, of which the Germans had foolishly allowed themselves to be deprived. The pope would simply accept the accomplished fact, or, acting upon the old theory still maintained in Rome of the pope's right to transfer the imperial dignity, would declare that he had deprived the Germans of the imperial title, half of them being heretical, to bestow it upon the French who were wholly Catholic. In Louis's able hands the international significance of the imperial dignity, which had now sunk into abeyance, would be revived; Paris with Versailles would become a second Rome, the centre of the Western world; the empire by degrees be centralised; and Louis would show the world what strength was latent in the idea of a supreme head and advocate over Christendom.

Louis asserts in his memoranda, that, had it not been for the dissensions of the royal family, France would long before have become the mistress of the world. The royal family was now united, all its princes as submissive to him as he could possibly desire. To the nation, above all to the clergy, and to the nobility who desired distinctions and titles, the transference of the empire would have been exceedingly welcome. To set aside once for all the anomaly by which the Holy Roman Empire was committed to the keeping, no longer of the foremost and most capable nation of the universe, nor of the eldest son of the church, but of a foreign race of recent origin, would in French eyes be the most glorious act which the king could accomplish. In the French empire of the Bourbons would be seen the exact counterpart of German history. Whereas the Germans had looked on, partly submissive and partly co-operating, whilst their kingdom was being ruined and the empire shorn of its privileges, the royal power and the imperial dignity would be protected and strengthened in the hands of the French; and the empire, in particular, would become in reality all that the Germans had asserted it to be in theory, but had practically suffered to be destroyed or forfeited. Louis de Bourbon as emperor would understand how to give effect to the image of the two swords, how to pose as the 'living law upon earth,' the secular head of Christendom and 'leader of kings'—as Alphonso of Naples termed the emperor—side by side with the spiritual head.

Louis had not originated his own views with regard to the empire and to the rights of the French crown over Germany; they had been held long before by both statesmen and jurists. As early as 1632, under Richelieu's government, De Cassan, a councillor of the tribunal of Béziers, had written a book to prove that the Kings of France, as the descendants of Charles and of the Frankish princes who had taken possession of Gaul, had the right of jurisdiction over Germany. Again, in 1662, a state paper drawn up by the parliamentary councillor Aubéry had appeared in Paris, which developed the same thought, founded on the legal maxim of the Salic Law, that territories obtained or conquered by the French Kings were acquired for the state, the continuity of which remained unbroken and its rights inalienable even when another dynasty arose.

The book excited great attention; but even in Germany we meet with similar views, although not founded perhaps upon such unhistorical assumptions. The great universal historian Herman Conring, after Leibnitz the most versatile and gifted scholar of Germany, longed for an empire under a new Charles the Great—who could be none other than Louis—as being, he said, the least of all evils. The pension granted to him by Colbert is supposed to have had to do with his writing in that strain, but to me his private letters appear to prove that, with the dread of Turkish ascendency still prevalent, he held a strong empire to be necessary for the protection of Christendom, and saw in Louis the only monarch capable of giving it practical shape.

The Treaties of Westphalia and the Pyrenees placed France in an extremely favourable situation. Louis quickly discovered that he had only to stretch out his hand to become more powerful in Germany than the emperor. The Electors of the Rhine had decidedly more to fear from him than from the emperor. The other princes were apprehensive lest by siding with the latter they might forfeit the advantages guaranteed to them at the time of the peace by France and Sweden; the more so, because Sweden was firmly united with France through common interest as well as through the influence of French gold. A German policy could not, properly, be said to exist. In Vienna the welfare of the state was constantly made subordinate to dynastic advantage. There was a Catholic and Protestant, a Saxon and a Bavarian policy; a genuine German policy had yet to arise. Louis himself at a later period did his best towards it—at least towards preparing the way for it.

It soon, then, became apparent that Louis nad broken with the policy of his grandfather and of the two cardinals.

They had secured the power and greatness of France, and placed her in the foremost rank on the Continent, by countenancing the Protestant cause in Germany and the Netherlands, and by helping to break down the threatening power of the Habsburgs. Cromwell had recently turned the policy of England in the direction of diplomatic interference in behalf of Protestantism, with such success that even Mazarin had showed himself compliant in the matter of the Waldenses. Where was now the power that could protect the Catholics? Spain was not in a position to defend even herself; the countries ruled by the Emperor Leopold were suffering heavily from the results of the long war and of emigration; he himself was in continual want of money and scarcely able to carry on the war against the Turks. Louis appeared to himself to be called upon to fill the void. He had been so frequently told, and was so firmly convinced, that this mission, the most exalted possible for a Christian ruler, devolved upon him by divine appointment, that it became an essential part of this belief that he should not consider himself bound by international treaties if they happened to form an obstacle in his appointed path. He considered it his office to impose treaties upon others, but not particularly incumbent upon him to maintain them conscientiously himself; that was not, he considered, to be expected, since promises, when they became inconvenient, ought not to be taken more literally than expressions of courtesy. This feature of his political system, with its attendant results, inspired more and more suspicion, and no accusation was more frequently or bitterly levelled against him throughout Europe than that of untrustworthiness and recklessness in breaking his promises.

The foundation and aim of his policy was this: that his house should assume the position and acquire the supremacy which the house of Habsburg had held for 130 years. That family had continued throughout that period to be the fighting arm of the Roman Church; by its help and under its shelter the reaction had set in which had led to the return of millions of perverted souls to the church. But since 1648 this supremacy had been broken, and no revival of it would be possible if Louis felt himself called upon to assume the diminished yet still indispensable dignity and responsibility of leader and protector of the Catholic states; to carry forward with the weight of his powerful arm the work of reaction or counter-reformation; and thus to follow the bright example left by the German house of Habsburg. Two things he considered were needful to him for this purpose: the imperial crown upon which Henry IV., and later, Mazarin, had already cast covetous glances, and an addition of territory from the Spanish inheritance. With a view to both of these objects, Protestant alliances were, at least for a time, indispensable to him, and so also was the goodwill or at any rate the peaceful attitude of Protestant states and princes. He thus found himself in a difficult position: on the one hand, he was desirous and determined to offer to the hierarchy by his actions some security that he was called and was worthy to be the successor of Philip II. and Ferdinand II., and therefore under the necessity of accomplishing a great work of conversion; on the other hand, he was hampered by the policy of religious toleration by which his grandfather and the two cardinals had made France great and strong. The most important point for him was to choose the right moment for showing himself to the world in his true character when, at the risk of being obliged to throw over his Protestant allies, he might enter upon the path of the Valois, of Ferdinand, and of Philip. He waited twenty-four years before he made the decisive step which left no further room for doubt.

It may be said that, in a certain sense, all the wars in which Louis engaged were religious wars, or at least that religion had to do with them—if it was not the first and most immediate motive—just as the great wars before his time, when not simply dynastic, most frequently sprang from a combination of political with religious causes. The Thirty Years' War was essentially a religious war, however much the fact may have been disputed, and remained so to the end, however much political interests and questions of might and right became implicated in it. The Peace of Westphalia, the repudiation of it by the papacy, and the questions upon which the earlier attempts at negotiation had failed, leave no doubt upon this point. For only after the heavy blows of 1647 and 1648 had fallen, and constant disaster pursued the imperial arms—only, indeed, when Austria was utterly exhausted—did the emperor give in to that which was inevitable, and consent to admit the principle of the equal rights of both churches, for the empire, though not for his hereditary dominions, and resolve to accept the consequences which must ensue.

But again, after the Peace of Westphalia, and even after the beginning of the eighteenth century, religious interests were mixed up with the question of European supremacy in every war that broke out. A Catholic monarch could only take upon himself and maintain the lead amongst the Catholic nations and states by making himself at the same time the advocate of Catholic interests and ecclesiastical claims ; a Protestant state could only aspire to leadership by putting itself forward as the guardian of Protestantism throughout Europe after the pattern of Gustavus Adolphus or Cromwell. If Louis's object were to supplant the house of Habsburg he must equal if not excel it in his zeal for the church. And, indeed, the majority of the people of France expected nothing less from him. France especially had been the theatre of bloody religious struggles. In the thirteenth century the Albigensian war, and in the sixteenth the struggle between the Huguenots and the League, were cases in which the religious question was paramount and other interests had been forced to conceal themselves under the mask of piety. The sentiments of the French which had instigated those wars had not fundamentally altered in Louis's time. The peace of the Edict of Nantes was a mere truce. The Peace of Westphalia had traced boundary lines and thrown up bulwarks that were needful for the security of the German peoples against religious coercion, but they were insufficient, as was soon apparent. It was well-nigh impossible that Louis or any of his coreligionists should acknowledge the right of liberty of conscience. From first to last the lesson had been impressed upon him that the monarch's duty was, not to tolerate error, but to use force if needful in driving back schismatics into the fold of the church. When his victories had brought new subjects under his rule, when his authority was sufficiently assured to permit him to dictate treaties and to impose conditions upon independent states, and to busy himself even beyond the frontier of France about seeking the advantage and extension of the church, and weakening and diminishing the number of the heretics, then any forbearance shown to the holders of other beliefs, or toleration of their rights, would seem like a neglect of the highest duties, and a damning proof of indifferentism. Consequently all the wars which Louis undertook, even those which he waged against Spain and the emperor, appeared to him to rest upon religious motives, a source from which he drew perfect justification for them. For he was convinced that Providence had raised him up to be in his time the true guardian and champion of the church; and, in order to spread the faith, he must enlarge his own kingdom and widen the limits of his power.

In his own day Louis was constantly accused of aiming at universal monarchy. The Spaniards were the first to raise the cry against him, for the sake of inducing other states to join in a coalition with them. This accusation must be considerably modified; Frederick the Great was not mistaken in declaring the project of a French universal monarchy to be a fiction, a bugbear invented to terrify the simple and to serve the designs of the Habsburgs. The period previous to the publication of the will of Charles II., and that which followed after the year 1700, must be taken separately. During the former period it had been Louis's aim to enlarge and fortify the boundary of France by the acquisition of the Spanish Netherlands, including a portion of the Dutch Republic, besides extending his frontier towards Germany as far as the Rhine. He contemplated planting his foot in Italy by means of an exchange of territory or through the acquisition by force of arms of Savoy and Piedmont, as well as of Milan, then still Spanish. It may appear strange that he never seriously undertook to obtain the concession of the country over which he had the most justifiable claims, viz. Navarre; he did indeed formulate his claims, but there the matter remained. France was to become the first power in Europe both on land and sea; the Mediterranean was to be turned into a French lake; and all this was to be crowned by the imperial dignity, which, if the Emperor Leopold had died sooner, before the whole of Central Europe had armed itself against Louis, the latter would certainly not have allowed to escape him. Such an empire as this would have made itself felt energetically in the internal affairs of Germany. The same fate—brought about of course more cautiously and by carefully measured steps—would attend the Protestant churches of Germany as had overtaken their brethren in France. England, before the year 1688, was considered by Louis to be safe and to require no check from him, the two Stuarts, Charles and James, being in his pay, and unable without his assistance to venture upon any considerable undertaking. He had promised that he would give substantial assistance, in men and money, to the designs of the two brothers for the catholicising of England, and he kept his word. England, Catholic and absolutist, or, if fortune were less favourable, distracted by ecclesiastical and political schisms, would have become still more dependent upon France than it had been at any time under the Stuarts.

The fall of James II. in England, the elevation of William of Orange, the great coalition against France—these severe blows annihilated many of his hopes; but he was not thereby shaken in his central idea of a French empire over the Continent; the prospect still remained to him almost certain of a great addition of territory and power whenever the event, now imminent, of the vacancy of the Spanish throne should occur.

The will of Charles II. summoned the grandson of Louis to assume the undivided possession of the Spanish Kingdom. At once the hopes which Louis had cherished for forty years of adding Belgium and Italy to France out of the Spanish inheritance, fell to the ground. Henceforth he consoled himself with the expectation that France, and Spain rejuvenated by his grandson, would, as two strictly allied kingdoms, maintain the supremacy over Southern Europe together with the mastery of the Mediterranean Sea—a position which would have opened a glorious future to the two Bourbon houses as the protectors of Southern Christendom against Osmanli oppression, and the pirates of Barbary. Things turned out otherwise!

Let us now examine more closely into Louis's policy. The experience of Piedmont and Switzerland showed that he well understood how to despoil the smaller neighbouring states and make them serviceable to his ends. Both these countries, in the prolonged struggle between the Habsburgs and France, had gathered strength by the prudent yet bold assertion of their independence. The Swiss confederation in particular had extended and fortified its frontier, and had been fortunate in preserving it intact, although its territory lay between the contending powers. Nevertheless the constant renewal of military capitulations and treaties of alliance (the last in 1663) by which the king was kept supplied with large bands of mercenaries, to such an extent that 32,000 Swiss were at one time serving under his standard, formed a pretext upon his part for bringing the country into a state of galling dependence upon France. Subsidies and pensions continually distributed, and forming a permanent revenue to the secret agents and paid creatures of Louis, had this result that they were to be found in all the councils of the cantons, and that his envoys were enabled to dictate measures to the confederates in a manner which made them sensible that the federation was dependent upon the offensive and defensive alliance of France. Even in the internal affairs of the federation he contrived to maintain a thinly veiled supremacy. The taking of Franche-Comté and Strasburg and the erection of the fortress of Hüningen before the gate of Basle completed Switzerland's dependence. His designs upon Geneva, which he thought to betray into the same fate as Strasburg, did indeed fail, thanks to the energetic interference of the neighbouring cantons; nor did he succeed as he hoped in procuring Neuchatel for the Prince of Conti; the Swiss decided in favour of the King of Prussia. But again, shortly before his death, Louis formed a tie which, had he lived, might easily have brought about the ruin of the free state. He concluded a secret treaty with those Catholic cantons that had been embittered by their defeat in the religious war of 1712, promising the assistance of France in every dispute with the reformed cantons, and specifying even the details of the advance to be made by the French army into Switzerland.

If money, diplomatic skill, and intimidation were the means by which he triumphed over the confederates, it was, in Savoy-Piedmont, rather by the sharpness of the sword and by a treatment similar to the wasting of the Palatinate that he aimed at making both prince and country the instruments of his purpose. Victor Amadeus II. had been reduced almost to the position of a French provincial governor in his own dominions, when the marriage of his two daughters with Louis's grandsons and the outbreak of the War of Succession raised him again to a more independent position, and the Treaty of Utrecht soon afterwards obtained for him, in exchange for his claims upon a portion of the Spanish inheritance, a large increase of power and territory, together with the title of King.

The Turkish Empire in the year 1661 had already passed the zenith of its power and begun to decline. France was the State towards which the Porte naturally turned after abandoning its old spirit of defiance; enmity towards the emperor formed a common bond between the two powers; the French ambassador obtained advantages for the Catholic subjects of the Porte, firmans for the security of the French flag against the pirate states, protective rights over the holy places belonging to the Latins in Jerusalem—rights which had hitherto belonged to the emperor. But the loss of reputation and honour which the king suffered by this friendly attitude towards the enemies of Christendom was not outweighed by these advantages.

In Poland some of the most influential nobles were in his pay; twice he attempted to obtain the election of a prince of his house to the throne, so that he might secure the alliance of this power, and thus be enabled to threaten the empire in the rear. A majority of the votes, secured by large sums of money, had already declared for the Prince de Conti, when a power, which now first began to equip itself for interference with the affairs of Europe, came forward to oppose him. This was Russia, under Peter the Great. Conti was thrown over and the Elector of Saxony was chosen. Louis's influence in Warsaw, however, remained always great and often decisive, and served him at times to reduce even Brandenburg to submission.

Louis was exceedingly skilful in the art of paralysing his opponents by raising up enemies in their rear. Thus he rendered the Elector of Brandenburg powerless by inducing Sweden to declare war against him. He fomented discontent in Hungary in order to weaken the emperor, and supported the rebels with money and advice. Portugal served his purpose as a check upon Spain, in humbling her, and in keeping her forces occupied on the Portuguese frontier. At the Treaty of the Pyrenees Mazarin had ignored the interests of Portugal and had thereby roused in Madrid fresh hopes of reconquest. But Louis soon renewed friendly relations with King Alphonso, concluded an alliance with him, and sent troops to his aid. Yet the doom which awaited his ambitious projects, in consequence of the acts of 1685 and 1688, was felt even here. Portugal needed the protection of a naval power; England, through the Methuen Treaty, succeeded to the position which Louis, after the battle of La Hogue, could no longer maintain, and in the War of the Spanish Succession Portugal was ranged upon the side of the opponents of the French King.

In England Charles II. was seated upon the throne which he had regained, but his position was rendered uncomfortable by his dependence upon Parliament. Convinced that in England, so long as it remained Protestant, unlimited monarchy such as he aspired to was impossible, he deceived himself with the idea of imposing Catholicism upon his subjects combined with a despotic government. A double revolution of the sort could only be undertaken with the aid of his cousin Louis both in men and money. The secret treaty concluded through the mediation of Charles's sister, Henrietta, Duchess of Orleans, at Dover, in 1670, arranged that upon the receipt of four million livres Charles should declare himself a Catholic and should take part in the war which Louis was preparing to carry on against the Netherlands. In the event of the change of religion causing any disturbance the descent of a French army upon England was promised. However, nothing of all this came to pass; for Charles soon perceived that as a national measure the change of religion was impracticable, and as a personal step it would cost him his crown. In Louis's eyes the return of England to Catholicism, with the corresponding political transformation, was merely a question of time, as he knew that the Duke of York, already a Catholic, would take the work in hand as soon as he ascended the throne, and that he, the powerful neighbour, would be called upon to play an important part in it.

Upon the pretext of a claim which had devolved upon him through his Spanish wife, Louis in 1667 seized upon the Burgundian frontier and thus occasioned the formation of the first coalition against him. The triple alliance between England, Holland, and Sweden, his own former friends and allies, was a combination which either Richelieu or Mazarin would assuredly have found means to prevent. Still, the acquisition of such towns as Lille, Courtray, Douai, and Tournay was of incalculable value, and this was secured to him by the Peace of Aix la Chapelle.

Four year later Louis entered upon a war which eventually led him much further than he wished or expected, and revealed to watchful politicians a glimpse into the secret designs of his policy. Suddenly, and without assigning reason, he descended upon the Dutch Republic, having first with consummate diplomatic skill contrived to isolate it entirely. This was not, as has often been said, an act of revenge and of warlike restlessness. He detested the republic which, founded upon a revolt from king and church, had rapidly risen to a marvellous pitch of prosperity, to the position of the first naval and commercial power of Europe, and the guardianship of intellectual freedom. Numerous publications, which would never have been allowed to appear in France, found their way from thence over the border.

Hitherto the most useful ally of France, the Dutch Republic had yet been the stronghold of Protestantism on the Continent, and a school and intellectual arsenal for Louis's heretical subjects. Its annihilation would have been hailed throughout Europe as a brilliant triumph for the church. The overthrow of Holland was to have been the preliminary step to the change on the other side of the Channel, which with Louis's help was to transform England from a Protestant and parliamentary state into a Catholic and absolute monarchy. An arrangement had been made with Charles II. The Netherlands were to be partitioned between France and England; the former naturally appropriating far the larger share. This accomplished, the Spanish or Belgian provinces would all the more surely fall into the power of the French monarch. The plan was frustrated through the noble self-sacrificing resistance of Holland under William of Orange.

The year 1685 was an important turning point in the political plans of Louis. By revoking the Edict of Nantes and by decreeing the complete extirpation of the Protestant Church in France, he made the plainest avowal to every Protestant nation and cabinet of his intention to use his power as opportunity occurred, even beyond the French border, to injure their religion and to serve his own church.

In proclaiming the revocation of the Edict of Nantes Louis declared that from henceforth no dissenters from the faith were to be tolerated in France, but that all must belong to the king's church. His idea of the unity of the faith to be brought about by him was as much political as religious, for to his mind religious and political interests were inseparably united. His predecessors like himself had laboured to establish the unity of the royal power upon a solid foundation; he had himself thoroughly broken the power of the French parliament as a political body, leaving to it only that of a judicial tribunal; he had the Catholic clergy completely in hand; he disposed freely of persons and property; of immunities there was no question; his warrants of imprisonment and decrees of banishment, frequently with no reason given, struck priest and layman alike. The Protestants therefore, with their consistories and synods, presented a sharp contrast and were an eye-sore, a republican discord in the great monarchical harmony, however peaceably and humbly they might demean themselves. The *non licet esse eos*, which the Christians of the second and third centuries had so often heard from the Romans, was at bottom the opinion of the French Catholics also. Every system of ecclesiastical or secular despotism must, by an internal law of its nature, ceaselessly strive to widen the sphere of its power, and to overthrow remaining barriers. And Louis, too, was accustomed in spiritual matters to find all things bend before him without breaking; he had been often assured that a summons or a decree from him would suffice in a single day to turn thousands of heretics into good Catholics. The revocation of the edict was after all only the conclusion, long and anxiously expected by a portion of both clergy and laity, of a series of preparatory measures which had been commenced in the very first years of his reign.

It was the true despotic instinct, also, that prompted him to reject the plans for negotiation and reconciliation between the two churches suggested by eminent men like Leibnitz, Bossuet, Molanus, Bishop Rojas de Spinola, and others, and to condemn them as a perversion of principle; although Richelieu, whom he otherwise esteemed so highly, had determined upon seeking to restore unity in this way, by concession, and by the abolition of ecclesiastical abuses. The idea of concession even in things not touching the substance of dogma was repulsive to Louis. In his eyes it contained a dangerous germ, as there would remain room for the converted to suppose that the authority of church and king had gone too far in the arbitrary enforcement of these things, and had therefore erred. Herein he was more orthodox than his court theologian Bossuet, upon whom otherwise in questions of doctrine and church discipline he bestowed implicit confidence, and he was wholly in accord with the popes who placed uniformity in church ritual, at all events in the West, above all other considerations. It had been Bossuet's wish to concede to the Protestants the reception of the cup at the Lord's supper. Louis and his ministers would hear of no such proposals; neither could he endure that any of his subjects should believe their religion to be better than the king's, and should cherish sympathy for foreign co-religionists in defiance of the antipathy felt for them by the king. No part, therefore, of their church life should be left to the converts which might warrant their retaining any religious peculiarity.

The chain of circumstances which followed the fatal 22nd of October, 1685, holds together link by link, leading up to the final annihilation of the lofty project of a European hegemony, or rather of an autocratic monarchy. At the Peace of Nimeguen, 1679, the power of Louis stood at its greatest height; a military promenade had put him in possession of Franche-Comté, and a large part of the Spanish Netherlands, with sixteen fortresses, besides Freiburg in Breisgau which had been ceded to him. Directly afterwards Germany, wanting in energy or corrupted by bribery, permitted the 'Chambres de Réunion' to carry on their work; Strasburg and Casale were besieged in 1681, Luxemburg seized in 1684, the Palatinate twice desolated. For the sake of proving to the world that oppression and persecution of aliens from the faith were part of his mission, he offered troops to the Duke of Savoy to assist in the persecution of the Waldenses, whom Cromwell and Mazarin had formerly protected, and ordered Catinat to organise a massacre of these harmless inhabitants of the Piedmontese valleys. Meanwhile his Protestant subjects who had emigrated and were scattered through other Protestant countries, carried with them the news of the dragonades, rousing fear and disgust everywhere. Holland and England were filled with wild excitement, whilst Louis's most faithful, devoted ally, James II., relying upon the powerful arm of his French cousin, blindly advanced from one deed of violence to another, and awoke to the idea that with the help of Louis he might imitate the deeds of Louis. Thereupon James's son-in-law, William of Orange, was invited to come to the assistance of the imperilled religion and constitution of England. The French King committed one of his most fatal mistakes; instead of throwing his army upon Holland, he sent it into the Palatinate. William was consequently able to take his troops over to England, a North-German army was marched into the places vacated by them, and an enterprise succeeded, the failure of which would have caused the history of the world to take another direction. James, determined that no parliament should compel him to renounce his despotic claims, saw himself at once forsaken by the nation, and fled to France. In vain Louis, for the sake of upholding him and the principles that were at stake, sent an army to Ireland; the cause of the two kings was lost at the battle of the Boyne, and through the naval victory obtained by the English and Dutch fleets over the French at La Hogue, England won the mastery of the seas which she has ever since retained. Thus recoiled upon himself the words which Louis had uttered in the intoxication of his first successes, that 'battles, won by divine decree, revealed the heavenly counsels as to who should bear rule and possess the land.' His star was rapidly on the wane. When, after a few years, the utter exhaustion of France obliged him to seek for peace, he was only able to purchase it at Ryswick in 1697 by a series of humiliating concessions and renunciations. Yet official voices in France contrived to extol even this peace as a triumph obtained by the king. Germany, divided and distracted, was vanquished; Alsace and Strasburg remained in the possession of the French; and an article in the treaty stipulated for the re-introduction of the Catholic religion into the districts upon the left bank of the Rhine. 'We receive what we have earned,' was the remark of Leibnitz at the time. But Louis gained the credit of having once again proved himself, even at the cost of his own advantage, the support and benefactor of the church.

His mission had by this time become more than ever a political necessity, and the indispensable means of maintaining his power. For now the decision of a question which had formed the end and aim of his whole life, and entered into all the calculations of his policy, was imminent. When the Spanish succession should be declared, the conviction must prevail in Rome as well as in Madrid that the welfare of religion and the aggrandisement of the church had been the supreme law of his conduct.

Before becoming king, Louis Philippe once remarked

that men, as soon as the crown is on their heads, are blindfolded. Louis XIV., as his writings prove, was an intelligent ruler, deliberate and clear-headed, who in many things saw correctly. Yet it cannot be denied that at critical moments of his career he acted blindly. The greatest benefactor to France and to the king would have been one who, with the authority of a prophet of old, could have confronted Louis in the year 1685 and have warned him in some such terms as these: 'Revoke not the Edict of Nantes! Thou wilt forge thereby the first link of an interminable chain of abominable oppression and violence; thou wilt make more hypocrites than believers; thou art compelling them to desecrate sacrilegiously the holy ordinances of the church; driving thousands of the most useful and conscientious citizens, of the most industrious subjects and artisans, out of the country; strengthening the hands of thine enemies present and future; and forfeiting the friendship of those princes and peoples who have hitherto been thine allies. Driven by thee into exile the men who were thy faithful subjects will gather round foreign hostile standards to fight against thee and the cause that thou representest. Out of the dragon's teeth of hypocrisy, lying, and dissimulation which thou art now sowing broadcast will spring up a faithless and hostile generation to thy successors and the church. It will overthrow the throne which thou hast thought to set up so high; it will persecute and lay waste the church which now presses into thy hands the weapons and implements of punishment against the sons of thy people.'

During the twenty years which elapsed between the day of the Revocation and the death of the king, many of the consequences indicated above came to maturity. Many were concealed from Louis or were disregarded. He moderated secretly some of his severest measures with a view to counteract in some degree the mischief brought about by the ruin or flight of so many families. But in their main points the laws remained in force which declared the Protestant religion to be dead and extinct in France, and denied existence as citizens to those who clung to it. Thus matters remained until sixty years after the death of Louis.

By the close of the century France no longer possessed either friends or allies. Fear, mistrust, or hatred were the sentiments which animated the neighbours and former allies of the king and of his people, when at length the long expected event, fraught with terrible consequences for Southern and Central Europe, came to pass.

The sickly life of the last of the Spanish Habsburgs had expired, and his will named the grandson of Louis as his heir; as King of Spain he was to enter into possession of the whole undivided empire, Naples and Sicily, Sardinia, Lombardy, the Catholic Netherlands, and the American possessions. For forty years had Louis looked forward to the opening of the great question of the Succession, and in all his dealings with the house of Habsburg, as well as with the naval powers, had kept it carefully before his eyes. Spain itself, a feeble and degraded monarchy, had been treated by him, now as an enemy, now as a vassal, and occasionally with a certain amount of consideration due to its value as a future prize. He had striven to secure not the whole, but a certain amount of the inheritance for France. His glance naturally turned, more especially at first, towards the Netherlands, but it was directed towards Italy as well. Thrice already he had concluded treaties of partition. First, in 1668, he had succeeded in a marvellous way in persuading his opponent, the Emperor Leopold, to enter into a treaty of the kind, and to suffer his only weapon to be wrested from him by his powerful rival, by giving his assent to the invalidity of the renunciation made by the Infanta, the wife of Louis. This treaty, which for a while tied the hands of the court of Vienna, inducing it to adopt a tortuous and evasive line of policy, was a few years later cancelled by the formation of a coalition against Louis. After the death of the Bavarian prince whom Charles II. had appointed as his universal heir, Louis had concluded a secret treaty with the naval powers, allotting Spain, with the colonies and the Netherlands, to the emperor, and Southern Italy to the king. The assent of the emperor had not been obtained. Meanwhile, in Spain it was recognised that the partition of the monarchy, which was regarded by all with abhorrence, could only be avoided by summoning a French prince to the throne. Pope Innocent XII., upon being consulted by Charles, had given the same recommendation, partly out of preference for the Bourbons, partly because it was thought in Rome that if Southern Italy became a French dependency, the introduction of Gallican principles would inevitably follow—an evil much to be deprecated. The court of Vienna caused this danger to be vividly represented to the pope, but had itself so far contributed towards its existence that Innocent recommended the selection of the grandson of Louis rather than of the Austrian Archduke. If the monarchy were to remain united under a French prince, whose government would be carried on by Spanish ministers and officials, then in all probability Spanish views and institutions would remain dominant.

Louis made up his mind to accept the will, thus resigning the hopes and plans which he had cherished hitherto, of making parts of various Spanish provinces serve for the enlargement of France, but satisfied because a second splendid crown would be acquired for the house of Bourbon. Once more a triumph after his own heart awaited him, when the Junta, which carried on the administration in Spain during the interregnum, with the two presidents of the High Councils of Aragon and Castile, besought him, 'the most Christian King,' to assume the direction of affairs in Spain, assuring him that he would be as implicitly obeyed there as in France. It was the last ray of sunshine which illuminated the evening of his life, darkening already to its close. For now he was hurried on into a twelve years' war, which, with the insufficient resources of a country weakened and exhausted by forty years of constant warfare, and without allies—excepting the King of Bavaria who was speedily subdued—against the combined powers of the emperor, the two naval powers, and other princes, brought France to the very brink of ruin. And now Louis, being burdened with the alliance of the Spaniards in their decay, found himself in the predicament of having to defend the countries appertaining to the Spanish crown. It was a cruel Nemesis that he, who in his first three wars had been the unjust aggressor and yet had carried them on with a series of splendid successes and in the end remained the victor, should now, in his fourth war, with the right on his side, suffer such fearful reverses and defeats, and in the end owe his deliverance to a change in the English cabinet brought about by a caprice of Queen Anne. But even now, at the critical moment which was to decide the conduct of England, he allowed himself in his zeal for the church, and perhaps through female influence (see p. 367), to be led, against the advice of his ministers and contrary to the terms of his treaty with William of Orange, into the disastrous mistake of recognising the son of James II. as the legitimate King of England. This he did at the moment when he was nevertheless most anxious to avoid the war which was impending upon the Spanish question. Resentment at his want of faith had the immediate effect of uniting the contending parties, and of causing England to throw her whole weight upon the side of the emperor and his son. Even after the peace, in the last six months of his life, Louis again sought to stir up a rebellion in England and supported the Pretender. And yet the repeated blows which had befallen him in consequence of the step he had taken, had brought him so low that he even offered to pay a million monthly to his enemies, to defray the expenses of dethroning his grandson.

The war of the Spanish Succession was the first since the Reformation which had nothing to do with religious interests and principles but was purely political and proceeded from the jealousy of states and the impatience of oppressive despotism. But in the personal judgment of Louis the consideration of the advantage of his church still had full weight, and, so far as was possible to him with very reduced power, he threw it into the scale in every international question.

History has pronounced its verdict upon Louis XIV. It has denied him the title of 'Great,' and thus has not ranked him with Alexander, or Charles the Great, or Frederick II. of Prussia. Real genius and the eagle eye of the born commander, such as Napoleon I. possessed, were denied to him. The educated portion of his people rightly speak of him as *le grand monarque*, but they only; for in the remembrance of the masses his name no longer holds a place either for praise or blame; according to the testimony of Count Gobineau scarcely a peasant could be found anywhere in France who cherished his memory. Nevertheless a monarch, whose influence upon the course of the world's history was so powerful that an epoch in the progress of civilisation has been called 'the age of Louis XIV.,' deserves to be spoken of as 'the great monarch.' He added a splendour and a charm to royalty—he may be said to have enriched the meaning of it. He was truly the first monarch since the times of the Romans whose life, in its nobler features, afforded a public example for the imitation of kings. It testified to the much-neglected truth that to govern requires persevering labour—that, by the highest law of the modern state, a king who would be worthy of the name must apply himself energetically to all departments of human enterprise, to science, to art, to education, as much as to politics and the material benefit of his people. In thus combining the qualities of a great administrator with those of a Mæcenas, Louis had no equal either on his own or any other throne. By extending the authority of the crown, and by the exercise of the autocratic principle of reserving every point for personal decision, he rendered the burden so excessive that his own successors, at best but moderately endowed as to powers of mind, inevitably succumbed under it. Even he, in his prime, was not equal to the self-imposed task, for it surpassed the average measure of human ability. By degrees the burden became too heavy for him. We see him for the last twenty-five years of his life, ill and weary, averse to business, yet, in the midst of disappointments and shipwrecked hopes, still toiling on in spite of weariness and disgust, such as he would have deemed impossible in his younger days. At the same time he experienced the aching void of a life surrounded by courtiers whose only studies were questions of etiquette and genealogy, and whose highest ambition was to carry the king's candle when he went to bed, or to hand him his night-shirt. The principle that the absence of all restraints is a continual danger to any human being and in the long run injurious to the moral condition of the soul, was by no means taken for granted in those days, and least of all was it to be looked for in a king into whose mind the contrary had been instilled by the precepts, example, and encouragement of the authority that he deemed the highest. Had he not governed absolutely he could not have kept the oath taken by him at his coronation. It is not therefore surprising if, according to Fénelon's description, he showed himself in later life hard, peremptory, and unsympathetic, always inclined to avoid facing the truth, preferring to take an optimist view of things and to flatter himself that they were as he wished them to be. In him the king ended by stifling the man originally capable of better things. Yet it must not be overlooked that his faults were only the outgrowth of royalty in the shape that the nation demanded, and for the sake of which it crippled itself by its own feverish efforts. There was, it seemed, a general conspiracy to spoil the king by every form of flattery; to lead him astray by false teaching or half-truths and by the habitual concealment of facts. With but rare exceptions, every one with whom the monarch came in contact, instructors and guardians, poets and orators, historians and theologians, were silent upon the immorality of his private life. As he once said of himself, no one was so open to flattery as he; and this all knew and took into account.

Death robbed him of his children, grand-children, and great grand-children; laid desolate his magnificent court, which had revelled in luxury and pleasure, and spared to him but one being whom he loved and trusted; he stood erect and solitary like an isolated tower in the midst of ruins. Vanquished, richer in shipwrecked hopes and disappointed plans than territories acquired or power increased, buffeted by external as well as internal blows of fortune, shaken in the belief in his own infallibility which he had cherished for years, he still remained the unflinching, dignified, unapproachable king who never betrayed a sign of weakness. Tortured by physical and moral suffering—for he was aware of the condition to which he had reduced his people—he sought and found comfort and peace in the thought that he was punished here in order that he might more surely find grace hereafter. This he once said, weeping, to Marshal Villars. Madame de Maintenon was on other occasions the sole witness of his frequent tears. The natural dignity and majesty, unaffected fortitude, and pious resignation, with which he prepared for death, and the calm resolution with which he made the necessary arrangements, have won the respect and admiration of men who have otherwise judged him severely. The Emperor Hadrian said that an emperor must die erect; Louis died standing upon the pedestal of majesty. It belonged to his vocation to show the world even in death the pattern of the real king. All the more undignified seemed the behaviour of the court: the expiring monarch was forsaken of all; hired hands closed his eyes; hirelings watched by the corpse. The nation, whose enthusiasm for him had long since been quenched in unutterable misery, breathed more freely as though a weight had been lifted from its heart.

Now if it be asked what effect has been produced by Louis upon posterity, and what was his share of responsibility in the Revolution which happened seventy-four years after his death, and in the course which it took, it might perhaps be said that Spain has better cause to honour and exalt the memory of Louis than France. He conferred a new dynasty upon Spain by giving to it his grandson, and thus drew that country into close and friendly connection with France, and gave that kingdom the opportunity of recovery from the abyss of misery and degradation into which it had been plunged by the policy of Philip II. and his successors. The Bourbons, Ferdinand VI. and Charles III., introduced better principles of administration, regulated the public finance which the Habsburgs had left in complete confusion, gave a lasting peace to the country after centuries of unprofitable and exhausting warfare, opened channels of communication by which fresh knowledge and wider views might be imported into the Peninsula from beyond the Pyrenees, and succeeded at last in welding together Aragon, Catalonia, and Valencia with Castile into one strong and united kingdom.

With regard to France itself, let us look first at the brighter side of Louis's administration. Without attempting to decide how much was due to Colbert and how much personally to Louis, the first part of his reign was in any case more fruitful of good and more brilliant than any period through which France had hitherto passed. A strong naval power was rapidly created, the trade of the country aroused and promoted, a network of highways and canals formed, and manufacturing companies called into existence under the patronage of government. The foundation of the state of Louisiana strengthened the position of France in North America, already rendered important by the possession of Canada, and shut in the English plantations upon three sides. The code of civil and criminal law, although still disfigured by barbarous harshness and cruel regulations, was a step in advance which at the time was much admired and elsewhere imitated. Many of Louis's enactments, although altered in form, have in spirit been perpetuated, and are still in force in spite of the Revolution. The skill and circumspection used by him in discovering and laying hold of every expedient for prosecuting his undertakings, and directing every lever to the right place, are worthy of admiration. He possessed, besides, the attractive talent of enhancing by well-chosen words the value of his gifts and favours.

But in contrast with these bright pages there are as regards France many dark leaves in the book of fate. Louis, in the latter part of his life, regretted his extravagant outlay upon buildings, as well as upon his unjust wars. That in autocratic wilfulness he should have squandered the national wealth which he had in the first instance helped to amass, and that he should now leave a burden of debt to his successors and an impoverished country, grieved him indeed; yet he never thought of compensating even private individuals for his private debts, and for the restitution owing to the country he relied upon the mercy of God. The spoliation of his Protestant subjects, whose wealth had flowed into his treasury, he seems to have considered even on his deathbed as perfectly justified by the piety of the motive.

Before the outbreak of the last war, all classes in France with the exception of the clergy were exhausted and impoverished by various arts of extortion which financial acuteness alone could contrive and practise. Fénelon declared that every one must now live on the king's bounty, since the wealth of the country had utterly disappeared. Such a condition of things could only be possible where the revenues of the country and of the ruler were not separate. Louis was in his own opinion the sole proprietor of all France, and justified in turning the screw of taxation to any amount, and he had gradually increased the number of taxes and dues payable to the state by the towns to the number of 10,000. With a debt of

2,000,000,000 the population had decreased by several millions, and in the year 1700 was reduced to 19,000,000. The remnants of the army had degenerated into robber bands. Famine followed upon famine. Despotism had found a limit in the failure of funds, and Louis, like other tyrants, was fated to learn by experience that even despotism might be powerless to carry out real reforms or to reorganise a kingdom in decay; that reforms, in fact, are only possible with the help of vigorous institutions and energetic men. But France possessed neither the one nor the other. Out of consideration, besides, for the aged king, and to spare him additional sorrow, much was kept secret. Of his later ministers, at best but indifferent men of business, and by no means equal to Lionne, Colbert, or Louvois, none was capable of taking a comprehensive view of affairs; it was felt more and more that the pilot was wanting in the ship of the state. The system of centralisation, embracing every act and enterprise of social life, had accustomed and indeed compelled every one to expect and demand everything from the government; all spirit of enterprise and self-reliance had been crushed, and the government itself stood helpless and powerless before the magnitude of the evil.

The nobles, ruined by the extravagant outlay which Louis exacted from them at Versailles, had been reduced to the dependent position of the king's pensioners, and of mere servants in the palace; yet they retained numerous privileges, irritating and burdensome to the people, which at a later time were the cause of their ruin.

To the French Church, which the king had so highly esteemed and so carefully cherished, governing and administering her affairs with the best intentions, he bequeathed as a legacy that apple of discord, the bull *Unigenitus* and the coercive means for its enforcement. By this the very vitals of the Gallican Church were poisoned; a lasting breach made between the clergy and laity; endless conflict stirred up between the bishops and parliaments, and between the latter and the cabinet; corruption and the germs of dissolution introduced into those ecclesiastical institutions which had been heretofore an ornament to the church. The system of coercion and repression exercised henceforth by and over the clergy, estranged them more and more from serious studies, causing them to shun knowledge, and reducing them to a state of intellectual impotence which rendered them utterly incapable of entering the lists in the literary contests provoked by the powerful and aggressive adversaries of religion which arose in the secular world.

The parliaments had been embittered by the insult lately put upon them by the king in forcing upon them the legitimisation of his bastard children. They were ambitious at the same time to raise themselves out of insignificance. A welcome opportunity presented itself in the terms of Louis's will, which they hastened to cancel immediately after his death. The king had reserved for his nephew the subordinate position of a member in the council of regency; the parliament of Paris proclaimed him sole regent with unlimited powers.

The unhealthy condition of the body politic was aggravated by the superabundance of officials. Louis, being in pressing need of money, created a number of offices and posts, for the most part superfluous, with the intention of selling them afresh upon each succeeding vacancy. The system was extended even into the villages, where the municipal posts, which had been elective hitherto, were henceforth put up for sale, thus stifling any impulse of self-government or public spirit which yet remained amongst the people. The traffic in these posts corresponded to the sale of public offices. The sale of patents of nobility, introduced at the same time, was profitable for the moment, but diminished the number of tax-payers, and increased the seekers for office and the crowds of servile flatterers, who, encumbering the complicated machinery of the administration, made the task of controlling and directing it impossible. It is a proof of national vigour that France did not altogether sink into the condition of an Oriental state.

The refinement of manners, the elegant adornment of life, and the aristocratic polish which prevailed at Louis's court, have been frequently praised; a beneficent influence, it is supposed, spread from thence throughout the nation, displaying itself in gentler habits and a greater regard for the comforts of life. The truth of this supposition is somewhat impugned by the fact—of which there can be no doubt since the appearance of recent publications, combined with the revelations of Saint-Simon and the letters of the Duchess of Orleans and Madame de Maintenon—that beneath the outward show of etiquette the court was a hotbed of every vice. In a treatise of Fénelon's of the year 1714 there is the following passage: 'The present habits of the nation inspire every one with the strongest temptation to attach himself to the holders of power by every kind of base and cowardly action, and even by deeds of treachery and shame.' The state of things at court was more demoralising and injurious to the middle classes in France than the corruption which prevailed at the same time at the court of Charles II. in London was to English people, because the latter for the most part concerned themselves little about the court, whereas in France the worship for royalty caused everything that proceeded from the court and from the vicinity of the great king to be looked upon as a pattern worthy of imitation.

In this realm of all-powerful despotism people became accustomed to expect nothing from equity or from persevering industry, but everything from favour and intrigue. Noblemen like the Count of Grignan, Madame de Sévigné's son-in-law, had no scruple in sending their wives to court to petition for presents in money or a pension from the king. Even hypocrisy had become a fashionable means of advancement, ever since Louis—for the first time in 1684—had let it be known that his favour was proportioned to participation in the observances of religion. All the more rapid and complete was the reaction which took place under the Regency.

The question before referred to, as to whether Louis XIV. is responsible for the Revolution and for the overthrow of the monarchy, would accordingly be more correctly replaced by this one: Was it still possible for the rulers who followed him to avert the Revolution? In this form it must at once be answered in the affirmative. It would have been possible, and not even very difficult, supposing that instead of his nephew, grandson, and Louis XVI., three capable and judicious monarchs had successively held the reins of government. This, indeed, would have been a phenomenon such as very rarely occurs in the history of dynasties. And Louis was not free from blame for the errors and vices of his nephew, whom he had brought up in enforced idleness and forced into a distasteful marriage.

We may in conclusion examine into the testimony of two men who, differing in nationality, in condition, and sentiment, yet both ranking amongst the greatest intellects of the century, exercised the sharpest criticism over Louis's actions, and upon the whole condemned his policy. The first of these is Leibnitz, the faithful but unheeded Eckart of the Germans, who with such quick foresight and warm eloquence called upon his countrymen to rise in arms and make common cause against the Western foe. His opinion of the king, expressed in 1698, was as follows: 'This great prince is himself the greatest wonder of our age. Posterity will envy us as his contemporaries. I am not thinking of his achievements in politics and in war, but of what he has done for learning, which would in itself suffice to immortalise him. I need not describe him further, he is too unique and too well known. Good fortune and merit are combined in him in the most astonishing way. Having been victorious everywhere, and having won peace and prosperity for his own country, not only has he nothing to fear, but he is in a position to benefit all mankind. His good intentions equal his power, and philanthropy, to say nothing of the love of fame, leads him to care for the alleviation of human sorrow down to the smallest detail. This is as glorious as his military conquests.' Leibnitz then expresses the further wish that Heaven may continue to favour Louis and to allow Europe long to remain in enjoyment of the happy peace with which he has crowned his wonderful undertakings. The German certainly knew little of the internal condition of France, or he could not have spoken in 1698 of the prosperity created by the king. But we recognise the impression which the king's personality produced, even on people who had had to endure the worst from him.

The second witness is the Duc de Saint-Simon. Over and above their historical value, his memoirs are well known as the best and most trustworthy authority for the personal history of Louis and of his court, as well as of the most notable men and women around him. He is unrivalled in his delineations of character and descriptions of court life. The French, not incorrectly, style him the Tacitus of their literature. He is not free from errors, from fanciful exaggerations, from conjectures which he states as facts, and from class prejudices; hatred and gossip divert his pen into many unjust statements. Since his work became known it has contributed, not less than Voltaire's well-known work, towards the generally unfavourable opinion which has been formed of Louis throughout Europe. Within the last two years, however, a previously unpublished work of Saint-Simon's has appeared—a comparison between Henry IV. and Louis XIII. and XIV. In it he praises the goodness and piety of Louis XIV., his unfeigned love of justice and truth, his constancy and courage; he admires the genuine and simple magnanimity, the humble yet dignified resignation, with which Louis to the very end met the hard blows of misfortune in his latter years and the gradual approach of death, and he lays the blame of the king's misdoings upon Madame de Maintenon and the bastard Duke of Maine.

The people of Germany will never forget that the rich classical literature fostered, and partly called into existence, under the shadow of Louis's throne, furnished their fathers with an indispensable source of culture during a period of literary destitution in their own country. They followed a wise inspiration when they entered this school, and learnt to emulate the French and to appropriate their versatility of form, clearness of style, and purity of language. The treatment which Germany suffered at the hands of Louis, and the wasting of the German provinces, should not hinder us from recognising the bright side of his character and actions, and from taking into account extenuating circumstances for many of his misdeeds. The year 1870 has in no slight degree made the practice of this duty easier.

XII

THE MOST INFLUENTIAL WOMAN OF FRENCH HISTORY

Long ago it was observed that according to the testimony of history, women—born in France or transplanted thither—have, in a certain sense, succeeded in cancelling the effects of the Salic Law. In no other country have women interfered so extensively or so effectually with politics as in France. This is not surprising if we accept as true the estimate which Madame Emile de Girardin, the clever authoress of 'Letters from Paris' (1844), gives of her sex. Ambition, she says, is the very life of the women of France; to possess weight and influence is the object of their dreams. How could they avoid meddling with public affairs, and even aspiring to the direction of them, when in France it is the prerogative of the women, conceded to them by the men, to govern in the family and in society? When Buonaparte came to Paris, in 1795, he remarked that there, and there only, did women deserve to stand at the helm; the men thought of nothing but of them; lived by and for them; a woman must spend six months in Paris to know her rights and how to govern. That, moreover, was immediately after the Reign of Terror, when the court, in which, up to that time more than elsewhere, women had displayed their power of taking the lead, had been overthrown and dispersed, and had fled to foreign lands. French women understood better than others how to wield the weapons, whether good or bad, peculiar to their sex; and the ambition which can only be satisfied with real power, as contrasted with flattery and homage, was more frequently apparent amongst them.

The series of queens who, as widows or regents, held the reins of government, commences with the mother of Louis IX. Blanche of Castile, with masculine energy, managed to carry to a successful issue a seven years' struggle with the great vassals of the kingdom. Her memory, however, is tarnished by the part she took in the war against the Albigenses, and in establishing the Inquisition in France.

In the most distracted and comfortless period of French history, when the kingdom appeared to be on the brink of ruin, and, under the imbecile Charles VI., was torn by the dissensions of the princes and nobles, two female figures rise before us in as strong contrast with each other as light with darkness. One of these, the wife of the king, Isabella of Bavaria, is a shameless, voluptuous, mischievous woman, who attempted to rob her own son of the throne that was his by right, and to transfer her crown, with the hand of her daughter, to the King of England. The other is a maiden of the people, pure in conduct, endowed with a heroic, vision-nurtured confidence in God, who rekindled the courage of her desponding countrymen, and prepared the downfall of the foreign government.

With the death of Louis XI. the political influence of women begins to increase in France, amounting repeatedly to complete ascendency; indeed the interval between 1483 and 1590, exclusive of the reign of Louis XII., may be described as a period during which the government was in the hands of women and favourites, the kings were phantoms, either led by their cleverer wives, or misused and preyed upon by their mistresses and the men whom they made their favourites. During the minority of Charles VIII. the government was carried on by his elder sister, Anne of Beaujeu, herself but twenty-two years of age. She apparently inherited the political talents of her father, Louis XI., and, although unsupported by any legal right or position, succeeded by the wisdom and vigour of her administration in making her authority recognised.

Widely different was the behaviour of Louise of Savoy, the mother of Francis I., whom he followed blindfold to his own detriment and still more to that of France. The influence of this avaricious, extravagant, and vindictive woman—it is impossible to forget the Constable of Bourbon—was continually adverse to the interests of the nation, and, besides her, the king's favourites, the Countess Chateaubriand and the Duchess of Etampes, helped to aggravate the evil. 'The women,' says Tavannes, 'make everything, even the generals.' He might have added, 'even the bishops,' after the signing of the concordat, and even before that.

Henry II., the son and successor of Francis, continued up to the day of his death in the toils of a widow of forty-eight, Diana of Poitiers, whom he had created Duchess of Valentinois. He allowed her free interference in public affairs, as well as the disposal of the public treasure, and of all posts, ecclesiastical and secular, and she surrounded herself with all the attributes of power. She it was who levelled the path by which the Lothringian house of Guise attained to power, and she was equally successful in her efforts to bring Protestants to the stake.

With Catherine de Medici Italian elements of the basest description were imported into the court of France. Catherine possessed the political instincts of the Italians of her day; she was a pupil of the school of Machiavelli, in which all her family had been trained. The fundamental principle of this policy was that everything is allowable for the sake of power. Several of her countrymen of kindred views followed her to Paris and were raised by her to the highest posts. Such a one was Birago, who, in reward for the active part he played in the massacre of 1572, was advanced to the dignities of chancellor and cardinal. Addicted to astrology and to every kind of pagan superstition, she trod in the path of her father-in-law Francis, filling the court with a bevy of women versed in the arts of coquetry, who served her as tools in maintaining her power. It is well known that the massacre of St. Bartholomew was planned and executed chiefly through her agency.

Not less baleful for France was the influence of another daughter of the Tuscan house of the Medici, Mary, the wife of Henry IV. and mother of Louis XIII. A spendthrift, the slave of her passions, continually occupied with herself and her adornment, suspicious, yet singularly open to the suggestions of flattery, the period of her regency marks an epoch of misfortune to France. Herself the daughter of an Austrian Archduchess, she reversed the policy of her husband, and sought to reduce France into dependence upon Spain. No sooner had her son assumed the government than she endeavoured to stir up enemies against him everywhere; incited his own brother and sister-in-law to resistance, and embittered his whole life. Violent and inconsistent in hatred, fickle and capricious in her attachments, she did all in her power to procure the overthrow of Richelieu, although she had herself caused his elevation and introduced him into the cabinet. She lent herself to various conspiracies, and died at last in a foreign land unreconciled with her son, the victim of her own folly.

France was yet again destined to experience the full meaning of female government carried on in the name of an absolute royalty, and to tide through the dangers and catastrophes entailed by female interference in politics. In appointing Mazarin as prime minister during the minority of her son, the Queen Regent Anne of Austria was not only following the impulse of her heart, for he had won her love, but the calculations of policy, for she counted on his continuing the policy of Richelieu, and reckoned that as he was unshackled by party ties, he would depend upon her, would serve her only, and would relieve her of the burden of public affairs, whilst leaving her the consciousness of unlimited power. The foreign favourite was both detested and envied, as Richelieu had been, but less feared. Four distinct parties formed themselves against him, and three times plunged the country into civil war; drew down upon it a

Spanish invasion; and caused a massacre in the Hôtel de Ville in Paris, upon which occasion one hundred and fifty corpses were thrown into the Seine. A state of anarchy ensued, produced by the competition of private ambition with the interests of public bodies. For men like Retz and Condé the only considerations were the possession of place and power. The attempt on the part of the parliament to assume a position of permanent mediation between the monarchy and the nation, and to place legal barriers to the despotism of the crown, was of greater national importance.

Mazarin said that of the women who interfered there were three competent to govern the kingdom or to overthrow it. Yet Mazarin well knew how to play off women against each other, to disarm them or to win them by money or places at court. Anarchy was the result in the long run, and high treason, in the shape of a compact with Spain, the hereditary foe of France. Mazarin shed no blood, but the resources of his cunning and his skill in the art of bribery were unlimited, and absolute monarchy came forth established and strengthened from the assaults made upon it.

The education of Louis had been much neglected by the fault of his mother and of Cardinal Mazarin. He had learnt nothing profitable. Neither the habit of reading, nor the love for any study, had been instilled into him. His ignorance made him averse to associating with men of culture and science. Accustomed from childhood chiefly to female society, he continued into old age to feel the necessity of surrounding himself with women, and of being accompanied by them upon his frequent expeditions. The first who seriously engaged his affections was Maria Mancini, niece of the cardinal, but he was compelled to forego his inclination for her. Mademoiselle de la Motte d'Argencourt was separated from him and shut up in a convent. But shortly after his marriage with the daughter of Philip IV., whom he never loved, begins the series of ladies upon whom Louis, sometimes simultaneously, bestowed his favours: De la Vallière, de Montespan, de Fontanges, de Soubise, and others less notorious. In the beginning these liaisons were kept secret. But gradually, first at court and then in public, with pomp and pageant, as if to defy the opinion of the world, he caused himself to be accompanied by his mistresses wherever he went; he afforded them the spectacle of sieges and blockades, he permitted them the utmost extravagance in expenditure, and regarded with pleasure the homage paid to them, holding, however, strictly to the rule of allowing them no influence in political affairs.

At length Françoise d'Aubigné made her appearance at court, and before long attracted his attention. This woman, who was three years his senior, though little noticed by him at first, slowly but surely, with silent but irresistible force, took possession, for a time in company with others, but afterwards exclusively, of the monarch's heart and mind. She became indispensable to him, and from henceforth no other woman had any attraction for him.

This remarkable personage, who died one hundred and sixty-six years ago, still lives in the pages of history. During her lifetime and even since her death she has exercised an irresistible power of attraction upon all who have been concerned with her. Nevertheless, scarcely another individual of her sex, either in life or death, has been so misrepresented or so unmercifully dealt with as she. Even in our own day, in Germany as well as in France, opinion with regard to her is divided, tending from one extreme to the other; she remains, in short, an historical riddle. To assist in some measure towards the solution of the riddle by bringing into notice points in her life which, though hitherto neglected, are yet full of instruction and weighty as evidence; to amend by a more impartial distribution of the lights and shades the misshapen image of her which is frequently presented—this, rather than to offer an apology for her aims and motives, is my design.

The numerous misrepresentations of her history and the

unfavourable judgments that have hence been passed upon her have sprung from three sources. First, the work of La Beaumelle, who composed about 150 years ago a detailed history of the lady in question, and gave to the world a great part of her letters. La Beaumelle was an impudent and unscrupulous impostor; he forged a number of the letters, mutilated others, and interpolated many passages. This, although previously suspected, has only lately been conclusively proved by Lavallée, who had all the originals in his hands. By this it has become evident that the very passages which have been most frequently quoted as characteristic of her nature and ways, and regarded as descriptive of her individuality, are forgeries. The proof of this has been established since 1866, but the original falsifications are none the less persistently cited on both sides of the Rhine, and continue to form the grounds upon which she is judged and condemned. La Beaumelle's falsehoods were principally fabricated with a view to make Madame de Maintenon appear as a clever, cold coquette, who artfully calculated upon gradually setting Madame de Montespan aside and taking her place. He has, besides, by forging letters purporting to be from her to the famous Ninon de l'Enclos, cast suspicion upon her early life, which all her contemporaries acknowledged to have been blameless. In the fictitious letters he frequently makes her express herself in the half frivolous, half sentimental fashion of a Parisian lady of 1750; evidently desiring by such spicy additions to make the dish that he sets before his contemporaries more palatable. A considerable time will yet elapse before the false Maintenon who has become stereotyped in history and literature will have disappeared. Our most trusted historians still allow themselves to be misled by this *ignis fatuus*; Ranke even has not kept himself free from it. The Duke de Noailles' great work upon Madame de Maintenon has been likewise distorted by frequent quotations from the forged letters and interpolated passages. Notwithstanding that her correspondence down to the year

1701 has been for twenty years before the public in its genuine form, there has been no lack of new books of late years, even down to the present day, into which the La Beaumelle fictions have been introduced.

Meanwhile, the exposure of La Beaumelle's extensive forgery, the date of which coincided with the fabrication of a heap of similar impostures, notably of some pretended autograph letters of Marie Antoinette, awoke a hypercritical tendency in Paris to declare the Maintenon letters newly published by Lavallée to be unauthentic. Grimblot, who undertook to prove this,[1] built his hypothesis upon supposed contradictions between the statements of these letters and those of Dangeau's diary of the same date. The discrepancies, however, were merely the result of the arbitrary addition of dates by a later hand, in some instances by Lavallée himself, to letters which had been undated originally. The supposition that the letters were fabricated a few years ago is entirely disproved by the existence of the manuscript in the possession of the Duc de Mouchy.

In France the person who next to La Beaumelle has contributed to mislead public opinion with regard to Madame de Maintenon, is the Duc de Saint-Simon. This great master in the art of narration and delineation of character, her junior by many years, never, or scarcely ever, came into contact with her personally. He hated her because, in the first place, in his opinion she had presumptuously thrust herself into a position destructive of the hierarchical system of the court, thereby lowering the king in the eyes of all Europe. He hated her because, in

[1] *Les faux autographes de Madame de Maintenon* (Paris, 1867). A German critic, in Von Sebel's *Historische Zeitschrift*, xviii. 231, forthwith imagined that Grimblot had fully proved his point. However, since the appearance of Geffroi's inquiry in the *Revue des deux Mondes*, 1869, vol. lxxix. p. 302 ff., scarcely any one would continue to doubt the authenticity of the letters in question. The impress of Madame de Maintenon's spirit and of the circumstances in which she was placed are unmistakable in them. Geffroi, moreover, particularly shows, after careful comparison with the originals, that Lavallée has never allowed himself to be deceived by unauthentic matter.

the second place, he saw in her the governess and protectress of the legitimatised princes whom he cordially detested. That gossip, back-biting, and slander should beset the footsteps of a woman universally envied and shrouded moreover in mystery—a woman who must of necessity refuse so many wishes and petitions—is comprehensible. Saint-Simon in the case of those whom he hated was very ready to accept reports and tales hatched in the poisonous atmosphere of Versailles, and touched up and circulated by chamber-women and valets ; how little he is to be trusted, particularly upon the history of Madame de Maintenon, Chéruel and Ranke have already proved.

To these two false or doubtful witnesses may be added a third—which, so far as Germany is concerned, is evidently most important testimony—the letters of the Duchess of Orleans, Elisabeth Charlotte ; and accordingly it is upon them principally that opinion in Germany has been founded with regard to Madame de Maintenon, whilst at the same time they have continued to form the greatest hindrance to a more correct estimate of her. This princess of the Palatinate was, without herself being certain of it, the sister-in-law of Madame de Maintenon. The two women lived side by side for thirty years in constant intercourse, yet, from a fundamental difference of character, totally estranged from each other. Like almost all the German princesses who married into France, Elisabeth Charlotte was thoroughly unhappy ; her husband, the king's brother, was a copy of the last Valois, Henry III., as effeminate, vain, and vicious as he had been, entirely governed by unworthy favourites, whom he allowed to torment and persecute his wife. She was terribly sinned against, and in this even the king himself was not free from blame; but she sought and found another individual upon whom to lay the responsibility and to vent her hatred, and that was Madame de Maintenon. Her utterances with regard to her sister-in-law are full of contradictions and palpable falsehoods. She represents her as a fury in human shape, a murderess and poisoner, who has sowed mischief and dissension in all directions; a hypocrite who has supplied the dauphin with mistresses. Madame de Maintenon, according to her, has with the help of the midwife made away with the dauphiness —the Bavarian princess—has led astray the Duchess of Burgundy whom she brought up, has bought up corn as a speculation, to enrich herself in the famine of 1709. She has poisoned Louvois and the architect Mansard. She is the cause of all the evil which has come upon France. Even in the year 1719, when living in retirement at Saint-Cyr, she caused the castle of Lunéville to be set on fire, merely because the Duke of Lorraine did not belong to the partisans of the Duke of Maine. So also from her retreat in Saint-Cyr she has formed or fostered all the conspiracies against the regents. The duchess is perfectly positive upon all these points; she does not indeed name her authority for them, but she hints at other and more disgraceful things of which she has received intelligence or which she suspects.

We here encounter one of those unfathomable abysses of the human heart which sometimes baffle the historian. All these monstrous accusations are so entirely at variance with the real story that no one would be willing to waste time in a serious examination of them. Saint-Simon's charges have nothing in common with this catalogue of crimes and abominable deeds. The fierce hatred which breathes through the letters of the duchess during a period of thirty-five years is not, however, without remarkable changes and interruptions. To render such a state of feeling comprehensible we must reflect that the duchess, in order not to remain entirely apart from her husband, was forced to live in a morally pestilential atmosphere; that she was obliged to tolerate the society of his favourites, such as the Chevalier de Lorraine, D'Effiat, and their companions; as profligate a crew as could be found even in a corrupt court in those days. In her letters, as a rule, she shows herself fair in judgment, well informed, by no means credulous or fond of scandal. Her judgment of persons around her tends most often towards moral indifference. But where her passion interferes she is ready forthwith to adopt and spread any malicious gossip or unfounded invention to be gathered out of the sink of iniquity which certainly she has at hand. As she made no secret of her aversion for Madame de Maintenon, her attendants vied with one another in furnishing welcome sustenance for the feeling. At a time when the poisoning plots of Brinvilliers and Lavoisin had their ramifications in the highest regions of society; when for years whole provinces were the theatre of outrageous crimes committed by the nobles and long left unpunished; when at court the Chevalier de Lorraine could poison the king's sister-in-law (Charlotte's predecessor), and yet be more than tolerated, even favoured, by the king—we can to a certain extent understand how the duchess, with her imagination fertilised by such association, might credit a like tissue of infamy.

Charlotte herself informs us that she has given herself much useless trouble in endeavouring to secure Madame de Maintenon's favour and to obtain admission to her evening circle. She does not appear to have felt how much by this confession she weakened her own accusations. Her hatred flowed principally from three sources: from mortified pride of rank, from jealousy—she herself declared to the king that it was for love of him that she hated Madame de Maintenon—and from an erroneous fancy that the latter caused her to be suspected by Louis on account of her religious connections.

At a court where the length of a mantle or the triple grades of distinction in a seat—stool, chair, or arm-chair—were weighty questions for earnest discussion, Charlotte jealously insisted upon the tokens of precedence which were due to her, both as a German princess and as the sister-in-law of the king. But now, as she herself tells us, she was forced to see even the royal princes esteeming it a favour, and every one an honour, to be allowed to wait upon the widow of Scarron, and the princesses performing the duties of ladies in waiting, whilst she, the duchess, who took precedence by rank, sat alone and neglected in her own apartments.

It is a manifest exaggeration when she says, 'The Maintenon is absolute mistress of all his thoughts and feelings.' How little this was the case, how cautious Madame de Maintenon often had to be, her letters to Noailles and others show. The lukewarm Catholicism of his sister-in-law, the recollection that she had changed her religion only under constraint, her attachment to her Protestant relations and constant correspondence with them, her undisguised preference for German habits, interests, and people, besides some unfeminine traits in her disposition and the cynicism of her expressions in writing and conversation—all these were repulsive to the king, and continually excited his suspicions. The consciousness, besides, that he had upon two occasions, first with regard to the claims upon the Palatinate, and secondly upon the marriage of her son, deeply injured this woman, whom his brother had already made miserable, widened the breach. She could forgive him, but he could not pardon one whom he had so often and so deeply wronged. She, and she alone, of the whole family was excluded from the holy of holies, as she calls the apartment of Madame de Maintenon, where the king spent his evenings. This was natural enough because, both in religious and political matters, she was credited with independent sentiments, and was also justly suspected of making confidants of her relations in the north—of the Electress Sophia of Zell for instance, the natural opponent of the Anglo-French policy—as to all that she could glean in that circle. It was known that she spent whole days in letter-writing. In addition to all this, her own husband, as she complains, and even her son, calumniated her to the king. She was surrounded by spies, in want of money, neglected and shunned, continually tortured and hurt in her innermost feelings; and so she gathers up all her grievances and mortifications as in a vessel, to pour them upon the detested head of the woman whom she envied. This she does in the most passionate way and with the most vulgar expressions; she often seems to be quivering with rage as she writes. Madame de Maintenon, on the contrary, who never indulges in unfavourable remarks upon other women, seldom mentions the duchess, and if she does so, always with respect. 'She has qualities which might make her happy,' she says. 'She hates me, yet shows me more consideration than is due to me.'[1] Charlotte often stood in need of her interposition and made her the mouthpiece of her wishes to the king, and so outward deference and attempts at reconciliation alternate with passionate outbreaks of fury and abhorrence. She recks not of the self-accusation that is contained in her information, when she pities herself for having taken so much trouble in vain to win the favours and friendship—to get into the 'good graces,' she says—of the same person whom at the next moment she proceeds to depict as a demon in human shape capable of any enormity. Madame de Maintenon she imagines has deprived her of everything she valued. First of all of the king's love; she loved him on her part, according to her own account, tenderly, as a father; but this father was only fourteen years her senior, and the handsomest, most irresistible man in France. Once, in the year 1676, he had paid her some attention, but never again. Since the queen's death, the widow of Scarron had become the first lady in Versailles; treated by the court like 'a goddess,' says Elisabeth Charlotte. This, as the dauphiness was a nonentity, ought to have been her destiny. She soon got into the habit of ascribing every mortification that came to her from the king, such as rebukes for her too great freedom of speech, to the influence of this detested rival; for the king only loved and hated as she dictated to him. Whilst Madame de Maintenon is for ever lamenting the slavery in which she lives, Charlotte imagines that the most wilful monarch in Europe is a puppet in the hands of

[1] *Letters to Madame des Ursins*, i. 291.

his wife. It never occurs to her that her capricious and in many ways repulsive nature—a perpetual source of discord at that court—would, even if Madame de Maintenon had not been there, have displeased the king. She betrays, moreover, the tainted source from which she drew her accusations, the vicious favourites of her husband, the Chevalier de Lorraine, D'Effiat and his companions, men whom she herself loathed, and of whose slanderous talk, if it had concerned one of her German relations, she would not have believed a word. But the fervour of her hatred had, as it were, distorted her otherwise clear-sighted intelligence, and produced in her, with regard to this one individual, a species of monomania, a diseased appetite for calumniation.

At the death of Charlotte's husband in 1701, Madame de Maintenon showed herself so sympathetic and helpful that the duchess, following the wish of the king and her own impulse of the moment, was reconciled to her, and afterwards wrote her a letter in which, with assurances of the most sincere friendship, she begged for advice and instruction. Shortly afterwards she again wrote, 'All the king's benefits to me come through her, and my friendship will soon equal the respect I owe her.'[3] Nevertheless there is presently a relapse into the old animosity with the usual invectives; and the paroxysm lasts several years, until the marriage of her daughter with Louis's grandson, the Duke of Berri, which was partly the work of Madame de Maintenon. Now again it is recorded, 'She has behaved very well in this affair, and I have nothing to say against her.' Finally came the death of the king and the triumph of her son as regent over Madame de Maintenon's favourite, the Duke of Maine; and although she paid a visit to that lady after her retirement to Saint-Cyr, her letters indicate that the old bitterness has broken out again with, if possible, redoubled force, which even the death of Madame de Maintenon cannot mitigate. One is reminded of the proverb

[3] The letters are printed in the *Journal des Savans*, 1861, p. 760.

of Larochefoucauld: 'Envy is even more implacable than hatred.'

The grandfather of Madame de Maintenon was one of the most famous Frenchmen of his time. This was Agrippa d'Aubigné, a leader and champion amongst the reformers, as bold with his sword as with his pen, the friend and companion-in-arms of Henry IV. His unworthy son, who early in life had fallen under sentence of death, had been led by well-merited misfortune into the prison of Niort, and there Françoise was born. Poverty and bitter privation surrounded her earliest awakening to consciousness. She was taken as a child by her father to America, and a few years later brought back to France by her then widowed mother. The poverty of the mother induced an aunt, Madame de Vilette, to adopt the girl, and to bring her up as a Protestant; but after some years Françoise was placed in a convent by another relation, where, after a prolonged resistance, she yielded and became a Catholic. She subsequently related how, at twelve years old, Bible in hand, she made the business of her conversion a tough one to the priests, and how it was two years before she gave in. By the death of her mother, she was left alone in the world and utterly destitute, a good-looking girl only fifteen years of age. To avoid taking the veil, she consented to marry the comic poet Scarron. Owing to the age and the crippled condition of the man, the marriage was one only in appearance; Françoise served him as both nurse and secretary, and he became her instructor; she was indebted to him for the education of her mind, and for the knowledge of three languages, Latin amongst the number; she enjoyed, besides, the society of a circle of authors and friends of literature, both male and female, who were in the habit of gathering round the invariably cheerful and witty poet. After some years, on Scarron's death, she again became free. The young widow lived for a considerable time in Paris in moderate circumstances, but welcomed and generally esteemed in the highest literary circles of which the capital could boast. Madame de Montespan now invited her to undertake the education of the children whom she had secretly borne to the king. Madame Scarron consented, upon condition that she should receive the commission directly from the king, and she then forthwith took up her abode in a remote, isolated house in Paris, where she fulfilled her calling in quiet seclusion.

When, in 1673, the king acknowledged the children and caused them to be brought up in his vicinity at Versailles, Madame Scarron was suddenly transplanted to the court, which she at first found very attractive. For a considerable time she received little notice from the king; he looked upon her as a somewhat cultivated genius; but when he gradually perceived the care with which she watched over the welfare of his children, particularly that of his favourite, the sickly Duke of Maine, he endeavoured to retain her in his service. The two women, however, could not endure each other. Madame Scarron knew, or believed, that Madame de Montespan, who alone possessed the king's ear, prejudiced him against her by accusing her of caprice; Madame de Montespan could not endure the presence of a lady whose opinion, even if unspoken, of her doubly guilty relation to the king she either knew or divined. To Françoise the situation became so painful that for a time she hesitated whether to give up the position and leave the court. However, her confessor, the Abbé Gobelin, to whom, in letters which are still preserved, she described the torment of her position, advised and exhorted her to persevere, for the sake of the good she might effect at court. By degrees the king began to find pleasure in the conversation of an unassuming woman of refined mind. She introduced him, as Madame de Sévigné expresses it, 'to an entirely new country,' the peaceful intercourse of friendship without the excitement of passion. Madame de Montespan had accustomed him to violent changes of humour—stormy outbreaks alternating with tender submission—to witty, but malicious comments upon others; here he found modesty and reserve, coupled with genuine womanly worth; a cultivation of mind superior to his own; agreeable conversation, combining gaiety with seriousness.

Soon a royal grant transformed the widow Scarron into Madame de Maintenon, the owner of a country seat of the same name. After a time the king, whose affections now inclined more and more towards her, appointed her as lady-in-waiting (*dame d'atour*) to the dauphiness, thus putting an end to her distasteful relations with Madame de Montespan, and securing her an almost independent position at court. In 1680 she already stood so high and secure in the monarch's good graces that she wrote to her brother that she would ask nothing of the king, since he loaded her with riches, honours, and benefits of every kind.

Even in the early days of her rise to favour, in 1675, she had ventured, encouraged by clerical advice, to draw the king's attention to the scandal of his doubly adulterous relations. This she did without any *arrière-pensée*; for the queen was still alive, younger than herself, and perfectly healthy. Her words, as yet, made no impression; Madame de Montespan gave birth to a daughter by the king two years afterwards. Even in 1684, the very year of his marriage with Madame de Maintenon, the king was still in the habit of visiting Madame de Montespan twice a day. These visits, however, were only for the sake of his children. Madame de Maintenon had used her influence to bring him back to his long neglected and much injured Spanish wife. In this she succeeded, and the queen gratefully acknowledged that she was indebted to her for this happiness. Madame de Sévigné mentions, as early as 1676, that Madame Scarron had then gained universal admiration in her arduous position, and in the three years from 1680 to 1683 she stood at the height of her fame; all paid homage to her, all bowed down before her, and, as Madame de Sévigné expresses it, she was the soul of the court—of that court which at the time was the quintessence of French society. These must certainly have been the happiest years of her life.

On July 30, 1683, the queen died, and, after a brief delay, in the beginning of 1684, Madame de Maintenon, now fifty years of age, became the wife of Louis, the marriage ceremony taking place secretly at night. The marriage had been resolved upon in the September of 1683, as is proved by a letter from Madame de Maintenon to Gobelin, referring to the peace of mind which she is now enjoying after a period of inward distraction and painful hesitation, and observing that she stands in need of the strength that comes from God to make a good use of her happiness. The king had previously, in a cabinet council, declared that he did not intend to enter upon a second marriage—meaning one of equal birth, which would have given a prospect of an increase of the royal family, already numerous. Had he been a German prince he would probably have adopted the form of a morganatic marriage, which would have conferred upon the object of his choice the position and consideration of his wife before God and the world, although without political rights. That this was not the case, and that the marriage was not made known, was a sacrifice on the part of Madame de Maintenon to which she doubtless resigned herself with difficulty; for she knew full well that she was injuring her reputation, which she had hitherto guarded so carefully, and that, at any rate at a distance, both in and out of France, she would appear as only the last on the numerous list of royal mistresses. But here the authority of the church, always paramount with her, intervened. The priests to whom she had entrusted her conscience, Gobelin and Godet des Marais, told her—and the success she had already achieved warranted the idea—that it was her vocation, her mission, to labour at the side of the king, for the salvation of his soul, and for the welfare of the church and the nation. Two or three bishops, and—according to a tradition preserved in Saint-Cyr—the pope himself, joined in persuading her, and this fact is now placed beyond doubt by the papal letters addressed to the lady containing the permission or dispensation from Rome.

According to statements afterwards repeatedly made by contemporaries, she ardently desired the public announcement of her marriage, and twice almost persuaded the king to grant her wish; but the bishops and ministers of whom counsel was asked—to Louvois she is said to have gone down on her knees—dissuaded the king from it. The thing is hardly credible. Shortly after her marriage Madame de Maintenon wrote to her brother: 'I shall never advance a step higher, I have already been raised too high.' In a letter from her director, Godet, she is said to have willingly sacrificed an earthly kingdom for a heavenly one; for she had been taught to regard the renunciation of the avowal of her marriage as a sacrifice to be offered up to God. She accordingly destroyed all letters and records which gave testimony to her marriage, saying to her confidential friend: 'None shall learn what I have been to the king.'

The German historian who has rendered most justice to this lady, and has appreciated her with the finest discernment, Karl von Noorden,[1] is uncertain whether a religious marriage took place, although he deems it probable, and lays stress on the fact that Ranke also—wisely, as Noorden remarks—has avoided any precise assertion as to her being the lawful wife of Louis. But the letters of the Bishop of Chartres, who was in the secret, the exhortations contained in them that she should not refuse to the king his rights as her husband, and the letter to the king himself from the bishop, in which he alludes to his happiness in possessing so excellent and loving a companion for life,[2] leave no further room for doubt.

[1] *Europäische Geschichte im 18. Jahrhundert*, iii. 17.

[2] 'Vous avez une excellente compagne, pleine d'esprit de Dieu et de dis-

Let us now endeavour to picture to ourselves, both upon their good and bad sides, this wonderful pair, who, although so strongly contrasting in character, yet passed thirty years in uninterrupted harmony.

Louis was a magnificent man, perfect in bodily proportion, with regular and beautiful features. Whatever he did was done calmly, with grace and dignity. He possessed, to an eminent degree, the gift of saying the suitable, agreeable thing to every one, and he never said what could hurt. He was patient, was complete master of his emotions and countenance, never lost his temper, seldom found fault, and then without harshness. Irresistibly attractive, yet dignified in his friendliness and condescension, he played the hospitable host at Versailles, was always indulgent to the feelings of those around him, and solicitous in providing pastimes and amusements both of the finer and coarser sort. He combined in himself so much that was attractive to men and women that their admiration often took the form of adoration, as though he were a demigod.

To reign for Louis signified to command. He felt himself a ruler both over minds and bodies, and the source of all justice and honour. None in France should be anything save through him. To see him and to be seen by him was the most serious occupation which he could devise for the nobles who thronged his court. He was not so much the father of his country as the master of it, in the widest sense of the word. Care for his royal dignity, for his personal prestige, was supreme with him. For in him the state, the national power and greatness, were concentrated and embodied; without him France would have been only a heap of individual atoms. His views were part of the religious opinions in which he had been educated, and were carefully fostered by the clergy.

cernement, et dont la tendresse, la sensibilité pour vous sont sans égales. Il a plu à Dieu que je connusse le fond de son cœur. Je serais bien sa caution, Sire, qu'on ne peut vous aimer plus tendrement ni plus respectueusement qu'elle ne vous aime.' *Corresp. Mme. de M.* iv. 196.

France, according to him, has the leadership of all Christendom as the oldest, most powerful, and most important Christian kingdom; the king is consequently styled 'the most Christian,' the 'eldest son of the church;' and, by virtue of his office, is the foremost defender of the Catholic religion and church, her right arm, the born adversary and extirpator of every heresy. The more power and wealth he acquires, the more his name is feared, the further the borders of his kingdom are extended, and so much the better he is enabled to fulfil the high responsibility entrusted to him. The wars which Louis waged thus became to him religious wars; from the first, in the expedition against the Netherlands, he asserted this, and announced to the Catholic powers that the object of this campaign, so completely at variance with the previous policy of France, was the extirpation of heresy. Hence, when he affirmed that his own aggrandisement was his most agreeable occupation, his satisfaction was enhanced and sanctified by the thought that the aggrandisement of France was a gain to religion and the church as well. Even later, when, by the Peace of Ryswick, which was considered a disgrace in France, he had to relinquish territory that he had conquered, he contrived to introduce amongst the articles of the agreement a clause, upon the strength of which hundreds of Protestant communities were deprived of their religious liberties.

Pride was the most prominent feature of this man, a pride which often degenerated into boundless arrogance, and laid, as it were, a thick bandage over his eyes. He prided himself in the thought that, in spite of his miserable education, he had raised himself so high by the power of his own will; and had made himself such a master in the art of government. He had, as he fancied, educated his ministers himself, and had then with their help made France into the first naval and military power of Europe, the keystone of the European hegemony. He was proudly conscious of the charm which, in spite of the excessive burdens laid upon his people, he exercised upon all classes of Frenchmen; proud of the victories which his plans had prepared for his armies, as well as of the triumphs of diplomacy which wisdom and gold had secured under the direction of one who so thoroughly understood the art of stifling or extinguishing foreign rights, and of discovering French claims upon foreign territory.

How much there was to nurture this intoxicating self-confidence and to carry it beyond the limits of sobriety! In flattery and homage the clergy, with the bishops at their head, strove to outdo every other class. The nobility, which but recently, in the time of the Fronde, had proved so turbulent and insolent, now thronged his antechamber for the mere hope of catching a gracious glance from him. Every one must become a courtier to deserve his notice and share in the outlay of a showy and extravagant court; to be enabled to do so most of them were assigned pensions from the king, and were all the more willing in consequence to renounce all political rights and participation in the administration of public affairs.

The egotism so constantly ascribed to Louis was the inevitable consequence of his position, the logical result of absolutism which is accustomed to deny itself nothing, which cannot help referring everything to itself, and regarding all men in the light of the use they can be put to, or the services they can be made to render. It was the same with the suspicious temper which everywhere accompanied him; almost every one, says his minister[6] Torcy, was an object of suspicion to him; to every one he was ready to impute impure motives. His daily impressions were gathered from a thoroughly corrupt court, but he certainly did not remember that the court, and all that it had become, was peculiarly his own work. The stage on which he passed his life, its surroundings and its mephitic atmosphere, explain to us exactly why he so often mistook obstinacy for

[6] *Journal inédit de M. de Torcy* (1881), p. 170.

firmness, violence for energy, and without a twinge of conscience wasted thousands of human lives.

Yet Louis was a man of contrasts. Whilst all Europe credited him with boundless arrogance, he showed himself in his immediate circle gentle, affable, even yielding. Boileau, who knew this from experience, said that at home, in his own circle, he seemed passive and inclined to follow suggestions rather than to dictate to others. In 1707, when years of misfortune had come, and heavy blows of affliction had broken his haughty spirit and lowered his confidence in victory, his wife declared that she could use more freedom in reproaching him for his mistakes than she could have done with thousands of others. He did not consider himself indispensable, and thought that another would do as well in his place, that is to say, would equally be led by divine inspiration.[7] But in saying this she forgot that it was she alone who could presume to remonstrate with him, and even she only upon certain things. For a man to have ventured upon anything of the kind, was inconceivable with a king who, from his youth up, had displayed aversion and shyness for every person of superior intellect, and a preference for the compliant and cringing. This characteristic was emphasised by the efforts of his ministers to keep at a distance any man who might become influential. Men conscious of their own worth seldom cared to approach him, since, as Saint-Simon remarks,[8] to be acceptable to him it was necessary to appear penetrated with the sentiment of one's own nothingness, and of the fact that one was indebted to him for everything. All greatness must be only an emanation from his own.

Continually suffering from gout, vertigo, and other ailments, and constantly in the hands of physicians and surgeons, he yet possessed sufficient strength of will to maintain the appearance of robust health and to attend incessantly to business. The man was often sick or suffering when the

[7] *Lettres historiques*, ii. 199.

[8] *Mémoires*, ed. of 1843, xxiv. 75.

king appeared to be in health. Himself sorely in need of remedies, he was yet persuaded that he possessed the royal gift of healing others, and regularly, after receiving the communion, touched hundreds of unfortunate beings afflicted with scrofula and other evils, who swarmed to Versailles in expectation of the benefits to be received thereby.

Louis was always well satisfied with himself, nay more, he candidly admired himself, the wisdom of his administration, and the magnificent results of his actions. When success failed to follow his undertakings, his self-confidence was not thereby shaken; on the contrary, he intimates to us in his memoirs that he carried with him that satisfaction 'which a great mind must feel when he has satisfied his own virtue.' He could certainly no longer hide from himself, after the year 1690, that through his wars, through his mania for building, and his unprecedented extravagance, the prosperity of the country had been destroyed, the people plunged into distress and poverty, he himself crippled in his resources for the future. But he had learnt from Richelieu's testamentary memoir—a work, according to the report of the Venetian ambassador, then highly esteemed at the court—that the people ought to be kept to a certain degree in poverty lest they should grow insolent; and he was also of opinion that, being the legitimate owner of all property in France, he might dispose of it all according to his pleasure. It was a great error, he said, on the part of a monarch to choose to possess separate property distinctly appropriated to him, since everything in the country belonged to him equally. Tellier, his confessor, had obtained a decision of the Sorbonne which corroborated this assertion by pronouncing it a theological truth. Just as firmly did he believe that he had the right to dispose of all church property, although he abstained from exercising this right even at a time of extreme distress, contenting himself with the sums granted to him by the clergy. It was a principle with him, likewise, that each individual and corporate body was bound to obey his orders without question (*sans discernement*) : hence his contemptuous and overbearing behaviour towards the parliaments. He believed in absolute unlimited monarchy, not by any means as being one form of government amongst others equally legitimate, but as the only form agreeable to the will of God. But he likewise entertained peculiar views upon the sincerity and upon the observance of sworn contracts. Superior political considerations and well-weighed motives of self-interest, he said, ought to enable a man simply to set himself above them or to weaken them by skilful interpretations. He so frequently put this doctrine into practice, that his faithlessness became on all sides a standing reproach, and delayed negotiations for peace, or rendered them more difficult, often to the disadvantage of France.

We are assured by his wife that Louis was exceedingly solicitous for the happiness of his people and anxious to mitigate the public distress of which he was well aware. But the desire went no further than words, and never ripened into deeds. Still it must be remembered that, from the year 1702 until the time of his death, both the leisure and the power were wanting to him. Meantime, both at Versailles and Marly, he continued to indulge his passion for building, whilst thousands of his subjects were, through his fault, dying of starvation, and want of money was crippling the military power of the state then struggling for its very existence. These characteristics which are here apparent—stubborn hardness, unmerciful selfisiness, and disregard for human life—meet us too repeatedly in his history to allow us, as others have done, to lay the responsibility on his ministers and on them alone. He was too thorough an autocrat for that; no minister, not even Louvois, would have dared to damage the reputation of the king by cruelties committed on his own responsibility. When in a time of profound peace (1670), and in defiance of the law of nations, Louis suddenly fell upon the Duke of Lorraine and took possession of his country, he commanded that the prisoners, men who had only done their duty, should be sent to the galleys; on the remonstrance of his minister Lionne, he merely reiterated the order.[9] The barbarous fashion in which the war was carried on by Louvois' orders, with the consent of the king; the burning of villages, even of whole towns; the laying waste of large districts with no strategic purpose, as in the Palatinate, in Piedmont, and in the Netherlands; the wholesale executions in Gascony and Brittany, where the people had been driven to revolt through the intolerable weight of taxation; the order given to the commissioner appointed to inquire into a rebellion of the kind, that he should cause at least twelve hundred persons to be executed before beginning his investigation—for these things history must reckon with him, and it is moreover obliged to admit that this hardheartedness at times wore the semblance of a gloomy fanaticism, as if he had taken the Duke of Alva or Simon of Montfort for his pattern. This is sufficiently indicated by all that Rousset[1] relates of his utterances and orders with respect to the Waldenses in Piedmont.

If the object before us is to draw a true picture of Madame de Maintenon, and if we look around for information in the accounts given by her contemporaries, we must, as we have already shown, set aside on many points the testimony of the two principal witnesses, Elisabeth Charlotte and Saint-Simon. They furnish us, however, with many a detail evidently truthful, as well as many an undesigned admission which cannot be overlooked. We are otherwise somewhat destitute of contemporaneous information. Although Versailles was the centre of the universe at that epoch, we can distinguish only a few voices of any weight. Contemporary history and biography could scarcely be written, such was the severity of the censorship. La Bruyère's saying, that it was difficult for a Frenchman of his time to

[9] *Journal des Savans*, 1860, p. 220.
[1] *Histoire de Louvois*, iv. 28.

find trustworthy material for his pen upon any subject, applies above all to the materials of history. The diaries of Dangeau and Sourches are each of them a dry collection of facts, and abstain from all expression of opinion. The numerous authors who took refuge abroad knew but little, and their reports were coloured by party spirit. The Duke de Berwick and the minister Torcy, whose testimony would be very welcome, are both of them silent. The Abbé Choisy has nothing of importance to tell us beyond the fact of the secret wedding at night. In the memoirs of La Fare, the epicurean of the Orleans faction, the whole of the statements with regard to Madame de Maintenon are false. The memoirs of Languet de Gergy are valuable and instructive. Through Madame de Maintenon's influence, he filled the post of almoner to the Duchess of Burgundy between the years 1700 and 1715, and was therefore constantly in the presence of his patroness, and in frequent communication with her, through her became Bishop of Soissons, and died as Archbishop of Sens in 1753. He was one of the men who enjoyed her confidence, and, as her letters show, received from her many commissions as to church matters; he was also for some time her confessor. We should be glad to forget that this man was also the author of such a book as the famous biography of the nun Alacoque; he also left memoirs which, although not intended to be printed, offer a picture in which every shadow is wanting. Nevertheless, as authorities they are a source of inestimable value, for not only does he speak as an eye-witness and with the intimate knowledge of a spiritual counsellor, but he had access to records, since lost, proceeding from Madame de Maintenon herself, or made use of by her in her own memoranda, and his statements often coincide with those of Saint-Simon, with this difference, that the latter was fond of putting an ugly interpretation upon things which in Languet's eyes appear quite natural and commendable.

The reports of foreign ambassadors, Venetian and German, who were about the court, are likewise worthy of credit. Foscarini says in the year 1683 that Madame de Maintenon enjoys the highest reputation at court; is universally esteemed, and lives very quietly in great retirement; that she has won the affection of the king through her vivacity and the refinement of her mind, through her accommodating spirit and tact in sympathising with the feelings of others; that the high favour in which she stands is considered a matter of rejoicing, because it is believed that she may impart to the king some of the kindliness and amiability of her own nature. Girolamo Venier makes mention in a few words of her influence over the king in the interests of peace and in favour of religious institutions (1688). Pietro Venier confirms this in the year 1695. He thinks the principles upon which she acts to be the best and fittest; that her influence is altogether beneficial, and that she lives a very modest and retired life. Erizzo, finally, in 1699, calls her a woman of remarkable intellect and sanctified life, who is very far from misusing her power and authority in any way.[2] Oddly enough, none of these men seem to have suspected that this lady was really married to the king.

A memorandum[3] drawn up for the future King of Prussia by Ezekiel Spanheim, a German diplomatist, in 1690, is less favourable; yet even he finds no particular cause for blame, excepting as to her behaviour in the persecution of the Protestants, and considers her marriage with the king to be almost a certainty. Count Sinzendorf, in a report destined for the emperor in 1701, has no doubt as to the marriage, praises her 'indescribable retirement' and abstention from all display, but shares with Saint-Simon and Elisabeth Charlotte the suspicion that the leading motive of her policy was the desire to have herself proclaimed queen; whereupon he relates a foolish story, probably imparted to him by the Duchess of Orleans, to the effect that the king was dissuaded from doing this by Fénelon, whose fall was a

[2] *Relazioni di Francia*, ii. 363, 448, 519.

[3] In Dohm's *Materialen für Statistik*, 1781, vol. iii.

matter of revenge on her part. He does not otherwise mention a single trait prejudicial to her.[4]

Upon the whole the more we inquire into the opinion of eye-witnesses and contemporaries the more we are impressed with the fact that those who judge her most favourably are the best, and amongst them those who had known her longest and most intimately. Thus, amongst the women, Madame de Sévigné; Madame de Miramon, who was revered as a saint and who begged for her presence upon her deathbed; the Abbess of Fontévraud, sister of Madame de Montespan; the Queen of England; Madame de Dangeau, Princess of Löwenstein, who, is described as both beautiful and virtuous, even by Saint-Simon; the Duchess of Lorraine, otherwise her implacable enemy. The language of admiration which the Princess Orsini adopts in her letters to her is evidently not flattery, but the expression of sincere conviction. The same may be said of the letters addressed to her by Marshal Villars. The tone of deference which runs through Fénelon's letters to Madame de Maintenon is due not merely to her position, but to her personal qualities.

No woman in history has been more loved and admired, and none more hated. But the hatred has been invariably produced by envy. 'Her position,' says Sévigné, 'is unique in the world; there has never been, nor ever will be again, anything like it.'[5] The idol of France belonged to her exclusively, and the wishes and aspiration of the feminine world at the court were hence once for all extinguished in a country where, according to the statement of the Duchess of Orleans,[6] 'the women are jealous of their husbands more from ambition than from love; wishing to rule over all and to make all things subordinate to them, so that there is not a kitchen-maid who does not

[4] *Archiv für Kunde Oesterr. Geschichtsquellen*, xiii. 11.

[5] *Lettres* (éd. Monmerque, 1862), vii. 280.

[6] *Briefe a. d. Jahre* 1720 (Tübingen, 1879), pp. 178, 209.

suppose herself to be intelligent enough to govern a kingdom.'

Both husband and wife, so closely united in unbroken harmony, and yet so widely different in thought and feeling, reveal something to us of their nature in the course of their writings: Louis, in his memoirs, written, as it were, before the mirror, filled with naïve admiration of his own reflection; Françoise, in the important series of her letters, to which many have recently been added, as well as in the papers and notes which she wrote for Saint-Cyr. Louis's memoirs—the genuine production of his own sentiments, but written in a style of which he himself was not capable—were in all probability composed with the assistance of his wife, or were at any rate revised by her. That this was believed to be the case is reported by the Venetian ambassador;[7] and the editor of the memoirs in 1806 admits the co-operation of Madame de Maintenon in certain portions of them. In any case the king gave them to her to read. Thus she drew her accurate knowledge of his thoughts and aims from his writings, as well as from his conversation. The discovery on her part followed as a matter of course that she had—within the limits, at least, prescribed to her by her director—espoused the opinions together with the person of the man she had married.

The letters of Madame de Maintenon are among the best that French literature has to offer, and, although differing entirely in tone and purport from those of her friend Madame de Sévigné, are worthy of comparison with them. Her style is clear, terse, refined, often sententious; her business letters are patterns of simplicity and pregnant brevity. They might be characterised as womanly yet manly, so well do they combine the warmth and depth of womanly feeling with the strength and lucidity of a masculine mind. If some of them, especially those to her brother, who was far inferior to her in moral worth, give the

[7] *Relazioni* (ed. Barozzi e Berchet, 1865), pp. 111, 364.

impression of a certain calculating coldness and dry utilitarianism, this is the exception called forth by the character of the person she addresses; most of them touch us by the warmth and natural sincerity of feeling, the hearty human kindness, the gentleness and forbearance, displayed in her judgment of individuals, the absence of all that comes under the description of polite tittle-tattle. They are not free from an occasional hardness, which we shall presently explain; but, all things considered, it may be asserted that they are the reflection of a noble, excellent soul, rather above, than of, its time.

The prevalent conception, that Françoise d'Aubigné was an exceedingly clever, calm, cold, shrewd woman is to a great extent erroneous. She was extremely vivacious and highly sensitive in feeling, possessed by an imperative necessity for loving, and an almost passionate longing to commend herself to others by the services and sacrifices she was ready to perform for them. She had, she relates, as a young girl, such an ardent love for her instructress, the nun Céleste, that, when she was dismissed from the convent (of Niort), she prayed to God that she might die, so intolerable did the separation from this nun appear to her.[8]

Early habits of piety had led to daily self-examination and sifting of conscience; she had by this means acquired unusual control over her senses, as well as over her feelings and will. She was, she affirms, by nature impatient, yet during the forty years that they lived together she never gave the king any proof of it, although she often feared she should break down before him from sheer exhaustion. In these characteristics is revealed the secret of that pre-eminence in the art of education to which she attained, without herself having been a mother—or perhaps because of this. For she possessed in the highest degree the art of being all things to all men, of understanding and

[8] *Entretien sur l'éducation des filles*, par Mme. de M., éd. Lavallée 1854), p. 314.

sympathising with the peculiarities of each individual, of advising, awakening, and directing consciences, of even making herself a child with children, so that she became an excellent teacher, and, sensible of her talent, exercised it readily in village schools such as those of Avon and Fontainebleau.

Personal impressions, as Fénelon remarked, counted for more with Louis than acknowledged principles. The impression which Madame Scarron made upon him, the mixture of personal attraction, admiration of her power of mind, and pleasure in her conversation which he experienced in her society bound him to her with an ever-strengthening tie. He became aware that she was devoid of selfishness, striving after nothing, asking for nothing, careful only for him, for his health and amusement, and, above all, for the welfare of his soul. Her piety and conscientiousness made her seem to him as a guardian angel in female form, ever at his side, commissioned to counsel and to warn, to cheer and to comfort him. The hours that he spent with her were the most agreeable in the day. Distrusting every one else, and accustomed to solicitations expressed in words and sighs and glances from all around, it was with her only that he enjoyed the sweets of unrestrained confidence and felt the full value of an unselfish love devoid of self-interest. For the first time, the opportunity had been granted to him—who until then had seen life only through the incense-laden atmosphere of the court—of learning from the lips of one belonging to him the truth and reality of things. Such a friend as Henry IV. had possessed, a king like Louis could never have; at the best he could only have an intellectually insignificant favourite like Villeroi.

Now, at length, Louis had obtained that which hitherto he had never enjoyed—a peaceful, unconstrained, agreeable private life, the intimacy of home, in which he could rest from the endless burden of having to play a part.

Even adulation and flattery end by becoming wearisome, and the most luxurious monarch must at times long for more wholesome entertainment, and for an interval in which he may lay aside the yoke of etiquette—a yoke which deprives himself, as well as the princes, princesses, and courtiers, of the free use of their hands and arms and of their free will, and transforms even pleasure into toil. Truly he himself wore with fortitude and dignity [9] the iron fetters which he had forged for himself, whilst his wife experienced to the full the torture of the daily constraint, and feared sometimes that she must sink under it, although always obliged to conceal it from him.

'Never,' says Elisabeth Charlotte, 'was a young and beautiful favourite so worshipped as this old woman; so enamoured is the great man of his treasure.' [1] 'She was,' says the duchess in another place, 'mistress over all his affections and thoughts.' It is a matter of fact that from the time she became his, no other woman succeeded in insinuating herself into the king's favour, nor was he ever unfaithful to her, although he continued to seek the society of women and chose to be accompanied by ladies upon his journeys. Royal gifts and favours fell to the share of the ladies of the court henceforth chiefly through her interposition. In public she appeared as a private person, or simply as a lady of the court, claiming no token of higher rank; but in her apartments she was forced to consent to princes and princesses doing homage to her as to a queen, waiting upon her and surrounding her with attentions, divining her wants and vying with one another in satisfying them. The homage which was thrust upon her whenever she showed herself in public, or paid a visit, induced her to keep as much as possible in the background; even to her friends she found it

[9] Upon the whole, the outbreaks of temper and cynicism, which Saint-Simon reports, may be considered as exceptional.

[1] Ranke, *Werke*, xiii. 171, A.D. 1699.

necessary, as she expressed it, to be as one dead. Yet in her own apartments she could wield the sceptre with as much grace as dignity.

The craving of the king to be continually in the company of this woman of his choice is difficult to explain. It was as though some subtle, beneficent influence flowing from her communicated itself to his being; as though her glance, and the tone of her voice, calmed and refreshed him. In 1698 Madame de Maintenon, then sixty-three years of age, writes that the king comes regularly three times a day to her apartment. Soon afterwards she laments her want of time, and how inaccessible she is to others, as the king is scarcely ever out of her room,[2] though indeed, as she remarks, she scarcely ever talks to him, for he is generally immersed in the most serious political business. To her no small inconvenience he had his writing-table placed close to her bed, and would carry on his work there, even with his ministers, whilst she listened, lying in bed. Torcy mentions one occasion when, during a discussion, she exhorted him from her bed to follow the advice of the minister.[3] She was even obliged to accompany him during a campaign. We may therefore well believe that she gradually assimilated much of Louis's way of thinking, just as he, on the other hand, received much from her. We are reminded of the magic ring of Fastrada, which cast a love-spell about the heart of Charles the Great, and which, when Turpin threw it into the fish-pond at Aix, detained the king there by its magic power. True it is that Louis admired the marquise more than she admired him. 'She is a saint,' he wrote; 'she has every perfection, and more intellect than most men.' If she happened to be present at his deliberations with the ministers, he was certain to ask, 'What does your Wisdom think of this? How does this strike *votre solidité!*' She, on the other hand, told her director that her views and principles were so much at

[2] *Corresp.* iv. 253.

[3] *Journal inédit.* (publ. par Masson, 1884), p. 125.

variance with those of the king that her situation was made much more difficult thereby.

Françoise had to take the king as he was; she could neither hope nor venture to dissuade him from his delusion that royalty was divinely inspired. His mind had already been under her influence for twenty years, when in the memorial addressed to his grandson, the King of Spain, he exhorted him never to decide except for himself, because if his intentions were good and he gave no heed to the opinions of others he was sure of the divine illumination. She held fast to the resolution to express her opinion only when called upon to do so, and this was in keeping with her own inclination; but, as time went on, her opinion was more and more frequently asked, even on public affairs, and the divinely inspired king, after deciding, usually discovered that his Egeria had thought and advised exactly in accordance with the will of God. Her omnipotence, about which Elisabeth Charlotte, Saint-Simon, and the foreign ambassadors have so much to say, consisted mainly in that. He set all the more value upon her opinion, even on public business, because he was persuaded that in his long daily discussions with her he had put her through a course of instruction and had initiated her in the great questions and aims of his policy and administration. In the same way he had, as he believed, by his instructions educated his ministers to become useful men of business. He thus waived nothing of his own dignity when, relying upon the solidity of her judgment—*votre solidité* he used to call her—he inquired into her views and agreed with them.

Her influence, however, was powerless to make any change in the course of his policy, or the continuance of the war, up to the time of the Peace of Ryswick. When she sighed for peace she was informed that the enemy was obstinate, and that hostilities were carried on for the use and profit of the Catholic religion. So the directors of her conscience believed, and so they assured her. Her confessor,

Gobelin, wrote enthusiastic letters to her upon the subject, full of daring hopes. She, meanwhile, willingly allowed herself to be deceived by these delusive pictures; what could be more agreeable or elevating than the consciousness of being the loving and admiring wife of the most distinguished hero of the faith of that era, the new Louis IX., the chosen warrior, who contended for the welfare and extension of the church! It did not disturb her to know that this champion of the faith and of the church was in alliance with the arch-enemy of Christendom, and supporting the Turkish arms in the invasion of Christian countries in the East.

It is scarcely needful to observe that under no circumstances and at no period of the more than thirty years that her influence lasted could she have ventured to call in question the merits of unrestricted royalty, as it had been planned and carried out under the rule of the two cardinals, and systematically developed by Louis. The question might present itself to her mind whether such a system could be termed Christian; she may also have had doubts instilled into her by Fénelon during the period of their intercourse. But the church herself had created the system; her bishops and preachers had commended and sanctioned it in the pulpit. She knew that Bossuet, the foremost teacher of the church in the kingdom, had declared that this condition of self-glorification and absolutism rested upon the divine order of things, and was the old and permanent constitution of France. Nor, again, could she have dared to meddle with the system of arbitrary imprisonment by royal warrant, although now and then, in a few cases, she succeeded in preventing a sentence of imprisonment or banishment, or at any rate in shortening it. The pernicious custom of the sale of public offices she durst not call in question, seeing the condition of the finances. Nevertheless there remained to her a large and comprehensive sphere, in which she could at least attempt to soften severities and to obtain a milder application of coercive measures; yet not infrequently she must have been met with the remark that such and such a thing was traditional, that it had always been so. Since the king laid considerable stress upon her judgment of persons, and was convinced of the purity of her intentions as well as of her devotion to himself, it occasionally happened that an important office was filled up on her recommendation—not always happily, as, for instance, in the case of the honest but incapable minister Chamillard. At a later date she lamented that her endeavours to bring the best men, such as the Duc de Chevreuse and the Duc de Beauvilliers, about the king had ended unfortunately for all concerned. Her efforts often failed on account of the king's old aversion for superiority, whether in intellect, science, education, or natural gifts, which might overshadow him, or perchance expose his ignorance. Least of all could she find fault with the king's partiality for building, which had now grown to be a passion. Once, at a moment of great financial distress, having allowed herself to make some remonstrance as to the building expenses at Marly, when Versailles already had cost four hundred millions, she experienced an unfriendly rebuff.

There is no contradiction in saying that a woman to whom homage was paid as to a queen, and whose slightest gesture was instantly obeyed, nevertheless lamented the condition of slavery in which she lived. The Bishop of Chartres, in writing to her, says by way of consolation that it is God's will that, although free-born, she should be a slave. It was a matter of course that Louis, just because he rated her so highly and trusted her so implicitly, gradually put more and more upon her, especially things that were disagreeable to himself—those, for instance, which concerned the female portion of the royal family. She had to look after the princesses, to lecture and reprimand them; and these ill-educated, capricious beings, of whom, as she says, not one came to any good, were not seldom seen to come from her apartment weeping. So entirely had she given herself up to the king's service that she might well declare that she did not keep back from him one moment of her life, and that she never knew until ten o'clock at night what she might have to do on the morrow. Godet pointedly recommended her to exert herself in entertaining and cheering the king, that by such means she might obtain a more favourable hearing on serious matters. He wrote to her to the effect that by gaiety, of which the king was so fond, he must be prepared for truths that were distasteful to him.[4] She followed this advice and invented novel forms of social pastimes; concerts, dances, took place in her apartments, whilst she herself, as she says, was deeply sorrowful at heart over the course of events and the condition of the country; for the king, she observes in one of her letters, desires only to amuse himself and to forget everything. Yet a time came when the king, *blasé*, over-satiated, broken in health, saddened by political and family misfortunes, was no longer capable of amusement—*inamusable*, she says—and yet could not endure to be without her company. Then, when this monarch, who of all men in his time had been the most admired and feared, spent his days in weeping and in seeking comfort and encouragement from her, it required all her strength of mind to bear up under the burden of her own grief and that of others, and not to sink under the constant strain put upon her.[5] She had to become a heroine of patience, forbearance, and comfort.

[4] 'Ayez donc une grande confiance; marchez dans la joie du St. Esprit en la répandant sur le roi; car il a besoin de goûter la douceur et la liberté de la bonne conscience. Il regard encore trop la vertu et la perfection de son état, par ce qu'il y a de plus austère et de plus rebutant pour la nature; quand il verra la personne qu'il aime et qu'il estime le plus, dans une joie et une liberté d'esprit continuelle, dans une continuelle innocence et dans un amour ardent des bonnes œuvres, Dieu lui fera la grace d'aspirer au même bonheur. La femme fidèle sanctifiera l'homme infidèle, dit St. Paul, combien plus le mari chrétien.' *Lettres de l'évêque de Chartres* (1757), p. 173.

[5] 'Quand le roi est revenu de la chasse, il vient chez moi; on ferme la porte et personne n'entre plus. Me voilà donc seule avec lui. Il faut essuyer ses chagrins, s'il en a, ses tristesses, ses vapeurs; il lui prend quelquefois des pleurs dont il n'est pas le maître, ou bien il se trouve incommodé. Il

Small wonder if her letters are full of lamentations. Though standing in the place of a queen, she had not so much liberty as the wife of a simple citizen; the king whom she loved was often her heaviest cross; she needed repose in the feebleness of her advancing years, but was compelled to live an active life.[6] To judge by her letters, the longing for death seems to have been her strongest and most persistent feeling.[7] From an exalted idea of duty and an exaggerated power of self-tormenting she sometimes reproached herself for still wishing to be loved, and fearing that the king loved and valued her quite too much.[8] In another place she complains that under the plea of conscience—her director had imposed this upon her—she was too much occupied with her health, and that, oppressed by the weight of suffering and sorrow, her senses seemed as it were blunted.[9] So entirely unique, and (so to speak) incongruous a position demanded a tension of mind and physical exertion beyond her power. She complains that the long hours of standing when receiving visits of ceremony were almost unendurable to her —she had to struggle perpetually against nervous attacks (*vapeurs* was then the term for what was later called *migraine*). This grew worse as the years wore on. She suffered continually from feverish attacks, which the king's physician, Fagon, otherwise her devoted admirer, called 'fanciful' because in reality they were produced by mental excitement and distress of mind. When fifty-five years of age she was already so ill that she believed her death to be imminent. But she resembled the king in this: namely, that her will enabled her to overcome physical weakness and infirmity. Her bodily suffer-

n'a point de conversation. Il vient quelque ministre qui apporte souvent de mauvaises nouvelles; le roi travaille. Si on veut que je sois en tiers dans ce conseil, on m'appelle; si on ne veut pas de moi, je me retire un peu plus loin, et c'est là où je place quelquefois mes prières de l'après-midi.' *Lettres hist. et édif.* ii. 163.

[6] *Lettres de M. de Chartres* (Glasgow, 1756), 180.

[7] *Idem* 74. [8] *Idem* 73. [9] *Idem* 194.

ings, she said, she could find means to endure, if only she might lead a life in keeping with her age; but continual change of place obliged her to live as if she were a woman of twenty. The king, thinking only of himself, did not see this.

Madame de Maintenon thought it her vocation, and one of the duties laid upon her by the king, to maintain or restore harmony and peace amongst the numerous members of the royal family. She developed in the performance of this task that fine womanly tact of which she was mistress; no one had studied more carefully the human, especially the female heart, in all its recesses. Disputes of every kind were rife in this circle; almost all the children, nephews, and cousins of the king had been badly brought up by Louis's fault, and, the king's brother at the head of them, set an example of serious excesses and even of shameful vices. She has recorded what a burden it was to her to have to entertain these royal personages, who paid her interminable visits merely for the sake of distraction, and, blunted and worn out by dissipation, took no real interest in anything.

As the king led a wandering life, moving from one royal residence to another—Versailles, Marly, Clagny, Trianon, Fontainebleau—his wife was obliged to accompany him everywhere, and often to inhabit unhealthy rooms which had been but a short time completed. She complains that in the construction of them more attention had been paid to architectural effect than to making them habitable. The consequence to her was increasing ill-health, and it is astonishing that, in spite of her repeated attacks of fever, she should have lived to so great an age. 'We shall perish for the sake of symmetry,' she once wrote, not without bitterness. The king's love for her was sincere, but in his selfish want of consideration he paid no attention to such things, and she was afraid of being troublesome to him.

Besides all, there was the Sisyphus-work of labouring to satisfy the insatiable thirst for amusement and enjoyment of the princes and princesses of an idle court. She knew well by experience that these pleasures fly faster the more eagerly they are pursued, and leave only weariness and vexation behind them.[1] She could not, however, entirely withdraw from them, but was forced to take part in them personally, and to be continually inventing something new because the king wished it.

The instinct to help and to benefit others was strong within her. In the village of Avon she taught the peasant children their catechism, and looked after the sick. As she had made a rule to herself not to ask the king for money, she was often compelled to limit her small gifts, or to suspend them till she again had a sum of money at her disposal. Since the king had designedly reduced the nobles to poverty, and nevertheless obliged those whom he had attracted to court to be lavish in their expenditure, he, whose system of finance had brought the whole riches of the country into his own hands, was obliged to assist the feudal lords, now transformed into needy courtiers, by frequent donations in money, and by allowances. In Dangeau's and Sourches' diaries, numbers of these presents are specified, many of them amounting week by week to 50,000, or even to 100,000 livres. That Madame de Maintenon should be solicited to present petitions from men, and yet more from women, was a matter of course in her position, and with her reputed omnipotence. As all donations were mere acts of grace, a refusal amounted to disgrace, and became consequently a double mortification. The king was indifferent to such grievances, but they were most painful to his wife, and a never-ending source of vexation and enmity. She took pains in the selection of candidates to apply the standard

[1] 'J'ai passé le temps de Fontainebleau dans une grande solitude, dont je me suis très-bien trouvée ; je la veux continuer ici. Je n'ai nulle raison de me montrer, et j'en ai mille pour me cacher ; je suis vieille, sourde, souvent triste, malade, ennuyée du monde, connaissant trop les courtisans ; je n'ai plus ce qui m'intéressait à tout, qui m'est devenu indifférent, excepté ce qui regarde la personne du roi et le bien de son état.' *Lettres de Mme. de M. à la Pr. des Ursins*, ii. 320.

of moral behaviour, and since the yearly sums available for donations in money progressively diminished, owing to the continually increasing outlay consequent upon the prolongation of the war, the crowd of malcontents proportionately increased, causing invective and slander to be heaped upon her, who might infallibly, as they supposed, have obtained what was wanted from the king, had she only chosen to make the request in earnest. The echo of these murmurings is perceptible in the letters of Saint-Simon and of the Duchess of Orleans. Madame de Maintenon herself said that nothing could be sadder than to be always having to say 'No' to persons whom one would willingly serve; in the Valley of Jehosaphat she would be fairly judged. She thought little of herself and her future as far as money matters were concerned; so little, indeed, that she had not even secured for herself a jointure. 'What will become of her?' asked Louis on his deathbed, 'for she has literally nothing.' Yet something she had: an asylum in Saint-Cyr, and the thought of that institution which had grown so dear to her, the hope of ending her days there far from the bustle of the world, far from the intrigues and wickedness of a corrupt court, amongst her beloved daughters, who, as she said, were pure and good as angels; this it was that sustained her in the latter years of care and sorrow, and amid increasing infirmities.

Madame de Maintenon was fully aware that lampoons upon her, lies and calumniations, derisive ballads, and such like, daily sprang up in Paris and Versailles like mushrooms from the ground. But she calmly resigned herself to the inevitable; 'We live here upon slander,'[2] she once said; and again, 'We are accustomed to live upon poison.' She knew also that it was her inevitable destiny to share in the general hatred which her royal husband's system of government had drawn down upon him with accumulating force since her union with him; the people could see her power but could not perceive its limits, nor the helplessness with

[2] 'Nous vivons ici d'injures.' *Lettres hist. et édif.* (1856), ii. 211.

which she sorrowfully contemplated the diseases of the state.

As if to enhance the cares and burdens of her life, the exiled King James II. of England and his consort Mary settled in her neighbourhood in 1688. Madame de Maintenon soon won the confidence of the latter, a princess of Modena, who claimed her intervention in all her affairs and troubles. The two women soon became (yet not to the advantage of France) the warmest friends, so that, as Madame de Maintenon says, she had sometimes to receive two courts, the English and the French, together in her apartments. Mary wrote to her, 'We confide in you in all things.' The result was that Madame de Maintenon persuaded Louis, at a highly critical moment, by an act of perjury, to proclaim and acknowledge the Pretender, James III., as King of England, a step which at once had the effect of rousing the whole English nation to energetic participation in the preparations for the War of the Spanish Succession, and entailed the most injurious consequences upon the French King and his people.

The piety of Madame de Maintenon did not in any way interfere with her social charm; she was as serene and cheerful in her days of health as she was courteous, modest, and obliging, and so found a welcome in the most exclusive circles, winning both men and women by her amiability. Withal, she was most strict in her own conduct, and, by her simple yet dignified deportment, understood how to repel all undue familiarity and to maintain a spotless reputation. In after days she related to her pupils at Saint-Cyr that what preserved her from going wrong was not so much piety, as the ambition, the passionate desire, to be highly esteemed by every one, and to be blameless in the eyes of the world. She had never known any one who approached her in this quality. This thirst for recognition, praise, and sympathy, remained to the end an ineradicable feature of her character, which she herself summed up in the expression that she was a 'glorieuse.' Nevertheless in the end she sacrificed one ambition to another by voluntarily accepting her ambiguous position before the world, thus exposing herself to the evil suspicions of many persons. This, she was assured, was a sacrifice imposed upon her by a higher duty; it was made with the sorest repugnance, but she never regretted it.

But Madame de Maintenon aimed at a higher degree of piety than was customary in her day. A distinction was then made between piety and devotion. The great mass of pretenders to piety contented themselves with outward obedience to the precepts of the church and with the observance of the usual religious ceremonies. The 'devout' desired to take religion seriously; it was to be the rule and supreme motive of their whole life. Every one in Versailles who approached the king must have a confessor, and Louis insisted on knowing from all, who in any way attracted his notice, to whom they went to confession. The merely pious used frequently to change, but the devout kept to their original choice, and had also a director, who, being credited with special experience in the art of directing souls, gave general instructions as to behaviour, advice as to ascetic observances, prescribed and conducted special religious exercises, and was appealed to in difficult cases of conscience. Men only exceptionally had a director, but women frequently, and he was usually the man upon whom they bestowed the fullest confidence and to whom they yielded the most implicit obedience, often far too much at the expense of the husband's rights, for blind submission and complete renunciation of their own judgment was deemed essential under the circumstances. Madame de Maintenon had been taught to regard obedience as the highest virtue of the spiritual life, and every work, however small and insignificant in itself, as meritorious and holy if performed in the spirit of submission.

The marquise had bestowed her full confidence upon the Sulpicians, an order of priests recently founded, without monastic vows, and devoting themselves principally to the education of the clergy. These men sought to assume an intermediate position in the church controversies of the day. Like the Jesuits, they were the opponents of all who were suspected of any leaning towards Jansenism, advocating unquestioning obedience to the papal chair and its decrees, but disapproving of Jesuitic casuistry and the system of penance. The fact that Madame de Maintenon joined herself to them and shared their views to the extent that in her last years she still called herself a 'complete Sulpician,'[3] and that she consequently became their protectress and advocate with the king, has exercised an important influence upon the history of France.

Godet des Marais was the priest whom she chose for her director. He retained the post for thirty years, even after that, through her influence, he became Bishop of Chartres, and until his death in 1709, and from this circumstance he became, next to the royal confessor, the most influential man in the Gallican Church, and the most powerful of the French bishops, without, however, misusing his power. She herself said that without her director she would not be able to exist.[4] He was to her the personification of her conscience; he shared the burden of responsibility in a position full of difficulties and temptations, and pointed out to her exactly what she should do or leave undone, and how, in this or that situation, she should conduct herself. So long, she says, as she had acted upon her own choice, she had been continually afraid of doing now too little, and now too much, or of not doing the right thing at all. But at last, in obeying her director, she had found peace. Her pupil and friend, Mademoiselle d'Aumale, tells us that it often filled

[3] *Lettres hist. et édif.* i. 350 ff.

[4] 'Grâce à Dieu, j'ai un directeur de bon esprit, et qui me décide de gros en gros ce que j'ai à faire, et quand une fois il m'a dit ce que je puis faire en sûreté de conscience, ou ce que je dois éviter, je m'en tiens à sa décision; autrement je ne vivrais pas, et j'aurais des peines infinies.' *Lettres hist. et édif.* ii. 276.

her with confusion and astonishment to find Madame de Maintenon consulting her director in perfectly simple things upon which nobody could feel uncertain. But it was the merit of obedience that she sought. She sent him month by month a report of the state of her soul, of her temptations, and her spiritual joys and sorrows. We gain a knowledge of these reports (*redditions*) from the answers to them, conveying comfort and encouragement. She is evidently most conscientious, unsparing, and searching in her self-examinations. She found the numerous claims and difficulties of her situation an overwhelming burden; she is often at her wits' end how to cope with the whirl and press of the multifarious occupations into which she is drawn, and upon which she is expected to give an opinion, however strange they may be to her. She ought, Godet writes to her, to be at court the light of the world and the salt of the earth; she must be the stay and comfort of the church. God has committed into her hand the welfare of the state and of the church, and the spiritual well-being of a great king; she is the harbour of refuge, and the guardian angel of the monarch; the king has himself entrusted her with the treasures of his kingdom. Godet winds up with the assurance that it is her mission to reform the world. Parallel with this runs the exhortation, oft repeated, to continue under the yoke of obedience, especially to the priesthood, and not to allow the king's zeal for the extirpation of Protestantism and Jansenism to grow cold. In his anxiety to console and encourage her, he touches the borders of flattery, and even now and then oversteps them in the emphatic recognition of her virtues, of the blameless purity of her life, and in the certainty of her future salvation. She herself deprecatingly represents to him that his praises foster her self-love. Thereupon he assures her that she has entirely overcome and laid aside pride and vanity, whilst all the while she is aware of the contrary. He sets before her that it is under his direction that she has arrived at what she is. We are reminded of Praxiteles, who, in the image before which he knelt, worshipped the work of his own hands.

Next to Godet, another man, peculiarly fitted to be a director and religious guide of men, exercised great influence over Madame de Maintenon for some years. This was Fénelon, whose great qualities she had early recognised, and whom she had attracted to the court. Partly owing to her advice he had been nominated to the post of tutor to the prince and heir to the throne, the Duke of Burgundy. Like Godet, Fénelon belonged to the school of St. Sulpice, and was his intimate friend, but far superior to him in intellect. To him also the marquise opened herself without reserve, beseeching him to enlighten her as to her faults, and the true remedies for them. His answers[5] give some insight into the relative position and dispositions of the three individuals concerned. Living close to her, and having become thoroughly acquainted with her by constant intercourse, his remarks upon her, like those of her detractors Saint-Simon and the Palatinate princess, carry great weight, although, unlike the comforting and flattering Godet, he takes her severely and seriously to task, and is even too exorbitant in the demands which he makes upon her. She is too cold and dry towards persons who are distasteful to her; is still, without being aware of it, 'glorieuse;' too sensitive to everything that touches her vanity; she sets too great value upon the esteem and approbation of the well-disposed, and upon the consciousness of her own virtue. In short, Self is still with her an unbroken idol. He admits at the same time that her piety is genuine; that she has never taken part in the wickedness of the world; has long since abjured its errors, and that she is universally credited with a sincere love of goodness, although men reproach her for intolerance with their faults. Her mind is better qualified to judge in public affairs than she herself supposes: she ought not, indeed, to interfere in politics, but to study them, and carefully and prudently to

[5] *Correspondance de Fénelon* (1827), v. 470 ff.

use her influence with the king according to the opportunities which Providence has granted her. She ought, he says, systematically to control the king, since he would have her do so; to rule him, as he wishes to be ruled. She ought, at the same time, to seek out the most able men in all professions, and prepare the way for them to office; to protect the king from mischievous influences, to stand upon the alert, like a watchman in Israel, and, in short, to do more than the most experienced statesman could have done. But to the burden which he heaps upon her he adds yet another, still heavier: she, who from her natural vivacity and sensibility strongly felt the need of female friendship, must forego this natural affection and the desire of her heart, since it is but a refined self-love, and therefore of the devil. She must devote herself instead to the 'pure love' of God. Thus he wrote in 1690. It was premonitory of that which she was destined to hear from him and to read in his writings six years later, when the dispute broke out between Fénelon and Bossuet upon 'pure love.'

We must here make some mention of a memorial composed four years later by Fénelon (1694), because it enables us to draw conclusions as to the way in which in her innermost heart she regarded the king's method of government and the fruits which it bore. It is the famous letter which in 1694 Fénelon addressed anonymously to the king with the object of moving him, if possible, to reflection, self-knowledge, and conversion.[6] Fénelon sets before him that hitherto his reign has been one long series of unjust wars carried on from ambition, avarice, and the desire for fame.

[6] Ranke (*Werke*, xi. 74) doubts its authenticity on the ground that Fénelon could not have said that he was unknown to the king. Yet he could say so with perfect truth, since the king at that time knew him only by name, not personally. He had only one audience of the king, and that, obtained through Madame de Maintenon, took place after the affair of the letter. See on this subject the pamphlet, *La France Catholique* (1825), ii. 194. Any one acquainted with Fénelon's letters and political writings will easily recognise his style in this letter; its authenticity is also generally accepted in France. Ranke was unaware of the testimony to it in the letters of Madame de Maintenon.

His faithlessness prolonged these wars indefinitely because the allied powers, convinced that Louis would forthwith violate the terms of peace, preferred the risk of continuing the war. France, utterly exhausted, resembled a great hospital devoid of comfort and of the necessaries of life; the king had ruined the nation to maintain his court in monstrous and unwholesome luxury, and by making himself the sole possessor of wealth, had surrounded himself with hosts of murmuring beggars. His greed of fame had blinded him; he was heedless of the decrease in the population brought about by misery, hunger, and epidemics, and of the threatenings of rebellion. His ministers, hard, arrogant, and dishonest, who left to him merely the semblance of autocracy, suppressed every outburst of violence. His religion consisted of fear and superstition. After a sharp criticism of the king's confessor (La Chaise), whom from a cloistered priest he had made a minister, and to whom was committed the entire disposal of church patronage, the marquise and the Duc de Beauvilliers are likewise blamed for weakness and timidity because, possessing the king's confidence, it was their business to have opened his eyes. This letter, which Fénelon managed secretly to convey into the king's hand through a friend, probably the Duc de Chevreuse, was communicated by Madame de Maintenon, who appears to have received it from the king, to the Archbishop De Noailles, with the remark that it was well written (*elle est bien faite*) but that Louis could not be converted by such truths; they only embittered or hardened him; therefore the letter was too severe. She appears to have had a suspicion as to the authorship, for she inquires of de Noailles whether he did not recognise the style. Severe, but true!—truly an important confession from her mouth, and a confession, too, of her powerlessness in the most weighty matters. It exonerates her to a certain degree from blame, for as a wife she was bound to submit and to witness in silence much that she disapproved of But by the light of this letter we measure the intensity of the longing which she so often expresses for flight and release, and the longing, too, for death, in spite of the sincere love with which she devoted herself to her husband. Scarcely anything could have been more disheartening and melancholy than that, after ten years of influence based upon the closest and most intimate ties, the condition of France and the spirit of the government should present itself to the eyes of the observer in gloomier colours than ever. If, as is probable, she guessed the author, she must also have known that his friends, the Duc de Chevreuse and Duc de Beauvilliers, two men whom she herself esteemed highly and had brought into the king's immediate circle, were of the same way of thinking.

The man who could say such things to Madame de Maintenon was clearly not fitted to remain the guide of her conscience; he would have driven her to despair. At a later period she remarked that she regarded it as a token of the gracious interposition of Providence, that she should have preferred the outwardly repulsive Godet to the brilliant and attractive Fénelon with his high flight of intellect, for indubitably he would have entangled her in the errors of mysticism. Godet fully atoned in other ways for his outward deficiencies. He appeared to her, and not to her only, to be a saint upon earth, and she was in the habit of so describing him. He understood so well, moreover, how to offer her comfort and consolation; he reassured her as to the reality of her piety and the certainty of her future salvation; he firmly believed that she was an instrument especially chosen and sanctified by the grace of God, and that her union with Louis was a miracle brought about by divine interposition. He also discovered in the king besides so many excellent qualities, vigorous faith, wisdom, and rectitude—things of which Fénelon could perceive nothing or saw only the reverse. Her heart willingly believed him, even if her head doubted. It was balm to her when Godet said that the king loved his people, although she must have daily seen how this love, belied by actions, expended itself in empty wishes. To Godet she consequently clung submissively during his lifetime, holding fast to his precepts and opinions as to infallible laws, and after his death (1709) giving her conscience into the keeping of the men whom he had recommended, Bissy and La Chétardie. The former became, through her, Bossuet's successor at Meaux and a cardinal; the latter she would willingly have made the king's confessor after the death of La Chaise, but he declined, and contented himself with being hers.

The outbreak of the Quietist controversy led to a complete estrangement between Madame de Maintenon and Fénelon—notwithstanding that the latter owed to her his elevation to the see of Cambrai—and caused her the bitterest grief, possibly the deepest of all her life. Her conduct towards Fénelon and the ecstatic prophetess Madame de Guyon is much criticised, even at the present day.[7] With respect to Fénelon, no ground for reproach is discoverable; she may be said, on the contrary, to have used much conscientious prudence and to have acted from the purest motives, and with all possible forbearance towards her friend. She did all in her power to avert and to mitigate the evil consequences of his imprudent publication. She held long discussions with both Fénelon and Bossuet; she read with the most careful attention the publication which had been so generally condemned; Fénelon himself left no means untried to win her to his opinions, but in vain. She trembled for Saint-Cyr, where Madame de Guyon, whom Fénelon had taken under his protection, had already initiated some of the nuns in her Quietist doctrines.[8] She could not familiarise herself with the idea of a pure, wholly passive love, renouncing every exercise of virtue, with a state in which the soul, detached from or unconscious of discri-

[7] Besides Sainte-Beuve, Guerrier has also lately (*Mad. Guyon*. Pari 1881) placed the conduct of Madame de Maintenon in an unfavourable light and has again made use of the fictions of La Beaumelle, although in other respects doing justice to her virtues.

[8] "La liaison qui est entre M. de Cambrai et Madame Guyon est fondée sur la conformité de la doctrine; on peut-on voir le danger, étant soutenue

minate acts, is rapt in the purely spiritual contemplation of the infinitely perfect, ineffable Being, and is even unmindful at times of its own salvation. This teaching, which the Archbishop of Cambrai had taken from the older mystics, and the delineation of a state which she had neither experienced herself nor perceived in others, appeared to her, as well as to most people with whom she held any intercourse, repulsive and dangerous; she thought that God had permitted this lofty and brilliant intellect to fall into error in order to humble him.

Fénelon used every endeavour to draw her to his way of thinking; in touching persuasive letters he put before her that in his writings he had merely propounded the doctrines of mystics and ascetics who had been canonised by the church. He entertained, it is very evident, a high opinion of her understanding and piety; he thought she was qualified to form an independent opinion upon these obscure questions, wrapt as they were in peculiar terminology and the subtleties of transcendental metaphysics. The intimacy between him and her had, indeed, been so great, that Elisabeth Charlotte of Orleans could say that, for a time, he had reigned with her.[2] His efforts, however, were in vain; Godet, despite the friendship which had existed hitherto between himself and Fénelon, declared strongly and decidedly against the book; all the other authorities accessible to the marquise gave the same opinion. Those who judged the book most leniently, she says, were yet of opinion that it had better never have appeared. Fénelon himself agreed with her to some extent upon this point; he ought, he wrote finally to her, not to complain that she believed the three great prelates (Bossuet, Noailles, and Godet) rather than

d'un homme de telle vertu, d'un tel esprit, et dans un tel poste? Nous l'avons caché tant que nous avons espéré d'y apporter du remède; nous l'avons découvert quand nous avons cru le devoir à l'église; voilà ce qui dépendait de nous, c'est à Dieu à faire le reste.' *Correspond. de Mme. de M.* iv. 266.

[2] *Ranke*, xiii. 159.

him alone, and that the safety of the church was dearer to her than his personal reputation.

The entire order of the Jesuits, with La Chaise at its head, in Paris as well as in Rome, took Fénelon's part; they saw in him their advocate and fellow-combatant against Jansenism, and their mystics taught as he did; but the allied bishops this time prevailed with the king, and La Chaise prudently gave way. They informed the king that the book contained innovations of a very dangerous kind. That was quite enough for a monarch in whom the very word innovation was sufficient to arouse terror and indignation. With the whole weight of his authority, he persuaded the pope, who had long hesitated and now only yielded with the greatest reluctance, to publish a solemn condemnation of the book. In threatening imperious letters he explained to the Curia that all he had demanded was such a condemnation, and nothing else; a simple dogmatic statement of the true doctrine he would upon no account admit into France. So the sword of Brennus was thrown into the theological scale. Both parties carried on the struggle in Rome, not always with the legitimate weapons; Fénelon did not scruple to charge Bossuet with Jansenism, and his agents in Rome at once included Noailles and Godet in the accusation; neither did he omit to put forward his own ultramontane views and devoted adherence to the Romish principles, in opposition to the author of the declaration of 1682.

Amongst the persons who drew upon themselves the king's displeasure upon this occasion was Madame de Maintenon herself. Louis was angry with her for having recommended this man to him—with whose sentiments she must have been acquainted long before the appearance of the book—for the prince's tutor and for the office of archbishop. Never, she says, had she been so near falling into real disgrace. She became seriously ill from grief and worry, so that the king, standing by her bedside, inquired at last whether she really meant to die of this affair.

Fénelon and his patroness never saw each other nor exchanged letters again. He submitted unreservedly after Rome had condemned twenty-three propositions drawn from his work. She, however, did not believe in the sincerity of this submission; she knew too well that his system had become altogether a part of himself. Fénelon amongst his friends made no secret of his conviction that truth and justice would rather have required the condemnation of his opponent Bossuet, who had so often opposed the doctrine of the pure unselfish love of God, to preach the self-interested love which rests upon the promise and the hope of salvation. 'He who has erred,' he wrote, 'has triumphed, he who was free from error has been crushed.'[1] He lamented that by this means, that is, in consequence of the Roman decision, the faithful were led astray; but his word was pledged, and he seems to have believed that in the conflict of two duties, the duty of witnessing to the truth and that of obedience to the church, precedence was due to the latter. Then another circumstance arose, which for Madame de Maintenon made reconciliation or accommodation of any kind impossible. 'Télémaque' made its appearance. She, as well as almost all contemporary readers, perceived in this romance, written ostensibly for the instruction of the prince, the design of setting him against his grandfather's method of government, and to place the latter in the unfavourable light of an ambitious conqueror and tyrannical oppressor of his people. In her eyes, this was unpardonable ingratitude, or even worse.

Madame de Maintenon would have succumbed to her

[1] 'Feu M. de Meaux a combattu mon livre par prévention pour une doctrine pernicieuse et insoutenable, qui est celle de dire que la raison d'aimer Dieu ne s'explique que par le seul désir du bonheur. On a toléré et laissé triompher cette indigne doctrine, qui dégrade la charité en la réduisant au seul motif de l'espérance. Celui qui errait a prévalu; celui qui était exempt d'erreur a été écrasé.' *Correspondance* (1827), iii. 246.

griefs much sooner, had it not been for Saint-Cyr, the institution which at her desire the king had founded in the immediate neighbourhood of Versailles, and richly endowed, for the education of the poor daughters of the nobility. She felt this to be the greatest benefit which he could have conferred upon her. Here was an asylum to which she could fly when Versailles became intolerable and her patience was exhausted. In this beloved spot the king allowed her to pass the hours which were not dedicated to him. They were the happiest hours of her life. There, as an instructress of youth, she felt herself thoroughly in her element. In her system of education religion entered into all things. Little by little her energy, guided by love and patience, accomplished all that she, in combination with her friend and confessor Godet, thought necessary or beneficial. Upon the teachers of the establishment, the Dames de Saint-Louis, she left the impress of her mind, so that the spirit of her teaching was preserved throughout the century that the institution existed.

Yet a great and serious change in the discipline of the establishment soon proved necessary, and was accomplished by the marquise not without bitter feelings of sorrow and self-reproach. In the necessity for providing distraction and entertainment for the king, she had been misled into permitting some of Racine's plays to be performed before him by the young ladies of Saint-Cyr. Evil consequences did not fail to show themselves. The girls, in whom the lavish applause of so distinguished an audience soon kindled feelings of pride, vanity, and coquetry, became worldly, dissipated, and neglectful of their former occupations. 'They have wit,' observed the marquise, 'and use it against us, and they are haughtier than would beseem princesses.' She at once set about expelling, gradually and without harshness, the worldly spirit which she had roused: theatricals were banished; the cure was complete, and her pupils became contented and happier. The teachers and governesses of the institution, the Dames de Saint-Louis, were, not without opposition, transformed into a religious body bound by vows. In this matter again she was following the suggestions of Godet. She clung to Saint-Cyr with the energy and tender affection of a woman who finds a suitable sphere for the exercise of her faculties and inclinations. Saint-Cyr continued to be the comfort and support of her life; there she breathed a purer air, there she could, for a few hours at least, forget the moral miasma of Versailles. The society of the Dames de Saint-Louis, and of the girls committed to their charge, acted upon her like a purifying and invigorating bath. There she could be that which fate had denied to her, yet for which she was so pre-eminently fitted, a tender careful mother overlooking nought which could minister either to the bodily or the spiritual health of her children; yielding herself up to the delights of unrestrained intercourse, beseeching, exhorting, warning—with unwearied patience if need were—commanding and enforcing; beloved and revered by almost all as a higher being, the slightest word from whose lips ought to be preserved. In connection with this institution of hers she cherished yet higher and bolder hopes; she saw in it a nursery of youth, from whence a blessing would flow upon family life, first amongst the nobility and gradually through all classes. Besides this, as many of the pupils of Saint-Cyr gave themselves up to the life of the cloister she anticipated that the higher tone of the instruction and training acquired at Saint-Cyr would by them be diffused amongst other convents employed in the education of girls.

Nevertheless Saint-Cyr, though so beloved and so full of consolation, was a source of anxiety to her; for when these girls, who had been brought up with such care, were ready to enter upon a new life, the question arose, what was to become of them? They were all poor, only a small number entered convents; for the majority husbands had to be found. 'We are in want of sons-in-law,' is the outcry of the motherly heart; the marriages, too, must be suitable as to rank, the husbands consequently of noble birth. But the nobles were completely impoverished, and had no calling in life but the army, the court, or the church ; filled no political posts, and were for the most part entirely dependent upon royal pensions, in the bestowal of which she had great influence, although, since financial distress had increased, the pensions had sensibly diminished. Add to this the immorality of the men's lives, to the extent of which she and all her contemporaries bear witness, was sufficient to deter her from willingly consigning her foster daughters into the keeping of such husbands. Her representations to the king upon this point appear to have been just as fruitless as were the exhortations from the pulpit calling upon him to check the evil. He tolerated it half willingly—upon system, if the statement of his sister-in-law is to be credited—half from necessity ; in any attempt at reform he must have begun with his own brother. The assertion of the marquise that in her experience by far the greater number of the marriages, in the class whose daughters she educated, proved unhappy, is probably correct ; and the opinion of another lady, Elisabeth Charlotte, whose observations were made in the same sphere as those of Madame de Maintenon, goes further, and says that out of a thousand marriages scarcely two turned out well. The marquise consequently did not hesitate to set before the pupils of Saint-Cyr a highly repulsive picture of men. In her private correspondence she alludes to the worthlessness of the men of her acquaintance in expressions which make it evident that she gathered her impressions and made her observations amid the same scenes, and in the same class of people, as Larochefoucauld when collecting the materials for his maxims.[2]

A variety of opinions have been formed as to the share

[2] 'Je serais bien fâchée, madame, que vous m'ôtassiez l'estime que j'ai pour le comte de Bergheitz, car je voudrais bien croire qu'il y a un fort honnête homme dans le monde ; je comprends pourtant bien qu'il n'y en a point de parfait.' *Lettres de Mme de M. et des Ursins*, iii. 133. This is only one example of the utterances from which her opinion of the men who came into her circle can be seen.

taken by Madame de Maintenon in public affairs, and as to her influence in the disposal of the highest offices; both have been either exaggerated or treated too lightly. Her spiritual adviser had prescribed for her a course of conduct which from its indefiniteness, and the way it partly encouraged and partly dissuaded, must have filled her with doubt and dismay. Where the interests of the church were concerned she ought to be unsparing in the exercise of her influence with the king. But in many cases secular things trenched upon the religious and ecclesiastical sphere—and here it was impossible to draw an undeviating line. Gradually a tacit understanding grew up between the marquise and the ministers of the crown, on the strength of which her hands were left free in church matters, whilst she kept herself aloof from secular affairs, or else in agreement with the ministers: in mixed questions a compromise was sought, or the king himself decided.

There was nothing contradictory in her assurance that she hated political affairs, and yet, as time went on, was more and more occupied with them, particularly after 1701, and she was supposed to have acquired boundless influence in this department. She hated public business all the more because she was conscious of her own deficient knowledge; she often found it to be the case that projects, which she had carefully built up in every detail, collapsed suddenly from some circumstance upon which she had failed to calculate; or when she desired to act she felt herself entangled as it were in the meshes of an invisible net of which she was unable to break the threads. In addition to this, no sooner did she in any way take part in the government, swayed as it was in those days by fiscal interests, than she found herself in conflict with her religious convictions.

Twice only in her life did it happen to the marquise to be present at a sitting of the cabinet council. In a letter to Archbishop de Noailles she describes the astonishment, mingled with terror and disgust, with which she perceived the principles and aims which guided the conduct of public business and the way in which it was carried on.[3] And yet at that time she saw but the prelude to the arbitrary acts and oppressive measures, by which in later years, during the War of the Succession, the unfortunate people were oppressed and driven to the brink of ruin and bankruptcy.

The first event which decidedly injured her in the public opinion was the Peace of Ryswick, by which the nine years' war was ended in 1647. Louis had brought about this war by his arrogance and his desire for his own aggrandisement; had made gigantic efforts to carry it on, to the utter exhaustion of his people and of the resources of the country; the French armies had been victorious in almost every battle; yet now he relinquished nearly every conquest which he had made. Madame de Maintenon had written to her friend Brinon, whilst the war was still going on, that it was the cause of God that the king was defending—can she have thought of the barbarities with which the war was being carried on in the Palatinate and Piedmont?—and the enemy would surely be overcome in consequence. The king also was certain that God would grant him success, and yet he was fully aware at the time of the misery of the people.[4] And now this humiliation had befallen the proudest of monarchs—his withdrawal from everything beyond the frontier of 1681, with the exception of Strasburg. It was the overthrow and condemnation of the whole of the policy followed since the Peace of Nimeguen. Surprise was universal, the matter seemed inexplicable. In Paris, in Versailles, throughout France, the influence of Madame de

[3] 'Quand on est du conseil, Monseigneur, on est mystérieux. Le roi nous a imposé silence sur ce qui se passa il y a quinze jours. Et en vérité, c'est un bien pour moi, et encore plus pour eux, que je n'ose dire tout ce que je vis, et tout ce que j'entendis. J'en suis tout affligée, Monseigneur, non-seulement par rapport à l'affaire présente, mais pour toutes celles que ces messieurs auront à traiter. Cet échantillon me fait voir que je mourrais de douleur si j'assistais au conseil. Que les rois sont à plaindre! Que les hommes sont mauvais! Enfin, Monseigneur, si l'on ne prenait patience en considérant celle de Dieu, on se désespérerait.' *Correspond. de Mme. de M.* iv. 263.

[4] *Mémoires de Languet*, 401.

Maintenon was thought to be the key to the enigma. It had, in fact, something to do with it, in so far that, as Torcy remarks, the utter exhaustion of the nation and the prospect of an immediate opening of the question of the Spanish succession, made the king's mind more accessible to her arguments. Be that as it may, she was supposed in France to be chiefly to blame; from henceforth, she complained, she must 'live upon poison, she must submit to be hated and reviled,' and Godet did not hide from her that public opinion was against her.[5]

The year 1701 ushered in important changes for Madame de Maintenon, as for the whole of France. It was the beginning of the War of the Succession, in which France, without allies, for twelve years withstood the assaults of half Europe. She was obliged now, despite her aversion, to take part in political affairs. She alone possessed that farsightedness which was wanting in the ministers and even in the king. Since the sins committed in youthful arrogance had begun to avenge themselves so fearfully, and now that numerous defeats had to be acknowledged; now, also, that in the midst of danger and distress, the most unwelcome measures must needs be adopted, the aged and infirm monarch had lost his taste for public business, and his wife felt that, if only to lighten the burden for him and to prolong as far as possible a life grown more than ever indispensable to the state, she must be at his side to advise and to labour with him. She mediated between him and the ministers, held conferences with them, assisted them in reasoning with the king, and occasionally shared in their defeat. She has been blamed for inducing the ministers to conceal important events of a vexatious kind from the king, and for the evil results which followed. Here the woman's nature predominated, allowing solicitude for his person to trouble her political vision. She now read despatches from the ambassadors at foreign courts, consulted with Chamillard and

[5] Spanheim certifies this in his report of 1689. See *Bulletin de l'Institut national Genevois*, t. viii. 186.

Torcy, and the lately published letters of the Maréchal de Villars show that this general fully confided in her judgment, and availed himself of her services in communicating with the king. From her long correspondence with her friend the Princess Orsini, who at that time ruled in Spain, we perceive that she also took an interest in Spanish affairs.[6]

Thus she lived through twelve years of torment, during which she was seldom free from the longing to be relieved by death from the heavy burden of ceaseless anxiety. With her excitable disposition and susceptibility for all painful impressions, political and military disasters were to her the occasion of physical suffering. She mentions in one place that the news of a threatened inroad of the Savoyards into Dauphiné obliged her to keep her bed for twenty-four hours. When informed that her friend Brinon dreaded the approach of death, she wrote: 'Is it possible? By me the announcement of death would be hailed with delight!'

Entertaining strong feelings both patriotic and religious, she was greatly perplexed by the victories of the enemy. It seemed to her inexplicable that God should bless the arms of the heretical powers, and should permit three worthy and zealous Catholic kings, as she terms the two Bourbons and the English Pretender, to be defeated. Yet the thought now and then occurs to her that the king by his haughty

[6] 'J'ai toujours à l'esprit l'Espagne presque perdue, la paix qui s'éloigne de plus en plus, les misères que j'apprend de tous côtés, mille gens qui souffrent sous mes yeux, et que je ne puis soulager; du côté de la piété, tous les excès qui règnent présentement, cette ivrognerie, cette gourmandise, ce luxe excessif, etc.; de celui de la religion, le danger visible où je vois qu'elle est. Je ne sais s'il faut porter le roi à pousser les choses jusqu'à un certain point, ou s'il faut le modérer; car qui sait si une conduite trop sévère n'aigrira pas les esprits, n'excitera pas une révolte, ne causera pas un schisme? D'un autre côté, qui sait si Dieu s'accommode de cette prudence humaine et de la politique des hommes, quand il s'agit de l'intérêt de l'église? Tout cela m'agite à un point inconcevable . . . en vérité la tête en est quelquefois prête à me tourner; je crois que si on ouvrait mon corps après ma mort, on trouverait mon cœur sec et tors comme celui de M. de Louvois.' *Lettres hist. et édif*, ii. 277.

violence, and the nation by its corruption, may have merited the divine chastisement. She knew full well where the chief delinquents were to be found. She daily saw how the covetousness, the intrigues, and animosities of the court interfered ruinously with the course of government, and were mixed up with the conduct of the war. To Archbishop de Noailles she wrote: 'Most people here betray and ruin their friends and relations simply for the sake of being able to say one word more to the king and to show him that they would sacrifice everything to him. In this terrible place (that is to say the court) there is nobody who is not infected with the general dishonesty; the court transforms even the best.' Elisabeth Charlotte from her own point of view made the very same observation in almost the same words.

When at length the Peace of Utrecht had unexpectedly been concluded to the advantage of France, leaving the kingdom intact and the dynasty upon the Spanish throne, Madame de Maintenon felt herself once more a genuine Frenchwoman, longing for the glory of her royal husband. Her first thought was not of the misery of the people, well-nigh ruined, and bleeding from countless wounds, but of the glory which Louis had gained in having arrived without loss of territory at the termination of a war in which half Europe had been ranged against him. Had she not been blinded some presentiment at least must have risen before her mind that the mischief done was now past all remedy, that the general corruption of the political and moral forces of the nation would, at no very distant period, lead to some tremendous catastrophe and to the downfall of the edifice!

However little in harmony it may appear with her character as otherwise known, one cannot help perceiving in her a certain hard-heartedness, and a fanaticism, apparently rather instilled into her than of spontaneous growth. Her French critics probably hint at this when they speak almost unanimously of her dryness (*sécheresse*). She has not a word of regret or sympathy for the twice devastated Palatinate, or for Piedmont given over to fire and sword. She encourages her brother to enrich himself by the acquisition, at a nominal price, of the properties of the Protestant nobles in Poitou. She reports, as a matter of business, to Cardinal de Noailles that several hundred more 'fanatics'—*i.e.* Protestant peasants fighting for liberty of conscience—have been killed in the Cévennes, and that it is expected that the whole of Languedoc will now be 'purged' from them. Here, it must be admitted, one fanaticism was pitted against another, but she had helped to kindle the flame.

We have still to take into consideration her whole attitude towards French Protestantism. The accusation most frequently brought against her is that upon her must fall the chief burden of responsibility for the revocation of the Edict of Nantes and the oppression of the Protestants. This accusation must in some respects be modified, in others emphasised.

To destroy the Protestant Church in his kingdom was Louis's first aim; he varied only in the choice of means to the end which he had set before him from the beginning. It belonged to the glory which was to encompass himself and his reign; if he were successful, he would stand high above his predecessors, whose efforts had failed in the beginning, and who had not had the courage to renew them. Was it to be supposed that he in his omnipotence could not bring about that which the Austrian Habsburgs in their hereditary dominions had, apparently at least, accomplished successfully? It was intolerable, that a considerable portion of his subjects should consider him as in error upon some of the weightiest matters; that they must wish success to his enemies in his wars with Protestant powers, which he himself, as well as the southern and eastern powers and the bulk of the nation, chose to reckon as religious wars!

The system of coercion and bribery pursued for twenty years had already achieved much when in the year 1685 the decisive blow was dealt by the revocation of the Edict of Nantes. Whether this was done by the advice of the marquise remains uncertain; anyhow, she did not venture upon any opposition. She related at Saint-Cyr how that once, when she had recommended some mitigation of the proceedings, Louis had said that apparently she still retained some affection for the opinions of her youth. In reality she thought, in common with every one else in France, especially the clergy except the Jansenists, that religious liberty was highly objectionable, and that coercion and force were not only most praiseworthy when employed against the unorthodox, but a duty incumbent on the monarch as the guardian of the church. This was the teaching of Rome, re-echoed from pulpits and professorial chairs, and recorded in episcopal pastorals. Even Pope Innocent XI., by no means amicably disposed towards Louis, commended the king's action as most praiseworthy and meritorious, and celebrated it in Rome with brilliant festivities.

It contributed essentially to the ill-will of the king and Madame de Maintenon towards the Jansenists, that they refused to share in the general rejoicings and were scandalised by the coercive measures. Besides this, Godet, being in favour of coercion, if not exactly of the dragonades, insisted that the new converts should be compelled to attend mass and to partake of the sacrament. Other bishops disapproved of this; they thought that many would thus become guilty of sacrilege, and even Madame de Maintenon recoiled from the idea with horror. Yet her memoranda for the year 1697 [1] breathe a striking harshness. She rejects any possibility of granting even the smallest measure of religious liberty; the reputation of the king forbade that he should make any retrograde step; the practice must be continued of depriving parents of their children to bring them up as Catholics. The

[1] Lavallée, *Correspondance gén. de Mme. de M.* iv. 199 ff.

memoranda prove how completely she shared the king's views upon this vital question, and that she agreed with the bishops who had extolled the action of the king in enforcing the faith. It would, she said, be incompatible with the king's honour and dignity to permit any of those who had emigrated to return; the converts would derive fresh hope from the permission, and would again leave the church; the complete extermination of Protestantism must be carried out. Without a word of disapprobation she mentions the breaking of the king's word, when in a second edict, after that he had promised the Protestants to abstain from coercive measures, he forthwith commanded the severest penalties and cruelties to be resorted to without mercy, including confiscations, dragonades, slavery in the galleys, imprisonments, and abduction of children from their parents. All that she would have granted then is expressed in the words 'imperceptible mitigation.' Attendance at divine worship is to be enforced by the severest penalties; and since the penalty of death was then in force in such cases, it is evident that she gave her consent to that. She remained, in short, the worthy disciple of her director, Godet, excepting upon one point: she could not approve that the hundreds of thousands who had been forced to abjure their faith should also be driven to the sacrilegious reception of the sacrament. Her spiritual instructor, Godet, insisted on this, because, he thought, it was impossible to allow a large section of the population to remain entirely without religion, and to suffer a generation of atheists to spring up: true, indeed, it was that men were forced thereby into deadly sin, hypocrisy, and the desecration of all that was holiest: but for that the responsibility fell, not upon those who exercised compulsion, but upon those who suffered under it. This was too much, however, even for a woman of her blind credulity to accept; and she therefore took the part of the prelates who, like the Cardinals de Noailles and Le Camus and the friends of Jansenism, rejected compulsory confession and communion as blasphemous and ungodly. In helpless perplexity the bishops conferred with one another; none knew how to discover a reasonable way out of the labyrinth into which the king, with the bishops and clergy, had been led by the heads of the church.

After the lapse of several years bishops and intendants announced the fact, which, however, was for the most part concealed from the king, that the only result arrived at had been to make the people utterly irreligious and to cause countless acts of sacrilege to be committed; true conversion was as far off as ever. Some variation was made in the methods of persecution; and a few of the coercive measures which had proved ineffectual were allowed to drop. Then, again, the most fearful punishments were ordered to check the wholesale emigration. The treatment of the Protestants was like that of a sick man whom an unskilful surgeon tortures and mutilates with cuts and stabs first in one direction and then in another. Everything was done to make their existence in France unendurable. When, at length, about 100,000 of the wealthiest and most industrious families in France had taken refuge abroad, and their loss to the country was becoming yearly more perceptible, covert endeavours were made to introduce some relaxation of the regulations in force, and to induce some of the exiles to return. The attempt failed. As to the opinion of the marquise it cannot be denied that it helped to bring about the outbreak of war in the Cévennes, which necessitated a division of the French forces just at the time of the last great war, cost the lives of 100,000 men as well as the destruction of 500 townships, and brought upon the king the deepest humiliation he had yet suffered, viz. the necessity of treating with the rebels, and of making concessions to them. It is a dark page in the history of Madame de Maintenon. Here, as in other cases, the king and she alternately excited and deluded themselves. Hence the inconsistency and arbitrariness of the measures resorted to. The most severe and mischievous of the regulations were not enforced whenever, from the pressure of foreign affairs, any aggravation of the situation was feared. But as soon as the danger was removed all the most odious measures were once more put into execution. For Madame de Maintenon, as well as the king, the ministers, and the bishops, the fundamental idea remained ever the same, namely, that Protestantism must be exterminated.

In the reports of the crown officials, and even of the missionaries, though they were only intended to increase the king's satisfaction as to his spiritual triumphs, there were yet features to be found which might well have served to bring the court to its senses. It was observed that the Protestants, as is usual with oppressed minorities, were in general more moral, and consequently more thrifty, than the Catholics, and it had to be granted that by compelling them to deny their belief, their morality, which was entirely founded upon religious principle, was completely destroyed. It was reported, besides, that the members of a community accustomed from childhood to an evangelical form of divine worship, conducted in the vulgar tongue, could not be brought to content themselves with what appeared to them the incomprehensible and theatrical rite of the Catholic mass. Even Bossuet was anxious to concede to them the reception of the sacrament in both kinds, and he considered that negotiations might be opened with the Holy See to that intent. Madame de Maintenon, however, whose change of religion had taken place early in life, had lost all sympathy with the views and needs of Protestantism, whilst the king would not endure the bare thought that any one in France should possess a religious privilege that was denied to himself. It must be understood that not the slightest peculiarity could be tolerated which would disturb the symmetry of absolute submission; and, consequently, the overtures in favour of unity, put forward simultaneously by the bishop Spinola and Leibnitz, were straightway rejected. Afterwards when the quarrel over the bull *Unigenitus* was raging, it was remarked that the religious world in France was distinguished by the anomaly that those who desired the communion (the Appellants) were denied it, whilst those who abhorred it (the Protestants) were forced to partake of it. Even to the Catholics the whole proceeding was in the highest degree injurious. The mass of the people were brutalised and demoralised by the sight of the violence so frequently practised upon many defenceless and innocent beings, and by the assistance which they were called upon to render towards it. The tribunals, forced to abet such lawless cruelties, suffered in reputation. All sense of justice must have been stifled when, between 1686 and 1757, people could calmly allow over 7,000 men to be condemned to the galleys simply because, for the sake of their faith, they had attempted to quit France; and when the rule was laid down that Protestant galley slaves should never be set at liberty even when their period of punishment had expired. The clergy also lost credit and influence amongst the people. When 'the Angels' Bread,' the most sacred Christian ordinance and most precious gift of the church, for partaking of which steadfast faith and moral purity ought to be indispensable, was daily thrown away upon men who received it with inward repugnance, and even with aversion, the inevitable effect produced was twofold: contempt for the men who, as stewards of the sanctuary, played so unworthy a part; and a growing disregard for the desecrated gift. The years 1685 and 1793 stand in closer relation as cause and effect than might appear to the superficial observer.

Madame de Maintenon considered her highest duty and most sacred task to be the conversion of the king. God, she thought, had providentially ordained that she should be placed at the side of Louis that she might raise him out of a dead, fruitless belief and mechanical observance of precepts and ceremonies to a living and effective faith, founded upon the love of God and of his neighbour. A prayer composed by her has been preserved, in which she desires that God may open the heart of the king, that God may enable her to please, to comfort, and to encourage the king, and even, if it were to God's honour, to grieve him; that she may hide nothing from him in matters of which he ought to be informed by her, and which no one else would have the courage to say.*

It was her purpose to exercise a priestly office towards the king, and to act as a better physician and guide to his soul than the one whom he had chosen, and whom he only retained, as she thought, out of consideration for his feelings; she would organise a small household church with a view both to stimulate and to edify him. This, indeed, succeeded only for a short time; Louis soon became restive, and excused himself, saying: *Je ne suis pas un homme de suite*—it was not given to him to persevere in such things. In her bitter disappointment she exclaimed that God might well have not deemed her worthy of so great a happiness. Her ceaseless endeavours to breathe a Christian spirit into the king remained unsuccessful. She acknowledged regretfully that he was only moved to the performance of religious exercises by the fear of hell; and all his contemporaries who knew him intimately agree in this. Even foreign ambassadors such as Spanheim and Sinzendorf were struck with this trait in him. When Bossuet upon one occasion mentioned to Louis the necessity of the love of God for obtaining forgiveness of sins, he, a man of sixty years of age, who had been to confession a hundred times, and as often received absolution, replied that 'he had never heard of it.'

The marquise would not allow herself to be discouraged. Hopeful and untiring, she continued to labour for the religious reformation of the king; but the impressions he had received in early youth from his Spanish mother and his confessor remained ineradicable. Louis punctiliously observed all the forms and gestures prescribed to him,

* *Lettres*, iii. 319.

recited prayers, observed seasons of fasting, attended mass, wore relics under his clothes, suffered no unorthodox person about him, reckoned amongst obligatory observances for the expiation of his sins the extermination of heretics and the defence of the church; but sanctification, as his wife termed the evangelical spirit, found no place in him.[9] She succeeded only now and then in arousing him for a moment, although, during the sorrowful times of the War of Succession, she had often to dry his tears.

Opposed to her in this matter stood Père La Chaise, a man who long before her day and through most critical times had been the proved, complaisant, long-suffering guide of the king's conscience, building upon the foundation which his predecessors, Dinet, Paulin, Ferrier, and Annat had laid in Louis's soul. The order in whose name and under the shelter of whose authority Père La Chaise performed the onerous duties of his office, enjoyed the king's hearty and unreserved confidence; he saw in it a bulwark of the royal power and a spiritual army prepared to do battle for the interests of France in the east and west, as well as in the south. To the royal confessor the chief doctrines of his order, especially the doctrine of attrition—namely, that the mere fear of hell, without love, was sufficient to merit absolution and the assurance of salvation—and of probabilism—*i.e.* the art of transforming serious sins into light ones, or even into innocent transactions—were for Louis's case remarkably serviceable. La Chaise was for many years the most powerful man in the French Church, as the royal patronage—that is to say, the disposal of all ecclesiastical dignities and benefices—was centred in him. On this account the whole of the nobility, whose younger sons were to be provided for in

[9] 'La religion est peu connue à la cour; on veut l'accommoder à soi, et non pas s'accommoder à elle; on a toutes les pratiques extérieures mais non pas l'esprit. Le roi ne manquera pas à une station ni à une abstinence; mais il ne comprendra pas qu'il faille s'humilier et prendre l'esprit d'une vraie pénitence, et que nous devrions nous couvrir du sac et de la cendre pour demander la paix.' *Correspond. de Mme. de M.* iv. 308.

the church, were devoted to him and to the order, and the dependence of the bishops and clergy upon the favour of the order was likewise a matter of course. The marquise came to see in this father the most effectual hindrance to her efforts for the good of the king. He displayed, she said, more talent for evil than for good; he made the royal conscience too easy and comfortable; so long as he was there, nothing was to be hoped for. Moreover, as is generally known, he had inspired the king with the opinion that the pious (*les dévots*) were good for nothing, and he acted upon this principle in the disposal of bishoprics and benefices.[1] The aversion and religious mistrust of the marquise gradually extended to the whole order, the more so that she was aware that La Chaise, although a genuine son and representative of it, was upon many points of a somewhat modified type. The bishops whom she most esteemed, Godet, Bossuet, and De Noailles, strengthened her in her opinion as to the pernicious character of the order. In a letter to De Noailles she relates how Louis's vicious brother, in presence of herself and the king, had appealed to the fact that his Jesuit confessor, at a time when he had been living an even more immoral life than usual, always gave him absolution and urged him to come to communion; whereupon she had rejoined that this was the very cause of the general ill-will against the order, namely, that its members administered the sacrament without any regard as to the moral and religious condition of those whom they admitted to it.[2] Supported by the bishops and by public opinion, she actually presumed for a time to enter into a conflict with this most powerful body, chiefly for the sake of the king's soul; she even succeeded

[1] 'Le Père de la Chaise . . . a plus de talents pour le mal que pour le bien, et cela vient de ce que les intentions ne sont pas droites: peut-être aussi n'est-ce que faute de lumière. Il fit de grandes doléances au roi de n'être pas sous les évêques. Il surprend sa bonté par de tels discours; et ma malice répondit en face que ne pouvant être sous eux, il ne faudrait pas se déclarer leur ennemi.' *Correspond. de Mme. de M.* iv. 180.

[2] *Lettres*, iv. 315.

in diminishing the influence of La Chaise and in excluding the Jesuits from her beloved Saint-Cyr. In this she was helped by the general disesteem into which the Jesuits had fallen, in spite of their possessing at that time among them many eminent scholars and preachers; but this contempt and hatred were heightened by the fact that they were the objects of especial favour and consideration in high places. La Chaise himself reported to Oliva, the general of the order in Rome, that in France the Jesuits were altogether in the position of the primitive Christians; like them, they were regarded as the authors of all mischief, although they concerned themselves simply and solely with the conversion of heretics and the spread of the faith.[3] Oliva comprehended the serious import of the contempt into which the order had fallen, chiefly on account of the misuse of the confessional; and when some of the bishops began to oppose, or to refuse, the granting of licences to Jesuits to receive confessions, he drew up an apology for the society and sent it to Louis. He represented therein that the suspicions directed against the order, in its most practical sphere of influence, touched the honour of popes, emperors, kings, and countless princes and notabilities who had entrusted the guidance of their consciences to the Jesuits, and besought the king to vindicate his own honour and that of others, upon the detractors of the society.[4] Their opponents thought that the favour in which the Jesuits stood spoke plainly enough for itself; it was only needful to look closely at Versailles and other courts.

Meanwhile, in 1695, an event took place which roused in Madame de Maintenon the most sanguine hopes. She succeeded in placing De Noailles, Bishop of Chalons, at the head of the French Church as Archbishop of Paris. She was connected with him by family ties, his nephew having lately married her niece. He would, she thought, go hand-in-hand with her in working upon the king; she would do

[3] *Chantelauze*, Le Père de la Chaise (Paris, 1859), 81.
[4] *Lettere di G. P. Oliva* (Bologna, 1704), ii. 129.

all in her power to awake and to foster the king's confidence in him; whilst he, on his part, would in intercourse with the king give weight to her words by laying stress upon her position, and upon her capacity to discuss every subject. More particularly in her struggle with the Jesuits he would be her fellow-combatant, together with the Bishop of Chartres. 'The Jesuits,' she says, 'declare war against us upon all sides; we are surrounded by their spies.'[5] She only awaited a signal from the archbishop that the right moment had arrived, to set to work seriously to procure their fall[6]—so persuaded was she of the corruptness of their principles, and of the pernicious character of their power in the confessional. She thought that as long as the king retained a Jesuit as the guide of his conscience, she would labour in vain to detach him from his mechanical observances, and to bring him to a knowledge of himself. But her hopes were destined to be wrecked. The Jesuits soon succeeded in casting a suspicion of Jansenism upon De Noailles, and the latter was, moreover, far too weak and irresolute a character to make a strong ally. Nevertheless he struggled hard; for years he wrestled wearily with the powerful order, here and there victorious, but more often defeated and giving way, in the endeavour to maintain his position. For a long time Bossuet and Madame de Maintenon remained faithfully at his side. But Bossuet died in 1704, and the marquise, whose numerous letters to the cardinal had overflowed with expressions of devotion, obedience, sympathy, and admiration, became henceforth more and more estranged from him. Godet, her director, had seen the ghost of Jansenism embodied in the work of Quesnel, which De Noailles had approved, and had addressed letters to her filled with the weightiest charges against the cardinal for sheltering the heretics. Godet's authority, as usual, prevailed, and she therefore gave active assistance to Tellier, the king's confessor, in persuading the king that a

[5] *Correspond. de Mme. de Maintenon* (1866), iv. 94.

[6] *Ibid.* iv. 94. 95. 'Quand vous voudrez que je travaille à leur ruine.'

bull was necessary. The result of this was to fill the lives of three persons, the cardinal's, the king's, and her own, with grief and bitterness. She herself lamented the fate which obliged her to break with De Noailles as she had already done with Fénelon.

The assembly of the clergy, held in the year 1700 in Saint-Germain-en-Laye, was another memorable event in the history of Madame de Maintenon. It was entirely due to her efforts that the bishops, headed by De Noailles, Bossuet, Godet, and Tellier of Rheims, secured liberty sufficient to enable them to condemn the corrupt morality of the Jesuits and the doctrine of attrition. Bossuet, whose vast theological learning made him the soul of the assembly, and who was the author of the decrees issued by it, determined not to let slip the fruits of so bold an undertaking, and spent six weeks between Versailles and Marly in visits to the marquise for the sake of securing her co-operation. In his opinion the Jesuitical doctrine that the love of God was not necessary to salvation was the most dangerous heresy of the age, answerable in great part for the prevalent growth of immorality and irreligion; he wished, as he wrote to De Noailles, to devote the remainder of his life to assisting him to combat it.[7] The bishops had selected from the moral and theological writings of the order a list of the most offensive propositions which they were anxious to condemn, and the utmost endeavours of the Jesuit fathers to avert the blow were this time in vain. And the king, persuaded by the marquise, permitted the bishops to proceed to the condemnation of their propositions gathered from the Jesuitical writings, only under the condition that the names of the authors should be concealed and the honour of the order remain thus unimpugned. Louis, profoundly ignorant in matters of religion, seems not in the least to have comprehended the question of attrition, or he would assuredly not have permitted a doctrine to be rejected upon the

[7] *Œuvres*, éd. de Versailles, xxxviii. 59.

strength of which his confessors had continually granted him absolution.

When the marquise reckoned it amongst her highest and most sacred obligations to stand beside the king—whose power over the church, as Fénelon remarked, was greater than that of the pope—as the protectress of the church and the organ and mouthpiece of the bishops, she was but obeying the injunctions of her spiritual advisers and acting in accordance with the wishes of the king himself. In one of her letters she says that as often as the discussion in council with the ministers turned upon the bishops, the king addressed his remarks to her. No parallel can be found in the whole of history to the marvellous authority possessed by this woman in the church. It even extended through the nuncio and certain of the cardinals to Rome. The popes claimed her intervention and sent letters to their beloved daughter full of the warmest expressions of praise. Clement XI. extolled her countless and brilliant virtues in terms only customary upon the canonisation of the departed. Well might it be said that her ante-chamber was the council hall of the Gallican Church, so many were the bishops to be met there. Her counsels and wishers were, to the bishops, commands. Even Fénelon and Bossuet submitted to her will, or invoked her judgment and assistance in theological matters. In 1703, a few years therefore after all intercourse with her had been broken off, Fénelon observed, 'If only Père la Chaise could have the management of half the bishops, and Madame de Maintenon of the other half, all would go well.' The observation referred to a fresh blow which was about to be levelled at the Jansenists. She must certainly have been a woman of strong mind, not to become intoxicated by the incense of episcopal homage. In a remarkable letter,* highly seasoned with flattery, her director, Bishop Godet, assures the king that God himself has raised up this woman, so largely endowed with

* *Corresp.* ii. 508.

the gift of discernment (*discernement*), to stand by him as his counsellor. She would never deceive him unless she herself were deceived ; her judgment was invariably based upon wisdom and justice. It might be supposed that a monarch such as Louis, the very incarnation of egotistic vanity, would resent such testimony. That this, however, was not the case may be seen in a paper addressed by Fénelon to Pope Clement XI., in which he says that of all the French bishops the Bishop of Chartres was held in the highest esteem not only by Madame de Maintenon but by the king himself. A totally unprecedented event now took place. The pope, knowing the king to be in such sure hands, sent him, in the strictest confidence, the scheme of his anti-Jansenist bull *Vineam Domini*, for criticism and approval. Rome and Versailles, after much stormy conflict and mutual recrimination, were at that moment upon the best of terms. What this was worth, if not to France, at least to the dynasty, was manifest in 1700, when King Charles of Spain consulted the pope, with regard to the succession to the Spanish Monarchy, as to whether he ought to decide in favour of the German house of Habsburg, or of the Bourbons. The pope, or rather the congregation of cardinals appointed by the pope on his deathbed, pronounced the best thing for Spain to be the nomination of a French prince as king ; and this advice was followed at Madrid.[*] No one had in reality contributed to this result more than Madame de Maintenon ; the connection of events was certainly at that time beyond any one's ken. In our eyes the fair fame of Madame de Maintenon is obscured by the fact that the immediate result was a war which lasted thirteen years, and which led France, alone, into collision with the superior forces of other combined powers.

The marquise exerted herself to wrest, if not all, at least some of the nominations to bishoprics out of the hands of

[*] Klopp, *Der Fall des Hauses Stuart*, viii. 510. In a report from Lambert, the imperial ambassador, to his court.

the Jesuits, because the order took advantage of this patronage to fill the episcopal sees with its own devoted adherents. She usually selected her bishops from what was still at that time a very limited circle of men, viz. the Sulpicians; but her candidates found general approbation, and at the end of her career she thought herself justified in boasting that she had not given to the church a single unworthy bishop.

One of the tasks imposed upon her by the Sulpician directors of her conscience was that of leading back the king, and through him the whole French Church, into complete subjection to the papal chair. For this purpose it was necessary to cancel the authority of the famous declaration of 1682 as to the relation of the French Church to the papacy. This declaration, in conformity with the decrees of the Councils of Constance and Basle, which the popes themselves had confirmed, repudiated the theory of papal infallibility on questions of faith and morals, and declared the power of the sovereign pontiff to have been limited by the laws of the primitive church.

During the whole of his reign Louis was oscillating in his sentiments towards the papacy, and he allowed himself to be drawn, partly by circumstances, partly through personal influences, sometimes to the Gallican, sometimes to the Roman side. Saturated as he was with absolutist principles, and accustomed to think of the church as a power possessing the right of enforcing its commands by temporal penalties, a despotic and infallible pope must have appeared to him perfectly conceivable. But the two cardinals, Richelieu in his 'Testament,' and Mazarin in his verbal instructions, had warned him to withstand the Curia as apt to found a new claim upon every concession; and in his Memoirs he likewise appeals to his own experience in the matter. The ministers, the parliaments, all the jurists, the majority of the theologians at the universities, were Gallican in feeling, and rejected papal infallibility, which Rome herself had declared to be inseparably connected with the right of deposing kings and of absolving peoples from their allegiance. It was this fact which, as Fénelon observed, weighed heavily with the king. Nevertheless, the power of the marquise gradually made itself felt here also; she worked upon him so effectually that, according to D'Aguesseau's expression, he trembled at the very name of the pope. At the same time his wife, directed by Godet and Fénelon, exerted herself to raise suspicion in his mind as to his ministers, whose advice upon questions of church policy was founded upon principles of worldly wisdom. She herself narrates how she used all her arts to do this in the case of one of Louis's cleverest statesmen, the Chancellor Pontchartrain. She succeeded so far that the chancellor resigned, and withdrew to a cloister of the Oratorians. The most effectual means in such a case was to give out that the man was infected with Jansenist leanings. Whilst acting upon Godet's suggestions she felt no anxiety of conscience, and regarded it as permissible even to deceive the king for his own benefit, and to conceal important facts from him.

It has not been duly taken into account that the promulgation of the four Gallican propositions of 1682 was a result of the Jesuit policy directed against the Jansenists. Upon the strength of the royal prerogative all dioceses were, during vacancy, placed under the royal patronage, and afforded to the confessor La Chaise and his intimate ally De Harlay, Archbishop of Paris, the opportunity of filling the vacancies with the partisans of the order and of its theological views. The pope himself had the reputation, not without foundation, of being inclined towards the Jansenists, and of being therefore unfavourably disposed towards the Jesuits; whilst declaring that there were no Jansenists in France, he cherished the design of making the most distinguished theologian and leader of the Jansenists, the famous Arnauld, a cardinal. The Jesuits therefore, under the guidance of Père La Chaise,[1] took the most active in-

[1] Compare what Fleury has reported as an eye-witness in his *Opuscules*, p. 214, published by Emery, Paris, 1818.

terest in the propositions, and, in startling contradiction with their former doctrines and aims, suddenly became Gallican, wrote against the papal system, and composed historical works with this intention, which were forthwith condemned in Rome.

Madame de Maintenon welcomed with feminine instinct a doctrine, which to theologians, jurists, statesmen, and historians seemed both repulsive and unacceptable, as being to her mind both comforting and agreeable; did she not already believe in the infallibility of her director? She therefore, according to D'Aguesseau's statement, summoned the whole of her influence to her aid, day by day, exhorting and urging the king to throw over the declaration. Under Godet's instruction she represented to the king that the Jansenists availed themselves of the propositions to shelter their teaching from the censure of Rome. The king, too, at length discovered that the political situation, with the question of the Spanish succession daily impending, pointed to the advisability of a reconciliation with the pope.[2] A friendly agreement was consequently arrived at in 1693, that the king should drop the obligatory character of the propositions, which made their teaching compulsory, and should permit the newly-appointed bishops, who had taken a part in drawing up the propositions, to make a statement of submission, without directly abjuring the Gallican teaching. Yet again in 1697 Louis caused his ambassador, the Cardinal Forbin-Janson, to declare that he would not tolerate the papal infallibility being taught in France,[3] and the Curia was obliged for the time to content itself with the meagre advantage it had gained, and silently to permit the Gallican doctrine with its consequences to predominate in all the theological schools down to the time of the Revolution. In this instance bishops and clergy, tribunals and statesmen, worked so unanimously together, and public

[2] *Œuvres*, xiii. 217.

[3] Floquet, *Bossuet de* 1670 *à* 1682 (Paris, 1864), p. 572, from the records of the Paris archives.

opinion upon the point was so strong, that even the Jesuits and Sulpicians were forced to submit, and to abstain at least from any open assault upon the doctrine. But in Rome, as Polignac, afterwards cardinal, reported in the year 1707, the French clergy were regarded with even less favour than any of the German Protestants.[1] At Rome it was well known, and the marquise was equally aware, that one can arrive by circuitous ways at that which is not to be reached by the direct road, and that theory may slowly but surely be undermined by practice. Jansenism afforded to her as well as to Rome the desired opportunity.

As early as the middle of the seventeenth century, any men and women in France in whom earnest piety and purity of life were perceptible, and who were known by a stricter standard of morality, were counted as Jansenists. Such people usually held aloof from court, or, when there, were excluded from all favours and benefits: neglected at first, and afterwards persecuted. Jansenism was nevertheless rapidly increasing. It laid hold upon all ecclesiastical bodies with very few exceptions, it predominated altogether in theological literature; all public schools that were not immediately under the Jesuits, or, as in Spain, under the Inquisition, held Jansenist opinions, at least so far as the majority of their theologians were concerned. In Rome itself this teaching was strongly represented amongst the cardinals, and letters from Rome often reached Paris and Lyons encouraging those addressed to stand firm in the doctrines officially prescribed. The long series of papal decisions issued against them seemed rather to promote than to hinder their propagation. Fénelon himself, whose letters for twenty years teem with lamentations and warnings on the subject of the ceaseless progress of this heresy, observes that it alone has already cost the church more preventive and precautionary measures and damnatory decrees than

[1] Noorden, *Europ. Geschichte*, iii. 131, from the records of the archives *des affaires étrangères*.

all other heresies put together. He then proceeds to explain the surprising fruitlessness of the result, by emphatically declaring, and in this he was fully in accord with the Jansenists themselves, that nobody knew—now that the controversy and the condemnations had gone on for sixty years—in what the erroneous doctrine exactly consisted; for the Roman court stuck fast to the principle of giving no definition of what ought to be believed, so that the same doctrine which it apparently rejected in one form, was unhesitatingly accepted at Rome itself when expressed in other though synonymous terms. Besides, it was an open secret that in Rome, under the very eyes of the pope, a party existed, including even cardinals, which was constantly favourable to the Jansenists and working in their interests. Thus chaotic confusion prevailed in all minds.[5]

As a matter of fact, in both camps, amongst the Jansenists as well as amongst their opponents the Jesuits, and the theologians of Molinist tendencies, the conviction was the same, viz. that what was called Jansenism, when confined to the doctrine of grace, was an impalpable ghost, a phantom, as it was said at the time, and as had been proved in writings which were never refuted. For the same thing which under one name was condemned, was under another, as the teaching of the Thomists or Augustinians, declared to be perfectly orthodox. The best theologians, the most intelligent men of both parties, were agreed as to this; Fénelon and even the Jesuits, not less than Arnauld, Nicole, and Pascal. Even popes, such as Innocent XI., and afterwards Benedict XIV.,[6] the latter only verbally, acknowledged to holding the same opinion. The later papal decisions of Benedict XIII. and XIV. settled this point. But impor-

[5] The Archbishop of Mechlin, De Precipiano, belonged to those who saw in the arbitrary decrees of the two kings of France and Spain the only means of rescue for the church from the encroachments of Jansenism. Nothing, he says in a memorial drawn up by him, is to be hoped for from Rome, since the pope (Innocent XII.) protects the congregations, and in these the friends and patrons of the heterodox opinions predominate. Gachard, *La Belgique sous Philippe V.* (Bruxelles, 1867), p. 12.

[6] The testimony of the Roman Jesuit Cordara. See my *Beiträge*, iii. 9.

tant hierarchical interests were connected with the phantom, and above all the imperative necessity of never making a retrograde step, nor any acknowledgment of mistake or error. Besides, the Jesuits were determined that so trenchant a weapon of assault, so effectual an instrument of ecclesiastical government, ought not to be abandoned. For fifty years it had rendered good service to the order, broken the power of numerous opponents, or forced them into silence, and placed the Jesuits in complete possession of the public schools and other institutions of learning, and made them the dreaded censors of all theologians, and particularly of all the religious orders which, in the opinion of the Molinists, were infected by the poison of the new heresy. In Rome, however, the method of procedure without any formal affirmation of church doctrine, contrary to the custom of the primitive church, was steadfastly adhered to in the questions of predestination and grace. Throughout the wearisome dispute such affirmation was ever carefully avoided; only certain propositions, drawn from some book, were condemned. And just because nobody could tell in what sense such propositions as those taken from the works of Jansenius or Quesnel were to be rejected, did they become valuable: for the whole question was turned into one of blind obedience and submission, without previous investigation. The Jesuit D'Aubenton, who as Tellier's agent in Rome had undertaken to procure that the passages selected from Quesnel's book should be condemned, repeatedly informed his employer that at Rome everything turned upon the papal infallibility; to get this passed whilst the king was ready to impose, by force of arms, upon the bishops and clergy the unquestioning acceptance of the papal constitution, was the only object; the theological aspect of the matter was neither especially considered nor rightly understood.

Madame de Maintenon firmly believed that Jansenism was pernicious heresy; in this matter she thought and acted in full accord with the confessors La Chaise and Tellier;

she strengthened the king in his delusion, and fanned the flames of persecution. She knew perfectly that the charge of Jansenism was the means daily employed to suppress rivals, and to exclude sincere and religious men from all dignities and offices in the state and church. She herself says that most men and women who became earnest in religion were at once decried as Jansenists. Yet evening after evening she read to the king passages from the papers that had been seized, belonging to the Oratorian Quesnel, in order to keep alive his zeal against the silently smouldering 'cabal.' At that time 'cabals' existed everywhere, and so, consequently, did suspicion and espionage; there was a Protestant and a Cartesian cabal, cabals of the followers of Arnauld and of Quesnel, of the Jesuits and of the Sulpicians. Even she herself, Madame de Maintenon, had her own cabal in common with a few bishops; she wrote in cipher and received visits from them which had to be kept secret, in order that they might not be employed as weapons against her by the Jesuits who were about the king.

A widely diffused and much-esteemed book of devotion by Quesnel, 'Considerations upon the New Testament,' had been selected as a holocaust at this time—a book which had received the approbation of the Archbishop of Paris, Cardinal de Noailles, and in commendation and defence of which Bossuet, the foremost theologian amongst the French bishops, had written a pamphlet shortly before his death. The Bishop of Chartres, the oracle of the marquise, pronounced it on the contrary to be saturated with heresy and highly mischievous, and his death, she declared, was caused by grief that his episcopal friends could not be brought to condemn it. The confessor and the marquise now persuaded the king that Jansenism was taking such strong hold on all sides, that a fresh papal bull to condemn it was an immediate necessity. Louis urged the pope to issue one without delay, but Clement XI. only yielded to the request upon the king promising to enforce unconditional submission to the bull from both clergy and laity by all the means and weapons of his sovereign power. Thus was prepared a deadly blow to the Gallican system, a system based upon the admission that bishops possessed the right of taking part in the examination and decision of dogmatic questions. A bull was now issued from Rome, condemning 101 propositions taken out of Quesnel's book, and designedly drawn up so as to contain a mass of obscurities and uncertainties which would inevitably stir up endless controversy. Thus a conflagration was kindled which was not to be extinguished, and was destined long after Louis's lifetime to continue to waste the best powers of the French Church, and, by the ruin which it caused, to assist in preparing the way for the Revolution.

Madame de Maintenon hailed the advent of the bull with feelings of triumph; at last that had come to pass which her 'saintly bishop'—so she was in the habit of calling Godet after his death in 1707—had so earnestly desired. But with surprise and terror she now recognised at the head of the heretics the very man whom she had made Archbishop of Paris, with whom for many years she had been intimately associated in advancing the interests of the church, and for whom she had previously wished at any price to secure the full confidence of the king, that he might counteract the influence of the Jesuits. She now complained that the archbishop was shortening the life of the king and embittering her own. She lived to witness the reaction in the time of the Regency, and such was the disastrous state of confusion in which she left the Church of France, that it must be owned that her conduct contributed more than Voltaire's mockery and the assaults of the Freethinkers to hasten the coming of the Revolution, and to imprint upon it that character of hostility to religion which still continues to exist in the present day, unenfeebled, if not increasing in strength.

A dark shadow falls here upon the marquise, and her influence was in a high degree injurious to the state—all the more so that it strengthened a characteristic of the king already mentioned, his aversion for persons of superior intellect. Mindful of the exhortations of the Bishop of Chartres, she held it to be her duty to see that only men of earnest piety should be put into government posts, and still further that none who could possibly be suspected of Jansenism or of sympathy with that school should attain to any position of importance. Upon this point, the triad—the king, his wife, and the confessor—were unanimous and watchful. Two poets, such as Racine and Boileau, who had leanings that way, might at a pinch be tolerated ; but to ruin a man at court it sufficed, as the Maréchal d'Harcourt says, to give out that he was a Jansenist. The consequences were, first, that many unprincipled aspirants, under the mask of dogmatic zeal against the doctrines which were banished from the court, wheedled themselves into office and were appointed to benefices ; and, secondly, that the best and ablest men were excluded if Augustinian or Jansenist opinions were once imputed to them. To have for confessor any one belonging to one of the religious orders supposed to be thus tainted was quite enough to rouse suspicion. Within the circle of the court only two societies were now accepted as altogether orthodox, the Jesuits, and the still small body of the Sulpicians. Into every other order the poison, according to Fénelon and others, had penetrated. It was asserted, besides, that all the secular clergy who had studied at the Sorbonne had imbibed the interdicted opinions. A flood of heresy had broken over France in the last fifty years, and was continually rising, and in Madame de Maintenon's opinion, which had been formed upon the teaching of the Sulpicians, this heresy was the most dangerous that had ever arisen in the church. She did her utmost therefore with the king—who, on religious questions, was always prone to take the side of violence and persecution—to embitter his feelings and fill him with suspicion, leading him to multiply the warrants for imprisonment, deprivations, and exile.

The life of this woman, when looked at as a whole, presents indeed a tragic spectacle. The best and most cherished of her hopes and plans were wrecked, some before and some after her death. She lived to see the king, her husband, who for thirty years had been the idol of France, descend into the grave laden with universal hatred ; his death was hailed as a deliverance by the country. As she survived the king by some years, she also saw, from her retreat in Saint-Cyr, how the Regency in almost all points strove for the very opposite to that at which Louis and herself had aimed. Concern for the families of the royal princes and efforts at peace-making had for years cost her infinite time and trouble, and now most of them had been snatched away in the flower of their age, and the rest were at variance amongst themselves ! Her favourite, the Duc de Maine, whom she had latterly again sought to place at the head of affairs, was excluded from them, condemned to inactivity, and, besides, had not fulfilled as a man the hopes which his brilliant gifts had raised in his boyhood. His imprisonment for high treason, so Elisabeth Charlotte asserts, hastened her death. With conscientious care and motherly tenderness the marquise had superintended the education of the Savoyard princess who had been brought at eleven years of age to the court as the bride of the dauphin ; she hoped to leave behind her a worthy queen for France ; but in 1712 the princess had been already torn from her and from the nation. The Duke of Burgundy, Fénelon's pupil, in her eyes as well as in those of the nation,was destined to make amends for and repair the faults of his grandfather's reign ; but within six days he followed his wife to the grave. Her affections had been so often deceived, so many ties of friendship which she had formed had been snapped asunder, that on her deathbed she said to her truest pupil and friend Glapion, that she was the only being who had remained faithful to her, and had not disappointed her.

The years which she had spent in continual endeavours to awaken the soul of her husband to a purer and truer religion had been spent in vain. Louis remained to the last what the order to whose guidance he had been committed as a child had made him. But since the authorities whom the marquise reverenced—popes, bishops, preachers, even her oracle Godet—were unanimous in praise of Louis's piety and faith, she too abated her earlier and loftier expectations, and by the time the great war broke out in 1701 was ready to imagine that Providence would give victory over the heretics into the hand of the devout and orthodox king. When the reverse took place, and year after year crushing blows fell upon the armies of Louis, then, as we have already said, she almost doubted the divine guidance of the universe; it seemed to her incomprehensible that her pious husband should be defeated by heretical powers. She calmed herself by degrees with the thought that the disasters and the general misery were punishments for the vices of the nation and the sins of the king. Louis himself acknowledged with tears that he had deserved his misfortunes, and that he recognised therein the chastening hand of God. And yet it was beyond her power to perceive that her own mischievous counsels—the recognition of James III. and the persecution of the Protestants—had most effectually helped to prepare the supremacy of England and the rise of the Protestant powers.

Madame de Maintenon, immersed as she was in active business and daily brought into contact with the theory and practice of government, would certainly not have endorsed the opinion of Fénelon, 'Despotism is the source of all our evils.' It was she who aggravated the yoke of despotism by countenancing the system of persecution which her husband introduced, and who, in the interests of an orthodoxy of Godet's style, took good care that victims should not be wanting, that acts of violence should be multiplied, and that the prisons should be filled with priests. She did not reflect that such tyranny would, like a poison, penetrate into other departments of the administration.

She had allowed herself to be persuaded that in meddling with ecclesiastical affairs she was fulfilling a mission from on high. Yet she subsequently appears to have felt some remorse for her conduct in this respect, for she wrote to her friend the Princess Orsini that she had interfered more than enough with the appointments of bishops. Here, what she built up with one hand she demolished with the other. It was her pet piece of handiwork, the bull *Unigenitus*, which became the means of degrading the bishops into convenient tools of the Jesuits, and of exposing them to universal derision by their discords and alternate utterance of complaints and anathemas. During the first years of her rule the French Church stood at the height of its theological prosperity; according to Bossuet's testimony it possessed more learned theologians than all other countries put together. But about the year 1715 Louis, with his wife and confessor, had already brought about its decline. The creatures of Madame de Maintenon, her Cardinals Rohan and Bissy, and their successors Dubois and Fleury, worked, in combination with the Sulpicians and Jesuits, all in the same direction. By the middle of the century things had gone so far that the Sorbonne was reduced to a shadow, and that the French clergy, when the time came for the struggle with the gathering hosts of the enemies of Christianity, presented a pitiful figure of unlearned impotence.

In the conversations that are recorded between the marquise and the ladies of Saint-Cyr, whole pages may be picked out which seem like adaptations of the words which the poet, in 'Faust,' puts into the mouth of his Gretchen:

> Doch Alles, was dazu mich trieb,
> Gott! war so gut, ach! war so lieb.

At the end of her career, a few weeks before the king's death, she wrote to her confessor: 'I have with the best intentions committed so many faults that I can no longer venture to meddle with anything;'[7] yet she straightway sets to work to persuade the king to make a will disposing

[7] *Corresp.* (1859) xii. 685.

of the succession to the throne, and makes a draft of it with the aid of Voisin, whom she had advanced to the important dignity of chancellor from the post of steward at Saint-Cyr. This will gave the title of regent to the Duke of Orleans, but practically made him a mere cipher, and disposed of the succession in a manner subversive of the fundamental laws of the kingdom by making the sons of Madame de Montespan, whom Louis had already legitimatised and thrust upon the list of princes of the blood, also capable of succeeding to the throne. This will, as is well known, was after the king's death at once set aside, and her favourite, the object of her hopes, deprived of all influence in the government.

In conclusion, let me be allowed to compare this remarkable Frenchwoman with a German, no less a person than the Empress Maria Theresa. Each was an ornament to her sex, each combined with a masculine intellect and judgment, all the feminine virtues; but the one ruled and issued her commands with the authority which was her birthright, the other, under the concealment of a strange name, upon account of which the Duke of Villeroi nicknamed her the mole, was compelled in most cases to arrive at her point by circuitous and covert paths, to petition, to persuade, to negotiate, where a word from the empress would have commanded obedience upon all sides. Each gave herself up wholly and unreservedly, Maria Theresa to the state, Madame de Maintenon to her lord and master, who could say with reason 'I am the state.' Each, lending a too willing ear to the suggestions of blind guides, approved or organised religious oppression or persecution. Both were pious and enthusiastic in the doctrines and the service of their church, but the Frenchwoman, stifling her own judgment, knew only how to follow implicitly the guides of her conscience, whilst the Austrian princess tolerated no interference in political matters from her confessor, and even in ecclesiastical affairs often followed other counsels. Each was convinced that she had received a mission from God and was an instrument in His hands, but the conviction operated upon each in a different manner. To Madame de Maintenon's excitable and highly sensitive nature every misfortune, every complication, was a source of painful anxiety, frequently even of physical suffering; Maria Theresa, on the contrary, thanks to her convictions, attained, as she tells us in her memoirs, even under the most distressing circumstances, to entire peace of mind as if nothing in the world could touch her. Both suffered much from the people nearest to them being governed by wholly different views: the empress through her son and co-regent Joseph; the marquise through her husband. Both, as usually happens in the case of imaginative and highly sensitive women, carried their wishes, which became hopes, their personal sympathies and aversions, far too much into politics. Both did much mischief in consequence: the empress, by making her daughter in Paris the tool of the Austrian house policy; the marquise, by inducing her husband at a most critical moment to recognise James III. and thus to break the peace. Both women, finally, left a mark upon the world's history, but of a very different kind. The memory of the great empress is still revered by millions, and outshines that of any of the male representatives of the house of Habsburg who have worn the two crowns. Any remembrance of the founder of Saint-Cyr has long since been wiped out of the minds of the people, although her letters will continue to hold a prominent place in literature beside those of her friend Madame de Sévigné. By the students of history she is sometimes lauded, sometimes blamed. The fatal effects of their actions have extended to the present day, and will continue to be felt in the future; only the chain of cause and effect, so far as Madame de Maintenon had a hand in it, will remain unrecognised by most. Yet we must not withhold from her this testimony, that although she erred greatly and did much harm, she also achieved endless good and scattered countless benefits around her with the purest intentions. She took heavy burdens upon herself for the sake of making the lives of others more endurable and worthier. Her best deeds originated from herself, her worst mistakes from too great a trust in the superiority of others. The rule which she gave her pupils, to be severe towards themselves, tender and considerate towards others, she invariably observed herself. The history of France does not produce any woman who surpasses her in the greatness and multiplicity of talents and virtues.

INDEX

I

J

K

T

U

V

W

X

Z

PRINTED BY
SPOTTISWOODE AND CO., NEW-STREET SQUARE
LONDON

www.ingramcontent.com/pod-product-compliance
Lightning Source LLC
Chambersburg PA
CBHW032304280326
41932CB00009B/686

* 9 7 8 3 7 4 2 8 9 5 5 2 3 *